The Ultimate Geography and Timeline Guide

by
Maggie Hogan
and
Cindy Wiggers

Timeline Figures and "Who Am I"
Liberty Wiggers

Cover Design
Michael Wheeler

We dedicate this book to our families
whose sacrifice made it all possible.

THE ULTIMATE GEOGRAPHY AND TIMELINE GUIDE

First Printing 1998
Second Printing 2000
Third Printing 2001
Fourth Printing 2003
Fifth Printing 2006

Copyright © 1998, 2000, 2001, 2003, 2006 Margaret S. Hogan, Cynthia G. Wiggers, and Michelle E. Wiggers

Library of Congress Catalog Card Number: 98-96194
ISBN-13: 978-0-9663722-0-5
ISBN-10: 0-9663722-0-4

Published in the United States of America by: GeoCreations, Ltd.
(877) 492-7879
Second Edition

Travel Notes

Welcome sojourner! You're about to embark on a journey like none you've ever taken. Your perception of geography is about to set sail on a new course. Never again will geography be the "find it, name it" subject you so dreaded. This book will guide you on an exciting adventure to a fuller understanding of the *true* meaning of geography. Whether you're a first time teacher or a seasoned pro, this book is just what you need to make geography a favorite subject.

Before you board
Take a mini-tour of this book. You'll learn how to:

- Teach geography
- Use timelines effectively

When planning a tour of the world, there are steps you must take before you board the plane. You'll plan your destination, pack your bags, and chart your course. Then you'll head off to see the world!

Just the Basics, Please!
1. While planning your destination you'll explore:
   Teaching styles, learning styles, cross-curricular thinking, and detailed information about the benefits of the student notebook approach. (You'll even use this information in all areas of teaching, not just geography.) You'll also be briefed on everything you need to know about geography supplies. To do the job right, you must have the right tools.

2. You'll pack your bags with a mini-refresher course in geography. Do you scratch your head when asked about the summer solstice? Fumble for words when defining meridians and parallels? Can you explain the difference between human and physical geography? If not, you're not alone! Few of us grew up in schools with strong geography programs. But fear not! Here's the information you need to finally master geography basics.

3. Chart your course as you learn to incorporate meaningful map work into your studies. If you don't already own great maps, you'll be inspired to get some. If you do have great maps, you'll be equipped with lots of practical and creative ways to use them. Student progress will soar when you start incorporating map projects into your school day!

Taking in the Sights
When you're ready to take off, you'll see geography in the real world with page after page of down-to-earth ideas to make the geography journey fun. These proven projects offer lots of different vehicles for building enthusiasm and knowledge. From wearing it, to collecting it, or even eating it - geography is everywhere!

Geography Through the Curriculum

We'll take you "Across the Great Divide" in your one-stop shop for incorporating geography into other subjects. You'll find simple ideas to full-blown lesson plans. Don't miss the complete literature study of *Hans Brinker or The Silver Skates*, or Blowin' Up a Storm, the volcano study in chapter eight. Geography Through History provides a complete outline describing which maps to use when, with United States history as an example. This foundation will help you establish your own world history mapping program.

Just Geography

Discover ready-to-go, comprehensive lesson plans. "Conquering the Continents" includes pure geography for upper elementary/middle school, and high school.

Reproducibles for Your Geotreks

We've included a plethora of reproducibles for your convenience - activity sheets, grids, charts, flash cards; plus a veritable treasure-trove of unique reproducible maps, designed especially for *The Ultimate Guide*!

Tour Through Time

An entire portion of *The Ultimate Guide* is devoted completely to timelines. If you've never used timelines and timeline figures before, or if you have a timeline and don't know what to do with it, jump into this lively method to help students visualize historical progressions. Read about the benefits of using a timeline, suggestions for variety, and build your own timeline notebook with the reproducible timeline! A super bonus: this tour through time includes a gold mine of over 300 historically accurate timeline figures and the "Who Am I?" game to introduce the figures.

Danger! Warning! Attempting to do everything in this book could be hazardous to your health! (Not to mention that of your students!) You hold in your hands literally years worth of information and activities designed to teach geography from grades K-12. Use the reproducible scope and sequence grid in chapter seventeen and the information from "Where Do I Start?" beginning on page one, to plan what needs to be taught each year.

Your mini-tour has now come to an end. Are you ready to begin the journey? Grab your planner and your highlighter, and get ready to take off on an exciting geographic voyage!

All Aboard!!

Please note:
- There are over one hundred fifty reproducibles in chapters twelve through sixteen. In addition, you may find you want to copy other pages to use as handouts or to place in a student notebook. Permission is granted to copy pages for your own personal use, not for an entire school.
- For ease of reading we have chosen to use male pronouns. This in no way indicates a male bias on our part.
- All facts, figures, and information given were up-to-date at the time of publication. If specific data is needed for your study we recommend using a current almanac from your local bookstore or library.

By learning you will teach; by teaching you will learn. ---Latin Proverb

Table of Contents

Acknowledgments

Mom - you've always been such an encouragement to me!

Bob - thanks for the late-night cappuccinos, the shoulder massages, the tech support, and most importantly: for your steadfast love and support. I wouldn't want to do it without you.

JB and Tyler - thanks for being diligent, independent learners when things got crazy around here! Thanks for keeping up with the laundry, the dishes, and phone calls. I'm so proud of you both. Can't wait to see you guys in print - you're both far more creative than I'll ever be!

Sherri - our editor with vision and skill - we appreciate your wisdom and enthusiasm. Your input has truly made a difference. Thank you.

And hugs to my friends who've prayed for me, listened to me, encouraged me, and dragged me to the YMCA at unreasonable hours of the morning! Janice, Celeste, Susan, and Beth - you're the greatest!

Special thanks to Cindy and Josh - who gamely took on this project, not knowing how it would take over their lives! It's an honor to work with you both.

Maggie

Josh - thank you for taking on the meal planning for these months: no one wants me back in the kitchen after your delicious colorful presentations! Thanks also for the late-night Expresso "a' la Joshs," developing all our maps to our (picky) specifications, establishing page formats, designing the cover and overlooking - always with patience - my fits of frustration from computer ignorance. This project would have never happened without the 100% support you gave. Thanks, hon.

Libby - thanks for all your work on the timeline figures and game. You excelled even beyond my wildest expectations! Proofing our mapping projects and filling in the gaps for my computer illiteracy was an added bonus. I'm so proud of you.

Hannah - thanks for gracefully accepting all of these changes to your routine and for preparing meals for the whole crew during final manuscript preparations. Your diligence to continue your studies without my support is a testimony to your character. Thanks, you're a real sweetheart!

Alex - you've been a real rock for three months while I "lived" in the office. Thank you for the many words of encouragement and hugs just when I needed them and for serving me above and beyond the call of duty!

To those who faithfully prayed, shared their input and suggested clever titles - thanks so much: Sally Ann, Dana, Christa, and Nancy. To our editor, Sherri, your contributions were first class.

To Bob and Maggie - your patience, diligence and creative "energy" made it all happen. Thanks for breaking me in! Bob, your research and submissions in the high school section were invaluable!

Cindy

Thanks to Tina Farewell - for giving me a starting point and sparking my enthusiasm.

To Jeanne Wiggers who drew pictures when none could be found - Thanks Grandma, they look wonderful!

Mom and Dad - thanks for pushing me to do my best, keeping me focused, and giving me ideas.

Thanks to God - for His energy and insight.

Libby "Liberty"

A note from Cindy and Maggie:

Some people pick up this book and almost instinctively understand how to incorporate it into their teaching. But the most common question we hear is, "How do I use this book?" We hope these next pages will help you in getting the most out of *The Ultimate Guide*. These charts are just a guide! Be flexible - trust your judgement!

Q. Where do I start?
A. Familiarize yourself with the Table of Contents. Read all of Unit One. Most of the chapters begin with valuable information for the teacher: peruse at will.

Q. How do I know what's appropriate for a ___ grader?
A. First, use what you know of your student's abilities and interests. Second, refer to the charts below and on the next page for a sample yearly teaching guide.

Q. How do I teach geography to children of different levels concurrently?
A. Pick a spot on the chart from the following pages that corresponds to an approximate middle level. Start there, or look at the chart below and pick chapters that fit most of your grade levels. The important thing is to start somewhere and to encourage your students to think geographically by noticing and talking about geographic topics.

Q. How do I know if I'm successfully teaching everything necessary for geography?
A. Many like using the Scope and Sequence charts on pages 255-262 to track what they have covered and what they plan to cover. Just remember, no one can teach "everything" or learn "everything." If you make a point to teach geography regularly and if your students begin using geography in their everyday lives, consider yourself successful!

T	1	Planning your destination
J, H, T	2	Packing Your Bags
P, M, T	3	Finding Your Way with Maps
P, M, T	4	Off to See the World
P, M, T	5	Geography in the Real World
T	6	Geography Through Literature
J	7	Hans Brinker
P, M	8	Geography Through Science
P, M	9	Geography Through Math
All	10	Geography Through History
M, H, T	11	Geography Through the Internet
T	12	Conquering the Continents
M	13	Pure Geography/Middle School
H	14	Pure Geography/High School
All	15	Maps
M, H	16	Walking Tours
T, A	17	Tools for the Tour Guide
T	18	Timeline Trekkin'
M, H	19	Tools for the Time Traveler

Suggested Levels
by Chapter

T   Teacher
A   All
P   Primary (K-3)
M   Middle (4-8)
J   Jr High (6-8)
H   High School

Simple Tips for Using *The Ultimate Guide*:

- Read through Unit One and the introductions to each chapter.
- Refer to the Scope and Sequence grids on pages 255-262.
- Starting with older students? Check for mastery of earlier levels.
- This is only one possible guide. Feel free to rearrange to meet your needs.
- We've intentionally overlapped grades to account for individual student development.
- Teach geography with history (chapter ten) yearly. Use the American history outline every time you teach that subject.
- Encourage your students to "think geographically." Look for geography in every day life.
- Don't be intimidated! Use what you want to use - don't be a slave to the book. Relax and enjoy geography and your kids will, too!

A Yearly Guide for the Less Than Confident

* Use atlases and outline maps with history EACH YEAR!

K-2nd*	
PAGE	**TOPIC**
61-65	Your choice of map activities
67	Your choice of hands-on projects from Unit Two
111	Introduce geography through science
89	Introduce geography through literature
2nd-4th*	
61-65	Your choice of map activities
67	Your choice of hands-on activities from Unit Two
111	Geography through science as appropriate
89	Geography through literature as appropriate
121	Introduce geography through math
263-284	Introduce "Stuff to Memorize" and selected flashcards
287	Introduce timelines

4th-6th*

PAGE	TOPIC
61-65	Your choice of map activities
67	Your choice of hands-on projects. (Prime years for collections!)
72-73	Begin current events
89	Geography through literature
23-53	Chapter two as it applies to your studies
111	Geography through science
121	Geography through math
263-284	Memorize appropriate flash cards and "Stuff to Know"
287-300	Work on timelines

6th-8th*

PAGE	TOPIC
23-53	Chapter two in more detail
263-281	Finish memorizing
44-66+	Compass and map skills
95-110	Hans Brinker: a study of Holland
239-253	Selected pages from chapter sixteen
151-197	Conquering the continents: middle school
141-147	Geography through the Internet
287-338	Begin keeping a student timeline
121-126	Finish Geography through math

9th-12th*

PAGE	TOPIC
23-53	Mastery of material in chapter two
151-155	Read chapter twelve
199-219	Conquering the continents: high school
344-348	Mastery of geography terms
338	Diligent use of timelines

*Use atlases and outline maps with history EACH YEAR!!

Notes:

Unit One

Just the Basics, Please!

PLANNING YOUR DESTINATION
CHAPTER 1

TEACHING TIPS TO PUT YOU ON THE RIGHT TRACK

Any journey begins by planning your destination. From establishing teaching methods and determining learning styles, to gathering supplies, this chapter will get you started on the right track.

Teaching geography can be the highlight of your school day if you've gained an understanding of the five themes of geography and realize that geography is much more than memorizing lists of states and capitals. You'll be able to discuss geography throughout the day. Five themes? Yes, and you'll learn all about them in the refresher course in the next chapter. It'll revolutionize your geographic thinking!

This planning session is designed to go over a few teaching tips that you can use in all class subjects including geography. Some ideas may serve as reminders and some will be new. So, let's start by developing a vision for teaching geography through a panorama of subject areas and instruction methods!

Geography Across the Curriculum

Geography is so all encompassing that it's easy to incorporate within the context of most any other subject matter. Your students will remember their geography better if it's associated with something else. As you gain a fuller understanding of geography's five themes, you'll awaken to opportunities to connect a current subject of study with a geography activity. Successfully incorporate geography throughout the curriculum and it won't be necessary to teach a separate geography class until high school, when a geography course is recommended for well-rounded global cognitive awareness.

Current Events

Current events provide perfect opportunities to learn geography through association. When is the best time to learn about China? When it comes up in the textbook, or when the president makes an historical trip there? TV news will flood the airwaves with images and special interest stories. Newspapers will provide a daily account of everywhere the president goes. Make a habit of associating events or other studies with geography. Your students will benefit with a fuller understanding of the subject, and improve their mental system for fact filing as well.

Memorization

Hands-on activities are absolutely wonderful because everyone benefits from the opportunity to be creative and thoroughly involved. However, there is a time and place for basic memorization! It can be done in a creative fashion, or it can be cut and dry; but however you choose to do it, it needs to be done. We don't get creative with math at the expense of basic math facts; let's not get creative with geography at the expense of basic geography facts.

Depending on the age and grade level of your students, choose a list or lists from those provided in chapter seventeen and help them make a concerted effort to learn as much as can be reasonably expected. (A well-thought-out reward system works well here.) This kind of information is both relevant and foundational to build a strong base of geographic understanding. The lists are divided by topics, both to help organize information, and to help students succeed by tackling bite-sized chunks. Also, part of the memorization has to do with finding places quickly on a map, rather than just memorizing place names.

Unit Study Approach

More and more teaching methods are including a unit study approach to help provide association. So many facts are learned in a lifetime that information is more easily retrieved when it's connected to a memorable experience.

Think about how a particular song takes you back to an experience you had. Retrieving stored knowledge is similar. When a student learns about world history he may quickly forget the facts after turning in the test. But that same student readily remembers what he learned while building a model boat, designing a chart, or when current events were associated. It's so very easy to provide association with geography! And through association, the student benefits from the "big picture" rather than separate, distinct pieces of a puzzle.

I hear and I forget. I see and I remember. I do and I understand.
--Chinese Proverb

Learning Styles

Many famous and accomplished people once labeled as "poor students" were probably not taught according to their learning style. But wow! Did they ever contribute to society anyway! Louis Pasteur was called a "dull student" by his art teacher, and his other teachers saw nothing remarkable in him. The headmaster of his school watched 13-year-old Louis and noticed that he worked slowly and carefully to complete assignments. He saw determination in Pasteur where others saw failure. With encouragement from the headmaster, Louis soon became head of his class. He attended the Royal College where he was rated a "mediocre student" in chemistry, yet he became the first to discover that germs were deadly. Pasteur developed the Anthrax vaccination and the pasteurization process that bears his name, along with many other great accomplishments.

If your student isn't "getting it," consider presenting the information in a different learning style.

Much more has been written regarding personality types and learning styles than could be contained in one small chapter, yet it's important to provide a brief overview. Recommended books are listed at the end of this section. This overview isn't intended to help you decipher the learning styles of your students, but instead to help spark an awareness that just as people are unique in their likes and dislikes, so also is the way they learn and process information.

When a student's learning styles and modalities don't match the teaching method, the student's mental aptitude can be underestimated. Thomas Edison was consistently at the bottom of his class. Teachers said he was too stupid to learn anything. Albert Einstein was declared mentally slow and expelled from school. Beethoven's music teacher said he was hopeless as a composer. Isaac Newton was a poor student in grade school. Leo Tolstoy flunked out of college. Edgar Allen Poe, Salvador Dali, William Randolf Hearst, and George Bernard Shaw were all expelled from school. Is it possible that each of these gifted individuals was simply misunderstood because he wasn't taught in harmony with his learning style?

Most children want to be successful in their endeavors. Research in the past few years has shown that each individual has a specific way in which he learns best. Often a child's desire to do well in school is stifled because teaching methods used don't match the way he learns. Increase your student's learning potential by gaining an understanding of basic learning styles. Then make sure your teaching methods take various learning styles into consideration.

Different authors and researchers give learning styles different names. From animal names, to Greek names, to cutsie descriptive names, to acronyms like "DISC" and "ABCD." For simplicity's sake, we'll call them "ABCD." Normally, people will display some, but not all, of the traits of a learning style. Sometimes it's difficult to peg a student who seems to fit a little of each.

Type A learns by doing, doesn't like deep thinking, is spontaneous, often creative, does not like sitting still looking at books, prefers games, competitions, short presentations.

Type B likes clear, structured, well organized tasks, wants everything done in order, wants "just the facts not opinion, thank you." He enjoys textbooks and works well with typical school curriculum. He is usually not creative or spontaneous, but is cautious.

Type C is a problem-solver, self-motivated, analyzes things, prefers logical subjects like math or science. He works independently, enjoys long term projects, and prefers well organized lectures. (Perhaps this was Pasteur?)

Type D is a social person. He is interested in the people, ideas and principles of the subject, not the events. He isn't a detail person, is vulnerable to conflict and criticism, and wants to understand "why."

In addition to these learning styles, information is transported to the brain through different modalities. The three most common modalities are:
- visual
- kinesthetic
- auditory

Another interesting "key" to determining style is by listening to the way people talk. They'll say things like:

- "I see" or "I can picture" for visual
- "I feel that" for kinesthetic
- "I hear what you're saying" for auditory

To "match" language with anyone in this way helps to create a successful rapport.

A **visual** learner receives information best through pictures, diagrams and other visual images. A person who receives best by hearing is an **auditory** learner and enjoys lectures, songs, stories and oral material. The **kinesthetic** learner understands best through touch and hands-on interaction.

This information will affect curriculum choices, homework assignments, how subjects are taught, and even how you assess a student's progress. You can see from these brief descriptions why some very intelligent students might do poorly in school and, in fact, will hate "learning" if taught by methods in disharmony with the way they learn.

For more information on this subject, the following books are recommended: *The Way They Learn* by Cynthia Tobias, *Learning Styles and Tools* by Alta Vista, *People Types and Tiger Stripes* by Gordon Lawrence, and *In Their Own Way* by Thomas Armstrong.

Lookin' It Up

Using a reference book such as the dictionary, almanac, or atlas isn't as dull as it sounds. Everyone has experienced the frustration of asking how to spell a word only to be told to "look it up" in the dictionary. You have to know how to spell a word to look it up, but if you knew how to spell it you wouldn't need to look it up in the first place! "It's too much trouble." "It's too hard." "I don't know where the dictionary is," are all common responses to the "look it up" decree.

Without pressure from a conscientious teacher, most students will become lazy in this area because of its seeming drudgery. Help your student develop sound, life-long learning habits by modeling the best "look it up attitude." When an unfamiliar word appears in an assigned reading, news report, or even in conversation, a quick trip through the dictionary will do wonders to increase vocabulary and understanding. Okay, most people will resist doing this, it's true. But the benefits far outweigh the short-term discomfort.

Short-term discomfort? Yes! It really doesn't take that long to look up a word in the dictionary or a place in the atlas. Go ahead! Grab a dictionary and prove it to yourself. Here's the scenario: While reading a sailing adventure, we find our fearless hero has spotted an island. Upon approach he discovers it's not simply an island but an archipelago. What's an "archipelago"? Note the time and look up "archipelago" in your dictionary. Now note how long this simple act took. Well, how long did it take? Fifteen seconds? A little more if you count the time it took to read the definition. Short-term discomfort, proven!

It wasn't really the drudgery you expected, was it? Now your students will more fully understand the next three chapters as the captain and his crew explore each island in search of fresh water. Sometimes the very act of looking up a word or a place in the atlas adds a sense of excitement, especially at the height of the story when they have to wait to hear the conclusion.

Dictionary use: make it a habit!

- Make the dictionary easily accessible to all. Then when a word needs defining, students will use thirty seconds to search for the word instead of ten minutes to search for the dictionary.

• Keep a light and airy attitude when your students moan about it. "Oh, it'll only take a few seconds, and it WILL be more interesting if we understand this word better."

• When finding the word, scan the definition for the right context of your lesson and read it aloud. Let one student repeat the definition in his own words or verbatim.

• Jump back into the reading with gusto - right back to the beginning of the paragraph where the word in question appeared.

• When the reading is completed, occasionally assign this word as a vocabulary word for the student to record in his vocabulary file, or the vocabulary section of his student notebook. Or combine this with penmanship, requiring students to record definitions weekly in their best handwriting.

Time Saving Tip
Using words that come up in the normal course of the day is a more effective way to increase vocabulary than memorizing an arbitrary list of vocabulary words.

Defining Dictionary Proficiency

It's a good idea to assess student proficiency with a dictionary. When students take advantage of a dictionary's organized layout they'll find words faster.

• Do students know how to use the guide words at the top of each page?

• Show them how to select the definition that matches the way the word was used.

• Require the definition to be written down, even in a shortened form.

• Remind them that, like any other life experience, the more it's done, the more efficient they become. Once developed, this habit is as easy as tying a shoe.

Lookin' It Up Atlas Style

Develop the same attitude toward looking up places and watch geography literacy explode! When the name of an unfamiliar place comes up in your reading, stop to find it in an atlas. Look in the back of the atlas for the name of the place. (Very small, insignificant places are only labeled in very big atlases. You may have to refer to a larger place nearby.)

Turn to the page indicated and look at the grid reference. If you're already familiar with where a place is located but want to show this to your students, skip the index and turn right to the section. Most atlases are organized by continents. First determine the continent, then the country, and flip to the right section of the atlas. Show students the map and location and point out any familiar places to help provide a point of reference.

As with dictionary work, the student can be held responsible to record this information on his outline map when the reading session is complete. Chapter three will show you how to effectively use outline maps, and chapter fifteen is full of outline maps you can copy. Keep a good atlas handy at all times. This can easily become a life-long learning habit for both you and your students.

Lookin' It Up and the "Osmosis Theory of Learning"
Have you noticed that when you look up a word in the dictionary or find a place in an atlas, that you found something else of interest? Maybe while locating the Bering Sea in the classroom atlas you've noticed Alaska is farther west than Hawaii. Not only that, but a part of Alaska's Aleutian Islands actually cross the international date line. You found what you were looking for - the Bering Sea - but like osmosis, other bits of information absorbed into your brain without any effort on your part!

This gradual, often unconscious process of assimilation or absorption of information is a phenomena that occurs regularly to those whose habits include "lookin' it up." Don't you just love when a student learns without even knowing it?

Amazing but True

Alaska is farther north, farther east and farther west than any of the other forty-nine states.

By modeling the habit of looking up information, you have profited the student in four ways:

1. You're showing that words are a very significant part of life. Understanding the words to which we are personally exposed improves our discernment of the world around us.

2. Having the "look it up" attitude yourself shows your students that it doesn't take long to look up a word in the dictionary or a place in an atlas.

3. Osmosis learning is taking place.

4. You're promoting the value of being a "lifelong independent learner" yourself!

THE STUDENT NOTEBOOK

A Student Notebook:
- Develops personal responsibility for learning
- Improves organizational skills
- Develops higher levels of critical thinking and reasoning
- Offers an outlet for artistic abilities and writing
- Hones research skills
- Develops note-taking skills
- Increases pride in school work
- Produces true learning
- Benefits all learning styles

There's much to be said for the higher level of critical thinking and real learning that keeping an individual student notebook provides, as opposed to the fill-in-the-blank approaches which often provide a reactive type of learning. Students often arbitrarily fill in workbooks without reflecting upon how the information applies to real life.

The notebook approach is *proactive.* It stimulates the student's reasoning and response abilities. Ideally, the notebook requires the student to write in complete sentences, most often stimulates original and independent thought processes, and provides a means for the expression of *true learning*. The notebook provides an opportunity for the student to record through essays, drawings, diagrams, and any other way that expresses the individuality of the student what the student reasoned for himself from the material he learned.

When the material covered in a unit or subject of study is kept together and displayed neatly in a notebook, folder, or composition book, the student tends to take his work more seriously. Filled with his summaries, research, essays, drawings, map work, diagrams and vocabulary, his notebook becomes a source of pride. A thorough notebook is also an excellent resource to use in studying for the (dreaded) test, even though an individual notebook may contain much more information than what the teacher or curriculum chooses as test questions. If you normally test to determine a student's progress, you may even be able to eliminate some testing by using the student's notebook to gauge what was learned. Certainly what a student develops for himself he'll be much more likely to remember and apply.

The Student Notebook is:

- The student's property, his expression of time, labor and stewardship.

- A record of individual progress, productivity and responsibility.

- Proof to the student that he can discipline himself to accomplish a goal.

- A valuable study tool.

Well, gee! If there are so many benefits, why aren't all students required to keep notebooks? There must be some drawbacks, right?

Keeping a notebook requires **self-discipline** and **perseverance** for both the teacher and the student. You cannot carbon copy a notebook and pass it out, or dictate exactly what the student will learn. The teacher is the student's guide, encourager, the one who makes assignments, and the one who must check daily for progress. Assessment isn't simply a matter of checking-off workbook pages or reviewing questions answered.

Keeping a notebook is laborious, especially for children with poorly developed writing skills. Since these skills vary widely, expect students to work at the upper end of <u>their</u> capabilities. Hold them to <u>their</u> personal best, not to someone else's. It's challenging, and requires that the student be willing to accept responsibility for his own learning.

If you've never used notebook methodology and think you want to give it a try, commit to follow through for one unit. You'll see that the benefits listed only scratch the surface of what you and your students will accomplish. If you decide to continue with this method, learn from your experience and blaze on! Each notebook is a new experience for both the teacher and student, and each new experience carries with it its own learning.

Notebook Basics

There are different kinds of notebooks and different ways to compile one. Choose what works best for the topic, your classroom, or your student profile. Feel free to use the following information as a guide for your own creative ideas. Each teacher and each student is unique and offers the class much in individuality. This may be the greatest benefit of the notebook approach: gifts of individuals have a medium in which to grow and flourish.

A notebook can be compiled in a three-ring binder with dividers, or developed right into a sewn composition book. Notebook paper can be placed in a smaller report folder with a clear cover when the unit of study is completed. It's recommended the student design a colorful cover for the first page, and leave room, if using a composition book, for a table of contents.

What Goes Where?
The information your student is learning can be organized into sections. These sections include, but are not limited to, lecture or research notes, summaries and essays (the student's written conclusions of what he has personally researched, read about or learned in lecture, audio or video presentations), map work, daily journal entry, vocabulary, drawings, assignment sheets, and tests. Usually only final copies of written assignments should go into the sewn composition book.

Attitude is (almost) everything! Be an adventurer and encourager!

Notebook Sections Can Include:
1. Personalized cover
2. Table of contents
3. Notes of research and lectures
4. Written work
5. Work sheets, handouts, tests, assignment sheets
6. Map work
7. Vocabulary
8. Daily journal entry
9. Drawings, diagrams, charts (optional)

Three-Ring Binder
When using a three-ring
notebook, choose a
binder with a clear
pocket to slide a cover
page in front. Tabbed
dividers can separate
sections. The vocabulary

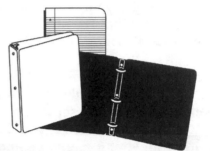

section can dedicate a page for each letter of the alphabet, or
you may choose to place words in the order they are used.

Composition Book
When using a sewn composition (comp) book, leave the first six
pages (three individual pieces of paper) blank and ask students to
number all other pages on the lower outside corner of the page.
The first page will be used as a cover page, and the next two for
a table of contents.

Vocabulary Section
Use the last five to ten pages for the vocabulary section, placing
the word "VOCABULARY" on the top center of the first page of
the section. Each vocabulary word is then placed in that section
of the notebook in the order used.

If you simply MUST have words in alphabetical order you can prepare the last thirty pages to place new words on the appropriate
page. Place the capital letter of the alphabet in order on the upper
outside corner of the first twenty-six of those pages, and leave
the last four as extras to use later (should a page get filled and
more space is needed.) To clarify, each side of a page is counted
as one page, so your vocabulary section will use fifteen pieces of
paper. The first thirteen will have each successive letter of the
alphabet on the upper outside corner, and the last two pieces of
paper will have only the page number written on them.

Maps, handouts, and any drawings not drawn directly into the
book can be taped to the appropriate place in the comp book
when that part of the project is completed. If a map is larger than

the comp book, simply tape three sides into the book and fold in what remains. You may wish to photograph larger maps and projects and affix the photos into the notebook as well.

Grade Levels and Guidelines

Typically, students in grades five and up will be able to keep a thorough student notebook. Younger students can begin as soon as they're writing their first sentences. Let them draw a picture to go with their sentences, or have them write a sentence to go with their pictures. If your student is drawing pictures before he can write, print the caption for the picture yourself. Allow the student to dictate what he wants to go with his picture. Keeping a picture book such as this provides a wonderful foundation for future individual notebook preparation.

Instruct students to keep their work neat and tidy. Most writing assignments require several drafts before the final copy. Only the final copy will be placed in the notebook. There should be no scribbling or doodling in this special notebook. This book will reflect the student's personality, his interests, and his level of educational responsibility. Each student should be encouraged to use his best penmanship at all times with the exception, perhaps, of note taking, when taking accurate, legible notes should be the focus. All words should be spelled correctly, and any misspelled words should be corrected as soon as they're discovered. Students can draw a straight line through mistakes, erase completely or use white-out liquid, whichever the teacher desires. If something is to be underlined, a ruler should be used to form a straight line. Cursive writing should be preferred when the student is capable, and any labeling on maps, charts or diagrams should be neatly printed. Questions should be answered in complete sentences.

There's no substitute for establishing good writing habits.

Students who are poor writers will see their greatest improvement over the course of the school year if they're faithful to their notebook. There are students who will require much patience and understanding from you if they are to succeed. Often, the very act of keeping the notebook will change the student's attitude toward writing. Reluctant writers can be encouraged to draw more pictures or submit photographs, but only if they are accompanied by written text. Much encouragement and commendation is needed to keep this student going until the excitement and pride in their notebook takes hold. It's tempting to accept lower quality work from the reluctant writer, and it may even be necessary to get them started. Be sure to raise the standard once the notebook has become "old hat." It is important, however, to require students to write in complete sentences.

Many students enjoy using a variety of pens or gel rollers to add fun and colorful additions to their notebooks.

Famous people who kept similar notebooks include:
- Benjamin Franklin
- Thomas Jefferson
- George Washington
- John Quincy Adams
- Nathaniel Bowditch
- Leonardo da Vinci

Artwork

Artwork should be put on unlined paper whenever possible with final copy only placed in the book. Sometimes the first draft of a sketch will be neat enough. When this occurs, the student can neatly tape the paper into his comp book or onto paper to place in the notebook. Enhance drawings, diagrams and maps with colored pencils, or outline with fine tip felt markers and erase pencil lines. Drawings can be placed in the notebook in a separate section labeled for drawings, or you may prefer students place them with the topic depicted. Artwork should either be titled or labeled, or placed opposite written information regarding the picture.

It's common for a student to feel totally inadequate when it comes to drawing. It's okay to allow him to copy a picture in the book, but don't allow tracing unless this is absolutely the only way the student is able to submit an entry without great agitation. He may be quite surprised at what a good job he can do when that extra effort is made and he's permitted to copy a picture from the book. His future drawings may come about without quite so much grumbling! Remember, the goal is to build the student's confidence to eventually draw without copying. Students need to understand that their picture may not be perfect or look exactly like the one being copied, because those artists had many years of practice. With practice, your students will improve, too!

It's a Wrap

Continue to add to the notebook throughout the year or for the duration of the unit of study. Many topics can be placed in the book at once. Other sections can include science, nature, spelling bears (frequently misspelled words - spelled correctly, of course!), history, government; whatever you're studying. Even handouts can be kept together in the notebook. When an opportunity arises, let the student design and draw a cover for his notebook and place in the front page of the comp book or slide in the clear pocket of the three-ring binder. Finally, complete a table of contents for the book with page number references.

There's a comprehensive unit on teaching geography while reading the novel *Hans Brinker or The Silver Skates* in chapter seven. Specific instructions and assignments are given for using a student notebook. If you should choose to use the Hans Brinker study, you'll have a grand opportunity to establish the student notebook. (Best for fifth grade and up.)

If some of the guidelines sound too strict and demanding, use your own judgement. You know your students and what you can expect from them. You'll find that the higher you set your expectations, the higher their performance will be. Always, always commend neatness, effort and responsible behavior. This will go a long way towards their development as life-long learners. Show-off their notebooks whenever possible, and treat the student notebook as the valuable tool that it is. The notebook should be stored conscientiously in an assigned place to eliminate misplacement.

With patience and discipline, students will reap the benefits of this individual learning experience and it may become a life-long habit.

Want help getting started with the notebook approach?

See Resources for:
• *Student History Notebook of America.* Students use it as a guide to record research, diagrams, map work, and much more.

• *Trail Guide to ... Geography* series companion student notebook CD-ROMs. Printable maps, templates, and more make creating geography notebooks a cinch!

GeoTrekkin' Supplies

You wouldn't try to canoe without a paddle, would you? Teaching geography without the proper tools is attempting to do just that. All classrooms should be supplied with the following: World and USA wall maps, student atlas, outline maps, colored pencils, colored pens or fine-tipped markers (for paper maps), or water-based markers (for laminated maps). A globe, an almanac, and an assortment of other atlases are very beneficial but not absolute necessities. Each item is discussed in detail below.

Globe

A globe is a great tool for seeing the whole world and the relationship between continents. However, because globes are limited in size, they lack the details needed for most studies. If you must choose between a globe and a wall map, get the wall map because its scale is much larger.

Maps

Maps are a must! You'll use maps for reference and activities, but don't stop there. Put up lots of different kinds of maps in lots of different kinds of places. Write on them, touch them, stick interesting stamps and stuff to them. Use them! Change them often. Post them on the back of the bathroom doors, on ceilings, on sides of desks, on the school door, in hallways, wherever kids congregate! Place a map on a big table and cover with plastic from a fabric store. Students of all ages love exposure to the world.

World Wall Map
Every home and classroom should have a world map prominently displayed. Choose a colorful current map of the world with the Atlantic Ocean positioned in the center of the map. This posi-

tioning is best, because it places the Western Hemisphere on the left (remember, west is left when north is up) and the Eastern hemisphere on the right. Avoid world maps which place the Western Hemisphere in the center of the map. It's confusing to see the East split into two parts and placed on both sides of the map.

It's important to choose atlases that are age-appropriate and current.

USA Map

A good classroom map isn't cluttered with unneeded information. It isn't necessary to have highways on a classroom USA map, for example, unless you're planning to do a lot of travel. Choose a map that's both colorful and concise.

Atlases

It's vital to have a wide range of atlases available to your student, especially when using outline map activities. It isn't possible for any one atlas to include every bit of information available. One may be great for locating finer details of the USA and continents, but scarce in providing information needed for specific countries. Small textbook maps just don't do the job. Often, it's necessary to open two or three or even more atlases until you find the one that gives the detail needed. Don't be discouraged! Keep looking!

Types of Atlases

A general world atlas or classroom atlas will be used most in your studies. Match atlas to age level! An atlas which includes latitude and longitude coordinates in the back of the book or in the gazetteer is recommended. Also, look for one that has both political and physical maps, and thematic maps such as population density, rainfall, or agriculture and natural resources. The Rand McNally's *Classroom Atlas* (elementary), *Answer Atlas* and *Premier World Atlas* (jr. high and up), and *Goode's World Atlas* (high school and up) are good general reference atlases. A general USA atlas is helpful to use when studying individual states.

Historical atlases are also helpful in your classroom. There are several types of historical atlases available depending upon the detail provided by the publisher. Historical atlases depict political boundaries, kingdoms, and empires throughout historical periods. A good Bible atlas is also helpful when studying ancient history, as they depict ancient civilizations well.

Time Saver Tip
Check out map information before presenting your lesson so valuable time isn't wasted figuring out which atlas to use.

Outline Maps

There's hardly a better hands-on tool for learning geography, history and many other subjects than an outline map. Chapter three is dedicated to guiding you to the many uses and advantages of outlines. Be sure to take advantage of the many unique reproducible outline maps in chapter fifteen.

Students can make their own outline maps of any area by tracing from the textbook or atlas. If you have access to an overhead projector, you can change the map scale. To get the right scale, trace the section of the map needed onto a piece of clear plastic overhead projector sheet. This can then be projected onto the wall into whatever size needed by moving closer or further away from the light source. Tape a blank sheet of paper to the wall and trace the map in the size needed. This map can now be used to fill in information for the duration of the study at hand.

Trekkin' Tools

- World map
- USA map
- Atlases
- Outline maps
- Colored pencils
- Water-based markers
- Globe
- Almanac
- Patience

Paper or Laminated?

Both paper maps and laminated outlines are effective; each serve a different purpose. Know your purpose before giving an assignment.

1. Laminated maps are durable and reusable. If you use water-based markers such as Vis-a-Vis overhead projector pens, the map can easily be wiped clean (with a damp paper towel or sponge) for future projects.

2. Paper maps are a better choice when finer detail is desired, since it's hard to place small details on a plastic map with an overhead projector pen. On a paper map younger students can use colored pencils. Erasable colored pencils are best, because the student can erase mistakes without smudging. Older students may prefer to use fine-tipped colored markers. The student may wish to have his map laminated AFTER the project is complete. Then any future information can still be added with the water-based pen on the same map.

Almanacs

It's amazing how much information is packed into an almanac! For a nominal fee you can have a comprehensive, up-to-date source of almost everything you'd ever want to know about world facts: facts about over 180 countries; about the people, language, geography, government, economy, flags, transportation and history. An almanac includes many more facts about the United States: health and nutrition, astronomy, calendars, science and technology, and maps. Don't let it get dusty sitting on some bookshelf - almanacs are meant to be used. There are a number of good almanacs. Check out the information offered, ease of use, and clarity of print. Some are crisper and easier to read than others. Also, check out children's almanacs, especially for the younger set. *Facts Plus* by Susan C. Anthony is an excellent choice for all students.

Hundreds of pages of small print can be intimidating to the uninitiated - both teacher and student. In order to become comfortable and familiar with almanac usage, follow these three simple steps:

It's Simple

1. First, look on the outside for a general list of contents. What do you see that you might find useful?

2. Next, look inside at the general table of contents. Most break it down to a more specific table of contents. Look these topics over.

3. Now, take a brief tour of the general index. Stop and look up one or two items that catch your eye.

Have contests: pick questions that are relevant to a subject being studied, pertinent to your class in some way, obscure, or even amusing; then see who can find the information the quickest. Have students make up lists of questions to ask with an answer key. Feeling brave? See if they can stump YOU!

The *Trail Guide to U.S. Geography* provides 30 weeks of daily questions for high school students to answer using an almanac. With this daily drill (two questions per day) students develop valuable research and critical thinking skills. See Resources.

Check out "Almanac Trek" (chapter 16) for a fun almanac activity sheet with questions your class can use for practice. (No answer key is provided because of differences in each year's almanac.)

Kingfisher

The *Kingfisher History Encyclopedia* is another excellent resource for history and geography because it has good, simple-to-follow maps when trying to label historical events as you study. The key word here is "additional." This type of book won't replace a good atlas but is suggested as an additional asset to your library.

Patience

You can't buy it at your local bookstore, but patience is an essential part of teaching! Students can become frustrated and discouraged when working with maps; whether identifying features or labeling an outline map. If your student puts up too much of a complaint or his face is more blank than the map, pull out your patience. He may need help to get going. He may need to look at a sample or require more guidance. Help, but resist the temptation to do it for him. He NEEDS this experience for his own educational development.

PACKING YOUR BAGS

CHAPTER 2

YOUR GEOGRAPHY REFRESHER COURSE

Singing the "Where In the World Is It Geography Blues"? Then this section is just for you! Some information is elementary, so if you feel completely confident about your ability to teach geography, go ahead and skip it. The rest of you take heart - it's not as confusing as it seems! This chapter will help to set some basic facts in order. There are a lot of vocabulary words here, so pay close attention if they're unfamiliar to you. Listen up, teachers - there'll be a test at the end of this unit!

High school students should read this refresher course in conjunction with the high school geography chapter.

What's the first thing you think of when you hear the word "geography"? Maps? Globes? Carmen San Diego? You're not alone - those are the three most common responses in our geography seminars!

What is geography, anyway? Maybe this definition from the National Geographic Society will help:

> Geography: A knowledge of place names, location of cultural and physical features, distribution and patterns of languages, religions, economic activities, population and political systems. Physical regions and physical phenomena, such as tectonic activity, land form, climate, bodies of water, soils and flora and fauna. The changes in places and areas through time, including how people have modified the environment. Cartographers' tools, such as maps, instruments, graphs and statistics, are also a part of geography.

Wow! Maybe a better question might be "What isn't geography?"

The word "geography" is from the Greek word *geographia*, meaning "writing about the earth." The word "earth" used here is all inclusive regarding people, places, and the relationships between people and the places where they live and interact. So first and foremost, throw out the thought that geography is simply knowing countries and capitals!

Geography can be broken into two main divisions: geography of the earth (physical geography) and geography of people who live here (human geography).

- **Physical Geography**
  The Earth in Space
  Time Zones
  Climate Zones
  Globes, Maps, Atlases
- **Human Geography**
  Race
  Nationality
  Language
  Religion
  Government
  Culture

- **Physical Geography** includes everything about the earth itself; its make-up, its position, and its movement in the solar system, the moon, seasons, its heat energy from the sun, the atmosphere, all natural features of the earth, water, rocks (geology), weather patterns and other natural processes that shape the world. See how this is intertwined with science?

- **Human Geography** is all about human lifestyles, beliefs, growth and development, the interactions of people to the earth itself and with other peoples who dwell here. It's understanding where people live and why they live where they do, how they communicate, what they eat, how they dress, how they use their resources, how communities develop, and how people impact their own environment. It's all about how these choices are related to the physical geography of the earth.

After going over some basics in these two groups, you'll begin to fill the gaps in your own foundation of geography.

PHYSICAL GEOGRAPHY: LET'S GET PHYSICAL!

Space...the Final Frontier

Amazing but True

One out of every five adult Americans believe the earth travels around the sun once a day! Hang onto your hats!

Let's start with basics about our planet and the solar system that is home to the earth. Earth is the third planet of nine in the solar system located in the Milky Way Galaxy. It's the only planet in this system known to support life. The Milky Way Galaxy is a gravitational spiral nebula made up of over 200 billion stars. It's so large it would take light 100,000 years to travel from one end to the other. The Milky Way is one of millions of known galaxies in the universe. The center of the solar system - the sun - is 109 times larger than the earth; its farthest planet is over 3.5 billion miles away.

The earth is almost 93 million miles from the sun, and travels in an elliptical path around it at about 66,700 miles per hour while spinning on its axis more than 1,000 miles per hour at a 23.5° tilt! Whew! It takes the earth 365.25 rotations on its axis to make one complete trip around the sun. This orbit and the earth's tilt produce the different seasons and variations in daylight hours.

Hemispheres

To make it easier to study geography and locate places, the earth is divided into **hemispheres**. The imaginary line running horizontally around the broadest part of the sphere, called the equator, divides the earth into **Northern Hemisphere** and **Southern Hemisphere**. The circumference of the earth at this point is 24,901 miles.

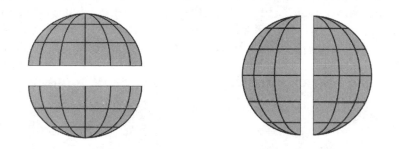

Another imaginary line runs around the earth perpendicular to the equator and through both north and south poles. Its circumference is 24,855 miles. This divides the earth into the **Eastern Hemisphere** and the **Western Hemisphere**. The Western Hemisphere is commonly defined as North and South America. Now you know why Americans live in the "West," and you can guess why the "Far East" is called the Far East!

Summer Solstice and Winter Solstice

During that 66,700 mile per hour trip whirling around the sun, the different positions of the earth in relationship to the sun causes seasons and varies the length of days.

In June, the Northern Hemisphere is tilted toward the sun, where it receives the most direct rays. On June 21st, the **Summer Solstice** occurs, marking the first day of summer when the Northern Hemisphere experiences the longest day of the year in sunlight hours. The sun is directly overhead at noon at 23.5° north of the equator. Geographers have marked this with an imaginary line running parallel to the equator and have named it the **Tropic of Cancer.**

Have you ever wished you had more hours in your day? Plan a trip north of the Arctic Circle during the Summer Solstice and you can! That's right - the sun doesn't seem to set for a full day, and when it does, it's back in a flash until the Northern Hemisphere's position in its orbit around the sun is no longer tilted directly at the sun. Have you ever heard Alaska referred to as the "Land of the Midnight Sun?" Now you know why!

GeoBit says:
Geo-nuts may have already noted the earth isn't exactly spherical in shape, or both circumferences mentioned would be the same. The earth is actually a sort of flattened sphere, bulging at the equator. Although this shape is more accurately termed a "geoid," for the sake of simplicity it's commonly referred to as a "sphere." (But feel free to add this to your Scrabble arsenal!)

Imagine what's happening in the Southern Hemisphere at the same time. It's tilted AWAY from the sun. Winter! Another interesting thing takes place at this time. Maybe you've guessed it already.... places below the **Antarctic Circle** are experiencing *night* all day long! If you got up at sunrise there, you'd be sleeping all day.

Now, if you followed the description of the Summer Solstice, the **Winter Solstice** will be a breeze! Imagine the earth six months later, in December. It's at the farthest distance of its rotation around the sun, and the tilt of the Northern Hemisphere is 23.5° away from the sun. The noon sun is directly overhead at 23.5° <u>south</u> of the equator, and the night hours outnumber the daylight. It's now winter, the shortest day of the year, the Winter Solstice.

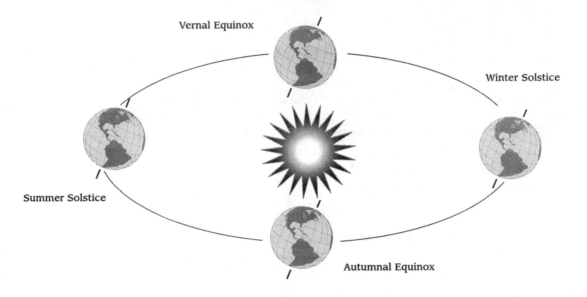

This location (23.5° South) is marked on the globe by geographers with a horizontal line running parallel to the equator, and is named the **Tropic of Capricorn**. While the people in the Northern Hemisphere are shoveling snow and skiing in the mountains, those in the Southern Hemisphere are basking in the sun on sandy beaches sipping kiwi juice. Now the long daylight hours are experienced by people living south of the Antarctic Circle, while north of the Arctic Circle it's a twenty-four hour night. (Time for a nap!)

GeoBit says:
Does anyone REALLY live below the Antarctic Circle? Only scientists live in Antarctica.

Equinoxes

The length of day and night is always equal at the equator, but as you can see it varies elsewhere, according to the position of the earth's orbit around the sun. There are two times when daylight and nighttime hours are equal everywhere else on the globe. One is in the fall, when the noon sun is directly overhead at the equator. This marks the beginning of autumn and is aptly named the **Autumnal Equinox**. Likewise, six months later the direct rays of the sun again hit at the equator, marking the beginning of spring. This is called the **Vernal Equinox**. Consider yourself educated!

Eclipses

An eclipse occurs when the earth and moon are positioned in a straight line with the sun during their orbital patterns. When this happens, the sun casts a shadow on the earth or the moon, causing the light to be hidden (eclipsed). A **lunar eclipse** occurs when the earth is directly between the moon and the sun. The earth casts a shadow on the moon, blocking the light of the sun from the moon. A **solar eclipse** occurs when the moon is directly between the sun and the earth. This blocks part of the sun's rays from shining on the earth. Eclipses occur several times a year and can be seen with the naked eye. Consult your almanac for dates, and remember to never look directly into the sun!

Time Zones

You think you have it tough keeping appointment times straight? Before 1883, communities each set their own time by the sun. In 1883, railroad companies in the United States divided the U.S. into four different time zones in order to be able to synchronize their schedules. This eliminated the confusion experienced by travelers (not to mention train conductors) who were traveling across country. The following year the whole world was divided into time zones.

It's easier to read a time zone map when you know the following facts. The twenty-four time zones are marked off every 15° from the **Prime Meridian** at Greenwich, England. The time is established from noon at the Prime Meridian. Every 15° east of Greenwich is represented by hours + or added to **Greenwich Mean Time** (GMT), also known as **Universal Time**. Every 15° west of the Prime Meridian is represented by hours - or subtracted from Universal Time. For example, if you look at a time zone map, you will see that Florida is at -5. Simply subtract 5 hours from noon and you get 7:00 a.m. When it's noon at Greenwich, it is 7:00 a.m in Florida.

There are some exceptions to this basic description. Lines aren't always drawn straight, in order to keep communities in the same time zone. Daylight Savings Time throws it off an hour, and in some countries the time changes by two hours or by half an hour instead of by one hour. The **International Date Line** separates the calendar dates. It's at about 180° in the Pacific Ocean. A person traveling west crossing the international dateline will lose a whole day and must advance his calendar by one day. When a traveler goes east through this line, it's a day earlier!

Time Zone Facts

- Greenwich Mean Time = GMT = Universal Time
- There are 24 time zones
- Time zones are designated at every 15° of rotation
- Zones represented by negative numbers are that many hours behind Greenwich
- Zones represented by positive numbers are that many hours ahead of Greenwich

Climate Zones

"Climate" refers to all weather conditions for a given location over a period of time. Scientists continue to work on understanding the complex relationships that constitute a climate. Besides average temperature, there are many other variables to consider: solar radiation, humidity, precipitation, atmospheric pressure, wind, latitude, elevation, topography, vegetation, and more.

Classifying Climate Zones

Understanding climate has been a topic of interest even as far back as Aristotle's time. He established one of the oldest methods of determining climate by dividing climatic regions according to temperature only. This outdated system is misguided. The three climate zones he established didn't take into consideration other factors such as wind pattern or precipitation. They were:

- Torrid
- Temperate
- Frigid

The twentieth century climate classification system developed by Russian-born climatologist Wladimir Koppen is widely used today as a general climate guide. Koppen observed that the type of vegetation in a region depended largely on climate. Modified several times, the Koppen classification now uses six letters to divide the world into six major climate regions based on annual and monthly precipitation and temperature. It's further divided into 24 different subcategories. The six regions are:

A. Tropical
B. Dry
C. Mild mid-latitude
D. Continental (severe mid-latitude)
E. Polar
H. Highland

We've included a modified summary of Koppen's classification on page thirty.

Climates defined by Precipitation and Temperature

"Tropics" is used most often to describe the region that lies between the Tropic of Cancer and the Tropic of Capricorn. Tropical climates receive the most direct rays of the sun. Since the sun's heat makes the water evaporate, the tropical zone has a high amount of precipitation. Tropical wet areas have lots of rain

GeoBit says:
Atlases may use thematic maps reflecting climate in a number of different ways. Read the key carefully!

throughout the year. Tropical wet and dry areas are known for their monsoon rains, but have relatively dry periods the rest of the year.

For further climate studies check out these websites:
• www.geography.about.com
• www.geographic.org

National Geographic publishes excellent geography materials that also cover climate.

"Polar" climates are frigid and all precipitation is in the form of snow. They receive the least amount of direct sunlight. Winters are long and dry; summers are short and chilly. Examples of polar climates can be found in the areas above the Arctic Circle and below the Antarctic Circle.

Mild and continental climates together are sometimes call "temperate" climates. They are found between about 25 and 70 degrees latitude. Temperate climates experience moderate temperatures and all four seasons with a distinct cold season.

Vegetation and Clarifying Terms

The same term may be used to depict both a vegetation and a climate. For example, a **"savanna"** is a tropical grassland. The weather is very rainy two times during the year, and then the rest of the year is quite dry. Conditions are harsh. Grasses grow well but dry quickly and become fuel for fire. Few trees can survive in that climate. The baobob tree has a thick, fireproof trunk that stores water like a sponge. The acacia tree has broad, flat crowns that shades its lower leaves. You may see a savanna region on a vegetation map. This refers to the type of vegetation that can thrive in that climate. This is why one atlas may refer to savanna as a vegetation and another atlas may call it a climate.

Similarly, the word "tundra" may be confusing. Tundra has been defined as a flat, treeless area of the northern Arctic regions. In the Rocky Mountains, the area above which trees cannot grow is also called the tundra. It's a cold, windy climate where the temperature rarely rises above 32° and there is very little precipitation. Few plants thrive in those conditions. The tundra vegetation includes mosses, lichen, and other shallow root plants. (It's amazing, by the way, to see the many very tiny flowering plants that do survive the harsh climates of the tundra.) As you may have noticed, the same term - tundra - is used to define both a climate and a vegetation.

GeoBit says:
A tundra is both a flat, treeless vegetation region, and a cold windy climate region.

Finally, all climate charts offer general guidelines, not definitive rules. Think of borders as transition zones. A climate chart can't encompass everything that makes up a climate. Charts will continue to evolve as climatologists continue to learn about the earth.

KOPPEN'S CLIMATE CHART: SIMPLIFIED

Climate	Temperature	Precipitation	Vegetation
A. TROPICAL Rain Forest	hot	100"/yr	hardwood trees, heavy undergrowth
Monsoon	warm	6 mo of heavy rain	tree ferns, palms, bamboo, mosses
Savanna	very hot at times	either very rainy or very dry 10"-30"/yr	sparse trees, tall grass, low trees, poor soil, prairie, grasslands
B. DRY Steppe	short, wet season	less than 20 in/yr semi-arid	bushes, wiry grass few trees
Deserts	very hot days 100° cold nights 20°	little rainfall less than 10"/yr	sparse vegetation succulent plants
C. MILD MID-LATITUDE Mediterranean	warm, dry summer warm, rainy winter	3X rain during wet season than dry	shrubs, evergreens, olive trees
Cool, Dry Summers	72°-50°	3X rain during wet season than dry	
Humid, Warm Summers	av. summer temp is above 72°	plentiful year round	short grass, low, thorny bushes
Marine West Coast	cool summer mild winter	plentiful	
D. CONTINENTAL Humid Warm Summers	av. temp above 72°	spread through year, no dry season	fertile agricultural lands
Very cold, Dry Winter	av. summer temp is less than 72°	severely dry snowy winter	coniferous trees
E. POLAR Tundra	rarely above 32°	very little	mosses, lichens berry bushes
Ice Cap	always below freezing	snow	very few plants
H. HIGHLAND - Exceedingly diverse.			

Globes, Maps and Atlases

Globes

A **globe** is a spherical model of the earth, and maps are a flat representation of the earth's surface. A globe is the most accurate map representation of the earth you can get. The information on a globe is true in all four characteristics of importance to cartographers: direction, distance, shape, and area. Although a globe is most accurate in its representation, it's not usually the best source to use when studying geography. Only one side of the globe can be seen at once, and even a large globe provides too small a scale to include much information. Besides, globes are awkward to carry around! A globe is great to use as a reference; however, detailed information will be better gleaned from a good atlas.

Map Basics

Meridians and Parallels
Okay! This is a good time to explain those imaginary lines around the globe we keep talking about. Lines are drawn on the globe to form a grid to help you locate places easier. Lines running parallel to the equator are called **parallels** or lines of **latitude**. They're measured in degrees (°) seventy miles apart and tell you how far north or south a place is away from the equator. The equator is at 0°. The **North Pole** is at 90° north of the equator, and the **South Pole** is at 90° south of the equator.

Lines of **longitude**, or **meridians**, are lines drawn around the globe from the North Pole to the South Pole. Longitudes are also are measured in degrees. The line through Greenwich, England is at 0°. Remember, this is the Prime Meridian. Any place located east of the Prime Meridian is measured in degrees east up to 180° and is located in the Eastern Hemisphere. Likewise, any place west of the Prime Meridian is measured in degrees west up to 180° and is located in the Western Hemisphere.

You'll see this grid on all globes and most good maps. The grid provides a kind of "global address" for any location on earth. The N or S degrees (°) are given first, followed by the E or W degrees (°). For example, Denver, Colorado is located at about 40°N 105°W and Athens, Greece is about 38°N 24°E. Take a moment to check these addresses for yourself in your own atlas.

GeoBit says:
A cartographer's greatest challenge is to depict the spherical shape of the globe in each of these points as true as possible:
- Direction
- Distance
- Shape
- Area

Each 15° represents an hour of rotation of the earth. Serious geography students may wish to investigate rotation in minutes (').

A gazetteer is an index in the back of an atlas with references to geographical names.

GeoBit says:

Latitude is first both alphabetically and when giving latitude/longitude addresses. Memory help: think "ladder" for latitude and "long" for longitude to keep the two terms straight.

For additional practice in using grids, see "Co-ordinate Grids and Number Lines" starting on page 124.

Finding Your Way Around

Did you find Athens in your atlas? If you can't find your way around in an atlas, that's about to change! If you don't already have it handy, stop and get an atlas now and take this quick lesson. Open the atlas to the back section called the **gazetteer**, or index. The gazetteer lists all places referenced in the atlas in alphabetical order. It will give the "global address" or a grid location and the page number where the place can be found.

For practice, look up Athens, Greece in the gazetteer. Note page number and location. Your atlas may list a reference labeled 1, 2, 3...or A, B, C... This is a grid reference. Turn to the page indicated, look for the grid on the map, and follow the path where the letter and the number cross. That's the grid section where you'll find Athens. If you're looking for the latitude/longitude of a place and your atlas doesn't give it in the index, you can figure it out yourself to a pretty close degree of accuracy. Look up the place given in the grid reference, and locate the latitude and longitude referenced on its borders.

The location in your gazetteer may say "38°N 24°E." If you know the longitude and latitude of a place you can find it on a map in the same manner. Using Athens again, find the right page. Locate approximately 38°N from the side border of the map (remember, this tells you that Athens is north of the equator by 38°.) Now, locate approximately 24° at the top of the map. If you trace both those lines across and down, your two fingers should bump into each other right near Athens, Greece.

Knowing Your Legend or Key

Do you have a clear picture now of longitude and latitude and how they're marked on a map? What else is on a map besides grids? All of the different pieces of information on a map are represented by symbols. The symbol doesn't necessarily look like what it represents, so they're shown in the **legend**, a separate box on the page with information about the map. Symbols could include a series of dots, dashes, dashes and dots, thin

LEGEND/KEY
• Cities under 100,000 population
● Cities over 100,000 population
◉ Capital City
┼┼┼┼┼┼ Railroad
─·─·─· Country Border
▲ Mt. Peak
0   100   200 Miles
Scale = 1:10,000

lines, thick lines, color lines, circles, triangles. The legend will include the scale, distance, and what each of the symbols represent. The scale is usually written in a representative fraction, such as 1:10,000. The first number represents the unit on the page, and the second number represents the unit on the ground. In the USA, map scales usually represent inches. In this case, one inch on the map equals 10,000 inches on the ground.

Most maps are presented with north facing the top of the page. This should be indicated on the map somewhere with a "compass rose." The compass rose shows cardinal points of north (N), south (S), east (E), and west (W). These are cardinal directions. The compass rose may also show four other points: northeast (NE), northwest (NW), southeast (SE) and southwest (SW). Many maps will only depict the north point. Just remember, south is ALWAYS opposite of north, and east is ALWAYS right of north.

In case you were wondering, the term for the directions NW, SW, NE, SE is "intermediate."

Types of Maps

There are many different types of maps to meet many different needs. Maps can be divided into two groups: general reference maps and thematic maps.

General Reference Maps

General reference maps show general information such as countries, continents, cities, rivers, elevation , political and other features. These maps are found in encyclopedias, textbooks or in an atlas. Road maps are a type of general reference map that shows the kinds of roads and distances to help travelers choose the best route for their journey. Pilots use reference maps called "charts" to plan their course of travel.

Political Map

Physical Map

Special Maps or Thematic Maps

Special maps which show boundaries of places under one government are called **political maps**. A political map shows the political divisions of an area, such as countries, states, counties and cities. It may also include basic physical features, such as rivers or lakes. Many maps use different colors to represent each nation; others use different types of lines or dots and dashes to distinguish between borders.

Maps that emphasize the general roughness of the surface of the earth are called **physical maps**. Color is used to indicate elevation, and shading may also indicate land forms and other features of the earth's surface as seen from an airplane or satellite photograph.

Other special or **thematic** maps emphasize some particular feature, using color, shading, or symbols to represent differences. "Population density maps" show how many people per square mile live in the area. "Rainfall maps" show average yearly rainfall

Thematic Map
(Early Indian Tribes)

of a selected area. "Weather maps" use symbols to show weather patterns. "Product maps" are labeled with text, color, or symbols to demonstrate the type of products produced in an area. This thematic map shows the locations of early Indian tribes.

Topographic maps
Topographic maps are special maps designed to show accurately the contour of the earth's surface. Contour lines indicate elevation or steepness of hills, mountains, or valleys, and show rivers, ponds or any other body of water. Topographic maps are used by campers, hikers, hunters, or fire and rescue crews to plan their journey on foot.

Illustrated Maps
An illustrated map is a special map that shows an area graphically (a drawn picture). You've probably used one at the amusement park to find your way around. A Chamber of Commerce may provide illustrated maps depicting the city's downtown, including three dimensional pictures of buildings and other landmarks. Illustrated maps aren't usually drawn to scale, but are useful for finding your way around a smaller area. (Good for the mall, not Texas!)

Drawing a map helps students to pay closer attention to details while reading historical novels, studying history, or even during science class. They use higher thinking skills as they draw. Start small: draw a bedroom, then the neighborhood. It can be simple, like the inside cover of *Winnie the Pooh* books, or detailed, according to the ability and interest of the student. Remember, an illustrated map doesn't need to be accurate to scale, but it should be accurate in what it displays. It's fun to allow students to use a variety of art supplies, colored pencils, markers, or even stickers.

Map Projections

All maps depict the spherical shape of the globe on a flat surface, and because of that, every map has some distortion. A map can show one or more of the following: true direction, true distance, true shape, or true areas, but never all four at once. Only a globe can represent each of those four features as true. However, even a large globe has a super small scale and can show very little detail. Therefore, maps are a more functional representation of the earth.

Many different projections have been developed by cartographers which place the distortion away from the center of the map. If you look closely at the fine print near the border or legend of a map, you may be able to find the name of the projection used.

Mercator Projection

The "Mercator Projection" is used for navigation. Any straight line on the map is called a "rhumb line." Using the four points mentioned before, the direction is true along a rhumb line (the rhumb line isn't necessarily the shortest distance). The distance is true only along the equator; the shape and area of large areas are distorted and the distortion increases away from the equator. Despite all of these negative factors, the Mercator Projection, drawn by Gerardus Mercator in 1569, is still a very common map projection. Several variations on the Mercator

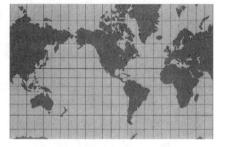

Mercator Projection

Projection have since been developed to minimize distortions in other areas. Many companies using a Mercator Projection will put the Western Hemisphere in the center of the page, splitting the Eastern Hemisphere into two parts.

Robinson Projection

The "Robinson Projection" is a more recent map, and is commonly used in the classroom. Presented by Arthur Robinson in 1963, it uses tabular coordinates rather than mathematical formulas to make the world "look right." The distortions are much less noticeable to the eye. There's a better balance of size and shape of the high latitude lands than Mercator's map. Directions are true along all parallels and the central meridian. (The central meridian is the meridian selected by

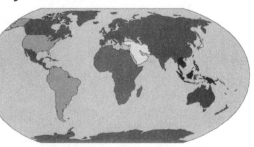

Robinson Projection

the map maker to be in the center of the map.) Distances are constant along the equator and other parallels, but scale varies. Distortion is minimal throughout, but greatest at the poles. Most

Just Ask!

Earth Science Information Center
US Geological Survey
507 National Center
Reston, VA 22092
888-ASK USGS
www.usgs.gov

- They have a great packet and poster teaching about different types of maps. It's called, "What Do Maps Show?"
- Also ask about their free Map Projection Poster

map makers using the Robinson Projection use a place in the Atlantic Ocean as the central meridian, without splitting the hemispheres.

More than you ever wanted to know about map projections? Actually, there's more - there are many other map projections besides the two mentioned here. The United States Geological Survey has a wonderful poster demonstrating the different projections, and normally provides them free of charge. The important thing you must understand, however, is that no map is without distortion. Only a globe can present the earth accurate and true in all four points. Now you know!

Show What You Know!
To explain this distortion to your students, try this experiment. Blow up a large balloon and draw a picture of a face with a felt tip marker or ink pen. It's best to hold the balloon closed rather than to tie it off, because when you've finished drawing the face you'll allow the balloon to deflate. Now, cut away the lip of the balloon and the opposite end as well. You should now have a sort of tube. Cut through the tube on the back side of the "head". This should be a rectangle shaped piece of rubber with a face drawn on it. If you take this piece of rubber and stretch it out, pinning all four corners to a cork board or a thick piece of cardboard, your students will easily see how distorted a round object is when made to lie flat. (This is even more effective if someone is artistic enough to draw the continents instead of drawing a face.)

Atlas Basics

An **atlas** is a book of maps. There are a variety of different atlases available. "General reference atlases" show current political boundaries and often also include thematic maps as well. "Historical atlases" include maps of political boundaries throughout historical periods. Historical maps may show explorers' routes, battle sites, and changes in political boundaries over time. They're invaluable in understanding the growth of nations and differing political dominions.

Atlases include more than just physical and political boundaries. You can learn about the earth's crust, plate tectonics, time zones, the solar system, and much more in many world atlases or student atlases. Your student can discern important information about the climate, agriculture, population density and more from the many special thematic maps in an atlas. Pay close attention to the legend and title on these maps to understand what information they provide.

Give your students a simple exercise to help them become familiar with maps in atlases. Have them choose six countries. Find and graph the population density and yearly rainfall of each country. Chart each country identifying its main vegetation, climate, agriculture, and latitude. Compare the facts gathered with each country's latitude. See what conclusions your students make about how the lifestyle and culture of people may be related to location.

There's your basic introduction to the complexities of physical geography. Continue to make use of maps, atlases, and earth sciences to develop and broaden your knowledge. Enjoy the journey, and your students will, too!

HUMAN GEOGRAPHY (No Aliens Here!)

Human geography, or cultural geography, focuses on the people of the earth and their interaction with their environment. It can be divided into several topics. To keep it basic, six main areas will be introduced here: race, nationality, language, religion, government, and culture.

Race

Race is a distinction based upon biological characteristics common to a population. There are many races designated by geographers. The eight main races are African, Asian, Australian (Aborigines), Caucasian, Indian, Native American, Melanesian, and Polynesian.

Nationality

Nationality refers to a group of people with citizenship in a nation or country. They share customs, ethnicity, and language, although there are certainly nations with more than one language.

Language

The world is home to nearly 4,000 languages, thirteen of which are spoken by more than 100 million people. These top thirteen (in descending order) are: Mandarin Chinese, English, Hindi, Spanish, Russian, Arabic, Bengali, Portuguese, Malay-Indonesian, French, Japanese, German, and Urdu.

Languages can be divided into sub-groups of families, branches and groups. About half of the world's population speak a language from the Indo-European language family, divided into eight main family groups. They are: Germanic, Romance, Balto-Slavic, Indo-Iranian, Greek, Celtic, Albanian and Armenian. The two

- **Physical Geography**
  The Earth in Space
  Time Zones
  Climate Zones
  Globes, Maps, Atlases
- **Human Geography**
  Race
  Nationality
  Language
  Religion
  Government
  Culture

- *Children Just Like Me* (Dorling Kindersley) introduces readers to children from 30 different countries in a typical day-in-the-life format. Pictures include each child's signature, clothes, home, toys, and more.

- *Travel the World Cookbook* by Pamela Marx (GoodYearBooks) has wonderful recipes from around the world and features culture notes, food facts, and an activity with each recipe.

- *Eat Your Way Around the World* by Loreé Pettit (Geography Matters) is a fascinating cookbook with delicious recipes for serving a complete meal from each of over 50 different countries.

most common groups are the Germanic languages developed from a language spoken long ago (German, English, Dutch, Swedish, Norwegian), and the Romance languages (Italian, Spanish, French, Portuguese, and Romanian) developed from Latin. A dialect is a difference in regional pronunciation and syntax. A blend of different languages is called "pidgin."

Religion

A basic understanding of religions is important because of its impact on world geography and history. Religion is any system of beliefs that incorporates worship and faith in a divine creative power. There are two primary types of religion:

1. Universal - open to all people. Its adherents, such as Christians and Buddhists, attempt to spread their beliefs to others.

2. Ethnic - includes a system of beliefs within a certain regional locality. Hinduism is an example of ethnic religion.

Although there are many, many different religions worldwide, more than 75% of the world's population belong to one of the groups listed below. The major world religions and their basic tenets include:

• Judaism
The Jewish people believe in one God as creator of the earth; they are His chosen as children of Abraham. Their holy day is the Sabbath, in which they celebrate the day of rest after creation.

Judaism isn't a large religion, but it's significant because of its political global importance and its roots in the establishment of both Christianity and Islam. Although Jews have been scattered all over the earth, their population is concentrated mostly in Israel, Canada and the United States. Major Jewish festival days include Passover (commemorating the deliverance of the ancient Hebrews from slavery in Egypt), and Yom Kippur (Day of Atonement).

Approximate number of believers: 18 million
Origination: Begun by Abraham around 1700 B.C.
Place of Worship: Synagogue

Primary divisions: Orthodox, Conservative, Reform, Hasidic
Type: Ethnic (Israel)
Book of Scriptures: Torah and Talmud
Spiritual leader: Rabbi
Symbol: Star of David

• Christianity

Christianity has Judaic roots and is centered on the belief in the death, burial and resurrection of Jesus Christ, the Son of God. Christians believe that Jesus willingly accepted crucifixion to pay the penalty for their sins. Those who accept Jesus are forgiven of sins and will have eternal life with God in heaven. Major Christian holy days include Christmas (the birth of Jesus) and Easter (His resurrection).

Approximate number of believers: Almost 2 billion
Origination: Around 33 A.D.
Place of Worship: Church
Primary divisions: Protestants, Roman Catholics, and Orthodox.
Type: Universal
Book of Scriptures: Bible
Spiritual leader: Priest, minister, pastor or preacher
Symbol: Cross

• Islam

This faith was founded during a time when people believed in many different gods. It was established by a vision of Mohammed, who was believed to be a prophet of Allah, the one true God. Muslims pray five times daily to Allah facing their holy city, Mecca. Muslims are found primarily in the Middle East, North Africa and Southeast Asia. The major Islamic holy day is Ramadan, when they give alms to the poor and fast during the daylight hours.

Approximate number of believers: 1 billion
Origination: Early 600's by Mohammed
Place of Worship: Mosque
Primary Divisions: Sunni Muslims and Shiah Muslims
Book of Scriptures: Koran
Spiritual Leader: Iman
Symbol: Crescent and star

• Hinduism

This is one of the oldest ethnic religions and incorporates many doctrines and deities. Hindus trust that all gods are part of a universal spirit called Brahman. They believe the human soul never dies but returns through reincarna-  tion. If a person lives a good life, he will be reincarnated in a higher state of life; if a bad life, he will return in a lower state.

Approximate number of believers: 750 million
Origination: More than 5,000 years ago
Place of Worship: Temple, shrine
Type: Ethnic (India)
Spiritual leader: Guru, yogi
Symbol: Sanskrit word "OM" used in meditation

• Buddhism

Siddhartha Gautauma, the Buddha "enlightened one," originated the belief that life is filled with suffering, but one can find nirvana (a state of happiness and peace) by living free from all material desires and worldly attachments.

Approximate number of believers: 335 million
Origination: About 500 B.C.
Place of Worship: Temple or pagoda, monastery
Type: Universal
Book of Scriptures: Tripitika
Spiritual leader: Monk
Symbol: Wheel of life (represents the Noble Eight-fold Path, right knowledge, right intention, right speech, right conduct, right livelihood, right effort, right mindfulness and right concentration.)

• Shintoism

A worship of the spirits and demons believed to have lived in plants, animals, and parts of nature. The highest god is the sun goddess, to whom the emperor of Japan was believed to have descended. He was worshiped as a god up until the 1940's.

Approximate number of believers: About 3.5 million
Origination: Native folk beliefs
Type: Ethnic (Japan)

There are several Chinese religions that make up the beliefs of 145 million people. They include Confucianism (more of a standard of moral and ethical codes), Taoism (simple life in harmony with nature), and Mahayana Buddhism. They worship at a shrine or temple. These are all primarily concentrated in China, Korea and Southeast Asia.

When studying world history and world events, these different religious beliefs have an impact on the culture of the nations and traditions of the people. Watch for ways the philosophy of the period affects the choices of people and development of nations.

Governments

People need rules to govern their lives, and those rules as they apply to a nation are established by their governments. There are different types of governments, because people are different and have different ideas about how government should operate depending upon the history, geography and culture of the region. There are three basic forms of government: rule by one, rule by a few, and rule by many.

• Autocracy

When a nation is ruled by one person, it's called an **autocracy**. There are at least two types of autocracy: monarchy and dictatorship. In a **monarchy**, the leader normally inherits the throne and retains power for the duration of his/her life. Familiar names given to monarchy include king, queen and emperor. A **dictator** usually comes into power during a crises and rules with complete authority. Examples of dictators include Benito Mussolini, Fidel Castro, and Joseph Stalin.

• Aristocracy, Oligarchy

When a nation is ruled by a few people, it's called an **aristocracy** or oligarchy. The aristocracy is generally of the upper class and may be members of royalty or wealthy landowners. One of the great revolutions in France came about as commoners rose up against the aristocracy and ended up performing the same distasteful acts they so passionately opposed. In an **oligarchy**, a small group of people hold power, ruling together as a dictator.

• Democracy, Republic

In a democracy and a representative democracy (this is called a **Republic**), the job of governing is performed by many people. A **democracy** is when everyone meets and votes on every issue together. Town Meetings of old were fashioned as a democracy, although not a pure democracy because not everyone was allowed a vote. It's often mistakenly said that America is a democracy. More accurately, in the United States we are governed as a republic. Individuals are elected by the people to represent them in the governing process. Each elected representative then votes on the issues.

Government Systems and Ideas

Within these forms of governments are various ideas of how a government should operate. When the power of government is used without the consent of the people, it's called **authoritarianism**. People have no freedom and are required to wholly submit to the authority. **Fascism** is a system of one-party dictatorship.

• **Human Geography**
  Race
  Nationality
  Language
  Religion
  Government
  Culture

Capitalism, Socialism, Communism

The method of governing a nation's resources varies as well. In America, our system is based on **capitalism**, or the free enterprise system. Here, our government allows an economic system in which private individuals and private businesses own most of the country's resources and industry. Ideally, competition keeps prices and profit margins reasonable. **Socialism** grew out of the belief that capitalism unfairly concentrates the wealth of a nation amongst the owners of the resources. In opposition to capitalism, socialists seek to have the government control the nation's land and resources through an orderly transition. Wealth is to be dispersed evenly among all people. **Communism** is socialism with a political twist. Communists advocate a revolutionary change from capitalism to total governmental control of land, industry and production, permitting no criticism of their ways.

Culture

Culture refers to human activities and achievements that people pass on from one generation to another. It includes language, clothing, diet, customs such as marriage and child raising, government and economic systems, and religion. Simply put, culture is the sum total of the way of life of a group of people. These choices and their diversities are commonly a result of the geography of the place where people have settled, what natural resources are available to them, and how they use those resources.

The culture of a group of people is reflected in their art, architecture, clothing, and food. Even a nation's flag, coins, currency and postage stamps bear symbols which reflect the history and beliefs of the people. When learning about any topic, remember to take into consideration the culture of the people who impact the topic at hand. Compare the aspects of their culture to your own. Watch for opportunities to tie in the geographical features of the area to the choices people made that helped form the culture.

Conclusion

Now that you know the fundamentals of physical and human geography along with teaching guidelines, you'll see ways to incorporate it into other areas of study. Use the tools suggested as you begin an exciting adventure into the world of geography, complete with the array of activities, ideas, assignments, and map projects provided in the remainder of *The Ultimate Geography and Timeline Guide* (from here on referred to as, *The Ultimate Guide.*)

The section that follows on the five themes will help clarify the distinct aspects of geography. Both physical geography and human geography will be reflected within each of the five themes.

THE FIVE THEMES OF GEOGRAPHY

By now you've seen a much broader concept of the physical and human side of geography. Geographers and educators have joined together to establish an understanding of geography by dividing geography into five themes. A basic knowledge of these will open a whole new realm of what geography is really all about. You'll quickly see that it's much more than simply knowing where a place is located.

If you teach with a unit study approach, considering these themes will help you provide geography activities or lessons within your unit. If you read historical novels, make bonus use of your reading time as you take advantage of all the many geography-related themes that will appear. Of course, studying history provides many opportunities for geography lessons, but knowing the five themes will help you become sensitive to those hidden lessons in other subjects as well.

What are Geography's Five Themes?

1. LOCATION: Position on the Surface of the Earth
Where is it Located?

 The first theme is the basis of how geography is normally defined by most people. Where is a place? You may locate a place in two ways: "relative location" and "absolute location." Relative location is a general location based on proximity. You may say that the grocery store is on Jackson Avenue across the street from the Tasty Cream Bakery. Absolute location is used to describe an actual spot on the globe, as in 45°N 16°E.

The Longitude and Latitude of It
The "where" in geography terms is measured in degrees longitude and latitude. (Some atlases do not use these coordinates, but simply place a grid labeled ABCD and 1234 on their maps.) Remember, lines of latitude identify degrees north or south of the equator. Longitude measures degrees from zero to 180 degrees east or west of the Prime Meridian. The Prime Meridian, an imaginary line designating the starting point, is located at Greenwich, England. Here's a quick math quiz: how many degrees longitude does the earth rotate in one hour? (360 degrees divided by 24 hours equals 15 degrees per hour.)

These imaginary lines form a grid that provides the basis for what is considered a "global address." What major city in the US lies 40°N 105°W? (Did you grab an atlas and check? If so, you would have seen the city is Denver, CO.)

The Five Themes

1. Location
2. Place
3. Relationship
4. Movement
5. Region

Hands-on Tip:
A great game to introduce the concept of a global address is "Atlas Drills."

It's Simple

1. Find the "address" of six places around the world and list them.
2. Show how to look up addresses in the index or gazetteer of the atlas.
3. Give your student an atlas and your list.
4. Student searches for the names of the cities listed.
5. Student competes against the clock or others.
6. Student submits "addresses" for others to find, or two students can swap "addresses."

Location Literacy: Maps, Maps, and More Maps!

One of the best things you can do to increase your student's geography location literacy is to use maps whenever possible. Remember the "osmosis theory"? Keep an atlas or globe handy to locate places in the news. Atlases are normally best for finding newsworthy kinds of places, since more information can be placed on maps in an atlas than on a globe. You'll find, with practice, that it takes only a minute to look up a place. Again, when you model this learning habit, the student will be more likely to develop the same pattern for his own life.

Let's say a news event has occurred in Calcutta, India. You grab the nearby atlas, open to the continent of Asia, and locate Calcutta near Bangladesh. (Go ahead, stop and get an atlas.) Did you notice that while looking for Calcutta, you discovered Sri Lanka is an island off the southeast coast of India? Or maybe you discovered another interesting fact. Osmosis theory at work!

Start map training close to home by using a state map and having students locate their own town on the map. Locate other places of interest in your state and in the city of your state capital. Compare the other cities to your own. Is the town north of your own or south? How far is it? You'll need to look at the map's legend (normally located at the bottom of the map.) Find the compass point on the map to see which direction is north. Most maps are drawn with north at the top of the page.

Obtain a map of your city for this activity. Locate your street and mark where your home or school is located. Now, begin to locate other familiar places: the bank, the church, the grocery store, library. Identify in which direction each place is from your own location (north, east, south, or west). What other identifying characteristics can you find?

Check Out This Example:
You've assigned your students to select the best route for a vacation to grandma's house. "This is where we are, this is where we're going. What roads shall we take to arrive at our destination?" One student may choose the scenic route, complete with gravel roads. Did she really not want to miss all the beautiful scenery, or was pink her favorite color? (Checking the key, you discover the scenic route was drawn in pink.)

Now you can see the necessity of determining an objective before choosing a route. Was the goal to arrive at grandma's as quickly as possible to spend more time with her, or was there sufficient time to see all those neat places along the way? If they hadn't seen grandma for a long time (or if grandma has a pool!), the student may have wanted to arrive as quickly as possible. This girl would then want to choose the green interstate highway lines (despite her affinity for pink!). Going over the legend of the atlas before beginning the project prevents misunderstandings.

When traveling by car, it's great for kids to have their own atlas in which to follow along with in the back seat. There are clever travel atlases for children that include crosswords and other activities at the bottom of the page. Children can learn about state flowers and other interesting facts. They rarely ask, "How much farther?" when they're busy watching exits and locating different cities for themselves. Without knowing it's happening, they'll remember more geography than you can imagine.

Using a Compass

Developing skill with a compass is easy and fun. Compasses can be purchased from the camping section of most department stores. Don't waste money buying a compass that isn't liquid-filled. Liquid-filled compasses come in all price ranges. An inexpensive one (under $15) should meet your needs just fine. On the other hand, a cheap compass will only frustrate you and the student. There's a fun compass treasure hunt described in chapter four.

1. Hold the compass level and the magnetic disk will rotate to the north.

2. Align the north arrow on the dial with "N" on the compass.

3. When you know where north is, other directions can be easily discerned. When facing north, south is behind you, west is to your left, and east is to the right.

Which Way is Which?

Become familiar with your own surroundings. Show students where the sun rises in the east and sets in the west. Notice the slight shifting in the sun's arch across the sky throughout the year. You'll find it doesn't rise exactly due east and set exactly due west all year. Notice how snow melts easier on south facing lawns and slower on north. From which direction does the wind generally come? Do the trees have moss? On which side of the tree does moss grow heaviest?

Directional skills can be encouraged from a young age in the home and school, simply by being careful to give instructions using the following words when possible: above, below, left, and right. "Put the blocks on the shelf above." "The plates belong to the right of the cups." "Please get the book below the craft shelf..."

Using cardinal directional terms instead of left and right adds an interesting twist to letting a child give directions to the park or home. Be sure you're familiar with these directions yourself, or confusion will reign.

Geography Games

Geography board games and computer games can greatly increase knowledge of where places are on the globe. Feel free to play with an open atlas handy. If the student can find the answer in a given amount of time, he can continue to proceed in the game. (When playing with the atlas open the game will take longer, but geography knowledge increases as well.)

In chapters three and five, you'll find some great game ideas to do with your students. As always, feel free to adapt our games to reflect your own creativity.

2. PLACE: Physical and Human Characteristics
What makes a place special?

Location of a place is only just a part of understanding geography. What is it that distinguishes one place from another? What characteristics make this place unique to other locations on the globe? There are physical characteristics such as climate, soil type, plant life and human characteristics such as culture, architecture, and population density, to name a few.

When beginning a history study, while reading a novel, or even when learning where gold is mined during science class, take a moment to consider the characteristics of the place. By doing so, you will better understand the history, the culture of the people in the story, or why gold was found in that area to begin with.

GeoBit says:

Play "find the object" with younger children by hiding an object and giving hints to go west or north, instead of saying "hot " and "cold."

Ask the following questions on your way to learning about a place: What's the climate like? What plants and animals live in that area? Are there any unique physical characteristics? What are the natural resources? What are the people like? What kind of clothes do they wear? What kind of food do they eat? Is there anything special about the architecture? What type of government rules the people? When you begin to consider these types of questions, a new understanding will develop about the place you're studying. That book you're reading will come to life, and perhaps a new appreciation of another culture will emerge.

Geography Terms
There are many geography terms to describe the physical characteristics of the earth. You'll find many of the physical geography terms defined in the appendix, as well as flash cards in chapter seventeen. Physical maps are drawn with symbols, colors and shading to demonstrate the surface of the earth. A geography terms chart shows physical features in a graphic form. Become familiar with these terms, and watch for their use when reading. Encourage students to observe the out-of-doors with these terms in mind. Elevation, soil types, plant types, kinds of animals, and climate all help to form the physical characteristics of a place.

To become familiar with characteristics of a place, study its weather. Remember, weather patterns and climates are associated with location. Weather maps, charts, cloud formations, and much more will help the student appreciate the complexities of how places are uniquely special. (A cloud chart is a great teaching tool. Knowing clouds and simple forecasting rules is certainly a useful, life-long skill.) Chapter eight includes information to serve as a start on studying weather.

Plant Life and Animal Habitations
Plant life and animal habitations contribute to the physical characteristics of a place. Notice the relationship between types of plants and the place where they grow. The climate, soil, and water all affect the biological life. What kind of animals live there? Study how physical characteristics affect plant life and animal habitation. See how animal physiology is adapted to climate. Notice that Africa is home to the largest mammals, with the highest orders in greater numbers both in species and individual types than in any other continent. Australia has the greatest variety of flora and fauna found nowhere else in the world, and many of its animal species are unique. South America has more reptiles and insects than any other continent, and its mammals are smaller than those of Africa. These kinds of facts, coupled with climate and location, can help students to reason the "whys" for themselves.

The Five Themes

1. Location
2. **Place**
3. Relationship
4. Movement
5. Region

Discuss how the different characteristics of a place affect the way people live. Identify characteristic changes that have been made by people. Human changes to the place could include landscape, bridges, agriculture, roadways, recreational areas, reservoirs. Notice how building structures often conform to weather or topography. A visit to your local historical, recreational, or natural places of interest makes observing human changes and physical features interesting.

3. RELATIONSHIPS: Human and Environmental
How do people and the environment affect each other?

 People relate to their environment and the land in different ways. These relationships between people and their surroundings form the basis for this third theme of geography.

While learning about other cultures, note how their food, clothing, habits, hobbies, religion, and relationships relate to the places where people live. It's easy to see that people help shape the places where they live and work. Certain physical features of the earth are used by people in diverse ways. For example, the rich plains of America's midwest are ideally suited to agriculture; especially for growing corn, wheat, and soybeans. What places in the world grow vast amounts of rice, and how has that influenced the culture?

Notice how the physical features of the place affect the culture of the people. The frigid winters of Iceland drew the people inside in groups to survive the long winter days together. For entertainment they told stories, or sagas, of their conquests, their ancestors, and their adventures. This culture was known for the accuracy of their stories and the people, even children, were very good at telling them in great detail. Most of what we know today about the Vikings come from these sagas. We don't usually associate this part of their culture with their climate and location, yet the characteristics of the place where they lived probably had more to do with this than any other factor. Encourage your students to consider how the characteristics of a place affect its culture. Compare places you're studying to your own hometown, state, and country.

Consider why people live where they do. Areas along rivers, bays and waterways are heavily populated. Notice in an historical atlas that areas along a source of water were the first to become

inhabited. Besides our basic needs for water, early transportation depended upon water to move goods. Notice also that areas with good soil and climate are selected for farming and agriculture. People with a focus on recreation may choose to live in California or Colorado where the physical features and climate support surfing, skiing or an active outdoor lifestyle. Those who thrive best with sunshine and warmer temperatures may choose to live in Florida or Arizona. These same kinds of factors play a role all over the world when it comes to where people settle the land.

The Five Themes

1. Location
2. Place
3. **Relationship**
4. Movement
5. Region

Once a land has been chosen to settle, people historically make attempts to control their surroundings and change their environment to suit their needs. Early settlers harnessed water power with waterwheels to build mills. Merchants assembled buildings to sell their wares. Streets were laid, trees were cut, sidewalks were built. Where land was swampy, people constructed drainage systems or planted rice.

Even in your own home you attempt to control and change surroundings by mowing grass, planting trees for shade, and putting in gardens. In some areas, people must water and fertilize their lawn to have lush, green grass. Other regions may naturally grow more grass than its occupants  want to mow, so the landscape artist is called to design lawns that require less care. Governments construct levees, dams, or dikes to control water. Farmers build fences to keep animals in. The list goes on!

The changes that are made for personal benefit may carry with them consequences. Often, these consequences must be weighed with overall benefits to mankind. In the Netherlands (Holland), for example, the land is actually below sea level. Innovative Dutchmen have been pumping water off the land and building canals for hundreds of years, and that nation will forever be known for its windmills as a result. What damage may have occurred to the natural wildlife or plant life to dig the canals was outweighed by the need to have agricultural soil, fields for sheep to graze, and land for people.

Challenge your students to watch for ways people control their environment. Take the opportunity to attend a state park or a national park, ranger-led program to learn about the area's natural features and how they've changed over time.

4. MOVEMENT: People, products, and information
What are the patterns of movement?

People, products and even information are being moved from one place to another all over the earth. Clothing from China, stereos and cars from Japan, oil from the Mideast, fresh fruits from California and Florida are shipped all over the US as well as to other countries. Most of us interact with other places in the world almost every day in one way or another. How did those goods travel to your home? What mode of transportation was used? Notice how products are transported. Compare items to types of transportation chosen.

Discuss different modes of transportation. Compare speed, cost and comfort of various forms of travel. Consider what benefits different forms of transportation have over others. Would you take a train to the library five blocks away or ride your bike? Why? How is fresh seafood from  the east coast transported to the midwest? Which mode of transportation would best preserve the freshness of fish: over-the-road truck, airplane, train, or car? Have students share what type of transportation they have personally experienced and why each form was chosen.

Younger children have trouble understanding the concept of city, county, state, country, continent. Some think their own state is the country, or that their city is the state. To help students become more aware of the world around them, have them search their homes for items made in other countries. Let them locate 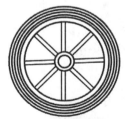 the "Made in..." on a number of items in the home or classroom and list the items and where they were made. Next, have them locate the countries on a map and draw a line from these places to their hometown. (Laminated maps are great for this!) When finished, the map should have many lines drawn from places all over the world like spokes on a wheel. Just the act of finding the item and locating the country it was from on a map will usually fix those particular places in minds much better than if you simply said, "Let's look up China on a map." There are other ways to reinforce this concept. You'll find some clever ideas in chapter five.

Information is transported around the world and within communities in different ways. Compare how information has been transported as technology has improved - couriers, the Pony Express, telegraph, telephone, television, the Internet.

Our American Heritage

In America, almost everyone has a heritage that began in another country. Study how families traveled to America. Students could interview their grandparents and great aunts for details of how the family traveled to America. In what city did they first land, and where did they go from there? What form of travel was used? See if students can find out how their family ended up where they are now. Why did they leave their country of origin?

On a world map, plot the route they may have taken. This can be put together in a booklet with the map, pictures gathered, and a timeline or family tree. The timeline figures in unit six include generic family figures to plot your family tree. Putting together a heritage family album with photo-safe materials provides an heirloom to pass on from generation to generation. Even Native Americans can use a USA map to depict their heritage from original tribal site to the place they call home, today. People in any country can trace their routes, even from regions within their country.

Here's a true story that may inspire you and your students to try a meaningful project:

Twelve-year-old Ian spent time composing a letter requesting his relatives to mail him a photo and their favorite recipes, especially ones that reflected their own background. He also asked for a warm memory related to the recipe. His mom's family came from Poland; his dad's were from the western states, and his stepfather came from Mexico. He received responses from relatives he (and his mom!) had never even met!

With help, he used a word-processing program to layout the recipes, photocopied in the pictures, added the anecdotes, and bound the finished product together into a very personalized cookbook! As a thank-you, he sent each contributor a copy of the cookbook. (Another student might need to add a small charge to cover printing costs.)

As a result of this semester-long project, Ian learned about his family, about places and cultures he had no firsthand knowledge of, and his extended family learned much about each other after receiving their copy of the final product.

High school students can even do an intensive genealogical search for a history credit. Most librarians are familiar with the basic research needed to get one started. Many books and great computer programs make the work even easier. Encourage them to take good notes and to present their finished information in a pleasing format.

The Five Themes

1. Location
2. Characteristics of a Place
3. Relationship
4. **Movement**
5. Region

5. REGIONS: How They Form and Change
What makes areas similar?

 Regions are areas that have a commonality: a sameness. They can be based on climate, culture, history, politics, religions, agriculture, economy, land forms and much more. In the United States, some regions are the heartland, the midwest, the high country, the plains, the corn belt, the Bible belt, the South. Hometowns have ethnic regions, socioeconomic regions and recreational areas. Consider into what kinds of regions the earth can be divided: continents, oceans, Third World countries, Spanish-speaking countries, etc.

Basically, regions are simply areas which share a variety of geographic or cultural characteristics that make them distinct, and these common features designate a region. Regions are not exclusive, for one kind of region can easily overlap another. Regions are depicted on thematic maps, since they demonstrate regional factors such as population density, rainfall, or agriculture. With physical maps, all similar physical regions are depicted in the same color.

Discuss regions of your community. Notice growth around lakes and parks. Regions are also demonstrated in the home: people eat in one region, sleep in another, and play in yet another. There's a region where laundry is done and where cooking is performed, regions in backyards for landscaping and for gardening.

Hands-On Tip

Regional maps are fun to make using blank outline maps. Use colors or icons to represent regional areas. When learning about the United States, younger students can color regions on an outline map, cover with contact paper, and cut out along colored borders to form a puzzle.

This section on the five themes introduces you to what geography is really about. Watch for any of the themes in action, and you'll be able to understand why most developed nations use geography as a core curriculum. It's easy to connect with almost any area of study, and it enhances the understanding of each discipline. Maybe American schools will once again recognize the importance of teaching geography, enabling students to gain an accurate understanding of the global state of affairs.

Well, you've just completed your refresher course. Now you're ready to get down to the basics of using outline maps. But first, there's one small detail yet to complete. You didn't forget now, did you?

The Five Themes

1. Location
2. Characteristics of a Place
3. Relationship
4. Movement
5. **Region**

Testing the Teacher

Let's see how well you fared on your geo-refresher course. Don't act surprised... you were told there would be a test!

True or False

1. _____ Students will fit exactly into one of the learning styles.

2. _____ All information needed to fill in outline maps can be found in one good atlas.

3. _____ You don't have to look up information in an atlas; just tell the students to do it.

4. _____ Laminated outline maps are always the best choice.

5. _____ The earth travels around the sun once a day.

6. _____ A Tundra is a measure of weight for Russian vegetables.

7. _____ The Prime Meridian is an expensive cut of beef.

8. _____ Physical maps can show where the gym is located.

9. _____ Political maps can reflect the politics of the nation.

10. _____ Geography is simply knowing where a place is located.

11. _____ Eclipses are visible only during a leap year.

12. _____ If you travel east via jet airliner at 350 mph nonstop from Taipei, Taiwan to San Fransico, California, you will have arrived before you left.

Answers:
The answer to questions 1-11 are false. The answer to number 12 is true. If you missed any of the first 11 questions you may want to go back and review. If you missed the last one you're in the majority. Crossing the international dateline is always a confusing experience. Just keep your time zone map with you!

NOTES:

FINDING YOUR WAY WITH MAPS
CHAPTER 3

CHARTING YOUR COURSE

Now that you've finished your refresher course, (how did you do on the test?) are you chomping at the bit to get started? Wait just a moment... you may want a quick education on outline maps. Here are instructions, map facts, map activities, and ideas to get you going! Chapter fifteen is packed full of brand new outline maps just for you.

Outline Maps: *How to Choose Them, How to Use Them How to Fuse Them into Your Curriculum*

Do you look at blank maps with a blank face? "How do I use this?" you may say. "It has absolutely no information on it!" Right you are. That's what makes outline maps fun - they're a great outlet for creative abilities.

What Exactly are Outlines?
An outline map is a simple black and white map which shows the shape of land masses only. It may include a nation's (or a state's) borders, but without any political details. Although some outlines may include geographical features such as rivers, there's no text (no labeling of places.) Don't be intimidated by blank space. It's really quite an interesting project to place information learned on the map. Using outlines, students will have an opportunity to organize geography and historical facts into a visual format. The information will be supplied by the student through a series of fun and interesting projects using atlases, history textbooks, and other reference materials.

Blank maps can be used across the curriculum. (Unit three is devoted to teaching interdisciplinary geography.) You'll find that almost weekly you can provide creative ways to incorporate mapping activities into your schedule. *The Ultimate Guide* provides you with an abundance of suggestions and lesson plans using outline maps. Don't try to do them all; but do try to use those that easily slip into your lesson plans. You'll soon see that outline maps supply some of the greatest cost effective, hands-on learning experiences your students can use. As you and your students get hooked, you may find yourself with enough completed outlines to paper your walls!

Why Use Outlines?

The benefits of using blank maps and adding to timelines are many. (Unit six guides you through the use of timelines and timeline figures.) Students who use blank maps gain valuable practice using reference materials. Learning to use reference materials effectively teaches one important, simple fact: we'll never know everything there is to know, but we can find the answer to any question if we know how and where to look it up.

Do your students forget much of what they've learned as soon as they've finished taking a test? Improve long-term memory retention by providing hands-on map activities associated with subjects. Much has been said about kinesthetic learners or those who learn by doing. The truth is, nearly everyone remembers better what they themselves have researched and recorded in an active way. Filling out an outline map or an outline timeline is just the ticket! (In unit four, you'll find "Conquering the Continents," an entire geography course for both middle school and high school written in just this style.)

Obtaining Outlines

Keep an assortment of outline maps in your resources file. Reproducible outlines in *The Ultimate Guide* are provided for use in your classroom. Included are maps of each continent, as well as a few other regional maps. If you'll copy them right away you'll have a file ready for use. When you want to use an out-line activity, simply check your file. If the area you're studying is too small on the map supplied, just choose the map that includes the area you need and enlarge it. Some projects will require a larger map. Try copying in quadrants and taping it together. Better yet, purchase large-scale paper and laminated maps. See Resources.

The Nitty Gritty

Paper maps or laminated maps - which is best? Both! Which you use depends on your objective, type of assignment, and your students. Here's why...

Laminated outlines

Laminated outline maps are durable and reusable. You may purchase maps already laminated, laminate your own paper maps, or cover them with contact paper. To write on laminated maps, use water-based pens. Overhead projector pens work best, because they leave a clear, bright line that doesn't bead up. Wipe clean with a damp paper towel or damp sponge. A damp sponge works best when trying to wipe off an area near another part you do NOT want erased. Wiping with the corner of the sponge is much easier to control than using a paper towel. Another advantage is that you can use a post-it note glue-stick with removable glue in order to post notes, stamps, postcards, etc., right onto the map. This special glue cleans off easily with warm water.

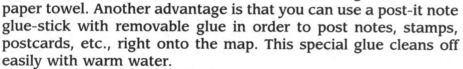

NEVER use dry erase markers on a laminated map. That's worth repeating: NEVER use dry erase markers on a laminated map! These markers are great for quick, write-on wipe-off presentations for corporate America, but not for students. Three reasons not to use a dry erase marker:

1. If you want the map to wipe completely clean, you can't leave dry erase markings on it for an extended length of time. They stain.

2. The fumes they give off can make your head spin - never a pretty sight!

3. Areas already labeled easily get accidentally bumped and smeared, causing tears of frustration (by students and teachers alike!) causing the project to lose its pleasure.

Amazing but True

Dry erase markers will stain a laminated map if not wiped off: use water-based overhead transparency pens instead!

Additional hints regarding laminated maps may be helpful. People with sweaty palms may find they're smudging the map when their hand touches a labeled part. Place a piece of paper on the map under the hand, and you not only provide a barrier from smudging but also a straight edge on which to write the next word. If you use your laminated map a lot, pen marks may begin to bead up. The hand's natural oils (or peanut butter and jelly!) may leave a residue that needs to be washed off. Laminated maps are easily cleaned using any mild window cleaner.

Besides reducing the number of dog-eared maps you own, the greatest advantage to using laminated outlines is their reusability. A large laminated USA or world map posted on the classroom wall can have information added all year long. Or wipe it clean with every new project and start all over. Use different colored pens to differentiate between projects or time periods. When laminated maps are used in the home, they can be stored flat under the couch and brought out when needed if wall space is at a premium.

Paper Outlines

Paper outline maps are versatile because students can do their work in pencil, correct any mistakes, and then trace over the pencil with fine tipped markers, pens, or colored pencils. Students enjoy making thematic maps or physical maps with color. Permanent mistakes are frustrating and can spoil the fun of a project in a hurry.

Although many prefer the durability of laminated maps, paper outlines can be covered with clear contact paper for inexpensive lamination after projects are completed. Often, students want to preserve their work this way, especially if they took great care in labeling the map and enjoyed doing so. Students may place maps in plastic sheet protectors and store in a three-ring binder when not in use. This adds protection, and the sheet protector can be drawn on and wiped off with a water-based pen.

Another advantage of paper maps is that larger desk maps can be folded and stored in the student's pocket folder notebook. Fine tipped markers are best for high school level detailed labeling. (A good, fine-tipped marker that doesn't get mushed is called Stabilo Sensor #189. It's available at office supply stores.) Other students who like finer details will enjoy coloring, labeling, and designing a legend with colored pencils. This is very difficult to do with overhead projector pens on a laminated map. (Use erasable colored pencils if possible.)

Now What?

Okay, so now you're no longer bothered by all that blank space and have even chosen which kind of map will suit your need. With marking pens or colored pencils in hand, you're ready to get started. But what goes on the map, and how is it done? What's the teacher's responsibility, and what's the student's job?

What Goes Where?
You may provide a list of what should be labeled as demonstrated in several chapters in *The Ultimate Guide*. Another way is to

Time Saver Tip

See www.geomatters.com for laminated and paper outline maps.

Chapters with specific map assignments:
• Ch. 7 - Hans Brinker study
• Ch. 8 - Science
• Ch. 9 - Math
• Ch. 10 - "What Map Do I Use When Studying...?
• Ch. 13 - 7 Continents: Middle School
• Ch. 14 - 7 Continents: High School

allow daily lessons to provide what should go on maps as shown in the *Hans Brinker* study in chapter seven. Or use any of the other great examples and suggestions given throughout *The Ultimate Guide*. With practice, you'll come up with your own brilliant ideas that include the effective use of outlines.

Students will use their own creativity when labeling their map, but it's best to get them started with clear directions. Specific guidelines such as, "Draw and label the Nile in blue, shade the Sahara with diagonal yellow lines, locate the Rocky Mountain range and indicate with brown triangles," leave no room for misunderstanding.

High school students will do very detailed map work and should use large-scale maps for their continent assignments (given in chapter fourteen). It's especially helpful when performing a lot of map activities to establish a format and stick to it. Let blue always represent water, mountains in purple etc. One student suggested that placing a star on the capital is too big; she uses red when labeling capitals. You may notice some atlas companies underline capital names.

Allow sufficient time for students to complete their map assignments. Please note that spellings of place names can vary from atlas to atlas. Have patience! It may take awhile to get oriented to finding the information and then figuring out where to place it on the blank map. But take heart, soon labeling will be a breeze!

Placing Your Own Grid on the Map

Sometimes it's hard to figure out where to put some features, like rivers, for example. Try placing a lightly shaded grid line on the outline, matching the grid on the reference map. Place a little tick mark on both horizontal borders of the outline map in exactly the same place they are on the reference map. Using a ruler, lightly connect corresponding tick marks. Repeat for vertical border. You should now have a grid very similar to the one on your reference map, making it much easier to figure out where to draw the city, river, or whatever on the outline. Remember, the more the map becomes filled in, the easier it becomes to properly place information required because you have increasingly more reference points.

A Good Teacher is ... Prepared!

When you use outlines in your lessons, it's very important to be well prepared in order for everyone to receive the best learning experience with the least amount of frustration. Be sure to have a variety of atlases available. Remember, you may go through three or four atlases before finding the one that provides what

Time Saver Tip

Tip: Many people find it helpful to label bodies of water first.

Good teaching is 1/4th preparation and 3/4ths theatre.

--Gail Godwin

you need. Atlases can be obtained from the library to fill in for what you may lack. Time permitting, it's always best to do the assignment first, checking for any potential snags. If you're certain the atlases you've chosen have the information your students will need, you're ready to dig in.

THE FIVE THEMES AND OUTLINE MAPS

Use the reproducible Map and Timeline Assignments sheet provided on page 254. Color-coding suggestions are given on the bottom of each section.

There are so many fun and interesting map activities you can do with your students using outline maps. In fact, each of geography's five themes can be demonstrated when using outline activities. These themes were introduced in chapter two. Here's how to apply them in your mapping adventures:

Location: During all subjects of study, make sure your students know the "where" of it. Whether talking about rocks and minerals in science, Alexander the Great's empire, the Gutenberg Press, the voyage of Columbus, the Holy Roman Empire, or the thirteen colonies, have students record the place or event on their outline maps. They can label the place, bordering nations, states, and bodies of water.

Place: Any physical features described about the place in question should be included on the map. Students can use symbols or colors to represent mountains, rivers, deserts, roadways, reservoirs, bridges, agriculture; absolutely anything learned that's associated with the land can be placed on the map. Any color coding or symbols should be represented in a legend designed and placed in an unused section of the page. Require bodies of water to be drawn and labeled, even if they're not mentioned in the study. They provide great reference points for future additions.

Relationship: Critical thinking will improve if students are encouraged to draw conclusions from what they see. Students can record information about a nation's population density, yearly rainfall, or land uses. By color coding population density on a map, students can easily reason for themselves that people tend to settle in areas along rivers, bays and other water sources. Code a map for soil type and climate. Add icons (or symbols) to represent types of agriculture. Students can draw their own conclusions for what type of soil and climate are needed for different types of agriculture.

Movement: Outline maps can be used to depict movement. Students can plot Magellan's route around the world, Lewis and Clark's expedition, or any movement taught. Discussions can follow regarding what method of transportation was used and why. Family heritage studies benefit from using outlines when the student plots the movement of his family from its country of origin to the United States, and further across the USA to his hometown.

 Regions: An outline map of the world can be used by the very young to learn the seven continents and four oceans. These large regions of the world are easily distinguished, traced, and labeled. Outlines can be used to learn geographic regions by outlining the regions and labeling them. Other regions, such as agricultural areas, cultural, or religious regions are also easily marked and labeled. You'll find many good thematic maps in an atlas that depicts these regions, as well as regions of population density, average rainfall, land usage, and more.

Map Facts

Do your students know these map facts? (Do you?!) Here's helpful information to understand before doing extensive map work. After review, use the "What Do You Know About Maps?" in chapter sixteen to see what information sank in!

- A person whose job it is to draw maps is called a cartographer.
- A symbol on a map that shows N, S, E, and W is called a compass rose.
- An arrow on a map denoting N usually points up, but may point other directions, too.
- North, south, east, and west are called cardinal directions.
- When you face north, you're facing the North Pole.
- When you face south, you're facing the South Pole.
- East is the direction the earth turns. It is the direction of the sunrise.
- If you know one direction, you can figure out the rest. Stand and face north. East is to your right, west is to your left, and south is directly behind you.
- There's usually a line on a map called a scale. Each inch on the map represents a certain number of feet or miles on the earth's surface.
- Maps also have a Legend or a Key. These are symbols and the "key" to what they mean.

Kids remember best what they can get their hands into!

Time Saver Tip
Salt Dough Recipe - So Easy!

2 parts flour
1 part salt
1 part water

(If it's still crumbly, add a bit more water.)

HANDS-ON MAPS

Here are some great map activities that will help your students with their geography and add interest to your school day!

3-D Topographical Maps

These maps are simple to make and promote learning in a true, hands-on fashion. Studying ancient Egypt? Photocopy the reproducible map of ancient Egypt. Glue it onto a sturdy piece of cardboard. Mix up a batch of salt dough. Color with food coloring before applying, or paint it afterwards. Using food coloring is simple: color dough blue for seas and rivers, green for the fertile crescent, and reddish orange for the desert. Or, paint it after it dries.

Making 3-D maps gives kids a great opportunity to learn how to read topographical maps. Are there mountains in Egypt? If so, where? Use a topographical map in an atlas to help define the fertile crescent, deserts, etc. After spending time with their hands making the map, they'll remember the lay of the land.

Salt dough can be used in other ways, too. Students can demonstrate their understanding by making a 3-D poster of geographic terms. Let them model an isthmus, build a peninsula, and craft a plateau!

Salt dough is easier to work with than most clay, although it does have a tendency to crack as it dries out. Despite that, it's an inexpensive, quick, creative way to learn about the lay of the land. Add twigs, pebbles and grass as needed. Add people for interest: use Legos, plastic figures, or make your own.

Jigsaw Maps: or "Putting it all together!"

Great for the kinesthetic learner! Using a copy machine, enlarge a map to the size you want. Copy onto card stock. The student can then label and/or color. Next, cover with laminate or contact paper. Cut it out according to specific state/country borders. (Or, make the pieces bigger or smaller, depending on the level of difficulty appropriate for your students.) Store in a resealable bag. Kids enjoy making their own puzzles, and putting them together reinforces the shape of the area you're studying. Older students can make these for younger children.

Blow It Up!

Blow up a map of the area you're studying using a copy machine. Then:

1. Make a giant wall map. Tape it together and color it in.
2. Tape to poster board or cover with contact paper and make a map you can walk on. Learning the states? "Walk" from California to Maine on your classroom floor!
3. Use it for a detailed map study with older students.
4. Use it as the sample map to point to so everyone can see what you're referring to on their matching student maps.

Another way to "blow it up" is to use an overhead projector. Tape a large sheet of paper to a wall, project a map onto it, and then trace the map. Now you have a mural-sized map!

In Living Color
Photocopy maps on different colors of paper or card stock. This is handy for telling students to "turn to the green map" or "the blue map," rather than "the map of Europe." Or use a color-code for different types of maps. For example:

- Copy each continent onto green paper and fill in with habitats around the world.
- Copy each continent onto yellow paper and make climate maps.
- Use pink paper for population, beige for religions, etc.
- Chart the similarities and differences between maps.

Map Books
Transfer maps to poster or card board and cut out to make "shape" books about the places you're studying.

Make an overlay, "see-inside" map book. This makes a terrific project for older students. It requires research and planning, it isn't as easy as it sounds. How to:

Supplies: acetate paper or overhead projector sheets and Vis-a-Vis overhead pens.

1. Trace the outline of a country on the first sheet.
2. On the second, make a political outline map.
3. On the third, make a rainfall map or physical feature map.
4. Make as many different types of maps as desired, laying each directly on top of the one before so that you end up with a "see-inside" map.

Why Draw Maps?
Many workbooks give children the chance to answer questions about maps. Rarely, however, do they encourage them to draw their own. Map drawing is a great way to:

- See what students understand about maps.
- Make them think. (Map making is harder than it looks - ask a cartographer!)
- Use math skills.
- Combine research with art.

Imagine That!
Suggest they draw a map of an imaginary place; great for the younger crowd. See if they remember to include a compass rose,

Amazing but True

The earliest known jigsaw puzzle was made in England in the 1760's by mapmaker John Spilsbury. He designed his "dissected maps" as a tool to teach geography to children.

scale, or key. As they gain experience, challenge them to draw a map of their room, their backyard, or their neighborhood. The bigger it is, the more complex the task.

Drawing to Scale

For older students, talk about scale and have them use the reproducible grid and a Vis-a-Vis pen to draw a map to scale. Drawing different types of maps also teaches much needed map reading skills.

Looking for Treasure!

What map is more exciting to a child than a treasure map? Follow these directions to make it antique looking. Suggest they tell or write a story to go with it. Or, use this activity after reading *Treasure Island* aloud:

Treasure Map Directions:
1. Steep a cup of dark tea. Dab tea unevenly onto a piece of high quality paper. Let dry.
2. Take a match and unevenly burn around the edges or hold over stove top until lightly browned.
3. Draw a large island. Include a compass rose, perhaps in the shape of a ship's wheel. Add a legend. Things they may want to include: harbor, ship, forest, cave, swamp, crocodiles, river, waterfall, directions to the treasure. Don't forget: "X" marks the spot!

Why Trace Maps?

Tracing maps is especially good for younger students and for those who don't like to draw. Tracing maps is:

- An excellent way to learn the shape of places - "learning by doing."
- A great way for non-readers to learn the shape of places. They can even trace in the names of places before they can write!
- A creative way to end up with an atlas of their very own, by systematically tracing a simple atlas.

On the Road Again...

Road maps provide real life experience. Have you ever been in a car with an adult who was unable to read a road map? What an important skill to teach our students! Ways to teach map reading:

Start simple; draw your own road map to someplace nearby. See if students can direct you there by reading it. Do exactly what they say, even if it's wrong! They'll get the hang of it. Hopefully, they'll also become proficient with "right" and "left." Better yet, have them say "north," "east," "south," or "west" instead! If going out in a vehicle isn't practical, draw and follow a walking map.

Let them make a map of the school and take turns with a friend following it to a pre-picked spot. Add compass skills and teach them how to orient a map. (See the compass section in chapter five.)

When they're comfortable reading a simple map, get a "real" road map of your town. (Your Chamber of Commerce may even have free maps to provide your class.) Look at the map together and point out where you want to go. Discuss possible routes and decide on one. Again, allow them to be the navigator. They'll learn as much from their mistakes as they will from their successes.

This is a fun family activity! Incorporate it into routine trips and even vacations. Eventually, they will become excellent map readers and much more confident when the time comes for them to drive away on their own.

Mapping the Oldies
Teaching about Ancient Egypt, Ancient Greece, and Ancient Rome is always exciting! Where did Hannibal and his elephants march? Memphis - I thought that was in Tennessee? Have you ever been frustrated trying to find suitable maps for these courses? We sure have! That's why we used a number of references to design these historical maps with places already labeled. Included in chapter fifteen you'll find maps for these three important time periods. Here are just two ways to use them:

1. With younger students, use the key to help them find each place on the map. Color in places as you talk about them.

2. With older students, allow them to use the key in order to become familiar with places, then provide a clean map with the key names blocked out. Instruct them to fill in the cities/bodies of water from memory.

Use the maps as a tool to understanding where events happened - not just a memorization exercise.

Touchdown!

Have a reluctant student who's a real sports enthusiast? Try giving this map assignment: Locate and highlight the states of each of the NFL teams on a blank outline map of the USA. Write the name of the city and draw the team logo. Draw the travels of a favorite team and record the score in each state they played. Check out the cool "NFL Mind Bender" in chapter sixteen. You can develop the same type of activity with any other sports league.

Just Ask!

Your local Chamber of Commerce may have free maps of your community. The state tourism board may have free state maps.

For more blank outline maps *Uncle Josh's Outline Map Book* contains over 100 different titles, including one for each of the fifty states. (See Resources in the back of the book.)

Lighting the (Olympic) Torch

Opportunities to turn real life events into a geography lesson abound if you only keep your eyes open. Every other year, either the summer or winter Olympics games are celebrated. If this isn't an opportunity to sneak in geography, nothing is!

Any of the following suggestions can turn watching the Olympics from a couch potato event into an intellectual odyssey. Place your focus on a popular event at hand or a popular athlete, and it's a natural transition to studying about the nation represented. Feel free to adapt these suggestions or come up with your own inventive project.

Assignments of Olympic Proportion!

- Using an atlas, locate countries as their particular athlete is honored. Label these on an outline map of the world.
- Draw country flags and attach to the outline map's border with a removable glue stick. Draw a line or attach yarn from the flag to the location of the country.
- Learn about the country that most piques your interest. Put together a travel brochure about that nation, including tourist attractions, history and culture.
- Record scores along with past records, and chart or place them on a graph.
- Write a short biography about an honorable athlete, and include information on how the location of his or her country and its physical features contributed to their interest, training and skill in the event.
- Fill out the "Let the Games Begin" country information sheet located in chapter sixteen, for countries which win a gold medal. Repeat for silver and bronze if you wish.
- Report about the city which hosts the Olympic event. How did its opening ceremony reflect the culture of that nation?
- During the parade of nations at the opening ceremony and again at the closing ceremony, watch for evidence of a nation's culture in its clothing.
- List any event that seems to be traditionally won by the same nation and consider why.

Watching the Olympics is certainly something many people enjoy. "Let the Games Begin" in your classroom!

Time Saving Tip

A wonderful resource awaits you at the library: Historical Maps on File by the Facts on File company are a treasure trove of information on both places and time periods.

Unit Two

Taking in the Sights: Fun and Games

OFF TO SEE THE WORLD

CHAPTER 4

GEOGRAPHY FUN IS EVERYWHERE

You've planned your destination, packed your bags and charted a course, and now it's time to see the world! This section provides specific ideas to make geotrekkin' fun for both students and you. From the simple to the complex, from early elementary through high school, these proven projects add excitement to any curriculum.

Off to See the World

"Around the World" studies that capitalize on cultures will engage students of all ages. After all, people are so diverse and interesting. Use this approach to:

- Teach about other places.
- Teach and practice research skills.
- Teach the best way to communicate what they've learned.

It's simple: choose a theme and learn about it from the perspective of people living in other places. The parameters are up to you, including length, amount of detail, and specific objectives. A class can work together on one or two themes, groups can work on a theme together, or individuals can pick their own theme.

Examples of interesting themes include:

Transportation Around the World	Wildlife
Transportation Through Time	Religions
Clothing/Costumes Around the World	Housing
Music Around the World	Flowers
Languages Around the World	Food
Languages Through Time	Flags
Currency or Stamps from Around the World	Sports & Games
Holidays and Celebrations	The list goes on!

Let students present the information they've learned through methods such as:

Collections	Multi-Media presentations
Posters	Mini-Museum with labeled items
Murals	Oral presentations
Collages	Books or booklets
Plays	Poems or rhymes
Songs	Learning station with hands-on
Games	components
Brochures	"ABC" book - find a corresponding
Dioramas	fact for each letter of the alphabet
Videos	

Reports do have their place; certainly in the upper grades. But it's wise not to over-do this method. Allowing students some freedom to choose their mode of presentation motivates them to gather materials and really learn about their topics.

There are quick and effective ways to show the interconnectedness between countries. From economy to lifestyles, we're becoming more and more connected to one another!

PASSPORTS TO DISCOVERY...

A pretty stamp, an unusual coin, a scenic postcard from a far away place... passports to discovery! Where did it come from? What does the symbol or picture on it mean? Is it an historical reference or an important person? How old is it?

Kids are born collectors. Using coins and such, parlay their natural interest into exploration! Never mind fancy collector albums; try pretty tins and jars, photo albums, and best of all - a great big wall map to stick stuff on.

Ask friends, teachers, and relatives to send coins, stamps, and cards when they travel. As students become intrigued with various mementos, have them do a bit of research. Read more about it at the library, attend collectors' shows, look for local collectors clubs, and check our your nearest stamp or coin hobby shop. The post office has good, free information about stamps. They may even know of the local philately (stamp) clubs. Spark an interest that lasts a lifetime!

Encourage students to bring in postcards for a class collection. Mount them in a notebook or on a giant map. Who went there? What was it like? What region of the world is it in?

Just Ask!

Check with the post office for free infomation about stamps. Ask for the booklet "Introduction to Stamp Collecting."

Stamps

When receiving a postcard or letter from out of town, students can soak off or cut out the stamp and tape it up near its place of origin on a large world map. This generates questions about the country, the sender, and geography in general.

Children can start their own informal collection by classifying stamps in a number of different ways: birds, animals, plants, transportation, presidents, countries, or historic events. Provide them with a composition book and let them paste in stamps according to their preferred classification system.

Design a stamp for the place/time you're studying. Showcase wildlife, famous people or events. What a great way to tie art into geography! For more information on stamp collecting, visit your local post office. The US Postal Service has a free booklet titled "Introduction to Stamp Collecting." Ask for it! Many post offices now have special Philatelic Centers or windows which carry a wide array of stamps and products for collectors. Ask where the nearest one is located. Post offices will often give a nice tour to your school group, too.

Currency: History In Your Hands!

Kids love foreign currency! Set it out on a table for awhile. Coins are cleaned, words and worth are guessed and looked up, bank notes are scrutinized, and the country is pinpointed on the big world map. Geographic subjects are often depicted on money: plants, transportation, maps, famous sites, and more. Coin collecting can lead you to lots of faraway places.

Students will quickly become conversant with units of currency from around the world. Even younger students learn that money differs from country to country, both in worth and design. Take an imaginary trip - how much would it cost? What's the rate of exchange? This is a great way to show practical uses for math in the real world. Calculate expenses for a shopping spree. Tie it together with a trip to the bank to exchange a few dollars for foreign currency. Create a folder to keep track of calculations and information.

Coin collections fascinate so many people. For the beginning collector, pick a theme for the collection. For example, use coins from Spain, coins commemorating the Olympics, coins with famous people, or coins from as many different years as possible, etc.

Take Me Out to the Ball Game!

Baseball cards are a great tool for geography studies. They can also be quite inexpensive to buy, since you aren't looking for valuable collector cards. It's quite possible to find boxes of them dirt cheap at yard sales. What do you do with them?

1. Use a map to locate the team's hometown. What does their name mean? (It often has a geographical reference!)
2. From where does the player come? Find his hometown and team town on the map.
3. Make a poster or keep a notebook with facts learned while researching information.

One enterprising mother got her baseball-loving son hooked on geography when she had him identify all the major league teams by marking their locations on an outline map. He looked up names and mascots and discovered their significance. He researched favorite players and learned many came from South America, Mexico, and other countries. That mom knows geography is more meaningful when it becomes personal!

Students can also choose from other favorites: NBA or NFL teams, actors, musicians, writers, and other famous people. Where do they come from? Are they on tour? Follow their tour route using removable glue sticks, posting a picture of them on a laminated outline map. Want to get those older boys interested in geography? Use the reproducible "NFL Mind Benders." Great Internet sites for hobbies can be found in chapter eleven, Geography Through the Internet.

CURRENT EVENTS

Amazing but True

National Geographic uses many current events topics in their Geography Bee questions.

Newspapers
Read the newspaper with an eye for geography and a number of things will jump out at you. Was there a terrible airplane crash in Asia? Read about huge brush fires in Australia, typhoons near Guam, a new train speed record in Japan, and many other things that may be pertinent to your studies. Share bits and pieces of information from around the world, find the location on a political map, and try to write it on the large outline map. It's amazing how many places will be written on that map, and how many details will be remembered. Instead of writing in the place name, use stickers or stars around places discussed. Occasionally look back and say, "Now, what was it that happened here?" It will keep everyone sharp!

TV News Shows

Older students can fill in a map or log in a journal of places mentioned in the news, and a brief summary of the event reported on. This keeps them both current on events and helps them to review and learn places around the world.

Use the Weather Channel and a big world outline map to discuss weather and upcoming storms. Charting hurricanes, following storm systems, and discussing droughts are just a few ways to improve vocabulary and core knowledge of places. The weather impacts man and the world.

Magazines

Subscribe to several news magazines, both for students and adults. They're an excellent source of information for current events. Pull items into class time as appropriate. For some students, the information stays longer if they read it in print than if they hear it. Of course, the opposite is true of auditory learners. Using a variety of sources will help meet various learning styles. Use magazines that write from different angles. Subscribe to both liberal and conservative news sources, and try to help students see and understand particular biases. This is a good place to teach them how to reach decisions based on facts versus opinion.

Other Opportunities

Certain radio shows, talk shows, and on-line resources can all be utilized to compare kinds of information, add to information, and present various points of view on current events.

By making a concerted effort to cover current events in at least a weekly format, you'll help your students see the importance of paying attention to the world around them - and the importance of knowing where the world around them is located!

Foreign Exchange Students

What's life *really* like elsewhere? Invite a foreign exchange student into your classroom and find out! Many high schools and colleges across the country host these students each year. They're encouraged to make presentations within their communities, and would likely welcome your invitation. Communicate clearly to what age group they're speaking, how long to talk, and any other parameters you may have. Invite them to stay and share lunch - that can be a good way for the kids to informally ask questions they may not have asked during a presentation. College students, especially, might appreciate being asked into your home for a holiday meal or visit when their classmates have gone home for break and they're on campus alone.

America is so culturally diverse! It shouldn't be hard to locate folks from other countries who would be happy to share their traditions, language, and cultures with your students. One month you might hear about holidays, another month religions, and another compare political systems, climates, or whatever you'd like! Ask guest speakers to spend just ten or fifteen minutes talking about a specific topic: native animals, growing up and going to school, music, etc. It's usually easier for the speaker if you provide a topic or a choice of several than to say "Tell us about your country." Prepare students ahead of time in terms of courtesy, hospitality, questions, etc.

Pen-Pals

Pen-pals are a time-honored way of learning about other people and places. Whether participating as a class through an organization or as individuals writing to friends-of-friends in far-off places, sending and receiving letters is one of the best ways to get a feel for other cultures. Here are just a few of the many pen-pal organizations:

ePALS
www.epals.com
Large, well-organized site, committed to offering safe, innovative ways for all learners to make contact with other cultures. It began as a simple idea to create a place where teachers and their students could connect with other classes interested in using technology to assist collaborative learning.

Student Letter Exchange
211 Broadway, Suite 201
Lynbrook, NY 11563-3265
(516) 887-8628
e-mail: custServ@pen-pal.com
www.pen-pal.com

(Both free services and services for a small fee.)

Intercultural E-Mail Classroom Connections
www.iecc.org
Free service by St. Olaf's College to link teachers and classes with partners in other cultures for e-mail classroom pen-pal and project exchanges.

Kids Space Connection
www.ks-connection.org/home.cfm
Award-winning, well-monitored Internet site for students through age 13 as well as teachers. Its purpose is to be a place where children worldwide can explore and communicate using technology.

(Remember: Use traditional rules of safety when contacting people you don't know.)

Wow!

Twelve-year-old Robin has a huge collection of letters and postcards from pen-pals around the world. She's honed her communication skills while getting to know kids from all over. With a hobby like this, going to the mailbox is always an exciting adventure!

GEOTREKKIN' THROUGH YOUR MIND

Travel... what an exciting way to learn about the world! Wouldn't it be great to jet to Egypt, sail the Caribbean, criss-cross America, or fly to ports unknown? A fortunate few do get to take these fantastic field trips, but most of us must be content with teaching with our imaginations, rather than actual travel. How? Armchair traveling! Through the use of maps, computers, books, videos, tapes, discussion, and best of all - other people, we can set our kids on fire with enthusiasm for learning about the world they live in.

Armchair Traveling: The art and science of steeping oneself in other locales without leaving home.

Flat Stanley

In the book *Flat Stanley* by Jeff Brown, Stanley is squashed flat by a falling bulletin board. One of the many advantages for Flat Stanley is that he can now see the world by way of the U.S. Postal Service. His escapades inspired the "Flat Stanley Project." There is an official website, www.flatstanley.com, and there are numerous Yahoo groups dedicated to helping children send their own flat travelers around the country and even the world. In exchange for sending your traveler somewhere else, typically you volunteer to host another family's traveler yourself. One family who participates in a Yahoo group consisting primarily of homeschooling families reported their flat travelers went to New Zealand and Canada, as well as to a number of states. They also hosted travelers in Delaware and even took a dozen with them to Williamsburg! (Hint: Hosting 12 at a time is way too many!) Currently there are about 47 countries taking part in the FSP. This is an exciting and painless way to learn about the world.

- http://groups.yahoo.com/group/flat_travelers_homeschool/
- http://groups.yahoo.com/group/FlatTravelers/

"The World is a book, and those who do not travel read only a page," attributed to St. Augustine.

Where's George?

Does your family enjoy coin collecting? Here's a twist: Participate in "Where's George?" This United States Currency Tracking Project provides the means for discovering where the paper currency in your wallet has recently been. Go to the Where's George website and follow the simple directions for registering your dollar bills. One dollar bill found with a "Where's George?" note on it had been to several states in a matter of days. Of course, some of your dollars will end up in a piggy bank somewhere, never to resurface, so the more you "release" the better your chances for tracking. Post a chart on the wall listing your dollars and where they have been "sighted." A large U.S. wall map or even an atlas will be useful for following "George" around the country. As of this writing, there are about eighty million bills registered at this website! Website: www.wheresgeorge.com

(Canadian folks can participate in their own tracking project at www.whereswilly.com.)

Letterboxing

Letterboxing is an appealing mix of treasure hunting, art, navigation, and exploring. Originating in England, it become popular in the U.S. after an article describing it appeared in *Smithsonian Magazine*, April, 1998. The premise is simple: Take a small, waterproof container, inside it put a journal and a stamp that in some way represents the area, and then hide it in a place that is legally accessible to the public. Write clues about how to find it and post these clues on the Letterboxing website for others to find. Or go letterboxing yourself. The website has clues available for most states and a number of countries. Bring along a family journal and stamp it when you find each box. Before setting out on a trip, check to see if there are any boxes hidden along your route and make time to hunt for them. This makes a great diversion for long car rides, and for many families this has developed into a hobby everyone enjoys.
Website: www.letterboxing.org

Geocaching

Geocaching is like Letterboxing for people who like to walk and love gadgets! It follows the same premise as Letterboxing, except instead of geographic, treasure hunt-style clues, you have to follow latitude and longitude coordinates with your handheld GPS unit. And instead of a stamp, many geocaches have little "treasures" in them. From baseballs and maps to CDs and even money, there is supposed to be a little gift as a reward for finding the cache. The hitch is – when you take a "reward," you are supposed to replace it with a different treasure for the next geocacher. These caches may be hidden in a nearby park or high on a rugged mountain or even deep within the ocean!
Website: www.geocaching.com

BookCrossing

The stated goal on the BookCrossing website is to "make the whole world a library." Imagine if thousands of homeschooling families shared their favorite works with the world. The concept is simple: Take a book you love, register it at the website, place the form from the website in the book, then "release" it for someone else to find and read. You'll be notified by e-mail each time someone records journal entries for that book. And if you make release notes on the book, others can go hunting for it and try to find it. So go ahead, buy an extra copy of *The Lion, the Witch, and the Wardrobe* and release it into the wild. Keep track on a wall map where your book(s) travels.
Website: www.bookcrossing.com

bookcrossing
n. the practice of leaving a book in a public place to be picked up and read by others, who then do likewise.

(added to the Concise Oxford English Dictionary in August 2004)

Trucker Buddies

Approximately 4,000 truck drivers participate in this program, founded by truck driver Gary King. Trucker Buddies matches truckers with classrooms and co-ops, allowing for an exchange

of information on a regular basis. Homeschooled groups are accepted if the number of students participating is twelve or more.

For example, the trucker assigned to your class sends a postcard or letter once a week. In it is information about his route: mileage, place names, geographic features he drove by (or under or over!), weather, and other interesting information. Think of it as a card from Great Aunt Hilda on vacation, but better! Engage students into learning more about our country from truckers who drive the length and width of it.

The possibilities are exciting! Here are just a few:

Geography: States and regions, mountains ranges and lakes, famous sites and more all come alive when presented in a first person, "Guess what I saw?" kind of format. Students can research places visited by their trucker. Let students ask their "buddy" questions; they're a wonderful resource!

Maps: Post a giant wall map and follow your buddy's travels. Use push-pins and colored yarn to trace various trips. Use highlighters on individual buddy maps.

Math: Ask your trucker to send mileage or even math questions for students to figure out. For example: "If I drove 367 miles today and it took me six hours, how many miles per hour did I average?" "If my gas mileage is seven miles per gallon, how much fuel did I use today?" Questions can include figuring the trucker's expenses, or cost per mile. The list is endless.

Language Arts: Improve letter writing skills, spelling and vocabulary from correspondence, creative stories about what your trucker might have seen or done on a trip, research and more.

Science: Pick a particular theme to follow through the year and ask your buddy to watch for information about it. For example, weather, animals, environment, ecology, or other things that would be fairly easy for the trucker to obtain.

For more great geography ideas visit
http://groups.yahoo.com/group/whole_hog

Other Great Ideas: Equip Trucker Buddy's Learning Centers with maps, a toy semi-truck that follows the route, a tape player for listening to and taping messages, a scrapbook with postcards and letters, brochures from places visited, books on big rigs, and more.

- Capture routes on huge wall maps.
- Create individual Trucker Buddy notebooks for each student, including individual maps.
- Invite a trucker in to talk about life on the road. Perhaps a "field trip" to his truck would be possible.

The good news? It's free! The bad news? There may be a waiting list to join. (Because of the demand for this program, they prefer to work with whole classrooms or co-ops.) Contact:

Trucker Buddies
P.O. Box 7788
Madison, WI 53707
1-800-MY BUDDY
www.truckerbuddy.org

Wait! There's More!
You don't need to "join" a program to do a project like this! You or a student may know someone who's a frequent traveler and would be delighted to participate. Consider participating with several people for a few months each. Think through your needs carefully, and then write them down. Effective communication goes a long way into making any relationship a success.

GEOGRAPHY IN THE REAL WORLD

CHAPTER 5

GEOGRAPHY IN DAILY LIFE: THE REAL WORLD

You've seen many aspects of geography - from maps to themes to activities and more. Here are some fun and games to plug into daily life activities.

Eat Your Way Around the World!

Eating your way around the world .... sounds fun (and fattening), doesn't it? It's amazing how much we can learn about cultures by discovering their recipes; clues to their natural resources, values and beliefs, lifestyles, and more. Hungry? Use these ideas to get started:

Cultural Neighborhoods
Little Havana's, Little Italy's, Chinatown, etc., abound in metropolitan areas. These are great places to collect information, interview immigrants, and discuss all the geographic questions you can imagine. Get ready ahead of time by doing research, preparing the students, and if possible, visiting the area or speaking to someone who has been there. Top the trip off with lunch at an ethnic restaurant.

For the less adventurous, or for those not near metro areas, many cities and towns have ethnic restaurants and grocery stores. Even older students benefit from a well thought out field trip and interview with ethnic owners and/or employees. Everyone enjoys a "food trip!"

Why are certain dishes predominant? What does it tell you about that region's crops, weather, lifestyle, etc.? This can be either a great kick-off for a unit or a memorable conclusion.
Field trips unfeasible? How about an ethnic lunch that you and

your students prepare yourselves? Invite that restaurant owner into the classroom. Perhaps he or she would bring "samples," or provide coupons or flyers for their restaurant. (Do make an effort to find someone who can communicate well in English and who is comfortable around students. Clearly communicate what you're looking for.)

Create an International Cookbook. Studying Africa? Gather favorite recipes from those you know of African descent, or use the library. Anecdotes or information about each recipe and country of origin will be a plus. How about a cookbook containing recipes from a family's heritage? (See American Heritage in Just the Basics, Please.)

Make a poster depicting the cycle of a region's most favored crop (rice, corn, wheat, etc.) Where does it grow? How is it harvested? What dishes are made with it?

Trace the history of corn or rice. They're closely intertwined with different civilizations. What crops originated in North America and which were brought here? What's the story behind the tomato? Make a chart comparing important crops across regions like corn, wheat, and rice.

Archaeology Geography

Here's a fun way to incorporate food into your history study. How do historians know what happened in the past? Besides things like written and oral accounts, archeologists contribute vast amounts of historical and scientific knowledge by discovering and piecing together artifacts. This activity gives students a small "taste" of the work that goes into an archeological "dig."

Time Saver Tip

Before running for the kitchen, read this section all the way through and make copies of the grids on page 244 and 245, if you'd like to use them.

Chocolate Chip Geological Dig

(with thanks to Kathy Bradford of Wilmington, DE.)

Cookie "Rock Samples" must be made at least one hour ahead so they're completely cool before the dig begins. This recipe yields about 18 delicious archaeological sites.

Cream together:	2 sticks real butter
	1 cup dark brown sugar
	3/4 cup white sugar
Add and beat till creamy:	1 tablespoon real vanilla
	2 eggs
Add and mix:	3/4 teaspoon salt
	3/4 teaspoon baking soda
	3 cups flour, one cup at a time

When well blended, add the following:
    1 cup chocolate chips
    1 cup butterscotch chips or raisins
    1 cup coarsely chopped nuts
    1 cup rolled oats (not instant)

For a more complex "dig", add as much of these as you wish: M&M's or other colorful, large candies; toffee chips, coconut, cherries, dried cranberries.

    Form large, two-inch balls.
    Place on greased cookie sheet, and flatten to 1/4 inch thick.
    Bake at 350° for 10-15 minutes until edges begin to brown.
    Remove and cool completely. (Test a sample or two to compare
        textures and make sure chips are solid.)Next, divide cookies
        into four quadrants. (You can do this with icing.)

The Actual "Dig"

With nut picks, toothpicks, clean paint brushes, tooth brushes, or anything you have that looks like a tool, let the budding "geologists" carefully dissect their "rocks."

Archeologists divide their "digs" into grids, faithfully recording where each item is found. It's time consuming work and requires much patience! The reward comes in the slow but remarkable piecing together of the past.

Let students get a feel for what recording at digs is like by recording their own findings. You'll find three reproducible "Chocolate Chip Geological Grids" in chapter sixteen. Each is for a different level.

How to use the grids:
Grid # 1 - Simple
    Make a key based on the ingredients in your
    cookies. Each child carefully finds chips,
    cherries, etc., and draws a picture of each
    one in the appropriate quadrant of the grid.

Grid # 2 - Medium
    Tally the amount of each item found in the
    appropriate columns. (six raisins in A1, nine
    nuts in B2, etc.)

Grid #3 - Advanced
    This is a different way to record findings.
    Consider the cookie as the entire quadrant.

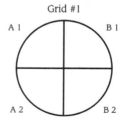

CHOCOLATE CHIP GEOLOGICAL DIG
Grid #1

Think of the chocolate chips as pottery pieces. An archeologist might ask:

- What is this substance? (Chips/pottery.)

- How many particles are in this quadrant? (Count all of the nuts in the cookie.)

- How much does it weigh? (Weigh all of the chips together on a small scale.)

This can be repeated for each different item in the cookie.

Finished? Now eat your project!

Compasses - What You Need to Know

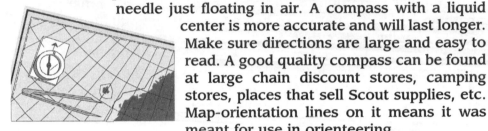

Buy a quality compass designed for years of use. Look for one with a liquid center, rather than a very cheap compass with its needle just floating in air. A compass with a liquid center is more accurate and will last longer. Make sure directions are large and easy to read. A good quality compass can be found at large chain discount stores, camping stores, places that sell Scout supplies, etc. Map-orientation lines on it means it was meant for use in orienteering.

Teaching Compass Skills

Having "N" on a map isn't very useful unless you know which direction you're facing. A map can't tell you that, but a compass can. How do you orient north on a map to north on a compass?

- Hold the map in front of you with the north arrow on the compass rose pointing directly away.

- Lay your compass on the map and wait until it's still.

- Slowly turn your body until north on the map and the compass needle are both pointing in the same direction: north.

- To double check: whatever is north on the map should be straight ahead of you. Look for a landmark east or west on the map and check to make sure that same landmark is to your left (west) or right (east).

- Through trial and error, students learn to hold a compass steady and level. Suggest laying it on a flat surface and waiting until the needle settles down.

GeoBit says:
It doesn't matter what direction the arrow on the map is pointing (traditionally it points up, but north isn't always straight ahead!) What matters is that the features on the map match your position on the earth.

- Initially, stick with the four cardinal directions: north, south, east, west. Add intermediate directions: NW, SW, NE, and SE later.

Treasure Hunt

Okay, you've taught the skills, now practice them with games. A treasure hunt is a great way to practice compass skills. By designing a course that calls for determining compass directions to identify landmarks, students learn how to get their bearings using a compass. They love it! (A "treasure" at the end is an added bonus.)

Directions: This needs to be planned in advance of class time.

1. Before class, place small treats in a treasure box to hide somewhere outside.

2. Using a compass and a pad of paper, write directions to the treasure. (Go east to the gate, then go west to the oak tree. Turn northwest and take five steps....) This is the part that takes some time, so be sure to have directions ready before the treasure hunt begins.

3. Send students out with a compass and your prepared directions.

4. Be patient! Ideally, they will find the treasure box, gain experience using a compass, practice their directions, and have a great time to boot! But in reality, this will take longer than you think - at least the first few times.

That Arrow Thingie is Pointing at "N"

The "Treasure Hunt" makes a cool birthday party game. This compass activity is just a bit sneaky. Kids think they're coming to a birthday party... you know: cake, ice cream, presents, games. They never suspect there'll be a geography lesson! And alas, even when the party's over, some of them will never know it happened. They'll only remember how much fun they had. (Tip: Make sure students take turns using the compass. And, of course, accompany them in case they really get stuck.)

GeoBit Says:

One set of directions people around the world all have in common is the rising and setting of the sun. When you face north, the east is to your right, west is to your left, and south is behind you. This is always true except at the North and South Poles.

For additional fun and games ideas, *Hands-On Geography*, by Maggie Hogan (Bright Ideas Press) provides specific instructions for activities, games, and projects. See Resources.

MORE FUN & GAMES

Benefits abound when it comes to playing good games: learning information in a fun setting, reading and following directions, and cooperation are all valuable educational experiences. Sometimes we forget that learning takes place in fun, informal settings, too. Use games to introduce a unit, as a research project, or as a lively way to end a study.

There are many geography games around, and several are quite worthwhile. Set up a Games Center and change games periodically to reflect your history, science, and geography studies. Allow students time to learn the rules and play.

Learn about the games that were played in the place or time period you're studying. Put together a "Game Notebook" of your findings. Compare games from different times or cultures, and then actually play those games!

Research the history of classic games like mancala or chess. Discover where and when they were played, and how they changed in various cultures and over time.

If possible, allow time for geography-related computer games. Keep a log for each student and set goals for them to accomplish.

Geography games can greatly increase your knowledge of specific facts - especially when it comes to where places are located on the globe. Feel free to allow students to play with an open atlas handy. If a student can find the answer in a given amount of time, he can continue to proceed. This may take longer to play, but geography knowledge increases as well. Additionally, this is a good way to allow people of different abilities to play together more fairly. For example, one student can use the atlas and take two minutes to find the answer, while the teacher or older student cannot use the atlas at all.

GeoMemory

Use the definitions flashcards in chapter seventeen to play this matching game for learning terms. It's played like concentration; the object is to match a word with its definition. Here's how:

1. Photocopy the vocabulary words and definitions onto colorful "card stock" and cut out each card.

2. Shuffle the cards and place face down in rows.

3. The first play turns up two cards. If they're both a word and its definition, the player removes both cards and goes again.

4. If they don't match, he returns the cards face down and the player to the left takes a turn. If his words match, he keeps both cards and turns over two more cards, and so on.

5. The player with the most cards when none are left to turn over, wins. Well, really everybody wins, because student vocabulary has just increased!

State and Capital Memory

Make cards (business card size) with state names on one side and matching capital names on the other. Place a large or desk-size outline map of the USA flat on a table or floor. Students place state cards on the correct places on the map. When states are known, turn cards over and place capital cards on the correct state.

Use the same cards as flash cards. Students can drill each other to name the capital that matches the state side or to name states that match the capital side.

Play a "concentration" game like GeoMemory. Cut fifty, 3 x 5 cards in half. Have students write the names of all the states on fifty cards and the name of every capital on the other fifty cards. Shuffle all cards and place face down in rows. Play follows the same rules as GeoMemory. Here you're matching the state card with its corresponding capital.

Name that Place!

The same type of game can be played with the focus on location. Students put the name of a place on one card and draw a map of its location on another. Play the memory game above, matching the name of the place to its map. Maps can be copied from the student's outline activities from the week, drawn by hand, or shrunk from a larger map when photocopying onto cardstock.

Stinky Feet Game

Everyone sits in a large circle on the floor. Warning: Don't do this after gym class or on a hot day! Have each person take off one shoe and throw it in the center. Next, everyone grabs a shoe that isn't theirs and looks on the tag to see where it was made. Make a list on the board where the shoes were made. Shoes tend to be manufactured in just a few countries, so you might not get a variety. But it does raise the question of why these countries are so popular for manufacturing.

Refrigerator Geography

Do this same type of activity with the refrigerator. A geography lesson in the fridge? Yes! Look in the refrigerator and list items and where they were grown or produced. Locate those places from all over the world on a map. Why are milk and eggs local but bananas aren't? How is each item transported to your community? Suddenly the idea that there's a whole world out there begins to take hold. Wow!

Peanut Butter Geography

All right, so you teach your kids not to play with their food, but here's a great exception.

Give them permission to take bites from their peanut butter sandwich to create state shapes. Start with Colorado – a sandwich is already about this shape to begin with. Nibble a corner off to form the shape of Utah. Nibble more and now you've got Indiana. See how many states can be formed from one sandwich.

Unit Three

Across the Great Divide: Geography Through the Curriculum

GEOGRAPHY THROUGH LITERATURE

CHAPTER 6

TEACH GEOGRAPHY READING NOVELS

Reading aloud to students of any age is not only fun but beneficial. Listening skills improve and relationships deepen. It's an excellent way to learn about other cultures or important people without it feeling like "school." Many teachers and parents have experienced firsthand these, and many other, great advantages of reading aloud.

In this chapter you'll learn how you can incorporate the study of geography while reading historical novels. You'll develop a better understanding of the five themes in geography and watch them unfold with the story you're reading. You'll be able to develop short assignments for your students to complete that follow along with your novel. By association with the novel, students will improve retention of the information learned and gain an increased understanding of other cultures.

Before proceeding further, it's a good idea to read unit one, "Just the Basics, Please!" It is especially important to have an understanding about the five themes of geography. Chapter three will give you instructions for doing the mapping activities. This will provide the foundation necessary to gain the greatest benefit for what follows.

Historical Novels

Historical novels are an excellent way to study geography. Learn about time periods or places from the perspective of one who lived there! It's common for the first few chapters of a novel to describe in great detail the physical terrain, climate, modes of transportation and more. As the story unfolds, you'll be exposed to the community involved, the culture, their foods, holiday traditions, and their spiritual beliefs. All play a role in understanding geography's five themes.

Supplies for studying geography through literature:
- Outline map(s)
- Atlases
- World map or globe
- Markers or colored pencils
- Terms Chart (opt.)
- Timeline
- Books about the place
- "Novel Activity Sheet"

Supplies

To get the greatest benefit from this kind of study, it's best to be prepared. You'll need a blank outline map of the location of the story (preferably one for each student), an atlas that depicts the area, a world map, a globe (optional but important), colored pencils (or water-based markers if using laminated maps), geography terms chart, timeline and any books obtained from the library about the country. Books with good pictures are very helpful to students who learn visually. When selecting library books, look for those that depict the clothing, architecture, and history of the area, as well as those that include good, large-scale maps. Don't forget to reproduce the "Novel Activity Sheet" in chapter sixteen for use by your students.

Terms Chart
There is an excellent color geography terms chart that illustrates topographical features on one side and defines over 150 terms on the other. It's a really effective visual for understanding the story line when plots of geographical significance take place. It's an essential part of this study, because we're not all familiar with how some geographical features look. It's likely that if a precipice was mentioned in the story, it will also serve a purpose later. If you or your students don't know what a "precipice" is, then later it might be hard to understand how the character fell off of it! It's imperative you look up all unfamiliar geography terms. The looking-up process is quicker and easier with a colorful terms chart. You may find a good one in your the classroom atlas, in a library book about physical geography, or call one of the companies listed in the back of the book for the one mentioned above.

Student Notebook
Establish a student notebook to keep all information learned in one place. You may choose to use a stitched composition book, a three-ring binder with appropriate dividers, or a report binder. The student notebook should contain all writing projects, research notes, vocabulary words, maps, drawings and any other completed projects. Students should always use their best handwriting and keep pages free from scribbles and smudges. Students tend to do a better job when they know their work will be presented in a finished report folder. It makes a great addition to a student's portfolio and adds a certain degree of pleasure to the work accomplished. The completed notebook will be a source of pride for both the student and teacher alike. For more detailed information, read the Student Notebook section in chapter one.

Outline Maps
All historical novels provide an opportunity to use outline maps. The maps in this book can be reduced, enlarged and copied for

your own use. If the area you're reading about isn't represented by a map here, simply have your student trace one from out of an atlas or library book on blank paper. The map project should include the country, boundaries of all surrounding countries or bodies of water, and any major rivers. Other major geographical features can be drawn with symbols. A series of triangles, for example, strategically placed would indicate a mountain range; a crooked blue line a river. Everything included should be clearly and neatly labeled. This is tedious work; praise and encourage students as they progress. Students can use any symbols they see on any atlas or book, or encourage them to design their own.

Timelines
Timelines improve the understanding of historical events as they relate to other events in the world. Using a timeline, plot historical events as they're presented in your story. Feel free to record corresponding events happening in other nations or in the United States contemporary to the events of your story. What composer was living at the same time? What invention or discovery took place? What philosophers influenced the thinking of people at the time? Unit six provides detailed instructions on using timelines and timeline figures. Use the reproducible "Notebook Timeline of History" page found there.

The Novel Activity Sheet
This is a reproducible in chapter sixteen which will help provide a framework for studying the place depicted in your novel. It includes questions for which students will use an almanac, atlas, other reference materials, and the novel to answer correctly. Feel free to add your own questions or activities. This should be placed in the notebook with the outlines and timeline pages.

Additional Projects

There are many interesting projects your students can complete as you continue to read the novel aloud one or two chapters a day. You may want to limit reading to four to six chapters a week to provide enough time to do the activities suggested and to keep up with a student notebook. Remember to fit the assignment to the learning style of your students. Examples include:

• Study and draw the symbols of the country. Explain what each symbol means to the natives of the nation.
• Design a travel brochure depicting the nation's attributes.
• Write a newspaper report as though you were there.
• Use a video recorder to capture an historical flashback type news report with a student acting as a "roving reporter." Choose an event in the story line or an historical event that occurred simultaneously.
• Study and report what life was like in the USA during the same time frame.

- Study the natural resources and plot them on the map.
- Write a journal entry daily (or weekly) from the perspective of one of the characters in the book.
- List plants and animals of this region.
- Keep a vocabulary list of new words learned.
- Purchase or prepare foods of the nation.
- Read other literature set in the place or time of your novel of choice.
- Find stamps from the country. Study what their symbols and pictures depict.
- Listen to music contemporary to the historical time period, or to what is popular to the area.
- View art from the area or of the same era.

Before Reading Aloud
Before reading the first chapter, talk about where the story takes place. Parentheses ( ) denotes five themes.

The Five Themes

1. Location
2. Place
3. Relationship
4. Movement
5. Region

- Using a map, let students identify the continent, the country, the latitude, and longitude of the location. Record this information on the "Novel Activity Sheet."

- Compare this to your own (location). Discuss if the weather or climate is similar or different from your own environment (place).

- Locate the country in an atlas and again on the globe.

- Notice what bodies of water are in and near it. Name any other major physical feature of the nation (place). Add to the "Novel Activity Sheet."

- Ask students what they currently know about the country, and how they came to know that information. What foods do they like that originate there? Are they aware of any natural resources there (relationship)?

Inspire students to pay close attention to any words that describe what the earth looks like. Challenge them to listen for geography terms which will provide clues to the physical terrain of the setting. Plan to look up all geography terms that are unclear, and keep a file card or notebook listing each new word.

Let's Get Going!
Read chapter one aloud. Consider using a file card as a book mark. When an unfamiliar geography term is spotted, jot it down on the card for use as a vocabulary word, or look it up immediately on your geography terms chart. Commend students for being good sleuths! These geography terms are now your vocabulary words for the week. Let students write a simple definition for each word using their best penmanship.

Follow this same procedure chapter by chapter. Watch for any of the five themes to surface. As the story unfolds, you'll begin to see modes of transportation (movement) and how people adapted their lifestyle or their surroundings to meet their needs (relationship).

Remember, you're identifying the culture, clothing, traditions, food, religious beliefs, weather, plants, animals; any characteristic of the people or the place directly related to the setting. Watch and see how often the plot is intertwined with geography-related subjects.

Students who learn best by doing can draw a picture of the description. Students may perform further research on any subject of particular interest that the story inspires. Many, many historical novels provide perfect opportunities to draw maps of the main character's neighborhood, journey, or of the main street. Students can draw the clothing, coins, flag, architecture; anything that distinguishes this place as special (region, place).

Great Books to Read Aloud

Since historical novels and stories with journeys help teach differences of climate and living conditions, show movement, and demonstrate physical and human characteristics, a few suggestions are provided below. Approximate grade levels and, if appropriate, study topics are given in parentheses after the author's name. These grade levels are arbitrary and can stretch in either direction. It's always a good idea to preview suggested books to determine appropriateness for your students.

Recommended Reading

Make Way for Ducklings by Robert McCloskey (K-2)

Winnie the Pooh by A.A. Milne (K-4)

Heidi by Johanna Spyri (all grades; Swiss Alps/Austria)

The Bronze Bow by Elizabeth George Speare (K-8; Israel)

Robinson Crusoe by Daniel Defoe (all grades; botany and survival skills)

Little House on the Prairie series by Laura Ingalls Wilder (3-7, Frontier America)

Little Britches series by Ralph Moody (all grades, early 20th century Colorado)

Journey to the Center of the Earth by Jules Verne (6-10, Iceland/Europe-geology)

Kidnapped by Robert Louis Stevensen (6-10, Scotland)

The White Stag by Kate Seredy (all grades; migration of Huns and Magyars to Europe)

Trumpeter of Krakow by Eric P. Kelly (6-10, 15th century Poland)

Hans Brinker or the Silver Skates by Mary Mapes Dodge (5-8, 19th century Holland)

Notes:

HANS BRINKER: A UNIT STUDY

CHAPTER 7

HANS BRINKER OR THE SILVER SKATES

Hans Brinker or The Silver Skates by Mary Mapes Dodge is a great classic to use to study the history and geography of Holland. It not only depicts the geography, culture, and history of that nation, but also provides excellent character models for your students. Consider pointing out how moral crises were handled, and ask students questions to help them see the value in making right choices. "What would you do?" or "What's the right thing to do?" "Where did you see honesty, or loyalty, or sharing in this chapter?"

A complete unit on *Hans Brinker* follows as an example. This unit should enable you to do this type of study with any other novel of your choosing. While reading the book, you and your students may see other examples of the culture or geography. Adapt this to your use and take advantage of other ideas that present themselves. This unit can be successfully completed by students in grades six through ten, depending on the assignments you choose.

WARNING! There are more assignment suggestions included here than you will ever need. Do only as much as your class and schedule permits and don't assign every suggestion given! As with any subject of study, the more time and effort put in, the more knowledge gained. It isn't necessary to make sure each area of study is complete before continuing the reading sessions. Remember to make this fun for your students! This may become the highlight of their day, so don't dampen it with so many requirements that the initial enthusiasm for the novel is lost.

Try to stay at least a chapter or two ahead of your read-aloud sessions. You'll be better prepared to point out important facts or ask the kind of questions that stimulate critical thinking. Consider giving vocabulary or research/study assignments a day ahead of the reading session. This helps to improve retention, and may help reading sessions to pass swiftly since words that would have stumped students will now be understood. The material that follows is so thorough that you may find it unnecessary to read ahead, but when you begin to prepare this kind of study on another book of your choosing, you'll need to.

Study and research time for your students will go more smoothly if you've already obtained necessary resources; however, if time isn't a factor, older students will gain more if they locate resources themselves in the library. If students are required to find their own materials, make sure they're well equipped to perform that research. Locating information for a study project is an excellent skill to develop, although it may be best for the sanity of the teacher if the student has somewhat matured in patience and tenacity first!

Getting Ready

TIP: Get this book with a copyright date of 1915 or renewal date of 1943 from a used book store or library. These older versions have excellent footnotes with added historical background and definitions of Dutch words used throughout the book.

Obtain the following supplies before beginning:

1. *Hans Brinker or the Silver Skates*, by Mary Mapes Dodge (preferably one copy per student).
2. Globe, atlases, maps of Holland.
3. Colored pencils and the outline map of Holland (from chapter fifteen) for each student. This map can be copied and taped into the composition book.
4. Geography terms chart (optional but handy).
5. Other books, travel brochures, or pictures depicting Holland (Netherlands) a century ago and now. Look for books that show the clothing, flag, canals, windmills, tulips and wooden shoes (klompen) that characterize Holland. Find a picture of a dike or bulwark. Travel books are very useful for this purpose.
6. Composition book (or three-ring binder and paper) to put into completed booklet with these sections: map, vocabulary, geography terms, drawings, reports.
7. Try and locate a copy of the *History of the Rise of the Dutch Republic* by Motley. This is mentioned in chapter two, although it can be read any time during your study.

Here's the Background:

Author: Mary Mapes Dodge was an accomplished writer by age seventeen. She wrote for an agricultural magazine published by her father for farmers. She married and had two boys, to whom she told many stories. After becoming a young widow, she was encouraged to publish her stories. Thus began her successful career in writing. Her children's stories were published, and she became editor of the magazine, Hearth and Home. She was selected as the first editor-in-chief of a children's magazine called St. Nicholas. St. Nicholas featured articles by Rudyard Kipling (which became *The Jungle Books*), poems which Longfellow submitted, and Louisa May Alcott's serial stories.

Amazingly, Mrs. Dodge wrote this book without ever having seen Holland! She performed a thorough research of the country, its history, and its culture. She had many long discussions with friends and acquaintances who were from Holland. *Hans Brinker or The Silver Skates* was so popular that in the first thirty years after its initial publication, it had undergone over one hundred printings and was translated into six different languages. When she finally had the opportunity years later to see the nation, she was awed herself at how keenly accurate a description her book portrayed.

Objective: Mrs. Dodge stated her objective for writing the book in the author's notes, and her purpose is restated here: "...that the reader would gain a lasting impression of Holland, its people, resources, culture and history, and develop a deeper trust in God's goodness and love."

The Kingdom of the Netherlands

Setting: The story takes place in the mid 19th century in Holland, mostly on or near the banks of the many canals near Amsterdam. Although the story is fictional, the history as depicted is accurate and the story of Raff Brinker is factual. The main characters are a brother and sister (Hans and Gretel), ages fifteen and twelve.

Location: The Kingdom of the Netherlands (Holland) is located in northwest Europe on the North Sea. The capital, Amsterdam, is at 52°N 5°E.

History: Julius Caesar conquered this region in 56 BC. It was inhabited by Celtic and Germanic tribes at the time. It became part of the Roman Empire and was eventually controlled by Charlemagne. After Charlemagne's empire split, the Netherlands, which included Holland, Belgium and Flanders, was divided amongst dukes, counts, and bishops. Eventually, William of  Orange helped bring about individual sovereignty. By the 17th century, the Dutch Republic rose to eminence in the arts, naval defense and economically. The United Dutch Republic was conquered by France in the late 18th century when Napoleon created the Kingdom of Holland and incorporated it into his empire in 1810. The Congress of Vienna restored the Kingdom of the Netherlands' independence after Napoleon's defeat in 1814, but the name "Holland" has been more widely used even by many Dutch people. Even though Holland seems to have two names, the "Kingdom of the

For more information about the distinction between Holland and the Netherlands see:
www.graphicmaps.com/aatlas/infopage/holland.htm

Netherlands" is the correct name of the country. Please note: This study uses the name Holland to avoid confusion, since it is the name used in the novel.

Government: The government of the Netherlands is a Parliamentary Democracy under a constitutional monarch. Queen Beatrix has reigned since 1980. The seat of government is The Hague.

The land: Mostly low plains with a few hilly areas west, half of the Netherlands is actually situated below sea level. Holland holds the title of the "world's lowest country." It is protected by dikes and special drainage systems. The clever Dutch built a dike at the mouth of the shallow inland sea called the Zuider Zee. This dike formed a lake where the former Zuider Zee was located and it was renamed Ijsselmeer. This shallow lake bed has been drained over the years to form "polders" or reclaimed land. The nation, in the last 800 years, has lost about 14 million acres of land to the sea and has reclaimed over 17 million acres - more reclamation than any other European nation.

Before Reading Aloud

Distribute a copy of the following to each student: outline map of Holland (from chapter fifteen); "Temperature Graph" and "Novel Activity Sheet" (from chapter sixteen), and two or three timeline pages (from chapter nineteen).

Guide your students to complete the following:

1. Look up Holland (Netherlands) on the globe. Find it also on a world wall map and in the atlas.
2. Identify the latitude of this nation and compare it to your own. What other countries are at this latitude? Begin to watch for daily temperature highs in Amsterdam from newspapers and television. Graph along with your own high temperature for two or three weeks. Add graph to the notebook.
3. Place the outline map of Holland in your notebook. If using a stitched composition book, fold the map in half and store in the comp book. When map activities are completed (after chapter 31), the map can be taped into the comp book. Have the student tape the north, west and south borders onto a right facing page of their comp book. The untaped side of the map can be folded into the book. If using a three-ring binder, hole punch the bottom of the map or the south edge.
4. Mark and label on the map all nations and bodies of water that share its borders with Holland. Know which is north, east, west, and south of Holland. (Zuider Zee, North Sea, Germany, Belgium.)
5. Draw in England in the appropriate place on the map.
6. Begin to fill in the "Novel Activity Sheet." Continue to add info.

Watching for the Five Themes

The five themes in geography can be studied using the following guidelines:

1. Location

You've already located the place, as listed previously.

2. Place

Since Holland is located so far north, you'll notice the weather is cold and icy during the winter. Watch for other signs to compare the climate at your latitude with the climate in the story. USA Today has a wonderful daily weather map. Encourage students to graph the temperature listed for Amsterdam. Also graph your own temperature and compare. Watch carefully for all descriptions of physical and human characteristics of Holland. What makes it different and unique? Many will be pointed out in the chapter-by-chapter outline below. Chapter two may require extra time for study, because there's so much in the way of rich description.

3. Relationship

Notice the relationships that develop between people and their surroundings. How do people cope with the difficulties caused by the location of this nation? Watch for examples of how people adapted their surroundings to fit their needs (windmills, dikes, etc.).

4. Movement

This story is an such excellent example of how the diversity of movement of people and goods can depend so fully on the geographical location of the place. Notice the movement on the canals in winter and in the canals in summer. Pay attention to how different information is moved in this place at this time in history compared to today. Challenge students to reflect on transportation as the story unfolds.

5. Regions

Notice that homes are clustered by income status. What other regions can students discover? Let your students watch for them as the story progresses.

Moving On...

While you're traveling through Holland with our characters, there are lots of interesting activities to do. Give students a genuine feel for the culture and a real sense of being there, even though they haven't left the classroom. Sample delicious Dutch chocolates. View the art of Dutch artists, examining carefully the scenery in the background. Look for feature films that represent the same period or that depict Holland. Hans Christian Anderson provides a peek into the life of the youth of the area, and he wrote during the same general time frame. Students who love reading can be encouraged to read on their own time. Obtain stamps from Holland or find Dutch stamps in a book. The philatelic history of the nation can stir interests and provide exciting subjects for further study.

Step By Step ...
A variety of questions are provided for discussion. They're followed by possible answers in parentheses. These questions and answers are by no means complete; but the guideline is thorough enough to get you started on your own path to seeing the five themes in action. Geography terms are listed, as well as plants, animals and vocabulary words. Notice there are fewer and fewer geography terms and vocabulary words towards the middle of the book. Plan to give heavier assignments then.

Many geographical terms can be found quickly on the geography terms chart during a short pause in your reading. The student can be expected to place the word and a short definition in the vocabulary section of his comp book. This is helpful, especially if when the word pops up again and a quick trip to the notebook, reveals the definition if forgotten. Forgotten? Well, it does happen!

The Journey Begins!

Chapter 1: Hans and Gretel
Describe where the story begins. (On the bank of a frozen canal.) What are the peasant women doing? (Carrying filled baskets on their heads as they ice skate to their destination.)

What does "lusty boy" mean, and how does he travel to town to work? (We don't normally use the word "lusty" in this way today; he skates on the canal.) Describe the importance of skating to these people. Hans showed he had ingenuity. Explain what he did to meet a need his parents could not provide. (Skating was so important to him that even though his family couldn't afford to buy skates for him, he found a way. He fashioned his own skates, and his sister's, out of wood and rawhide.)

What's the winter climate like in Holland? (Ice all winter.) Dutch homes and buildings often bear the date or a motto above the door or portal. Watch for this when looking at pictures of Dutch architecture. Ask students to speculate on the history behind wooden shoes, or "klompen." This would make for an interesting oral report. Describe the lay of the land. (Flat country, windmills, willow trees, dikes.) A zomerhuis is a summer house.
VOCABULARY: klompen
GEOGRAPHY TERMS: dike, canal
PLANTS: willow trees

Chapter 2: Holland
This chapter provides a detailed picture of Holland, its land, its history and its people. You may wish to spend extra time on this chapter or assign some of these activities during the following chapters.

The draining of the Zuyder Zee was considered as early as the 17th century, but was not feasible until 200 years later. In 1919, the actual work began. At the mouth of this sea, the Dutch built a dike that cut it off from the North Sea. This created a shallow lake the Dutch renamed "IJsselmeer." Portions of this lake have been drained to develop cities of reclaimed land. These cities are called "polders." So far, over 14 million acres of land have been reclaimed and the draining continues today. The Dutch are very proud of this engineering feat; it greatly improved drinking water, created recreation arcas, and opened land for new polders.

Amazing but True

The Zuyder Zee was a shallow inland sea at the northern border of Holland. Its more contemporary spelling is "Zuider Zee"; however, after changing the sea into a shallow lake, the Dutch changed its name to "IJsselmeer." Now you have three different words or spellings for the same place! Go figure!

How is Holland so different from most other parts of the world? (Large parts of it are below sea level. Where else have you heard of the keel of a floating ship to be higher than the rooftops or ships hitched to a doorpost, or freight received in an upper window from a boat?! There are more water roads than common roads, dikes, windmills...) Be sure students understand what sea level means. The author said that dikes "keep the ocean where it belongs." What does that mean?

How did the Dutch adapt their lifestyle to cooperate with the land and water? (Built canals, water fences, used green hedges instead of wooden fences, brought large stones from other countries to strengthen and protect the coast, windmills to pump off water for usable land.) Describe canal boats and how they move. (Looks like a house on a barge and is pulled by horses walking on the bank of the canal.) Describe the farm land. (Once great lakes, now pumped dry and useful because of windmills.) Notice how even the horses are affected by the soil and are shod with a wide stool to lift them out of the mire.

Sea Level - the level of the surface of the sea between high and low tide.

Additional information: A "kermis" is a fair. The water-omnibus (pakschuyten and trekschuiten) was a kind of canal boat. They looked much like a green house on a barge. They were towed by horses from along the banks of the canals.

Windmills are fascinating! Study how they work and what other uses they have. (To saw timber, beat hemp, grind, pump water.) How many windmills were depicted in this story? (9,900.) How many do you think there are today? How would you find out? (A good short term research project for one student to report to the class.)

Note: You may wish to reproduce the following pages for student hand-outs. This is why the wide margin has been eliminated from here on.

Why was the land a duck paradise? Give five recreational uses for water in this chapter. (Wading, sailing toy ships, rowing, fishing, swimming.) Describe dikes and why they're used. Draw a picture of a dike that's high, wide enough for a road, with trees and buildings. Describe a farm house. (Thatched roof, house on stilts.)

What problems were caused by the dunes? How did people deal with this situation? What were the results? (Sand storms blew sand on wet fields. Controlled by sowing coarse reed-grass and other plants to keep the sand down.)

What is learned about the Dutch as a people in this chapter? (They're a brave, heroic, and proud people. They excelled in commerce, navigation, learning, science, education, charities, public works, arts, music, literature, and engineering. Historically, they were known as a "safe haven," providing shelter for refugees throughout Europe from wars and battles.)

What would happen if priority wasn't given to public works? (The country would be uninhabitable, many people would die from flooding, and towns could be buried beneath water.) What kind of work is done to provide stability? (Dike repair, regulating water levels.) What's a "freshet"? (A stream or rush of fresh water flowing into the sea.) Why does springtime bring the highest danger of inland freshets? (When the ice begins to thaw, rivers are choked with ice blocks from one side of the dike, and the sea pushes toward the dike from the other direction.) How do they protect dikes from the ocean? (With straw mats pressed against the embankment, and with fortified clay and heavy stones.)

It may prove interesting to locate and read passages from *History of the Rise of the Dutch Republic* by Motley.

Describe how Hans and Gretel's father was affected by the water, his job, how he got injured, and how serious was his injury.
VOCABULARY: bulwark, verdure, polder, sluice
GEOGRAPHY TERMS: ditch, pond, river, lake, dune, inland freshets, shore
ANIMALS: duck, horse
MAP WORK: draw and label Zuyder Zee, the provinces of Utrect and Friesland

Chapter 3: The Silver Skates
Here we learn about the Brinker family and glimpse into the character of the children and their father. A grand skating contest is announced to celebrate Mevrouw Glick's birthday. (Mevrouw is pronounced MEFF-row and means Mrs. or Madame.) The prize: a brand new pair of silver skates for the best boy and girl skater.

The Dutch motto: "Learn, learn, you idler! Or this rope's end shall teach you."

How was the family supported economically? (Dame Brinker sold vegetables, spun and knitted, and pulled horses along the canal until Hans was big enough. Gretel tended geese. Hans earned a few stivers a day working with the towing boats. A stiver is worth about 2 cents.)

Describe Hans' character. (Hans took on responsibilities of his own free will by working the tow horses and insisting upon doing drudgery work when he was big enough. He was a hard worker, took teasing patiently, and was well behaved at school.) What was the father's character before the accident that changed his life? (Good and dependable, intelligent, wise, brave, and enjoyed singing.) How is the home kept warm? (Peat bricks for fuel.) What kind of bread do they eat? (Black bread.) Notice that all kinds people use the frozen canal for transportation, from stately men, professionals, to children, to women with baskets on their heads, even an old farmer without skates.

VOCABULARY: peat, burgomaster, stiver
MAP WORK: label Amsterdam

Chapter 4: Hans and Gretel Find a Friend
Wealthy Hilda shows a heart of kindness and concern for the peasant family. She encourages both Hans and Gretel to enter the contest. She even offers to buy them a pair of skates.

Why did Hans first refuse the money offered by Hilda? (Because he hadn't earned it.) How did Hilda gracefully convince him to take the money? (She asked Hans to carve her a chain like he had made for his sister so she could purchase it from him.) Notice the way Hans and his sister chose who should get the skates. Does it seem unusual to you that both Hans and his sister wanted the other to get the new skates? What would you have done?

Why was Hans so proud the next day? (His sister skated with new skates and a warm coat.) How did both Hans and Gretel end up with new skates? (Peter van Holp also bought a chain from Hans.) A kwartje is a small silver coin worth one quarter of a guilder or about ten cents. Jufvrouw (pronounced YUFF-row) means Miss or young lady.

Chapter 5: Shadows in the Home
We are introduced to a mystery which began the fateful night the father was permanently injured. He had given Dame Brinker  a silver watch to keep until he asked for it again, and before he could explain where it came from or why he had it, he had to flee to help save the dike from flooding. Alas; that was the night of the terrible accident, and he hadn't been in his right mind since. Dame Brinker never knew the story behind the silver watch.

Why did Dame Brinker refuse to sell the watch even when money was needed for food and medical care? (Faithfulness to her commitment to her husband.)

A large sum of money was missing since that night. Where did the money come from? (The Brinker's saved faithfully for their children's education.) When was the last time the money had been seen? (The night before.) What did they imagine may have happened to the money? (Stolen, misplaced, or hidden by the father.) What had more value to Hans than all the silver in the world? (His mother's happiness.)
VOCABULARY: guilder(s)

Chapter 6: Sunbeams
Hiereen Gract is a street in Amsterdam. Meester is a term for doctor used by the lower class.

What did Hans want to do with his skate money, rather than buy skates? (Pay for a doctor for his father.) How did the Brinker family plan to celebrate their Feast of St. Nicholas? (Dame Brinker would wear her festival dress, and they would rejoice at the new skates while enjoying a special waffle treat.)
MAP WORK: Dame Brinker had worked for a family in Heidelberg, Germany. Find it on a map in your atlas. What's its latitude and longitude? (49°N 9°E) How far is it, and in what direction is it from her home now?

Chapter 7: Hans Has His Way

Y (pronounced "eye") is an arm of the Zuyder Zee.

Hans happens to meet the great Dr. Boekman on his way to Broek to purchase the skates, and arranges for the doctor to see his father in a week. Why does the doctor agree to see Hans' father? (He likes the boy.) Where does the Brinker family live? (A mile south of Broek, near the canal.) How was the doctor to find the house when he arrived? (Ask anybody, everyone knows where to find the "idiot's cottage".)

VOCABULARY: automata, mosaic

GEOGRAPHY TERMS: rivulets

ANIMALS: cows

MAP WORK: label Leyden

Chapter 8: Introducing Jacob Poot and His Cousin

While skating on the canals, some of the boys plan a trip to The Hague. Although distances traveled are given in standard miles (5280 ft.) the Dutch mile is actually over 4 times as long.

MAP WORK: Label The Hague (Holland's capital - mark with a star, not a dot), Haarlem, England. (You'll see England's eastern coastline on your map.)

Chapter 9: The Festival of St. Nicholas

Compare this festival with Christmas. Remember, this festival is held on Dec. 6th. Compare St. Nicholas with Santa Claus. Notice St. Nicholas had a word of reproof and a blessing. Children desired to change their bad behavior after his words. Notice how shoes were filled as compared to stockings. Hendrick hit the doel. What do you think this is? (Bull's eye.)

VOCABULARY: mitre, crozier (crosier), august (august-looking), skullcap, ensign

PLANTS: birch

Chapter 10: What the Boys Saw and Did in Amsterdam

Amsterdam is the capital of the Netherlands. It has the greatest number of buildings in Europe; the oldest of which was built of wood in 1475. Amsterdam was home to famous artists Rembrandt and VanGough, and boasts of influences in the arts and music. Today, Amsterdam is known for its toleration to drug use and its red light district, its canals, and the arts. The boys visited a museum in Amsterdam. This was probably the famous Rijksmuseum (pronounced "rikes" museum), where today you can still view some of the same great works of art the boys in our story saw. (e.g. "Night Watch," by Rembrandt.) You may wish to locate any of Gerard Douw's art in books to show your students. Other paintings they saw were by Rembrandt and Van der Helst.

How long did it take the boys to skate from Broek to Amsterdam? (Half an hour.) Who kept the money purse for all? (Peter.) Describe the city and its relationship to the water. Draw a picture of a building in Amsterdam. Show any good pictures you may have found, and discuss the architecture. Notice the tall houses have gable ends facing the street where goods are lowered from and hoisted into upper warehouse rooms through a window.

What qualities were evident in Gerard Douw 's character? (Attention to detail, a good steward of his art supplies, thankfulness, patience. Taking three days to paint a broom handle or five days painting a woman's hand would require a good measure of patience!) Find out when Douw lived and add to timeline.

Write a daily journal entry from the perspective of one of the boys on this outing that will last through the next twenty chapters. Or design a travel brochure of Amsterdam, The Hague, or Leyden. Include all the places the boys visited while in each city.

VOCABULARY: panniers, locks
GEOGRAPHY TERMS: island
ANIMALS and PLANTS: Flanders horses, elm trees

Chapter 11: Big Manias and Little Oddities
Be prepared to show pictures of Holland's beautiful tulip fields. In a book about Holland, look for the Keukenhof. It is perhaps the world's most famous flower display with 70 acres of park land filled with tulips and other bulbs, beautifully landscaped with shrubs, trees, and lakes.

What was the duty of the guards? (Keeping the surface of the canal free from obstruction and garbage.) Notice the Dutch culture's respect for cleanliness. How did the Dutch tulip industry begin? What are polders?

Rotterdam is the place from where the Pilgrims departed to America in the Speedwell. (The Speedwell was found unfit for the journey and the Mayflower finished the trip alone.) The church where they had their last services is still standing. Add Pilgrims, 1620, to the time-line. Study Rotterdam. For what is it famous? (Largest port in the world.)

PLANTS: tulips, water lilies
MAP WORK: Find Constantinople (currently Istanbul) in an atlas. What are its latitude and longitude coordinates? (41°N 29°E.) How many miles away and in what direction is it from Holland? (Approximately 1,300 miles south and east.) Label Rotterdam.

Chapter 12: On the Way to Haarlem
Notice the great hospitality in the home of the strangers where the boys went to warm themselves. Could we do this today? Why? What is Zwanenburg Castle? Why was Brunings highly regarded by the citizens of Holland? (Great engineers are regarded as the highest of public benefactors.)

ANIMALS: eels
FOOD: gingerbread, sour wine, black bread, sauerkraut

Chapter 13: A Catastrophe
The boys arrive in Haarlem only to discover that all their money has been lost. How far had the boys skated from departure to arrival in Haarlem? (Seventeen miles.) How did Peter feel about losing the money? How did the others respond? What did they decide to do? What is tiffin hour? (Lunch time.)

Chapter 14: Hans
How is Hans viewed by Carl? On what does he base his opinion of Hans? How is Hans viewed by Peter? ("I like that boy, rich or poor.") Hans returns the lost purse, refuses any reward, and gains the assistance of Peter to find Dr. Boekman. Discuss honesty.

The father has gotten worse and cannot wait for a week to see the doctor. Discuss how it must have felt to see your father in such a state. Notice how each family member tends to support one another. Hans, though hungry, refuses to stop and eat with the boys, but instead returns home to care for his mother. Discuss loyalty.

Chapter 15: Homes

Notice the separation of class by region of the city and how this affected the attitude of Rychie Korbes and Katrinka toward "goose-girl" and others who are not of their class. What attitudes have you developed about people because of their clothes or income or where they live? Notice, also, how even Gretel struggles to love her father through his handicap.

VOCABULARY: coquette

Chapter 16: Haarlem - The Boys Hear Voices

How are the Dutch people informed of the death of a loved one? (The aanspreeker notifies friends and family. He also attends the funeral.) How do they learn of a birth? (Parents hang a red or white pin-cushion at the door as an announcement.) Here we use blue for baby boys and pink for girls. What are the colors in Holland? (Red for boy, white for girl.)

Retell the story of Handel playing the organ. A Vox Humana is an organ-stop that sounds much like a human voice.

Chapter 17: The Man with Four Heads

Who was Laurens Janszoon Coster? (Believed by Dutch to be the inventor of printing instead of Guttenberg.) Who was Dr. Boerhaave, and why was he so famous? Notice how proud the Dutch are of their heritage. Find when these men lived and add to the timeline.

ANIMALS: herring
PLANTS: elm
MAP WORK: locate and label Bloemendal

Chapter 18: Friends in Need

The famous story of the little boy putting his finger in the hole of the dike to save his city is retold in this chapter. Draw a picture from the description given.

VOCABULARY: burgher, ramparts

Chapter 19: On the Canal

There is much happening on the canal. Describe the iceboat Ben watched. Learn about the city of Delft. For what is it most known? (Blue Delft china.) Learn about Gouda and for what it is most known. (Gouda cheese.)

VOCABULARY: dowager, carillons
MAP WORK: label Gouda, Delft

Chapter 20: Jacob Poot Changes the Plan

Jacob, exhausted and cold, requires assistance to move on. The boys hitch a ride on an iceboat. Peter gives the skipper some coins to buy sweets for his children from St. Nicholas.

Chapter 21: Mynheer Kleef and His Bill of Fare

The boys arrive in Leyden, eat a meal, and secure a room for the night at the Red Lion Inn. Peter sets off to find Dr. Boekman. What is caviare?

VOCABULARY: roes of sturgeon, bolsters
FOOD: sausage, pudding, salmagundi, eggs, caviare, rye bread, potato salad, coffee

Chapter 22: The Red Lion Becomes Dangerous

The boys foil a robbery attempt and tie up the robber. The bedstead was laced with rope. Why? Do you think Carl was really running for help or running away from fear?

VOCABULARY: chrysalis, blunderbuss
GEOGRAPHY TERM: iceberg

Chapter 23: Before the Court
Notice how quickly the court hearing takes place. How does that compare to our country then and now? Write a court report of what happened to the boys at the Red Lion Inn and the results of the court proceeding.

Chapter 24: Beleaguered Cities
Much history of various cities is explored in this chapter. These historical events can be further studied and placed on the timeline. Who was Boerhaave? Van der Werf? Frederic of Toledo? Duke of Alva?

Describe what happened at the Ruine in 1807. (A barge loaded with 40,000 pounds of gunpowder exploded, killing people and destroying 300 houses.) Add to the timeline. Write your own story of Van der Werf. Be sure to include the role of the pigeons and the wind. Consider writing the story as a newspaper reporter.

Why did the boys not let out three cheers to Van der Werf? (It wasn't acceptable behavior to cheer in the street at midday.) With whom was Kanau Hesselaer compared? (Joan of Arc.)
ANIMALS: pigeons
MAP WORK: Find Rome in an atlas, locate its longitude/latitude coordinates. (42°N 13°E.)

Chapter 25: Leyden
The boys tour Leyden's Museum of Natural History, a tea garden, and Town Hall. What makes Breedstraat different than other streets there? (It's long and straight, has no canal running through it, and has colorfully painted houses lining its way.) How far were they now from The Hague? (13 miles.) What is a triptych?
MAP WORK: Draw the Rhine River. Find and list all countries through which it flows.

Chapter 26: The Palace in the Wood
The Wood is respected in the community, and no wonder!
GEOGRAPHY TERMS: ditch
PLANTS: oak

Chapter 27: The Merchant Prince and the Sister Princess
What historical event joined England and Holland? (The marriage of William of Orange of Holland and Queen Mary of England.) Who was Peter the Great? (Czar of Russia who worked as a shipwright to bring Dutch improvements in shipbuilding to his country.) Add to the timeline. Ben's knowledge of Dutch history throughout their trip has proven to be a great addition to the group's level of pleasure. How do you think knowledge can improve your own life and the lives of those around you?

Compare the furnishings of the van Gend home to that of the Brinker's home. Does either home lack for love? Read the description of the dekbed cover. To what could this be compared? (Down comforter or mattress cover.) How was Peter to inform his mother that they were going to stay in The Hague longer than planned? (By letter - no telephones or email!)
VOCABULARY: gnome, repast, artificer
MAP WORK: Locate and label Antwerp, Belgium. Give its longitude and latitude. (51°N 4° E.)
    How many miles and in what direction is it from The Hague? (About 60 miles south.)

Chapter 28: Through The Hague
This chapter provides an opportunity to talk of different modes of transportation to deliver goods: carts, ice boats, and walking alongside a cart pulled by a dog.

Speculate why there was no curb or raised pavement. Why do you think there were more sleds than wagons used on the brick pavement? How did the driver reduce the friction of the runners?

ANIMALS: stork

FOOD: fish, English roast beef, cheese, milk

Chapter 29: A Day of Rest

What kind of religious practices or traditions have you seen so far in this book? What are foot stoves? How do class distinctions show themselves in the church? (Specially designed pews for nobility.) What did Ben notice in the floor of the church? (Grave stones marking sepulchers.) What disturbed Ben about the Hollanders in church? (Wearing hats in the church was outrageously improper in England.)

VOCABULARY: sepulcher

Chapter 30: Homeward Bound

The boys depart for home and get in a little practice for the race, too!

Chapter 31: Boys and Girls

A Ysbreeker was a heavy machine with iron spikes used to break up the ice. Small ones were worked by men, but larger ones were pulled by as many as 60 or 70 horses! Describe the weather. (Windy.) What was the traffic like on the canal? (Not much traffic from Leyden and Haarlem, but a "moving throng" when they approached Amsterdam.)

Annie Bouman was friends with Gretel. What kept the other girls from befriending Gretel? (Gretel was the "goose-girl," too low-class for the other girls.) Why was Annie her friend? (Annie Bouman was a peasant girl, and closer in class to the Brinkers. She still took some level of teasing from the neighbor's children.)

VOCABULARY: skittles

MAP WORK: label Voorhout (between The Hague and Haarlem.)

Chapter 32: The Crisis

Surgery! Will it help the father or kill him? Notice Hans' respect for his mother in making the decision, and his support of her when she most needed it. She even commanded respect from the doctor! What kind of surgical practices would there have been at that time? (This would have occurred before Louis Pasteur's germ theory and even before Joseph Lister introduced antiseptic surgery, so it is probable brain surgery would have been performed without clean instruments; certainly not with sterile instruments. Today, the chance of survival of such a surgery in the home would be considered minimal.)

Chapter 33: Gretel and Hilda

Hilda gets past the class separation and follows her heart. She supports Gretel during the surgery. What is a thatched roof? How is it made and how long does it survive?

Chapter 34: The Awakening

The surgery is a success, and both the doctor and Dame Brinker give thanks where they believe it is due. To whom do you give thanks and why?

Chapter 35: Bones and Tongues
How had news spread of Raff Brinker's cure? Did it take long without telephones and e-mail? How did the community view these peasants now? Consider how we can choose when to embrace and when to scorn all to our own benefit. Does anybody really know what has happened? And yet the stories; half-truths borne out of speculation! How can someone prevent being a bearer of half-truths?

Chapter 36: A New Alarm
Can they provide the proper food and warmth for the father to heal? While Hans struggles over earning money to provide, the doctor sends help.

Chapter 37: The Father's Return
The father attempts to catch up on ten lost years. How old was Gretel when his accident left him a lunatic? (Two.)

Chapter 38: The Thousand Guilders
Hans and Dame Brinker dig for the hidden guilders with no success.

Chapter 39: Glimpses
Hans searches for work and sells his skates to buy peat and food.

Chapter 40: Looking for Work
List some of the industry found in Amsterdam. (Woolen, cotton and linen factories, making dyes and paints, diamond cutting, suppliers of meal, bricks, glass, and china.)
VOCABULARY: deportment

Chapter 41: The Fairy Godmother
The money is found.
ANIMAL: rabbit

Chapter 42: The Mysterious Watch
Raff Brinker shares the story of the watch, but can't remember to whom it belongs.

Chapter 43: A Discovery
What is the rumor about Americans? (Savages.) What's happening in America during this time? (Perhaps around 1850.)

Chapter 44: The Race
Note the clear description of the clothing of the time. Where could a Friesland family's treasure be displayed on a day like this one? (In the women's headgear.) A true Dutchman is never without what? (His pipe.) What would indicate the Dutch government's value of birds? (It's a legal offense to rob a bird's nest.)

VOCABULARY: gilt, pagoda, Mercury, Olympus
FOOD: doughnuts, bonbons
MAP WORK: label Schiedam, Texel. There's a French traveler. Have
   you labeled the French border already? If not, do so now.

Chapter 45: Joy in the Cottage
Raff Brinker remembers the name.
MAP WORK: Find Birmingham, England on a map.

Chapter 46: Mysterious Disappearance of Thomas Higgs
Who was Thomas Higgs?

Chapter 47: Broad Sunshine
VOCABULARY: reverie

Chapter 48: Conclusion
The end of the story is told. All have grown up, and each has reaped the seeds that were sown.

Journey's End
Your students have now amassed volumes of information about Holland and its history. They should have a map, timeline, drawings, a newspaper report, a journal and lots of vocabulary. Perhaps you'll want to test them on their vocabulary words. If you gave them a blank map, could they now label it with Amsterdam, Haarlem, Leyden, Rotterdam, Germany, and France? They may have drawn the flag, designed a travel brochure, and completed the Novel Worksheet.

Before laying this study to rest, be sure all information has been gathered together into a notebook. Encourage them to share their notebook with family and friends. Congratulations on a job well done!

When you repeat this kind of study with another novel, you'll be able to add your experiences and creative ideas. Enjoy the journey!

GEOGRAPHY THROUGH SCIENCE

CHAPTER 8

INCORPORATE GEOGRAPHY INTO SCIENCE STUDIES

 Although we tend to think of geography and history as the "perfect couple," geography and science go hand-in-hand as well. Earth Science is practically a detailed course in physical geography. The easiest ways to incorporate geography into your science program are to:

• Recognize when the topic you're teaching is also a geographic concept. (Watch especially in life and physical sciences.)

• Use an interdisciplinary approach when possible. For example - if studying the break-up of the Soviet Union, learn the political and physical boundaries, the environmental effect of Chernobyl, and the pollution problems faced by many former Eastern Bloc countries.

• Use maps as they relate to your science topics.

This chapter includes map ideas, lists of ways to correlate weather and geography, and a teaching unit on volcanoes.

The *Scientist's Apprentice* is one curriculum that uses this approach. See Bright Ideas Resources.

Maps and Science

Not only are maps a visual representation of information presented, they also serve as a reminder that the topic being studied has a correlation to geography. For example:

• Ecosystems and habitats - color code the areas in the world that share that habitat. Write in samples of animals or kinds of plants that live there. Make a key.

• Migratory patterns of birds make interesting maps. Seeing it visually leads to further areas of discovery.

- Chart weather on the map. Whether it's local or world, students should learn how to interpret various types of weather maps. Chart hurricanes during hurricane season.

- Include maps when studying oceanography. Show and discuss navigation charts used by boaters and maps of the ocean floor. How did we get that information? How are they different/similar to land maps? Use topographical maps for geology, ecology, and habitat studies.

- Maps for the solar system help us visualize where Earth is in relation to the other planets. It's easier to memorize planet order after seeing the information, instead of just reading about it.

Other topics that lend themselves to map use:

Earthquakes and volcanoes	Land forms
Natural resources	Geology
Water cycle	Climatic regions
Rock formation and weathering	Food supply
Chart mineral deposits	Plate tectonics
Ecology, pollution, and the environment	

Weather: Working up a Storm!

Geography and weather are intricately intertwined. Weather makes a fascinating unit with many opportunities for hands-on projects. Use the reproducible weather tracking chart, "Weather Report." Laminate and use a Vis-a-Vis pen for write-on/wipe-off use. It's great for helping students pay closer attention to weather and to signs of changing weather. (While making photocopies, don't forget the "Temperature Graph." Also, use the upper-level "Working Up a Storm" reproducible to challenge older students or as a research tool.) These reproducibles can be found in chapter sixteen.

Use these ideas and questions to put together a great weather unit!
- How does weather impact our lives?

- How do we find out about our weather forecast? What did our grandparents do before TV and the Weather Channel?

- Some people are very good at forecasting weather without using available technology. Why is that still important?
- Are there occupations today that still benefit from the ability to closely determine the weather?

- Interview someone who is knowledgeable about weather predictions. How did they learn to forecast? What information/clues do they use to determine the weather? How is that helpful to them in their everyday lives? (Try boaters, farmers, pilots, and anyone else who works or plays outside.)

- Track the temperature in the your region. Pay attention to the precipitation and wind, also. Chart your observations. Make predictions based on previous observations.

- How did weather play a part in the time and place of your history studies? How did weather affect the people living there and then?

- Take a field trip to a nearby weather station.

- Make a rain gauge using a skinny cup. Leave it outside and measure and record the findings. What's a drought? What places experience drought? How does this affect the population living there? Are there places where too much rain is a problem? How are the rainy seasons in India both a blessing and a difficulty? What causes a flood? Research a flood, its causes and effects. Report the findings.

- Rent a video about weather or storms. Try libraries or educational resource centers. The Weather Channel puts out an exciting video about storms. Watch it first without the sound.

- Write a poem about weather. Acrostics lend themselves well to topics. Look for weather-related poems from other cultures.

- Start a "Weather Journal." Take "weather walks" and record observations. Discuss what it would be like to live in the Australian Outback or on a research station in Antarctica.

- No weather station nearby? Try a military base or television station.
- Kids love to play in the weather! If it isn't dangerous, dress them properly and let them go.

- Severe weather is intriguing. Gather books from the library with factual accounts of floods, tornadoes, and hurricanes. Look for good photographs and eyewitness reports. What are some keys to survival? Does severe weather reoccur in the same regions? Why do people choose whether or not to live there?

- Make a weather poster. Include terms. Show differences in regions according to climate. How do people dress there and what kinds of housing do they live in? Why?

- Learn to identify clouds. Invest in a good cloud chart and use it. Is having a knowledge of weather predictions useful for the average person?

The Grand Finale!
Assign students to give oral weather reports - tape these "weathermen" presenting their "Action News at 6:00." Encourage them to dress appropriately for their topic and to ham it up. This is a memorable way to wrap-up the unit!

Volcanoes: Blowin' up a Storm!

This introduction to volcanoes works particularly well just following a unit on rocks and minerals. Included is both "teaching the teacher" information, as well as activities to do that explain concepts and explore different facets of volcanoes. Before starting, pull together a collection of interesting books with information and pictures about volcanoes for students to read and use for research. The bigger the variety, the better. When you're finished, use the reproducible in chapter sixteen, "Are You a Volcanologist?" (junior or senior edition) to wrap things up.

Volcano Notebook

During your volcano studies, guide the students in keeping a personalized notebook. Collect pictures and postcards of volcanoes, volcanic rocks, maps, and any other interesting, related pictures. (Old National Geographics are great for this purpose.)

One student may become fascinated with volcano names and pictures. Another may be more interested in the scientific study of volcanoes. A third might prefer rocks, and another the stories and legends about famous eruptions. Encourage them to include information that's meaningful to them, as well as the basic facts discovered during the course of their study.

Volcano Postcards

Kids are natural born collectors. Use that interest to further their knowledge of volcanoes and places. Write away to Chambers of Commerce in the areas where there are volcanoes and ask for postcards. Write to embassies of foreign countries and ask if they'll send a postcard of their most famous volcano. Or write to newspapers located in regions with volcanoes. The students can address their letters to the editor and explain that they're collecting volcano postcards. Would readers of this newspaper please send them one?

Postcards can be added to their volcano notebook, or they might want to mount them on a bulletin board with captions beneath.

Make a Volcano

There are many directions available for making a volcano. Before you decide on one, think about the purpose behind the assignment. Is it strictly an art project? Is it meant to be as scientifically accurate as possible? Is it a replica of a real volcano? Or is it just for fun?

Knowing your goal will help to define the activity and set the parameters for what, if any, research and preparation time is required. For example, although there are many activity books that suggest using vinegar and baking soda to simulate an eruption, that isn't a particularly scientific representation! The explanation and demonstration "What Makes Magma Erupt," on page 117, is more scientific than the ever-popular baking soda and vinegar demonstration. It's just that baking soda and vinegar is, well - a blast! Again, know your goals, and then make volcanoes!

When making volcanoes, consider giving students a clear idea of what's expected of them rather than step-by-step directions. Then allow for creativity in carrying out the assignment.

Eating Volcanoes? - Magma Fudge!

Food is always a good attention-grabber; especially if it involves chocolate! Fudge makes an easy visual aid for showing the difference between smooth, glassy basalt and rough, porous pumice. Use your favorite fudge recipe and then, while pouring half of the hot fudge into one pan, talk about how smooth and glossy it is. Ask how it might look when it hardens. Just before pouring the other half, whip it hard with a whisk until it's fluffy. As it pours, talk about the way it looks different from the first batch. Discuss the differences between the glassy basalt, and the pumice with air pockets in it. Which floats and why? Draw parallels between the hot fudge (magma) and the cooled, hardened fudge (lava). Then eat too much!

Read More About It!

There's more to volcanoes than included in this chapter, of course. For a deeper study with older students, learn about things like subduction zones and tectonic activity. However, basic information like this is a good starting place. A list of vocabulary is provided - pick and choose words appropriate for the grade level of the students doing the study. Volcanoes are naturally exciting; whet their appetite and they'll beg for more! ☺

The remainder of this chapter is written to the student. You may wish to reproduce these pages for placement in a student notebook. Don't forget about the "Are You a Volcanologist?" reproducibles in chapter sixteen. Answer key is in Appendix B.

Time Saver Tip
Make copies of pages 116-120 now for student notebooks.

VOLCANOES

Gas! Ash! Lava!
The word "volcano" comes from the Latin word "Volcanus" or "Vulcanus." This comes from the Roman fire-god Vulcan, who according to mythology, lived under Mt. Etna making thunderbolts for the god Jupiter. Proper spelling of volcano in the plural can either be "volcanos" or "volcanoes." Adding "es" appears to be more common.

What Are Volcanoes Really?
A volcano is an opening in the earth's crust from which molten rock is expelled, forming a conical heap or mountain. The opening is called the vent. The molten rock is called magma when it's under the surface, and lava when it hits the surface. If the magma that breaks through the earth's crust is thick with lots of dissolved gases like carbon dioxide, the explosion will be great. Thinner magma with less dissolved gas won't cause a great explosion.

How Can Rock Melt?
Hold a rock in your hand. Now, imagine it melting! How can that happen? The earth's core is approximately 3,950 miles down. It's surrounded by an outer core of liquid iron and metal. There are several other layers before the solid upper mantle and the crust. The temperature at the core? A whopping 5,000 degrees F; easily enough to melt rock! Melted (or molten) rock can rise to the upper mantle and break through when there's a crack in the crust.

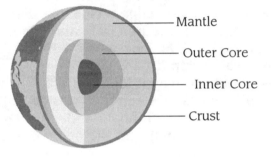

Where are They?
There are over 500 active volcanoes in the world, some of which are under the sea. Two major areas of volcanoes exist. (Earthquakes are common in these areas, too.) The first is called the "Pacific Ring of Fire." This area circles around the edge of the Pacific Ocean and has many active volcanoes. It includes the western coast of North and South America (including Mt. St. Helens in Washington state). It also includes Mt. Fuji in Japan, from Guam to Samoa, to New Zealand, then down and across to the southern coast of South America. The second chain forms a line along the Azores, Canary Islands, and east to Europe and Asia.

Map It
Find the Pacific Ring of Fire and draw it on the Pacific Rim outline map. Locate the second chain, also. Once you see the "ring" visually it will be much easier to remember where the major groupings of volcanoes are located. As different famous volcanoes are discussed, place a sticky note with the volcano's name written on it onto the map where it's located. This helps to see the pattern of volcanoes, and also to learn your way around the world. It may open a door to a future career - volcanologists, perhaps?

Volcanologists

A scientist who studies volcanoes is called a "volcanologist." This is an exciting, though dangerous profession. These scientists collect data and information in order to learn more about volcanoes, and to try and predict future volcanic activity.

These men and women monitor the size of volcanoes, recording any swells or bulges, with an instrument called a "tilt meter." They also record information on any earthquake activity using an instrument called a "seismometer." Another job is to collect data and samples of gas and lava. When they need to get close to craters of active volcanoes, they wear special suits to help protect them from the heat. These look similar to an astronaut's suit. Although these scientists are careful, volcanoes are very unpredictable. Volcanologists have been injured and even killed while studying volcanoes.

What Makes Magma Erupt?
Magma deep beneath the surface of the volcano holds gas. The pressure from the rock above keeps the gas dissolved. As magma flows upward, the gas begins to bubble as there is less rock pressing on the magma. As the pressure decreases, the bubbles continue to expand, giving rising magma explosive power! The following activity will demonstrate this concept:

Exploding Gas!

Materials:
1 or 2 liter bottle of clear carbonated water or soda
Red food coloring (optional, but more fun!)

Directions:
Remove cap, add a few drops of food coloring.
Screw top back on tightly.
Shake vigorously!
Hold bottle away from you and over a sink (or outside).
Slowly unscrew the cap.

What Happened?
Soft drinks contain a gas called "carbon dioxide." When sealed, there's pressure to keep this gas dissolved. When the cap is removed, so is the pressure. Bubbles form and the "magma" erupts!

Three Types of Volcanoes

1. Shield Volcanoes
Shield volcanoes have gently sloping sides. They're made of many layers of a kind of volcanic rock called "basalt." Basalt flows easily when hot and melted. When it comes out of a vent, it forms thin layers sloping away from the crater. The Hawaiian Islands are made up of shield volcanoes.

2. Cinder Cone Volcanoes
Cinder cone volcanoes are made up mostly of bits of volcanic rock called "andesite." The bits are called "cinders." They get blown out of the vent and harden in the air. When they land, they form a steep pile around the center crater. They're generally smaller than both composite and shield volcanoes.

3. Composite Cone Volcanoes
Composite cone volcanoes are made up of layers of cinders between layers of lava. The sides are steep. Look at a picture of Mt. St. Helens. It's a composite cone volcano. Now you know!

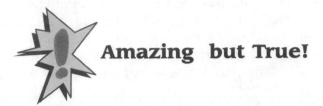

Amazing but True!

- On the ocean floor there are volcanic hot springs called "Black Smokers." These strange looking vents spew black steam. The mineral-rich water supports some very odd, sea-like tube worms and giant clams!

- In 1912 in Alaska, two volcanoes erupted at the same time. Ash so filled the sky that it was like night for three days. This area is still sending out hot gas and steam and is called the "Valley of Ten Thousand Smokes."

- Diamonds originate under the earth's mantle under extreme heat and pressure. Volcanoes can spew them out.

- Huge killer waves, called "tsunamis," are caused by a jolt to the ocean floor from earthquakes or volcanoes. They can speed across the ocean at over 450 miles per hour!

- Volcanic eruptions seem to affect our view of the sun in strange ways! It can appear to be blotted out or to look oddly blue or green.

- More than six million trees were flattened by the incredible blast of Mt. St. Helens in 1980.

- Over 3,500 people were killed when El Chichon in Mexico erupted. Its ash darkened the sky for forty-four hours.

- Each year there are about twenty-five major eruptions on land, and many more under the sea.

- A cinder cone volcano on the Indonesian island of Krakatau erupted in May, 1883. The violent explosion was heard 2,170 miles away! Tsunamis rose over one hundred feet high and crashed into villages along the coasts of Java and Sumatra, destroying them and killing over 30,000 people. Although Mt. Krakatoa collapsed, more than forty years later a volcanic island called Anak Krakatoa (meaning Child of Krakatoa) surfaced in the same spot.

- There's an active volcano in Antarctica called Mt. Erebus.

Add any new information you learn below.

Volcano Projects and Activities

See-Inside Volcano Book

Materials:
Two acetate pages (overhead projector sheets)
Vis-a-Vis overhead projector pens of at least two colors
Diagram of a volcano

Directions:
1. Draw, copy, or trace a diagram of the inside of a volcano on plain white paper. Label the parts.

2. Draw, copy, or trace the outside of a volcano the SAME SIZE as the first diagram. Label parts.

3. Place an acetate page over the first diagram. Trace it with a marker. Let dry.

4. Place an acetate page over the second diagram. Trace it with a marker. Let dry. Color in this volcano. Add trees, grass, wildlife, etc. The inside volcano should now be hidden by the outside volcano.

5. Label the top of the acetate page with "See-Inside a Volcano" by student's name. Place in a protective report cover.

Open the book, turn the page, and see the inner workings of a volcano!

Other books that can be made for volcanoes include a Make Your Own Pop-up Book, and an ABC Volcano Fact Book.

Volcano Research

Pick a famous volcano and conduct research about it. Make a poster, or in some other creative way show how the volcano affected the lives of the people who lived near it.

Bingo

Create a Volcano Bingo game, using research to come up with questions for other students to answer about volcanoes. Keep the game simple, or allow for more time and creativity in developing a game. Or use information in this section to develop your own game to share with other students - guaranteed to be more fun than a test!

Words to Know

Active: A volcano likely to erupt at any time.

Ash: Fine particles of matter spewed from a volcanic vent.

Basalt: A kind of rock that forms after lava cools and hardens.

Cinder: A fragment of lava from an erupting volcano; bits of rock.

Cinder Cone: Spew out burning cinders, ash, and steam from a single vent. Often violent and steep. Krakatoa is an example.

Composite Cone: Layers of cinder and layers of lava. Mt. St. Helens is an example.

Craters: The funnel shaped opening at the top of a volcano.

Crust: The hard outer layer of the earth.

Dormant: A "sleeping" or inactive volcano.

Eruption: An explosion of gas, ash, and lava bursting out of a volcano.

Extinct: A volcano that no longer erupts.

Fissure: A narrow opening or crack of some length and depth, usually occurring from a breaking or parting of the earth's crust.

Inner Core: A solid ball of iron and nickel at the center of the earth.

Lava: Magma that has reached the surface.

Magma: Red hot melted rock below the surface of the volcano.

Magma Chamber: A reservoir or pocket of magma under the earth's crust.

Mount St. Helens: A volcano in Washington which dramatically erupted in 1980.

Obsidian: Volcanic glass that is black or banded. Forms when thick, sticky lava cools quickly.

Outer Core: A liquid layer of iron and nickel at the center of the earth.

Pumice: A volcanic rock formed when frothy lava cools and hardens. Bubbles of air trapped inside allow it to actually float on water! Commercial uses include grinding it to powder for polishing and smoothing.

Ring of Fire: Area circling the Pacific Ocean where most volcanoes are located.

Seismograph: An instrument used to record an earthquake, how strong it is, and where it's located.

Shield Volcano: Gentle slopes made of many layers of rock called basalt. The Hawaiian islands are shield volcanoes.

Tilt meter: An instrument used to measure the size of the swell of a volcano.

Vent: An opening for the escape of a gas or liquid or the relief of pressure. Magma flows up the vent from the magma chamber to the surface.

Volcano Notebook Handout

GEOGRAPHY THROUGH MATH

CHAPTER 9

SPECIAL REPORT:
TEACHER USES GEOGRAPHY TO TEACH MATH!

Math? You thought this was a book about geography, and now we're talking about math? This isn't a tomato thrown into a basket of apples! In this chapter, we'll show you how to sneak in a bit of geography during a math lesson. We've included reproducible graphs, grids and charts to make your job easier.

There are several ways to incorporate geography into mathematics. Using the lessons already provided in your math curriculum, you can tie in geographical facts as data for solving problems. If you enjoy making up your own math questions using real-life situations, topics like currency exchange rates, time zone conversions, population densities, rainfall, and temperatures provide numbers you can draw upon.

Measurement, Time, and Distance

When teaching about simple measurements, time and distance, take figures from an atlas by using the scale from the legend. Students can determine the distance from one city to another and then calculate how long it will take to travel that distance by different means. Here's an example:

1. Using a map of Europe, determine the distance from Berlin, Germany to Paris, France.

   Note: To determine distance from an atlas, instruct students to measure the distance by marking on the edge of a piece of paper which is lined up at both cities. Put a mark where Berlin is located and again at Paris. Lay the paper under the mileage scale placing the Paris mark at 0. Mark off the miles on the paper until you've reached the mark for Berlin.

2. If you were to travel that distance by train (at 90 miles per hour), how long would it take? By plane (at 500 miles per hour)? On foot (at 3 miles per hour)? Which is the preferred method of travel?

Note: Time = distance divided by rate of speed

3. Use the inverse operation by giving the amount of time used to travel; what was the rate of speed?

Note: Rate = distance divided by time

4. Repeat these exercises using other places and also converting to kilometers.

Note: 1 kilometer = .621 mile
       1 mile = 1.609 kilometers

Charts and Graphs

When teaching how to construct charts and graphs, use geographic data obtained from your classroom atlas or an almanac. Create simple bar or pie charts showing numbers or percentages. Use the reproducible graphs and grids provided in chapter sixteen.

Comparative geographic data can be presented using one of several different types of charts. Try using line graphs, pie or bar charts, or tables to add variety and visual interest for your students. Use any of the following data to create charts and graphs:

- Population size of countries
- Percent of population by religious affiliation
- Relative size of continents, countries, or oceans
- Average monthly temperatures for countries north and south of the equator
- Average annual rainfall for various regions of the earth

Sample Problems Using Charts and Graphs

1. Using a pie chart, illustrate the total surface area of the earth. Sub-divide the pie chart with slices representing the surface area for each continent and the four major oceans. Use this example to demonstrate the relative size of the earth's major geographic features.

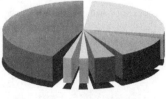

Time Saving Tip
Keep handy, copies of the various reproducible grids and tables found in chapter sixteen.

Note: To determine these divisions, instruct students to take the total surface area of the continent and divide by the total surface area of the earth. This will give the percentage of area of the earth for that continent. Repeat for each continent and for each ocean. You now have the facts to demonstrate on the pie chart.

2. One way to compare related data is to construct two pie charts side-by-side. One to show the relative size of each continent, the other to show the relative size of each continent's population. Compare size of continents to their population to determine population density for each continent.

3. A more advanced exercise involves determining the area and population of the ten most populous countries. Construct a bar chart that illustrates the relative size and population of each country. Next to each country's bar for size and population, add a bar that shows the population density per square mile or kilometer.

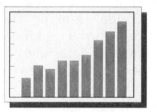

4. Draw conclusions on the ability of each country to grow sufficient agricultural products for its citizens. Which countries are likely to be able to export food products?

Money

Discuss currency from other lands. Compare values. Older students can do conversion problems. How much money will you need to take on a trip to Mexico? Shopping lists for the trip can provide simple money problems for younger students; upper grades can learn more about rates of exchange and banking. Exchange rates can be obtained from the daily paper, Internet, or an almanac. Sample questions: How many pesos equal one dollar? How many pesos do you need to purchase a pair of $52 athletic shoes?

Time Zones

Discuss the history of Daylight Savings Time in the USA How does it differ from time zones around the world? (Man-made versus a natural result of the earth's rotation.) Show them on a map. Use time zones as the basis for word problems, from the simple to the more complicated: If it's 6:00 a.m. in New York City, what time is it in Japan?

Visually demonstrate moving along the lines of longitude to different time zones to illustrate the concept. Upper grades need to know more about the role of the earth's rotation causing this - hold a globe with a flashlight shining as the sun. Rotate the earth and discuss what happens to daylight and nighttime as the earth rotates.

Temperatures

Use graphs to illustrate temperatures from areas being studied. Compare these with temperatures of your hometown. Use temperatures in word problems that relate to these areas. Discuss the effect of temperatures on the area: what living 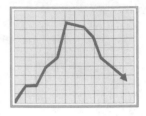 things would make a home in this habitat? Use temperatures when teaching mean, median, and averages. See the "Temperature Graph" in chapter sixteen.

Problem Solving

Using geographic information and data, present problems that require research and critical thinking. Simple questions can be formulated about the percentage of the earth's surface covered by water versus dry land, or determining the percentage of the South American continent below the equator.

For upper grades, create problems using import/export figures (gross tonnage or dollar value) and how they relate to Gross National Product (GNP). This can lead into an analysis of which countries are net debtor or creditor countries and the impact this can have on national wealth and the standard of living. Figures like these can be found in an almanac.

An inter-disciplinary approach between geography and other subjects will help your learners develop an appreciation for geography and its relevance to everyday activities and events. Try combining geography into practical exercises involving:

- Averages
- Sampling
- Statistics
- Banking
- Taxes

Co-ordinate Grids and Number Lines

You can use timelines when teaching concepts of positive and negative numbers (B.C. versus A.D.) on a number line. Many flat maps of the world and globes are represented with lines of latitude and longitude. These lines form a gridwork for determining co-ordinates for points of reference. This same principle is used in math when charting points, lines, or polygons on an X/Y chart.

Play games using grids to familiarize students with charting grid locations. A "Co-ordinate Grid" can be found in chapter sixteen, as well as a plain "Grid" to be used with the games listed below. Consider laminating these grids and use overhead projector pens to play the games.

Grid Stuff!

How do you find a particular road or place on a map? Cartographers often use a system called a "grid." An area is divided into square sections like a checkerboard. Columns are labeled with letters, and rows are identified with numbers. Locations on a map are given a grid reference, such as F4. To find the location, run your finger along the top of the grid and stop at the letter F. With your other hand, move your finger down the side with the numbers and stop at the number 4. Move your finger straight down the letter column and across the number column to find the square where your fingers meet: F4.

Battleship (A two player game.)

Copy the grid in chapter 16 so that each player has two. (Or you can use graph  paper.) Each player uses one grid on which to mark their ships. The other is used to mark the grids you guess your opponent's ships are on. Ships are identified on the grid by marking in two to five grid squares in a row, either vertically or horizontally,

 depending on the size ship, from a two square ship to a five or six square ship.

The object is to guess which grid squares contain your opponent's ships. During each turn, one guess is allowed. The opponent must respond as to whether you have hit a ship or missed a ship. Put a mark on your second grid to keep track of your guesses. You must guess all of the squares occupied by a ship before it's  "sunk." When you guess the last square a ship occupies, your opponent must identify which ship you sunk. The winner is the person who sinks all of the opponent's ships first.

Explorer (A two player game.)

Without letting the other player see your grid, write the letter "T" (for Trap) in 20-25 of the squares, or about 15%, depending on the size of your grid. Place your "T's" all around the grid in a random pattern. These squares mark Trap locations. You are the Trapper.

The object of the game is for the other player (the Explorer) to guess the location of squares that are clear and those that have Traps. At the start of the game, the Trapper must announce how many Traps are on the grid. (It's easier if the Explorer has his own grid to keep track of his guesses.)

The Explorer chooses one square at a time using the grid reference. If it has a T, the Explorer is trapped and the game is over. If it does not have a T, the Trapper says it's clear and identifies how many of the squares touching it have T's. Squares can be above, below, to the side or diagonal. Through a process of elimination, the Explorer tries to identify all of the clear squares without getting trapped. Take turns being the Trapper and Explorer, and see who can clear the Traps in the least amount of time.

Grid Mystery
Label the grid on page 252 with numbers 1 through 16 down, and A-J across. Instruct students to shade in the grid clues to solve the mystery of where to find the elusive Dr. Stealth.

E2, I2, E3, I3, E4, I4, F5, G5, H5, C6, D7, E8, F8, G8, D9, C10, B12, C12, D12, E12, F12, E13, D14, C15, B16, C16, D16, E16, F16

Students can create their own clues and send Dr. Stealth to a number of different places. This example uses letters to form the answer. Students may want to form shapes such as a boat or house.

(By the way, the answer is New York City: NYC)

Well, this journey actually took you through the land of mathematics to study geography. Isn't it amazing how much geography is incorporated into our daily lives?

GEOGRAPHY THROUGH HISTORY

CHAPTER 10

WHAT MAPS DO I USE WHEN STUDYING...?

History is such an absorbing subject! The people, the customs, and all the things that happen in a particular place or era can be absolutely engrossing. But, when we're caught up in the story we don't always think about the ways in which maps can present information in a visually memorable manner. Most teachers use at least some maps in their history studies. Here we give you much more than the same old thing: we give you ways to dramatically improve student retention and understanding through creative map work. Try it and see the difference!

Studying United States history? Whether using a textbook, resource package, or creating your own unit study, this chapter provides a strong framework in which to work. We've broken U.S. history down into time periods, we provide guidelines for which maps to use when, and we suggest ways in which to use them. We even provide the maps you need. You'll find them in chapter fifteen.

Choose activities based on your students' ages and abilities. Not studying U.S. History? No problem, the ideas here can be transferred to whatever you're currently studying in history.

Planning Your Lesson

When planning your lesson, check out the appropriate section, copy the necessary reproducible outline maps, and integrate them into the course work. Here are several ways to do so:

1. Before introducing the place or time you're studying, have students get their maps and together label major items of interest. This will help them visualize the information you're soon going to be giving them.

2. After introducing the concept, have students color in the appropriate information. This is particularly useful in order for them to "see" what you've just told them.

3. Invite students to show the information they've learned by creating a map "storyboard." This could be as simple as having them draw and label the original thirteen colonies, or as complex as a series of maps showing how the United States developed from the original settlers to the acquisition of all fifty states.

4. Maps can be an integral part of both reports and posters. Encourage their usage and show samples to get them thinking.

5. Summarize lessons by holding up large maps and reviewing pertinent information.

6. Assign map work for homework. (Make sure students have access to appropriate atlases or reference material.) It's a nice change from typical homework and it gives the artistic, left-brain thinker a chance to do homework creatively.

U. S. Historical Time Periods

There are many different ways to distinguish historical time periods. We've divided the U.S. history assignments into the following time periods:

- Exploration
- Colonization
- Birth of a Nation
- Civil War and Reconstruction Era
- 20th Century and Beyond

Feel free to adjust these periods to coincide with your own U.S. history curriculum. You may want to check off the boxes as your students complete each map activity. This is especially helpful to track if you're not covering these events in chronological order.

Most of the map work is layed out so that you can copy them as hand-outs for your students. You may want to copy them for your own record keeping. Since it's impossible to cover everything in U.S. history here in this chapter, we've selected what we felt was most important. Go ahead and add any other events you deem necessary.

All American History Volumes I & II by Celeste Rakes (Bright Ideas Press) is an easy-to-implement history curriculum for grades 5 and up. It uses a Student Reader, a Student Activity Book, and a fabulous Teacher's Guide to bring American history to life, piece by piece. See Resources for this outstanding U.S. History course.

UNITED STATES HISTORY: EXPLORATION

☐ **Explorations Before the Great Age of Discovery**

Maps: World
    North America

Explorers: Vikings (especially Lief the Lucky)
    Marco Polo
    Prince Henry the Navigator

☐ **Explorations from 1490-1530**

Maps: World
    Western Hemisphere
    North America

Explorers:
Columbus   Magellan
Cabot   Verrazano
Vespucci   Dias
Ponce de Leon   De Gama
Balboa

☐ **Explorations from 1530-1610**

Maps: World
    North America

Explorers:
Cartier   Raleigh
De Soto   Hudson
Coronado   Champlain
Drake

Using Maps for Exploration:

Begin with the World Outline Map, then move to close-up maps.

- Color code the explorers.
- Color code the nations they explored for.
- Draw a picture of the country's flag and put it in the key.
- Add dates and number of voyages as appropriate.
- Make symbols for what the countries sending explorers were looking for and paste them to the country or add to the key.
- What was their mission? Were they successful?
- Color code routes and places claimed.
- Make a boat for each explorer.
- Label New World and Old World.
- Label the continents.
- Label the oceans.
- Label the major lakes as pertinent to your study.

UNITED STATES HISTORY: COLONIZATION

☐ **The Thirteen Colonies**

Maps: World
North America
USA outline

USA, with state boundaries
Eastern Seaboard without state boundaries
Eastern Seaboard with state boundaries

1. Follow the London Company with John Smith on the Susan Constant, Godspeed, and Discovery. Make mini-ships and color code them. From where did they come? Begin on the World Outline Map, and then move to the North America or United States Map. Where did they land? What was the physical geography like there, and how did it affect their colony? What were they looking for? Did they find it? Learn what a peninsula is and what river their colony was near. What crop became important to them and why?

2. Follow the travels of the Pilgrims from England, to Holland, and to the New World on the World Outline Map. Color code them. Make a mini-Mayflower and move it from place to place. What is a "cape?" What geographic features did they wisely realize they would need? (Fresh water and a good harbor.) What skills did Squanto teach them?

3. Follow John Winthrop and the Puritans. Where did they come from, and where did they settle? How were Puritans different from Pilgrims? Follow Roger Williams as he left Massachusetts and founded Rhode Island. Follow Thomas Hooker as he left Massachusetts and founded Connecticut. How did New Hampshire become a colony, and for what natural resource was it settled? (Lumber.)

*As you discuss the New England colonies, remember that Vermont and Maine never existed as separate colonies.

New York

• Follow Henry Hudson and his ship, the "Half Moon." Where was he headed and who sent him there?

• Samuel de Champlain sailed from Quebec (which was being settled by the French) and claimed northern New York.

• Way back in 1497, John Cabot claimed the New World for England and they continued to claim it. Who got to keep New York?

Delaware

Delaware was claimed by: Henry Hudson who discovered the Delaware Bay; Sweden who sailed up the Delaware River and settled in New Sweden (Wilmington); and by England. Color code the different countries with claims, and add or erase countries throughout your study as claims were won or lost.

Pennsylvania

Who are the Quakers and where did they come from? William Penn chose a site to be Philadelphia. Why was this site a geographically good place for a city? What did Pennsylvania look like then? (Hint: King Charles gave Penn the land on the west bank of the Delaware Bay and River. Pennsylvania used to be much bigger.)

Maryland

Who was Lord Baltimore (also known as Sir George Calvert)? King Charles I gave him a colony in the New World for Catholics and any other Christians. The first settlement was St. Mary's. Can you find it on the map? What peninsula is it on? What land did Lord Baltimore try to take in order to add to his colony? (Hint: Delaware was almost part of Maryland.)

Calvert and Penn had a major boundary dispute which eventually went to court in England. It took nearly 70 years to resolve!

Interesting (Optional) Map Work & Research:

Pirates once sailed in the Delaware waters. Their attacks of various settlements provided the impetus for Quaker Pennsylvania and The Lower Counties (Delaware) to become two separate colonies. Read more about it and trace the French Privateers, Captain Kidd, Captain Blackbeard, and other pirates of the 1600's on the map.

North and South Carolina

King Charles gave this land to eight of his lords who wanted to make money by using the land for three products that were expensive to buy in England: wine, silk, and olive oil. Why did they think they could produce these in the Carolinas? Did it work? What climate do the coastal Carolinas share? What crops eventually became very important to the Carolinas? (Rice and cotton.)

Georgia

Who was James Oglethorpe, and what was his mission? King George II gave Oglethorpe permission to start a colony in the New World. The original capital city, Savannah, was well laid out. Compare a street map of Savannah to maps of other coastal cities. Can you discern which ones were planned and which ones grew haphazardly?

☐ Slavery

Maps: World
    Africa
    North America or USA

Where did the slaves come from? Most came from Africa. Notice this continent is more than twice the size of the United States. Most slaves came from a part of Africa called the Western Sudan. This is an area that extends from the Atlantic Ocean in the west, to Lake Chad in the East, and from the Sahara Desert in the north, to the Gulf of Guinea in the south. The Western Sudan was the birthplace of three powerful and highly developed black empires: Ghana, Mali, and Songhay (or Songhai).

A brief timeline would include the following:
- Ghana ruled much of the Western Sudan from the 300's A.D. to the mid 1,000's.
- By 1240, the Mali Empire had risen and taken over Ghana. Their most famous leader, Mansa Musa, encouraged his people to practice Islam.
- By the 1400's, the Songhay Empire was the strongest in the Western Sudan. They had well organized governments and a university in Timbuktu.
- In 1591, invaders from Morocco conquered Songhay.

Slavery was common in Africa during this time. However, it looked more like the serfdom of the Middle Ages than the slavery in early America. Slavery in Africa didn't mean you were inferior or stupid; it was possible to be a well-educated, accomplished slave. Slavery was not based on skin color.

1. Follow the Portuguese as they reached Africa. What deadly new element did they add to African slavery? (Guns.) African tribal kings quickly saw the advantages to guns and traded their captives for these weapons. Slavery quickly escalated into a major economic enterprise.

2. Trace on a map the route of Africans leaving Africa. Were the first blacks to North America slaves? (No, blacks were crew members on various Spanish exploratory expeditions, including possibly those of Columbus, Balboa, Ponce de Leon, Cortes, and Pizarro. Blacks also accompanied French missionaries to North America in the 1600's.) Which countries bought slaves? From where did the majority of the boats/sea captains come from who dealt in the slave trade?

Interesting (Optional) Map Work & Research
Make a map storyboard to follow the journeys of an imaginary slave family. It was quite possible they had stopovers on the way to the thirteen colonies. They may have ended up on a Caribbean island. Which islands had slaves? Which of the colonies had slaves? Did slavery proceed all the way across the United States? Are there states that never had slaves?

☐ **French and Indian War**

Map: North America

- Color in the land claims of the British, Spanish and English before the French and Indian War.
- Color in their claims after the Treaty of Paris.

UNITED STATES HISTORY: Birth of a Nation

☐ **The Revolution**

Maps: USA
      Eastern Seaboard

- As battles are looked at chronologically, add them to your maps. Number them with their names in a large key, and color code them as to who won.

- On a parallel note, trace the campaigns of famous generals as you read about them. (For example, have a separate map for George Washington, and a map for one of the British generals, perhaps Gage.)

- On a separate map, follow the sea movements of troops throughout the war. Why was the sea so vital to everyone's strategies?

☐ Western Expansion

Maps: North America
        USA

- What did the USA look like after the American Revolution? Draw in known boundaries. Color code where there were other peoples: French, Spanish, Indian, etc.

- Color in the Louisiana Purchase.

- Daniel Boone - trace the Wilderness Road. What were the geographic features that kept the vast majority of the population on the eastern coast? In what way was the Wilderness Trail important?

- Lewis & Clark - follow their expedition along on a map. Learn the names of rivers and mountains as you come to them.

- Florida - how did land become a state? Color code the Spanish and Indian presences.

- Construct a map of "Trails" including: Cumberland Road, Oregon Trail, Santa Fe Trail, Old Spanish Trail, and the California Trail.

- Make a Transportation Map. Include canals, railroads, stagecoach trails, Pony Express runs, etc. (It's getting a little ahead chronologically, but you could even include the Transcontinental Railroad and work your way up to our present system of interstate highways.)

- War of 1812 - follow the sea and land battles of this short war.

- Texas - continue the theme of the westward expansion with the Mexican War and theTexas Annexation, Mexican Cession, Gadsden Purchase.

- California Gold Rush - where was gold found? Put little gold nuggets in appropriate places on the North America Outline Map.

- Add the Oregon territory, Alaska purchase and Hawaii. Students will begin to visualize the shaping of America!

☐ Native Americans

Maps: North America
      USA without boundaries
      USA with boundaries

- Using the Historical Maps on File from the library, write in the various tribes living in North America before European settlement.

- Make maps depicting the Indian Removal Act of 1830, Trail of Tears, Seminole Wars, Indian Wars, and the current reservation system.

- Trace a particular Indian tribe or tribes from pre-colonization to present day.

United States History: Civil War and Reconstruction Era

☐ **Civil War**

Maps: USA
      Eastern Seaboard with state borders

- As events leading up to the war are discussed, use a symbol on the map depicting that event. Number the symbols.
- Number the battles and color code them according to whether they were a northern or southern victory.
- Color in slave states versus non-slave states.

☐ **Reconstruction**

Maps: USA with state borders

- Follow the events of reconstruction on the map.
- Label the homes of presidents and key people as you talk about them.
- Trace the origination and development of the Ku Klux Klan through modern times.

☐ **Inventions and the Industrial Revolution**
      Teacher Note: This unit begs for the use of a timeline! Use the "Notebook Timeline" in unit six.

Maps: Europe
      USA with state borders

- Show agricultural societies on the maps.
- Depict, using symbols, how these agricultural societies became industrialized.
- Use symbols to depict significant inventions (spinning wheel, locomotive, etc.)
- How did the Industrial Revolution change the United States? Can you depict this in map form?

☐ **Spanish-American War**

Maps: World
      North America
      USA
      (For an in-depth study, a map of Cuba and a map of the Philippines would be helpful.)

- Trace the events that lead to the war. How was Spain involved? How did the Philippines get into it?
- Trace the route of the Rough Riders from their Florida port of debarkation to their return to the USA.
- Color code the new acquisitions after the war: Puerto Rico, Guam, Philippines.

United States History: 20th Century and Beyond

Maps: World
      North America
      USA

South America
Europe

Africa
Eurasia

Divide the 20th century by decades. Here's a list of possible topics to study per decade. Pick and choose according to how in-depth the study is to be. Also included are several historical events that might be covered in an upper level history course. These are italicized.

☐ 1900 - 1919

Immigrants

Maps: World
      Europe
      North America or USA

- Trace the process of immigration into the United States. Color code nations from which large populations of people left to come to the USA.
- Color code the reasons people left their homelands.
- Color code the states that received large amounts of immigrants.
- What part did immigration play in the settling of the west? How did immigrants end up in places so far away from Ellis Island?
- In what ways did they travel and for what reasons?

Panama Canal

Maps: North America
      South America
      World

- Identify and color code the countries/nations involved with the building of the Panama Canal and the establishment of Panama as an independent country.

- Trace the oceanic trade routes from the major eastern and southern U.S. ports (include Boston, New York, Miami, New Orleans, and Houston), to the major shipping ports in Chile, Ecuador, California, Washington, British Columbia, Alaska, Hawaii, Philippines, Japan, India, and China.

- Calculate the distance saved by using the Panama Canal for journeys to each destination.

Spanish American War (If not covered earlier)

Oklahoma - 46th state

San Francisco Earthquake

New Mexico 47th state

Arizona 48th state

Titanic - 1912

- Trace the actual route of the Titanic on its voyage. Identify the intended route/destination of the ship.
- Identify the source of the icebergs that were in the path of the Titanic.

Prohibition - began in 1919

Maps: North America
      USA

- Identify the cities where major crime syndicates operated during the prohibition era.
- Identify major crime bosses of the era and mark the cities they controlled.

Russian Revolution

Daylight Savings Time

Maps: World

- Trace the twenty-four time zones around the world.
- Identify those countries that have Daylight Savings Time. What's the history behind it?

Wright Brothers

World War I

Maps: World
      Europe

- Identify the alliances that existed before the outbreak of WWI. Color code countries belonging to each alliance.
- Mark the location of the event that sparked the onset of WWI.
- Identify and mark the location of the major battles of WWI.
- Update your map to show how national boundaries changed at the end of WWI.

☐ **1919 - 1929**

City dwellers outnumber rural dwellers - 1920

Map: USA

- Research the population of seven major U.S. cities for each decade starting with 1860 and ending with 1930. Using different colors for each decade, chart the population growth for each city you have chosen on the map. Use stick figures or circles of a specific diameter to represent population size. Note the increase in the size of each city's population over the 70 year period.

Roaring Twenties

Charles Lindbergh

Stock Market Crash 1929

☐ **1929 - 1939**

The Great Depression

Dustbowl

Map: USA

- Outline the states whose farmland and agriculture were affected by the Dustbowl.
- Develop your own key or legend and identify the major agricultural products of each state affected by the Dustbowl.
- Identify states not affected by the Dustbowl that produce the same agricultural products.
- Using a scale of your own choice, graphically illustrate the production levels for each crop in an affected state for the year immediately before and after the Dustbowl.

1937 Ohio River Flood

Hitler Begins Expansion

Maps: USA
       Europe
       World

- Identify and outline the countries that came under German domination before the U.S. entered WWII.
- Identify and shade the portions of European countries with large segments of the population that were of German descent.

☐ **1939 - 1945**

World War II

Maps: World
       Europe/Middle East
       Eurasia
       Africa

- Identify and mark those countries that were part of the Allies and those that belonged to the Axis. Also, show the European countries that were officially neutral. Mark and label the capital of each country.

- Identify and label with a color code the colonies of the various major powers.
- List the rulers/presidents/prime ministers of major combatant countries around the world.
- Identify and mark the furthest extent of German occupation and conquest.
- Label the location of major battles and offensives. Color code the names/locations to identify the victor.
- Trace the various invasion routes and advances of the Allies in North Africa, Italy, and France.
- Mark the location and list the participants of the major wartime conferences of the Allies.

- Label and mark the location of major bombing attacks by the Allies and Axis powers.
- Locate and color code the major sea battles of the Atlantic, Pacific, and Mediterranean.
- List the major combatants with the number and type of vessels sunk or destroyed.
- Outline the furthest extent of Japanese dominion and conquest in Asia and the Pacific.
- Identify and mark the location of the city that was subject to heavy missile attack.
- Identify and mark the location of the cities where atomic bombs were dropped.
- Identify, list and mark the new countries or changed national boundaries that resulted after the war ended.
- Mark the separation of Germany into the different zones or spheres of influence that resulted from the victory of the Allies. Color code to show the controlling country.

☐ 1945 - 1956

Cold War

Maps: World
    Eurasia
    Europe/Middle East

- Draw and label the 'Iron Curtain' that ran through Europe.
- Identify and color code countries that were signatories or members of the North Atlantic Treaty Organization (NATO).
- Identify and color code countries that were signatories or members of the Central Treaty Organization (CENTO) Agreements of Cooperation.
- Identify and color code countries that were signatories or members of the Southeast Asia Collective Defense Treaty (SEATO.)
- Identify and color code countries that were signatories or members of theANZUS Treaty. (Australia, New Zealand and United States)
- Identify and color code countries that were signatories or members of the Inter-American Treaty of Reciprocal Assistance.
- Identify and color code countries that belonged to the European Common Market.
- Identify and color code countries that belonged to the Council for Mutual Economic Assistance (COMECON).
- Label countries that adopted communism as their form of government.
- Label countries that were colonies before WWII and show the year they achieved independence.

Korean War

Maps: World
    Eurasia

- Identify and label countries that supplied troops to fight in the Korean War.
- Mark the furthest extent of the North Korean/Chinese advance into South Korea.
- Label the capitals and major cities on the Korean peninsula.
- Label and shade the demilitarized zone running across the Korean peninsula.

H-Bomb (Hydrogen bomb)

Hostilities begin in Vietnam (See 1956-1976 for more information.)

Civil Rights Movement Begins

☐ **1956 - 1976**

American Involvement in Vietnam

Maps: World
      Eurasia

- Identify and label North Vietnam and South Vietnam, along with their capitals, major cities, ports, rivers, and mountains.
- Identify and label the other countries in the immediate area of Southeast Asia and the western Pacific Ocean.
- Label the military zones of South Vietnam.
- Trace the location of the Ho Chi Minh Trail and its entry points into Vietnam.
- Identify, locate and mark the location of major ground battles that took place in South Vietnam.
- Identify, locate and mark the North Vietnamese ports that were mined to reduce or prevent shipping into or out of North Vietnam.
- Identify and label the location where North Vietnamese patrol boats attacked U.S. navel units. This event led to the U.S. congressional authorization that escalated American involvement in Vietnam.

Castro, Bay of Pigs

Berlin Wall Built

☐ **1976 - 1999**

Camp David Accord

Iran Hostage Crisis

Energy Crisis

Falkland Islands

Grenada Invasion

Dismantling of Berlin Wall

Dissolution of Eastern Bloc Countries

Persian Gulf War - Desert Storm

Maps: World
Europe/Middle East
Africa

- Identify and label the countries in the Middle East area.
- Identify and shade Kuwait.
- Identify, locate, and label the sites of the major SCUD missile attacks.
- Trace the shipping/supply routes for U.S. troops to the Middle East from Europe and the U.S.
- Trace the invasion/attack route for the allied forces that resulted in the defeat of Iraqi forces.

Break up of USSR
Map: Eurasia

- Identify and label the republics that made up the former Union of Soviet Socialist Republics (USSR or Soviet Union).
- Label the capital city of each republic and at least eight major cities in the Russian Republic.
- Trace and label the major geographic features of the USSR including rivers, lakes, seas, and mountains.
- Using a legend of your choice, locate and label the major natural resources and agricultural products of each republic.
- Using a scale and legend of your choice, show the population of each republic and the major religious influences of each.

Break up of Czechoslovakia

Kosovo

Bosnias

☐ **2000-** _____

9/11

Afghanistan

Iraq

Hurricane Katrina

GEOGRAPHY THROUGH THE INTERNET

CHAPTER 11

GEOGRAPHY AND COMPUTER LITERACY

Are you using the Internet in your classroom? If so, you already know the advantages of having the largest source of information in the world at your fingertips! This chapter gives you ideas for developing your own lesson plans based on Internet research, a sample Internet search activity, and over fifty great sites to visit.

Before you begin you might wish to consult a book on using the Internet for educational purposes. There is a proliferation of Internet books; ask a teacher or librarian for their favorites. Look for one that gives you solid search tips. It's easy to waste large amounts of time doing unproductive searches!

Lesson Plan Objectives

When making lesson plans that require the use of the computer, have specific goals. For example to familiarize students with:

- the computer
- the Internet
- search engines
- computer research methods

To the teacher who's not "plugged-in," these goals may sound all vaguely the same. They aren't. It's important to take your students through the steps of computer and Internet usage. To just hand them a list of sites to browse is like handing them a good library book without teaching them how to find that book in the first place!

The above mentioned goals have to do with finding one's way around the computer and the Internet. Other goals for students would be to research topics or find specific information. It's impor-

GeoBit Says:
Remember - a well-educated student (and teacher) needs to be computer literate, too!

tant to think through your goals: are you trying to teach them to use the Internet, or are you simply using the Internet for retrieving information? A well thought out lesson plan is invaluable.

Let's walk through a lesson designed with several goals in mind:

- To introduce the student to a sampling of sites that will be useful for history, geography, or science research.

- To introduce them to the idea that the more specific the question, the easier it is to get an answer! (Browsing the web is fun, but it's easy to spend hours completing an assignment that should only take minutes if one has prepared specific questions to answer.)

GeoBit Says:
Learn great search tips to zip through your research. Go to www.google.com/about.html and click on "Help and How to Search."

Cyber Hunt

Sites such as Atlapedia and the CIA World Factbook are used to find answers to the following questions. Their addresses are listed on the pages that follow, along with many other great sites for geography, science, weather, history, and more. If your students are already familiar with using the Internet, consider adding a time element to this game to increase the challenge.

*Important! It's wise to complete this yourself first, in order to ascertain whether the sites are still active and to update answers, if necessary.

Here are sample questions for students to answer using the list of websites provided:

1. On what continent is Cameroon located?
2. What's the temperature today in Miami, Florida?
3. What's the population of Japan?
4. What's the name of Japanese currency?
5. When did the Battle of Gettysburg start?
6. How many species of worms are there?

Answers may vary according to the website used. Here are answers we found along with the websites we used:

Answer	Website
1. Africa	Atlapedia.com
2. Varies	Weather.com
3. 126,182,077 (approx.)	CIA World Factbook*
4. Yen	CIA World Factbook*
5. July 1, 1863	CivilWar.com
6. 4,400	Yucky.com

*www.cia.gov/cia/publications/factbook/

Another Cyber Hunt Idea
Design cyber hunts based on information you want them to find. Students will research questions on the Internet. Questions may relate to studies at hand, whether current events, history, science, government or other.

Go from site to site and write down specific items you want them to see. (For ideas, check out the "Scavenger Hunt" game at the Houghton Mifflin Social Studies site.) Or, your assignments may be traditional research questions about which they can retrieve up-to-date information from a variety of Internet sites.

It's essential though, that they learn to discern whether the site they're using has valid information. Students also need to learn how to cite information gleaned from Internet sources when writing papers and reports. Your librarian should be able to point you to articles on that topic.

Great Internet Sites

Of course, there are many, many more great sites on the Internet than those listed here, but these will get you started. Be sure to bookmark these and other favorite sites in order to easily to find them again.

NEWS, REFERENCE & RESOURCES

Library of Congress
www.loc.gov
Well designed site with tons of great links to follow.

About.Com
www.geography.about.com
A mega site with many, many subcategories. Each category has its own human "guide" that answers questions, sends free e-newsletters, etc.

Web Sites and Resources for Teachers
www.sitesforteachers.com
Just what it says - divided into nine categories. Includes lesson plans, online activities, and virtual trips to museums and countries around the world.

Ask Jeeves and Ask Jeeves for Kids
www.AskJeeves.com
www.ajkids.com
These are the places to go to get the tough questions answered. Check out their archived questions first - fascinating!

Google
www.google.com
A terrific search site! Did you know that if you click on "images" before you put in your search request, you will get images of your request along with their links? Type in "tundra" and see!

Awesome Library
www.neat-schoolhouse.org
Loads of well organized site lists.

USA Today
www.usatoday.com
News and weather.

CNN Interactive
www.CNN.com
News and weather.

Reference Resource
www.refdesk.com
Amazing, well-organized megasite.

Internet Public Library
www.ipl.org
Do research or ask the librarian a question.

GEOGRAPHY

Geography World
http://members.aol.com/geographyworld
Designed and maintained by a high school teacher, this is a well organized list of sites and resources for geography.

CIA World Factbook
www.odci.gov/cia/publications/factbook/
Everything you need to know about any country.

Atlapedia On-Line
www.Atlapedia.com
Great for key facts, statistics, and maps of countries. Useful and easy to use. Similar to CIA World Factbook but containing less information.

Time Around the World
www.worldtime.com
Pick a country - site displays a short fact file and the current time.

50 States
www.50states.com
Great site for state studies. Includes loads of information about each state, as well as thousands of links to relevant sites.

Google Maps
http://maps.google.com
Excellent easy-to-read street maps and directions.

Google Earth
http://earth.google.com
Google Earth combines satellite imagery, maps, and Google's amazing search engine to put the world's geographic information right at your fingertips. If you like maps, you'll love this site.

Houghton Mifflin Social Studies Center
www.eduplace.com/ss/index.html
Current events, games, contests, teacher helps and more.

U.S. Geological Survey Learning Web
www.usgs.gov/education
Downloadable lessons and activities for geography and science.

National Park Service
www.nps.gov
Educational information about US National Parks.

GeoLinks
www.tnris.state.tx.us/geolinks.htm
This site by a Texas state office is a gold mine of geographic links.

Geography IQ
www.geographyiq.com
Planning a trip? Perhaps you're interested in current events or are just curious about exploring the world around you. GeographyIQ is an online world atlas packed with geographic, economic, political, historical and cultural information. In addition, GeographyIQ brings together a number of other resources including maps, flags, currency conversion as well as climate and time zone information.

Geographia
www.geographia.com
Oooohh! Love this site! Great for browsing - part travelogue and part reference. Beautifully done!

HISTORY

The History Net
www.thehistorynet.com
Attractive, easy to use, and loaded with good stuff. Check out the riveting "Eyewitness Accounts" and archives.

The Digital Classroom - National Archives
www.archives.gov
Reproducible primary documents in user-friendly format with correlated teacher plans and student activities. A winner.

Hyper History
www.hyperhistory.com
The heart of this site is a gigantic timeline! It's a growing site covering over 3000 years of people events and maps. Many of the dates are linked to relevant sites. Great for planning a history course!

The History Place
www.historyplace.com
Includes: History Photo of the Week, Speech of the Week, This Month in History, and an eclectic mix of historical events.

Ancient Egypt Webquest
http://www.iwebquest.com/egypt/ancientegypt.htm
Fun site with lots to do. Elementary and junior high level. Great photos.

Internet Medieval Sourcebook
www.fordham.edu/halsall/sbook.html
This site is great for high school and up - medieval history presented in a complete outline form, with links to papers and source documents to most events in the outline.

Internet Modern History Sourcebook
www.fordham.edu/halsall/mod/modsbook.html
Set up like the Internet Medieval Sourcebook, this site begins with the Reformation.

World War I Trenches on the Web
www.worldwar1.com
Wonderful site!

History Book List
www.abookintime.com
Find historically based books, maps, timelines, and more.

American Philatelic Society
www.stamps.org
Learn about history and geography through stamp collecting.

BBC History
www.bbc.co.uk/history
A large, user-friendly site with an interactive kids' section. Includes "This Week in History" from a British perspective.

Love history? Love food? Visit this site:
www.historycooks.com

AMERICAN HISTORY

General Social Studies
www.socialstudiesforkids.com
Contains a wealth of information and is easy to navigate.

U.S. History Overview
www.ushistory.org
Created by the Independence Hall Association in Philadelphia.

American Revolution
www.americanrevolution.com
Includes many links.

U.S. Constitution
www.usconstitution.net
Includes a student version of the Constitution.

The Wild West
www.americanwest.com
All about the history of the states west of the Mississippi.

U.S. Presidents
www.whitehouse.gov/history/presidents
All things presidential!

Hypertext on American History
http://odur.let.rug.nl/~usa/
Links to primary source documents. Terrific for doing quality research.

Civil War
www.civilwar.com
Just what you need while studying this significant event.

SCIENCE

Creation Science Home Page
www.icr.org
Are you familiar with Creation Science? This site informs.

Exploratorium Home Page
www.exploratorium.edu/educate
This great museum site offers wonderful stuff for both kids and educators. Check out "Hands-On Activities" for quick and easy experiments. A winner.

The Yuckiest Site on the Internet
www.yucky.com
Terrific site includes "gross and cool body," "bug world," and much more. Parent/teacher center, games, quizzes. Kids'll love this site!

Mad Scientist Network
www.madsci.org
For older students and teachers. Includes "Ask A Scientist," Mad labs, Experiments, Guided Tour of the Human Body, and more.

The Franklin Institute Online
www.fi.edu/learning.html
Terrific site from an exceptional hands-on museum!

Science Whatzit!
www.omsi.edu/explore/whatzit
Answers science problems/questions but not homework assignments. Reading through previous questions is educational!

Brains Rule!
www.brainsrule.com
The place to learn about your brain! Play interactive games, ask questions for brain experts to answer, and meet a neuroscientist. Lesson plans available.

Biology
www.educationindex.com/biology
Great set of links to educational biology sites!

Volcano World
http://volcano.und.nodak.edu
Huge site with everything about volcanoes. Check out the "Kid's Door" for neat volcano stuff just for them.

Starport
www.space.com
Great ste for anyone interested in astronauts. Of course, you'll also want to visit NASA's site, too.

NASA for Kids
www.nasa.gov/audience/forkids/home/index.html
Loads of activities and information . . . about space, of course!

NASA
www.Nasa.gov
A great site - for teacher and older students.

The Weather Dude
www.wxdude.com
Wide range of information including weather basics, on-line quizzes, terms, and much more.

World Climate
www.worldclimate.com
Find out what the weather is *normally* like for thousands of places around the world!

Finding Websites
The websites listed were live at the time of publication. If you have any problems locating any of these recommendations, you can usually find the current URL by typing the title or topic into your favorite search engine.

Unit Four
Just Geography

CONQUERING THE CONTINENTS

CHAPTER 12

TEACHING PURE GEOGRAPHY: CONTINENT BY CONTINENT

By now you've completed your refresher course in geography and have learned how to establish a student notebook. You know the scoop about supplies, outline maps and atlases. You've taken a tour through a myriad of geography-related games and activities. And you've discovered a whole world of avenues in which to teach geography: through literature, science, math, history, and even through the Internet. But how do you teach just geography?

This unit provides a complete geography course through an overview of the seven continents. Obviously, there's enough material available about the world that one could spend an entire lifetime learning more about it. By introducing the world in bite-sized chunks you'll spark your students' interest. Lesson plans follow, divided into continent sections which include map activities for students to complete on outline maps. The high school level contains questions for students to answer by researching information using reference materials.

Depending on how much class time you have, map activities can be done during class or assigned as homework (assuming all students have access to a reasonably current atlas.) It works well to begin the map work in class and assign the remainder of it as homework. This gives everyone a good start and a feel for what they're supposed to do, yet allows enough teaching time to cover other information.

Regarding Atlases
An important point regarding map work: all atlases are not alike! It's unreasonable to assume everyone will find everything in their atlas. Unless you and your students are all working out of the same year and brand atlas, there will be differences.

GeoBit says:
The goal isn't to cram students' heads full of stuff they won't remember tomorrow. Give them a foundation, whet their appetites, and motivate them to be lifelong students of geography! Attitude is (almost) everything!

Remember, cartography is both an art and a science - no two cartographers will produce exactly the same map. Your students need to know this up front, or there may be frustration over not finding a particular place or finding places spelled differently.

One more reminder:
One atlas will not include **all** the information your students will need to perform these exercises. Having a wide variety of atlases will go a long way to ensuring student success.

The best way to begin this course:

- Introduce or review the information in the **Introduction to Geography** starting on the next page. Reproduce for placement in the student's notebook, read it aloud to the class, or present the information in a discussion format.

- Copy the "Geography Definitions Flashcards" in chapter seventeen. Students who've never learned geography terms can make use of the flashcards to learn their terms, and those who already have a strong foundation may want to use them for a quick refresher.

- Copy "Stuff to Know by Heart" from chapter seventeen and use as appropriate for grade and level.

- Copy outline maps and enlarge as necessary.

After students have learned or reviewed their basic geography information, they're ready to begin their journey through the seven continents.

We've divided the continent assignments into two sections:
- Upper Elementary/Middle School - Chapter 13
- High School - Chapter 14

The middle school lessons begin with facts and interesting information about each continent. Sample countries are further explored. You can add other countries using the same format.

It's a good idea to review each continent in the middle school level as an introduction to that continent for the high schooler. The main difference in the two levels is the high school student will be responsible to research answers to questions, whereas the middle schooler will learn most of his facts from class time discussions. The high schooler will also be responsible for much more detail in labeling his maps and will need larger sized maps.

The following pages can be presented as an introductory lesson to the class and copied for placement in a geography notebook.

INTRODUCTION TO GEOGRAPHY

Geography comes from the Greek, "geographia," meaning to write about or describe the earth.

The study of geography is the study of places and the complex relationships between people and their environments. There are many aspects of geography. Two broad subdivisions are physical geography and human geography. Physical geography includes natural features, along with climate, geologic and other processes that help shape our world. Human geography includes things like transportation, population, and how humans have impacted their environment.

Maps

Geographers must pull together information from many other fields of study without losing sight of the big picture: the interconnection of people, places, and things. Maps are one way geographers can share information.

- Cartography: the science and the art of making maps.
- Cartographer: a map maker.

As a science, cartography must be as accurate as possible. As an art, it requires careful use of color and design to communicate information clearly. In the 20th century, technology revolutionized cartography. Aerial photography, satellite imaging, and computers all brought cartography to new standards of accuracy.

Types of Maps

- **Topographic Map:** curving contour lines connect points that are at the same elevation.

- **Physical Map:** shows the elevation of a place by using a color code.

- **Political Map:** shows actual territorial boundaries in existence (i.e. a political map of the United States would show the boundary of each state.)

- **Climate Map:** shows the climate of a place by using a color code.

- **Vegetation Map:** shows the vegetation regions by using a color code.

- **Precipitation Map:** shows either annual or average monthly precipitation.

- **Population Map:** shows population by using a color code.

- **Street Map:** shows roads, important buildings, and places in detail.

- **Time Zone:** shows time zones by using both a grid and a color code.

- **Historical Maps:** maps that draw boundaries based on earlier time periods.

- **3D Landform Maps:** maps on which you can physically feel different geographic features.

These are just a few kinds of maps. Maps also show things such as land use, resources, types of population (i.e. Asian, Indian, etc.), income, unemployment, life expectancy, cancer rates, and much more.

GEOGRAPHICAL TERMS YOU NEED TO KNOW

Western Hemisphere: The region of the earth between the 160° east meridian and the 20° west meridian. Commonly defined as North and South America.

Eastern Hemisphere: The region of the earth between the 20° west meridian and the 160° east meridian. Commonly defined as Europe, Africa, Asia, Australia, and New Zealand.

Northern Hemisphere: Everything above the equator.

Southern Hemisphere: Everything below the equator.

Latitude: The distance north or south of the equator.

Longitude: The distance east or west of the Prime Meridian.

Prime Meridian: The line of O° longitude; the starting point for measuring distance east and west around the globe. It runs through Greenwich, England.

Tropic of Cancer: The line of latitude about 23° north of the equator.

Tropic of Capricorn: The line of latitude about 23° south of the equator.

Tropics: The term used to describe the region that falls between the Tropic of Cancer and the Tropic of Capricorn. The tropics are generally warm year round, with monthly temperatures averaging 77° - 82°F.

Subtropics: The zones between 23° and about 40° north and south of the equator.

Equator: An imaginary line around the middle of the earth.

*Add new terms below as you learn them:

MAP TERMS YOU NEED TO KNOW

Symbols: Simple drawings that show what things are. For example, a thin blue line may be the symbol for a river.

Key or Legend: Maps use either a key or a legend to explain what the symbols are. Look for the key or legend when beginning to decode a map. Sometimes it's called a "key," meaning it helps unlock the secrets of the map, and sometimes it's called a "legend" because it helps to tell the story of the map.

Scale: Tells the actual size of what's on the map. For example: 1:2,000 means that every one unit on the map stands for 2,000 actual units. Another way scale might be shown is by drawing it like this:

|_____|_____|
0   30   60 Miles

Four inches on a map may represent four feet, four miles, or even 40,000 miles! It's important to look at the scale when reading a map. It should be found within the key or legend.

Compass Rose: A circular and often ornate design used on maps to indicate the points of the compass.

Grid: Network of horizontal and vertical lines drawn over a map to help find places.

Coordinates: Tells us exactly where something on the grid is located. For example, in the game "Battleship," you know where to look when your opponent says "F6."

*Add new terms below as you learn them:

Notes:

CONQUERING THE CONTINENTS: MIDDLE SCHOOL

CHAPTER 13

PURE GEOGRAPHY FOR MIDDLE SCHOOL

Spend a month, spend a year, spend as much time on this as you'd like! How exciting it is to study the world! For just a taste of each continent, this can be done in eight, one-hour lessons with assigned homework. This just barely skims the surface, but it may suit your particular needs. The chronology is up to you; here's one possibility:

- Lesson 1 - Introduction to Geography and North America Part I
- Lesson 2 - North America Part II
- Lesson 3 - South America
- Lesson 4 - Europe
- Lesson 5 - Asia*
- Lesson 6 - Africa*
- Lesson 7 - Australia and Antarctica
- Lesson 8 - Wrap-up and Food Tasting Party

*Asia and Africa are each difficult to do in one lesson. Each would benefit from more time.

Included in this study are "Countries Close-Up," a more detailed look at a particular country or two within a continent. You could substitute a different country, add more countries, or have your students research and report on specific countries.

The key to a lively study - one students will remember and learn from - is your enthusiasm and ability to make places come alive. One powerful way to do this is by providing a "show-and-tell" for each continent and country. It is interesting to see big, dramatic pictures of people and places, examine currency, stamps, and postcards, have realia to pass around like clothing, toys, and souvenirs, hear the music and language, see the artwork, and sample

If you want additional lesson plans, *Trail Guide to World Geography* by Cindy Wiggers (Geography Matters) incorporates assignments and information from *The Ultimate Geography and Timeline Guide*. Students create an awesome geography notebook, to boot!

the food! (A food tasting party is a great wrap-up to this unit. Enlist the kids or parents to make or buy samples of foods from around the world.)

Preparation

Prepare for lessons by reading up on the continent and collecting books with great pictures that illustrate important features, places or people. Then gather memorabilia from other cultures. Label and store them in plastic tubs for future use. Call upon families you know who are from other lands. Most are delighted to share their heritage with others. Provide a schedule for when you're studying each continent in advance so students can bring in items to share. Students of all ages love to participate in this.

Of course, time is always an issue, so decide in advance how you'll administer "show-and-tell" time. One group of students could be assigned table displays. Another could arrange a "mini-museum" of Southeast Asia, another of Central America, etc. Remind them not to bring in Aunt Sophia's Faberge egg from Russia or any other valuable and/or breakable item!

Another important point in lesson preparation is having your own personal map work done ahead of time. If you can't find "Walla-Walla" on the map, chances are your students won't be able to either. By doing your homework you'll be able to spot troublesome areas to label, enabling you to effectively guide your students through the process. Have your map available, should you need to point out places students just can't find.

Here's one way to teach this unit:

1. Introduce the continent to be studied.
2. Show pictures of relevant places and people. Stimulate their interest! Use dramatic and colorful images when possible. The National Geographic Society has many excellent books and publications with eye-grabbing pictures.
3. Go over the "Fact File" for the continent. (As you progress, do mini-reviews and/or comparisons of the Fact File from earlier lessons.)
4. On a large world outline map, show the boundaries of the continent and some of the information you discussed in the Fact Files. (For example, draw in the longest river, biggest lake, highest mountain, etc.)
5. Pull out any realia specific to the continent you're discussing. Mention its significance, and pass it around.
6. Read and discuss the rest of the information related to the continent.
7. Begin the section called "Map-It."
8. Present "Countries Close-Up."

Time Saver Tip
Assemble each student's notebook ahead of time. Consider enlarging the reproducible maps or purchasing larger maps for the "Map-It" assignments. See Resources.

9. As with the continent, begin with relevant pictures.
10. Use a map to point out specific places, climate, vegetative regions, etc.
11. Discuss briefly the history/exploration/ancestry of the country.
12. Pass around any coins, stamps, postcards, or other realia brought in.
13. Read "I Didn't Know That!" while students are looking at items.
14. Have books available to borrow about that country or by a native author.
15. Do map work of that country. If possible, play a song or a language tape for a couple of minutes at the beginning of the map work.
16. Assign independent work.

Geography Notebook
You may reproduce the pages of the Conquering the Continents study and put together a notebook for each student in your classroom. Add the appropriate outline maps. It may be helpful to divide the notebook into sections. Some you may wish to include:

- Lessons
- Outline maps
- Activities
- Memory lists
- Geography Bee information
- Book list
- Syllabus and homework assignments

Other Notes:

Facts presented are current as of this writing, but it pays to stay informed. Countries in some parts of the world change boundaries (and names) on an almost regular basis.

Our **"I Didn't Know That!"** sections are just a beginning - feel free to add your own!

The **"Current Events"** heading under each continent (except Antarctica) is intentionally left blank; it's included for you and/or your students to add to as you hear noteworthy news. Keep a file for each continent and add items throughout the year. Challenge students to report on current events gleaned from a variety of sources.

For older students, consider leaving a block of information out in order that they research it themselves. For example, don't provide the climate or natural resources. This then becomes part of their weekly assignment.

Continent: North America

Fact File
Size (in relation to other continents): third largest
Land area: 9,500,000 square miles
Largest country: Canada
Smallest independent country: St. Kitts and Nevis
Most populous country: United States
Highest point: Mt. McKinley, Alaska
Lowest point: Death Valley, California
Longest river: Mississippi/Missouri

Geography
North America lies mostly between the Arctic Circle and the Tropic of Cancer, and between the Atlantic and Pacific Oceans. It includes: Canada, Greenland, United States, Mexico, Central America, and Caribbean Islands.

Climate and Vegetation
North America contains almost every type of climate and vegetation found in the world.

Current Events

Map-It
Identify the following places on your outline map of North America:

1. Arctic Ocean
2. Bering Sea
3. Gulf of Alaska
4. Pacific Ocean
5. Gulf of California
6. Gulf of Mexico
7. Caribbean Sea
8. Atlantic Ocean
9. Chesapeake Bay
10. Lake Superior
11. Lake Michigan
12. Lake Huron
13. Lake Erie
14. Lake Ontario
15. Hudson Bay
16. Baffin Bay
17. Missouri-Mississippi River
18. Arctic Ocean
19. Canada
20. Northwest Territory

21. Alaska
22. Baffin Island
23. Greenland
24. Rocky Mountains
25. Appalachian Mountains
26. Los Angeles
27. New York
28. USA
29. Mexico
30. Central America
31. Yucatan Peninsula
32. Baja Peninsula
33. Panama Canal
34. Sierra Madre Oriental (Mountains - Mexico)
35. Sierra Madre Occidental (Mountains - Mexico)
36. Jamaica
37. Puerto Rico
38. Cuba
39. Haiti
40. Dominican Republic

Canada Close-Up

Fact File

Area: 3,849,000 square miles (second largest country in the world)
Capital city: Ottawa
Main languages: English and French (a "bilingual" country)
Main religions: Roman Catholic and Protestant
Currency: Canadian dollar
Government: Parliamentary democracy

Ten Provinces

1. British Columbia
2. Alberta
3. Saskatchewan
4. Manitoba
5. Ontario
6. Quebec
7. Newfoundland
8. New Brunswick
9. Nova Scotia
10. Prince Edward Island

Three Territories

• Yukon Territory • Northwest Territories • Nunavut Territory

Climate and Vegetation

Ranges from humid subtropical on the west coast to dry highlands around the Rockies; dry steppe in the central provinces and temperate along the southern border with the USA. At the northern tip of Quebec province and in the islands of Nunavut and the Northwest Territories is the very cold polar region. In the far north, the vegetation is known as "tundra" with lichen and moss. Below the tundra is a broad band region running the full width of the continent. This area of coniferous forest is called the "taiga" region. Along the border with the USA in the east is a narrow band of temperate forest lands. The central region along the Canada-USA border has temperate grasslands.

Resources

Logging industries are concentrated there. The fertile center of Canada is known as the "Prairies," where vast fields of wheat and other crops are grown and farmers raise cattle and pigs. Further east around the Great Lakes are the most densely populated areas, where industry is centered. The Atlantic (or Maritime) Provinces are known for their seafaring industries.

Canada's wealth comes from manufacturing and from its many natural resources including: forests for logging and wood-processing industries, abundant fishing, uranium, zinc, gold, and oil. It's one of the world's largest producers of wheat.

Native Animals

Beaver, moose, and wolves live in Canada. In the arctic region you might find seals, polar bears, and walruses.

Exploration

Although the east coast of Canada had been visited by Vikings around A.D. 1000, this had all been forgotten by the 15th century. When John Cabot sailed from England to Newfoundland, he believed he'd reached China. The search for the Northwest Passage had begun! Many of the place names in the Canadian north are memorials to explorers; for example, Hudson, Champlain, and Baffin. And in the cold Northwest, Mackenzie, a Scottish fur trader, was one of the many fur trappers responsible for much of the exploration of the continent in the 17th and 18th centuries.

Ancestry

Most Canadians are of European descent - primarily from Britain and France. Both the English and French languages are used by the government. Each province has chosen which language it uses. Most French-Canadians live in Quebec and they strive to keep the customs and language of their French ancestors. Quebec Province held several votes in the 1990s in an attempt to secede from Canada. The native Canadians are Eskimos and First Nations. (The term "Indian" is outdated and considered offensive.) Eskimos, meaning "Eaters of Raw Meat," prefer to be called Inuits, meaning "People."

I Didn't Know That!

- Canada has two official sports: ice hockey and lacrosse.

- Quebec is the leading producer of maple syrup.

- Royal Canadian Mounted Police are often referred to as "Mounties." See: www.rcmp.ca/

- Books by Canadians you may enjoy reading: The *Anne of Green Gable* series, set on Prince Edward Island, and Sigmund Brouwer's *Lightning on Ice* and The *Accidental Detectives* series.

- Aurora Borealis: an aurora is a colorful light display that shimmers in the dark polar sky. Named for the Roman goddess of dawn, the lights in the earth's upper atmosphere shift gently and change shape like softly blowing curtains. (The same phenomena in the southern hemisphere is called the Aurora Australis.) Check it out when visiting the Canadian far north!

Map-It

Number each of the provinces on the outline map of Canada in their proper places.

Label and trace in green the St. Lawrence, Mackenzie, and Peace Rivers. Color Hudson Bay blue.

Write the following letters in their correct location on the map:
   A. Hudson Strait
   B. Baffin Island
   C. Gulf of St. Lawrence
   D. Vancouver Island
   E. Rocky Mountains
   F. Victoria Island
   G. Bay of Fundy (Hint: look between New Brunswick and Nova Scotia.)

Put a capital "T" where Toronto is located.
Put a capital "M" where Montreal is located.
Put a capital "V" where Vancouver is located.
Put an "XXX" by Niagra Falls.
Put a ^^ by Mt. Logan. (Hint: look in the SW corner of the Yukon Territories.)
Put an * by the Waterton Glacier International Peace Park. (Hint: look at the border of Montana and Alberta.)

Name the capital city of Canada: _____

United States of America Close-Up

Fact File
Area: 3,618,770 square miles (fourth largest country in the world)
Capital city: Washington, D.C. (District of Columbia)
Main language: English
Main religion: Christianity
Currency: US dollar
Government: Democratic Republic
Current president: _____

States and Territories
Fifty states
Alaska and Hawaii are not connected to the mainland. The other forty-eight states are connected, or "contiguous."
American Samoa - USA Territory
Guam - Unincorporated USA Territory
Puerto Rico - USA Territory
U.S. Virgin Islands - USA Territory

Let's look at the states by region. There are a number of ways to divide them. Here's one:

New England	Mid-Atlantic	Southern	Midwest
Maine	New York	Virginia	North Dakota
New Hampshire	Pennsylvania	North Carolina	South Dakota
Vermont	New Jersey	South Carolina	Nebraska
Massachusetts	Maryland	Kentucky	Kansas
Connecticut	Delaware	Tennessee	Missouri
Rhode Island	West Virginia	Georgia	Iowa
		Florida	Minnesota
		Alabama	Wisconsin
		Mississippi	Illinois
		Arkansas	Indiana
		Louisiana	Ohio
			Michigan

Southwestern	Rocky Mountain	Pacific Coast / Northwest
Texas	Idaho	California
Oklahoma	Montana	Washington
New Mexico	Wyoming	Oregon
Arizona	Nevada	Hawaii
	Utah	Alaska
	Colorado	

Native Animals
Sea lions, raccoons, chipmunks, bald eagles, armadillos, and turkeys are just a few of the many wonderful and interesting animals that live in the United States.

Exploration
The USA was originally inhabited by Native Americans. Later it was "discovered" by Europeans, including the Vikings. Christopher Columbus is credited with the discovery of America in 1492 that led to European exploration and settlement in earnest. Originally a British colony, the USA won its independence as a result of the Revolutionary War.

Map-It
Label and trace the Mississippi River, Missouri River, and Colorado Rivers in dark green.
Label and color the Great Lakes blue.
Label and color Salt Lake white or gold.
Label and color Lake Okeechobee blue.
Color the Mojave and Great Salt Deserts brown.

Put a ^^^ down the Rocky Mountains.
Put an XXX down the Appalachian Mountains.
Put a ////// down the Sierra Nevadas and the Cascade Range.
Put a triangle on Mt. Ranier.
Draw a circle around the Everglades.
Put a black diamond on Washington D.C.

If applicable, draw a heart in the state in which you were born.

Outline in black and then color in the following regions:
New England - light yellow
Mid-Atlantic - blue stripes
Southern - light red
Midwest - light green
Southwestern - light purple
Rocky Mountain - red stripes
Pacific Coast - pink

Which states touch Canadian soil? (Hint - there are eleven.)

Which states touch Mexican soil? (Hint - there are four.)

Mexico Close-Up

Fact File
Area: 761,604 square miles (fifth largest country in North and South America combined)
Capital city: Mexico City
Main language: Spanish (approximately five million Mexicans speak one of fifty Indian languages)
Main religion: Roman Catholic
Currency: Mexican Peso
Government: Federal Republic
States: thirty-one states plus one Federal District (located within the capital, Mexico City)

Geography
Two large peninsulas: the Baja California Peninsula on the west coast, at almost 800 miles long, is one of the longest peninsulas in the world. It has dry desert areas and high mountains. On the east coast is the Yucatan Peninsula.

Two key geographical features are the Sierra Madre Occidental and the Sierra Madre Oriental mountain ranges. These run down either side of the country, roughly parallel to the coast. They enclose the Central Plateau which covers about half of Mexico's territory. The Central Plateau contains the majority of Mexico's major cities.

Exploration and Ancestry
The people of Mexico are descended from the original Indian inhabitants of the area, and from the Spanish explorers who arrived in the 16th century. Most Mexicans are of mixed Indian and Spanish ancestry and are sometimes referred to as "Mestizos."

Climate and Vegetation
Mexico has almost every type of climate; hot deserts, rain forests, cold mountainous regions, and warm coastal areas that support a variety of vegetation. While most of the country receives too little rainfall, the Gulf Coast has too much - up to 235 inches per year! The fertile lands and temperate climate of the Central Plateau provide much of Mexico's food.

Resources
Corn, also known as "maize," has been the most important crop in Mexico for centuries. Every part of the corn plant is used - as food, fuel, or medicine. The most valuable export crop is coffee. Beef and cotton are also important exports. Mexico has valuable reserves of gold, silver, copper, lead and large oil fields in the Gulf of Mexico. Crude oil is an extremely valuable export.

Native Animals
Mexico has thirty percent more species of birds than the U.S. and Canada combined. However, as the economy has grown, so has Mexico's environmental problems. Air and water pollution and deforestation are concerns Mexicans are trying to deal with.

More than 100 million Monarch butterflies migrate each year from Canada and the U.S. to breed in a single forest in Mexico!

I Didn't Know That!

- Before the Spanish arrived in the early 1500's, the Mexicans had great ways of producing food for their large population (estimated to be around 30 million people.) The most interesting way was to build a "chinampa," or large floating island, in a shallow lake. Then they grew crops on it! These crops didn't need to be watered and would yield up to three harvests in one year. Now the only chinampas left are in a park near Mexico City.

- The early Indian societies used salt and cacao beans (from which chocolate is made) for money as well as food.

- Many ancient ruins can be seen in Mexico, including a Mayan temple at Palenque.

- Favorite sports are soccer and the very fast-paced jai alai. (Similar to handball but played with a woven basket-like glove called a cesta.)

- Fiestas and festivals are widely celebrated.

Map-It

Place a star on Mexico City.

Put a ^^^ on the three mountain ranges: Sierra Madre Occidental, Sierra Madre del Sur, and the Sierra Madre Oriental.

Label these rivers: Rio Grande (called Rio Bravo in Mexico), Rio Balsas, and the Rio Grande de Santiago. Trace them in blue.

Color the Yucatan Peninsula green.

Color the Baja Peninsula blue.

Identify and write in Gulf of California, Gulf of Campeche, and Gulf of Mexico.

Write in the following cities: Tijuana, Monterrey, Guadalajara, Acapulco, and Merida.

What named line of latitude divides Mexico almost in half? _____ ____ _____

Central America Close-Up

Fact File

Which countries are located in Central America? You can remember them in order from north to south with this sentence: "Great big elephants hide near city parks." Here's a list, along with their capital cities:

Country	Capital City
Guatemala	Guatemala City
Belize	Belmopan
El Salvador	San Salvador
Honduras	Tegucigalpa
Nicaragua	Managua
Costa Rica	San Jose
Panama	Panama City

Geography

Mexico is to the north, and South America is to the south. The Caribbean Sea is on the east and the Pacific Ocean is on the west. Much of the land is mountainous, but coffee and bananas are grown on plantations in the lowland areas. Timber is an important industry in some of the countries. Mahogany is an especially valuable export.

I Didn't Know That!

- Although Central America is part of North America, in customs and cultures it is more closely aligned with Mexico and South America than with the United States and Canada. Mexico, Central America, and South America are often referred to as "Latin America."

- Tajumulco, a volcano in Guatemala, is the highest point in Central America (over 13,000 feet).

- The Panama Canal, completed in 1914 and operated by the United States, was turned over to Panama in 1999. Interested? Read more about it!

Costa Rica Close-Up

Fact File

Area: 19,653 square miles (the smallest in Central America)
Capital city: San Jose'
Main language: Spanish (English and German are also spoken)
Main religion: Roman Catholic
Currency: Colon
Government: democratic

Climate and Vegetation

Costa Rica has two seasons: the dry season from December until May, and the rainy season from June until November. The lowlands by the Caribbean are tropical, and the interior plateau is temperate. Almost one third of Costa Rica is covered with forest.

Native Animals

Costa Rica is home to deer, monkeys, fifteen types of deadly snakes, a highly dangerous poison-shooting toad, lizards, parrots, macaws and many, many other interesting animals!

I Didn't Know That!

- Christopher Columbus discovered Costa Rica for Spain in 1502 during his fourth and final voyage.

- Ninety-two percent of the population is literate, the highest percentage in Latin America.

- Costa Rica has the highest standard of living in Central America and is probably the most stable country as well.

- In addition to two active volcanoes, Costa Rica also experiences earthquakes and earth tremors.

Map - It

Identify each country in Central America.
Label the following bodies of water: Gulf of Honduras, Gulf of Panama, and the Gulf of Fonseca.
Find the Panama Canal. Mark it in blue.

Caribbean Islands Close-Up

Here are a few countries to know, along with their corresponding capital city:

Country	Capital
Cuba	Havana
Haiti	Port-au-Prince
Dominican Republic	Santo Domingo
Jamaica	Kingston
Puerto Rico	San Juan
Bahamas	Nassau

Although some atlases refer to the "Caribbean Sea" and some refer to the "Caribbean Ocean," it's more often called the Caribbean Sea. The twenty-four countries within the thousands of islands are popular with tourists looking for pretty scenery, beaches, and a warm tropical climate. Islanders make their living from tourism, fishing, and farming. Sugar cane and citrus fruits are important crops. Some of the countries are extremely poor, like Haiti, and others are wealthy, like Barbados.

I Didn't Know That!

• Cuba is the largest Caribbean island.

• The Bahamas consist of 3,000 coral islands, of which only twenty are inhabited.

• Hispaniola is an island comprised of the countries of Haiti and the Dominican Republic.

Continent: South America

Fact File

Size (in relation to the other continents): fourth largest
Area: 6,900,000 square miles
Largest country: Brazil
Smallest independent country: Suriname
Most populous country: Brazil
Highest point: Mount Aconcagua, Argentina
Lowest point: Salinas Chicas, Argentina
Longest river: Amazon, 4,050 miles long
Largest lake: Lake Titicaca, Peru/Bolivia, the world's highest navigable lake
Longest mountain range: the Andes, which run almost the entire length of South America -
  the longest mountain range in the world
Driest place: Atacama Desert, Chile - driest place on earth
Highest waterfall: Angel Falls, Venezuela   world's highest waterfall

Geography

South America stretches from the Caribbean Sea, well above the equator, down to Cape Horn, the cold southernmost tip, which is just over 600 miles from Antarctica! The Andes run the length of western South America. The Amazon River begins in the Peruvian Andes and spans the continent west to east.

Climate and Vegetation

The Brazilian rain forest almost covers central South America. South of the rain forest are the plateau grasslands of the Pampas. To the west of the Andes lies the long and narrow Atacama Desert. Seasons in South America are opposite those in North America, because South America is in the Southern Hemisphere. For example, if you went to Paraguay in December for Christmas, it would be summer!

There are twelve independent countries in South America. Each country and its capital city:

Country	Capital
Argentina	Buenos Aires
Brazil	Brasilia
Bolivia	La Paz
Chile	Santiago
Colombia	Bogota
Ecuador	Quito
Guyana	Georgetown
Paraguay	Asuncion
Peru	Lima
Suriname	Paramaribo
Uruguay	Montevideo
Venezuela	Caracas

French Guiana (capital Cayenne) is a colony of France.
The Falkland Islands, off the coast of southernmost Argentina, belong to the United Kingdom.

Current Events

I Didn't Know That!

- The Atacama Desert in Chile, experienced no rain from 1570 until 1971.

- Ushuaia, Argentina, on the island of Tierra del Fuego, is the southernmost city in the world. It's less than 700 miles from Antarctica.

- Easter Island in the Pacific Ocean, although geographically a part of Oceania, belongs to Chile. It is known for its strange, giant stone-face monuments.

- Devil's Island in French Guiana housed the world's most notorious prison until it was closed in 1945.

Map-It

Write the name of each South American country on the outline map.

Identify the following places:
Draw the Falkland Islands.
Draw the Galapagos Islands.
Color Lake Maracaibo light blue.
Color Lake Titicaca dark blue.
Put a ZZZ by Angel Falls.
Put a ////// by Iguacu Falls.
Outline the Amazon River in green. (There are many branches, just give the general outline!)
Put an XXX in brown along the Andes Mountains.
Color the Atacama Desert brown.
Circle the Strait of Magellan.
Place a triangle at the Tierra del Fuego.
Put a "C" at Cape Horn.
Write in "Atlantic Ocean".
Write in "Pacific Ocean".
Draw the equator in black.
Label French Guiana.
Draw the Tropic of Capricorn red.
Draw the Tropic of Cancer blue.

Through which countries does the equator run?

1.

2.

3.

Brazil Close-Up

Fact File

Area: Over 3,280,000 square miles, the largest country in South America

Capital city: Brasilia (a new capital, built so the government would be situated in the center of the country)

Important cities: Sao Paulo, the previous capital and one of the most densely populated cities; and Rio de Janeiro, a beautiful coastal city popular with tourists.

Main language: Portuguese

Main religion: Roman Catholic

Currency: New Cruzado (written as CR$)

Government: Federal Republic

Geography

Brazil contains the largest area of tropical rain forest in the world. The Amazon, the world's second longest river, runs through Brazil. "Amazonia" refers to the area of 2.9 million square miles where the Amazon River and its 1,000 or so tributaries flow.

Climate and Vegetation

Because Brazil is so large (it covers forty-seven percent of South America) it has five different climate and rainfall zones! Most of Brazil has a tropical climate. It's cooler in the hilly areas and far south, which in winter can experience severe frosts or even snow. The northeast portion of Brazil is known for its droughts and harsh, hot weather. From the scrubby cactus covered regions in the northeast, to the lush abundant trees in the rainforest, to the sandy, palm tree-lined coastal cities, Brazil has a wide variety of vegetation.

Resources

Brazil has good supplies of gold, one third of the world's iron ore reserves, oil, and an enormous supply of timber, and water.* Chief products are steel, corn, coffee, cotton, rice, and diamonds. Exports include coffee, cotton, and machinery.

*The potential for hydroelectric energy in Brazil is enormous! It already provides more than ninety percent of Brazil's electricity.

Native Animals

A wide variety of animals make their home in the rain forest: sloths, jaguars, red-eyed tree frogs, toucans, and spider monkeys. The largest Amazon fish, piraibas, can grow to more than ten feet long and weigh over 400 pounds!

Transportation

For centuries, water was the most reliable way of traveling in Brazil. Even today, roads and railroads are just beginning to connect this vast country. It's expensive and difficult to build through Amazonia. One such road is the Trans-Amazonian Highway, 3,100 miles long. Ships are still well-used, bicycles are popular in urban areas, and on Marajo Island, water buffalo and carts are still in use.

Current Events

I Didn't Know That!

- Tropical fruit is so plentiful it's eaten at almost every meal.

- Rio de Janeiro is famous throughout the world for its "Carnival." Each year, thousands of people gather to dress in costumes and parade through the city. For many days there is dancing and singing in the streets.

- "Gauchos" are the cowboys of the southern grasslands, or "Pampas" of South America.

- The Amazon rain forests are home to many tribes of native Indians. They use blowpipes and bows for hunting. Destruction of the rain forests threaten these peoples and their way of life.

- The rain forest has five layers: forest floor, shrub, understory, canopy, and emergent.

- Despite Brazil's abundance of natural resources, many are extremely poor and live in slums. Thousands of children live on the streets and beg for their food.

- Soccer (called "futebol") is the national sport. Pele, one of the best known players in the world, is from Brazil. Brazil is the only country to have played in fourteen World Cup soccer tournaments.

- One of Brazil's dams, the Itaipu Dam, built jointly with Paraguay, has the largest output of any dam in the world.

- Brazil produces and consumes more ethanol fuel than any other nation in the world.

Map-It

Identify the following:

Place a star by Brasilia.
Place a square around Rio de Janeiro.
Place a circle around Sao Paulo.
Put an XXX in the area of Iguacu Falls. (Hint: on the border between
   Paraguay and Brazil)
Write in Marajo Island.
Trace the Sao Francisco River in green.
Draw the Tropic of Capricorn in brown.

Continent: Europe

Fact File

Size (in relation to other continents): second smallest but second most populated, after Asia

Area: 3,800,000 square miles

Largest country: Russia (Russia is in both Europe and Asia - the Ural Mountains are traditionally the dividing line)

Smallest independent country: Vatican City (followed by Monaco)

Most populous country: Russia

Most populous city: Moscow

Highest point: Mt. El'brus, Russia

Highest point excluding Russia: Mt. Blanc, between France and Italy

Lowest point: Caspian Sea (Asia-Europe) ninety-two feet below sea level

Largest lake: Caspian Sea

Longest river: Volga, Russia 2,194 miles long

Biggest island: Great Britain (England, Wales, and Scotland)

Geography

Think of Europe as an enormous peninsula stretching from the Ural Mountains, Ural River, and Caspian Sea in the east, to the Atlantic Ocean in the west; from the Arctic Ocean in the north, to the Mediterranean Sea and Black Sea in the south. Great Britain, Iceland, Corsica, and thousands of smaller islands off the mainland are also considered part of Europe.

Climate

The climate varies enormously, from the subarctic areas of the far north in Scandinavia and Russia, to the temperate central sections, to the warm and sunny Mediterranean climate of Spain, Italy, and Greece. (What U.S. state shares this same mediterranean climate? California.)

Recent Historical Changes

The European Union is an economic grouping of fifteen western European countries joined for the purpose of promoting economic cooperation and growth. Achieving a single currency is one of their aims. In 1999, a large step toward European unification took place with the introduction of the "euro" as the official currency in eleven countries.

Europe has been marked by sweeping changes since 1989. The old Soviet Union broke up in 1990-91, and its fifteen republics all became independent countries, including Latvia, Russia, Ukraine, Belarus, Armenia, Moldova.

East and West Germany, separated by the Iron Curtain and severe political and economic differences, reunited when communist East Germany collapsed.

Ethnic strife resulted in the break-up of Czechoslovakia into the Czech Republic and Slovakia.

Yugoslavia broke up, leaving the Yugoslav Republic and four independent countries. Ethnic tensions are still a factor in Croatia, Bosnia and Herzegovina.

Economically, there's a vast difference between the mostly wealthy western European countries, and the much poorer eastern European countries. Luxembourg has the highest per capita Gross Domestic Product (GDP) of $70,000, compared to Albania's GDP of $5706.

Current Events

I Didn't Know That!

- Switzerland is known for its numerous, wealthy banks and for its chocolates! The world's longest road tunnel runs through the Alps.

- Europe is the birth place of Western civilization and has had great influence on the rest of the world.

- Germany is known for its Black Forest, fairy tales by the Grimm Brothers, castles, the "autobahn," Oktoberfest, and for composers such as Bach, Beethoven, Brahms, and Handel.

- "Chunnel" is the nickname for the English Channel Tunnel. It runs for thirty-one miles, 150 feet below the English Channel, connecting England to France by train.

- The only volcano in Europe active in the 20th century is Mt. Vesuvius in Italy.

- "He's met his Waterloo" is a phrase that means "He's met his match and lost." It originated in Waterloo, near Brussels, Belgium, when Napoleon was defeated by British forces under the command of the Duke of Wellington. This defeat ended the Napoleonic Wars.

- In which European country are you likely to call a "water cab" to get someplace? Venice, Italy is built on 188 small islands in a lagoon at the top of the Adriatic Sea.

- Which country is called the "Bread Basket of Europe"? The Ukraine, with its flat plains (called "steppes") and its fertile soils, produces millions of tons of grain yearly.

- What is Lapland? Lapland, home to the Lapps, covers areas in northern Norway, Sweden, Finland, and Russia. The Finnish government has worked to preserve the traditional Lapp language and culture. Which animals are closely associated with the Lapps? Reindeers!

- St. Petersburg has changed its name three times in the 1900's: first it was St. Petersburg, then it became Petrograd, then Leningrad, and then back to St. Petersburg.

Map-It

Identify the following on your outline map of Europe:

Bodies of Water:
Caspian Sea (Hint - it's in both Europe and Asia)
Black Sea (Hint - its southern boundary is Turkey)
Aegean Sea
Adriatic Sea
Mediterranean Sea
Bay of Biscay
English Channel
North Sea
Baltic Sea
Gulf of Bothnia
Arctic Ocean

A Few Important Rivers:
The Rhine (or Rhein)
The Elbe
The Danube (begins in Germany, ends in the Black Sea)
The Rhone (France)
The Volga (Russia)
The Ural (Russia)

Selected Places:
Iberian Peninsula (includes Spain and Portugal)
Scandinavian Peninsula (includes Norway and Sweden)
Iceland
Ireland
United Kingdom
France
Germany
Poland
Spain
Portugal
Norway
Sweden
Finland
Ukraine
Russia
Italy
Sicily
Greece

Mountain Ranges:
Alps (across eastern France, Switzerland, Germany, Austria, northern Italy)
Apennines (the length of central Italy)
Pyrenees (the border between Spain and France)
Urals (in Russia)
Carpathian Mountains

United Kingdom Close-Up

Fact File

Area: 94,251 square miles
Capital: London
Main language: English
Main religion: Protestant
Currency: pound sterling
Government: Parliamentary monarchy

Sorting out the terms

The United Kingdom consists of Great Britain plus Northern Ireland.

Great Britain consists of England, Scotland and Wales.

The "British Isles" are a geographic reference, specifically referring to the United Kingdom, Ireland, and adjacent islands.

Some people are confused by these terms, but now you know which is which!

Geography

Located off the northwest coast of Europe, across the English Channel, the Strait of Dover and the North Sea. Consists of lowlands, rolling lands, and granite highlands.

Climate and Vegetation

The British Isles have a milder climate than northern Europe because of the Gulf Stream and ample rainfall. Crops include grains, sugar beets, and vegetables.

Map-It

On your outline map complete the following:

Color England yellow, Scotland purple, Wales brown, and Northern Ireland orange.
Color the Republic of Ireland green. (Think shamrocks!)

Label the following:
Put an "E.C." by the English Channel.
Write in Irish Sea.
Write in North Sea.
Put an "O" by the Orkney Islands.
Put an "H" by the Hebrides Islands.
Put an XXX on the Grampian Mountains in Scotland.
Put a star by London.
Draw in the Thames (pronounced "Tims") River.
Put a circle around Edinburgh.
Put a triangle by Belfast.
Put a "D" on Dublin.

France Close-Up

Fact File

Area: 210,026 square miles
Number of regions: twenty-two
Capital city: Paris
Main language: French
Main religion: Roman Catholic
Currency: Francs
Government: Republic
Highest mountain: Mount Blanc
Longest river: Loire

Geography

France is the largest country in western Europe. Low to medium hills and plateaus cover two-thirds of the country. France has several mountain ranges, from the small, round Massif Central and Vosges Mountains, to the tall Pyrenees and Alps. Twenty-five per cent of its land is covered with forest.

Climate and Vegetation

Most of France lies halfway between the equator and the North Pole. Because of this, most of the country enjoys a temperate climate. The southern areas experience a mediterranean climate of warm, rainy winters and very dry summers. The mountain areas experience rain and heavy snow. Southern France experiences hot, dry summers. In some places, droughts are a problem. Vegetation varies from shrubs to evergreen, deciduous, and coniferous trees.

Resources

Nuclear power is currently the main source of electricity in France, although hydroelectricity used to account for half its source. France grows fifty-seven million tons of grain per year - one-third of all grain grown in the European Community. In 1990, France produced more wine than any other country in the world, making grapes an important crop.

Native Animals

The government has opened many parks and preserves to protect animals. Species with special protection include wolves, wild horses, bears, eagles, and flamingoes.

I Didn't Know That!

- The French flag is called "le tricolore" because of its blue, red, and white stripes. It was first used during the French Revolution of 1789.

- The Eiffel Tower was finished in 1889 and stands 1,000 feet high.

- The warm and sunny French Riviera is famous for resorts, such as Nice and Cannes, and many wealthy people flock there from all over the world.

- The French are famous for their cooking! Ever had French bread? In France, it's called a "baguette." Other famous foods include crepes, pate', and escargot (snails).

- School often starts at 8:30 a.m. and finishes at 5:30 p.m. with a traditional two-hour break for lunch. Children often attend school on Saturday mornings, and in many places Wednesday afternoons are reserved for sports and clubs.

- France is also famous for fashion. Major design houses create and sell their own clothes and perfumes. Do Yves Saint Laurent, Christian Dior, Channel, or Givenchy ring a bell?

- Soccer is the most popular team sport. Rugby is also popular, as is horse racing. In bicycling, the Tour de France is a well known race. An old-fashioned game played there is "boules" or "petanque," and is somewhat similar to a combination of outdoor bowling and shuffleboard.

- Bastille Day is a national holiday celebrating the anniversary of the storming of the Bastille prison in 1789, leading to the French Revolution.

- A Mardi Gras is held here, marking the two weeks before Lent begins.

- Famous authors include Victor Hugo who wrote The Hunchback of Notre Dame and Les Miserables.

- Famous artists include Gaugin, Monet, and the sculptor Rodin. Famous works like the Mona Lisa can be seen in the world renown art museum, the Louvre.

- France has many colorful and interesting figures in its long history. Read more about Joan of Arc, Louis XIV, Marie Antoinette, Napoleon Bonaparte, and Charles de Gaulle.

Map-It

On your outline map complete the following:

Label Paris.
Label Nice.
Put an XXX by the Alps.
Color various mountain ranges purple.
Color hills and low tablelands yellow.
Color plains green.
Color Corsica pink; this island belongs to France.
What's the natural border dividing France from Spain (and Andorra)? _____

Russia Close-Up

Fact File

Official name: Russian Federation
Conventional short form: Russia
Area: 6,592,800 square miles, the largest country in the world
Capital city: Moscow
Main languages: Russian is official; many ethnic languages also spoken
Main religions: Russian Orthodox, Protestant, (communist for many years until the Religious Freedom Restoration Act went in effect in the 1980's)
Currency: Ruble
Government: Multi-party Federal Republic or Federation
Highest mountain: Mount El'brus
World's largest inland sea: Caspian Sea
Major rivers: the Volga and the Lena

Geography

Russia stretches from the Baltic Sea in the west to the Pacific Ocean in the east, and from the Arctic Sea in the north to the warm Baltic Sea in the south. It occupies a large area of eastern Europe and northern Asia. Some atlases include it in Europe; others in Asia.

Russia is the largest country in the world in terms of area, but it's unfavorably located in relation to the major sea lanes of the world. It's twice as large as Canada, the second largest country. The predominant mountain range in central Asia are the Urals, running north- south. There is a large mountainous region in eastern Russia. Many active volcanoes are also found along the Pacific Coast of the Far East and throughout the Kuril Islands. Russia also contains some two million fresh and saltwater lakes and rivers, as well as many glaciers in the Arctic and high mountain regions.

Climate and Vegetation

Around seventy percent of the total land area consists of broad plains. The far north is mostly tundra. There are vast coniferous forests called "taigas" in Siberia. Despite its size, much of the country lacks the proper soils and climates for agriculture. Throughout Russia, winters are cold, long, and snowy, while summers are hot or warm. Siberia has a subarctic climate. In the southern areas of the Far East, the climate is influenced by the Pacific Ocean, resulting in moderately warm and rainy summer conditions while winter is cold with little snow. Precipitation is fairly light.

Resources

Russia is rich in timber, hydroelectric power, and many mineral deposits. Oil is found in many areas. Mines in Siberia produce large quantities of diamonds. Coal and ore are abundant. Russia is also one of the world's leading producers of gold. Formidable obstacles of climate, terrain, and distance hinder exploitation of natural resources, however.

I Didn't Know That!

- Russia, formerly part of the gigantic Soviet Union, was a communist country. The Soviet Union (or USSR), had strained relations with the mostly democratic west. After WWII, a strong tension between the Soviet Union and the United States existed and was referred to as the "Cold War."

- On March 11, 1985, Mikhail Gorbachev was elected head of the Soviet Union. He embarked on a program which restructured the U.S.S.R.'s relations with the West. Gorbachev also established "Glasnost" (openness) as well as "Perestroika" (restructuring and reform).

- In April of 1986, a meltdown in the reactor of the Chernobyl nuclear power station in Ukraine sent radioactive fallout across northern Europe. Many people have died as a result of this tragedy.

- In December of 1988, an earthquake in Armenia killed some 50,000 people.

- After an attempted coup in 1991, Gorbachev resigned and the Soviet Union was dissolved. Boris Yeltsin, President of Russia, remained in power. A new constitution was adopted and many reforms have since taken place.

- Because of housing shortages, about one-fifth of city dwellers have to share their homes with another family.

- St. Basil's Cathedral is one of Russia's most recognized sites. It's made up of nine chapels, each with its own colorful and ornately decorated roof.

- A city of contrasts, Moscow has both food and housing shortages but its underground subway is elegantly decorated with marble, granite, and crystal.

- Moscow citizens eat about 170 tons of ice cream a day, even in the bitter cold winter. Sweet black tea is served with most meals.

- The Moscow Kremlin is the seat of Russia's government. The Kremlin isn't just one building, but a number of buildings.

Map-It*

Label and trace the Volga and Lena Rivers in green.
Color Lake Baikal (or Baykal) blue.
Color the Caspian Sea yellow.
Shade Siberia with light orange stripes.
Shade the mountain ranges in eastern Russia brown.
Write the following letters in their correct location on the map:

A. Sea of Okhotsk	D. Arctic Ocean
B. Bering Strait	E. Barents Sea
C. Kamchatka Peninsula	F. Black Sea

Put a capital "M" where Moscow is located.
Put a capital "P" where St. Petersburg is located (formerly Leningrad).
Put a capital "V" where Volgograd is located (formerly Stalingrad).
Put an "XXX" down the Ural Mountains.
Put a ^^ by Mt. El'brus. (Hint: look on the border between Georgia and Russian, west of the Caspian Sea.)

*Note: Since the land area of Russia is located in both Europe and Asia you may need to use both Europe and Asia outline maps to complete the Map-It.

Continent: Asia

Fact File

Number of Countries: forty-nine (including dependencies)
Size (in relation to other continents): largest and most populated
  continent
Area: 17,150,100 square miles
Largest country: (excluding Russia which is partly in Europe) China
Most populous country: China
Highest point: Mount Everest, Nepal/China
Lowest point: the shore of the Dead Sea, Israel/Jordan
Largest lake: Caspian Sea
Longest river: Yangtze River, China
Largest desert: Gobi desert

Geography

Asia ranges from the Mediterranean Sea in the west all the way to the Pacific Ocean in the east; from the polar regions of upper Russia in the north, to the islands of Indonesia in the South Pacific Ocean. Because of the immensity of this continent and the diversity of peoples and land, the map activities are first, and then Asia is divided into regions.

Map-It

Identify the following countries on the Asia outline map indicated:

MIDDLE EAST/ASIA	ASIA	SOUTHEAST ASIA
Israel	Iran	Thailand
Lebanon	Afghanistan	Vietnam
Jordan	Pakistan	Cambodia
Syria	India	Malaysia
Turkey	China	Philippines
Saudi Arabia	Mongolia	Taiwan
Iraq	Korea	Japan

Identify the following bodies of water:

Mediterranean Sea	Red Sea	South China Sea
Black Sea	Persian Gulf	Sea of Japan
Caspian Sea	Bay of Bengal	Sea of Okhotsk
	Aral Sea	

Put an XXX on the Himalaya Mountains.
Trace the Yellow River yellow.
Trace the Tigris River red.
Trace the Euphrates River blue.
Trace the Yangtze River green.
Trace the Mekong River gold.
Shade the Gobi Desert brown.

The Middle East Close-Up

Geography

The Middle East is the name of the region in Southwest Asia which lies between the Mediterranean Sea and the Indian subcontinent. Because of its location between east and west, there's a great mix of peoples and cultures there. A mountain range runs along the northern border of this region, from Turkey to Afghanistan.

The Arabian peninsula is a piece of land jutting out from this area into the Indian Ocean. On this peninsula are Saudi Arabia, United Arab Emirates, Oman, Kuwait, Qatar, and Yemen. This peninsula is bordered by the Red Sea, the Persian Gulf, and the Gulf of Aden. Most people there are Muslims who worship in mosques and speak Arabic.

Climate

The Middle East is temperate along the Mediterranean coast. Farther south, in the Arabian peninsula and central Iran, are hot and dry desert lands. Most of the people live in the coastal regions next to the Red Sea, the Persian Gulf, and the Indian Ocean.

Resources

Tremendous oil reserves located around the Persian Gulf have been a great source of wealth as well as turmoil, as countries and people fight to control the wealth. Although there are certainly industrialized, high-tech cities in places like Israel and Saudi Arabia, much of this area still remains in the past, with nomadic herders and poor, isolated villages. Immense wealth gained from oil has raised standards of living and education in these Arab countries.

Religion

This area is the birthplace of three main religions, and people from all three regard Jerusalem as a holy city: Judaism, Islam (followers are called Muslims), and Christianity. These religious differences have caused much conflict in the Middle East. In 1948, the modern-day Jewish state of Israel was established and has been hotly contested by its Arab neighbors ever since.

Asia Close-Up: Southwest Asia

Geography

The countries of Iran, Iraq, and Afghanistan are sometimes referred to as Southwest Asia. Iran and Iraq have become rich from oil, but Afghanistan is very poor. Afghanistan has had civil war since 1979. Russian occupation for part of that time compounded problems. Although Iran and Iraq are neighbors, they have had religious and civil differences that led to war from 1980 - 1988.

Religion

The Iraqis are Arabic, Sunni Muslims, whereas the Iranians are Asian, Shiite Muslims who speak Farsi, not Arabic. All Arabic men are required to pray five times each day at set times. They kneel and pray in the direction of Mecca (in Saudi Arabia), the birthplace of Muhammad. Friday is their holy day when all work is forbidden. Pork and alcohol are strictly prohibited.

South Asia Close-Up

Geography

This region is often called the Indian subcontinent. Can you see why when looking at a map? This area includes the huge country of India, as well as the smaller countries of Pakistan, Bangladesh, Nepal, Bhutan, and the large island of Sri Lanka off the eastern tip of India. "Monsoons" are torrential rains, and the monsoon winds govern the three seasons in India: hot, wet, and cool. Monsoons cause widespread flooding, but without them crops are ruined and famine is a real threat.

In the north are the snow-capped peaks of the Himalaya Mountains. Farther south are hot and overcrowded cities like Calcutta and Bombay. The populations in South Asia are huge and growing. Over 800 million people live in India alone, and more than 200 languages are spoken!

Religion

Hinduism and Buddhism began here. Today, India is predominately Hindu, and Pakistan is mainly Muslim.

Resources

Rice and wheat are major crops., and farming is done for survival. Spices are very important in Indian food. These spices were sought after by people from other countries, and the Spice Trade precipitated much exploration. Oxen are still used for heavy labor in fields. India is the world's largest producer of jute, used to make ropes, and one of the world's leading producers of iron ore.

I Didn't Know That!

- The Thar desert is India's largest desert.

- The Ganges River is considered to be sacred.

- India became a part of the British Empire in 1868 and did not become independent until 1947.

- Calcutta, India is now spelled Kolkata.

- Kashmir, an area at the northern tip of India, is a disputed territory claimed by India and Pakistan.

- Maharajah is a king or prince.

- Indians love cricket, kite-flying, polo, and chess.

- Darjeeling, India, is famous for its tea.

- Cows are sacred to Hindus and are never killed for meat. They are commonly seen wandering, even on city streets.

- It took 20,000 workers twenty-one years to build the Taj Mahal in India. It was finished in 1653 as a tomb for the wife of a Mogul emperor.

- Rickshaws, buses, and trains can be so overcrowded they seem dangerous. People routinely sit on the TOPS of moving trains and buses!

Southeast Asia Close-Up

Geography

Southeast Asia includes: Brunei, Cambodia, Indonesia, Laos, Malaysia, Myanmar (Burma), Philippines, Singapore, Thailand, and Vietnam. This diverse area includes ten countries with a population of over 450 million. Its land area is almost half the size of the U.S. It includes over 20,000 islands, mostly in Indonesia and the Philippines. The area includes the poor communist countries of Vietnam and Laos, developing democracies in Malaysia and Singapore, the rich monarchy of Brunei, and the military state of Myanmar. Six major religions are represented, along with about 1,000 languages! The Mekong River is the longest river in Southeast Asia.

Southeast Asia can be divided into two geographic areas: mainland and island. They're separated by the shallow South China Sea.
- Mainland: Cambodia, Laos, Myanmar, Thailand, Vietnam
- Island: Brunei, Indonesia, Malaysia, the Philippines, Singapore

This region lies over a fault in the earth's crust, causing earthquakes and volcanoes. There are over one hundred active volcanoes in Indonesia alone! The eruption of Krakatau, off the coast of Java in 1883, was the largest volcanic explosion ever recorded: the equivalent of 2,000 times greater than the atomic bomb dropped on Hiroshima.

The ocean plays an important part in the life of the Southeast Asians. Laos is the only country there that doesn't have a coastline. All countries lie between the Tropics of Cancer and Capricorn. At sea level, temperatures average 79 degrees. Rainfall, however, varies enormously, both in amount and by seasonal timing. It's rainfall, not temperature, that divides the seasons.

Laos, Cambodia, and Myanmar are three of the world's poorest countries, while Brunei is one of the richest.

Smokey Mountain is the name of a massive garbage dump outside of Manilla, in the Philippines. Entire families live in the dump and hunt for items they can sell.

Resources

Rice is the staple food and Thailand is known as the "Rice Bowl" of Asia. Other crops include coffee, sugarcane, and rubber. Major exports include timber and fish. Most of the countries are agricultural, and most are undeveloped. Singapore is certainly an exception - it is an international port and commercial center. Brunei is wealthy, and Indonesia exports oil and has a tourism industry.

I Didn't Know That!

- Papua (formerly Irian Jaya - the other half of Papua New Guinea) has the biggest gold reserve of any mine in the world.

- The temple of Angkor Vat (or Wat), one of the most beautiful buildings in Asia, holds the tomb of a 12th century Khmer king. Located in north central Cambodia, it's surrounded by a moat. The central building is in the shape of a stepped pyramid, culminating in a structure with five, pineapple-shaped towers.

- Insects are a common source of protein in many of these countries.

- Civil wars in Myanmar, Laos, and Cambodia have led to hundreds of thousands of refugees leaving for neighboring countries. These countries' governments are still considered unstable.

- Vietnam, Laos and Cambodia are communist countries. It was concern over the spread of communism that led the United States into the Vietnam War between 1964 and 1973.

China, Korea, and Japan Close Up

Geography of China and Korea

This eastern Asian region ranges from the Himalayas in the east to the Gobi Desert in the north, the East China Sea in the east, and down to Southeast Asia. Eastern China has fertile plains, crossed by two great rivers: the Yellow (Huang) River and the Yangtze (Chang) River. The Yangtze is the world's third largest river. The valleys of these rivers have been farmed for thousands of years. Most Chinese cities lie in the eastern half of China. Northern China is home to the Mongols and includes deserts and rolling grasslands. The mountains and deserts are inhabited by tribal peoples.

Climate

Because China is such a huge country, its climate varies considerably. It ranges from the bitterly cold northern part, down to tropical areas in southern China.

Resources

Although China is about the same size as the United States, it has four times the population! It's much poorer, too. Tea, rice, and silk are major exports. China is the world's biggest producer of wheat. There are some natural resources also, including a large supply of coal. Oil exploration is taking place now. There's some industry located in Beijing and Shanghai. Mostly though, China is a poor agricultural society.

I Didn't Know That!

- There's a conflict over who rules Tibet; Tibetans or the much more powerful Chinese. The 14th Dali Lama, spiritual leader of Buddhists, became ruler of Tibet in 1949 just before the Chinese army began to invade his country. Since 1959 he has lived in exile in India, advocating non-violent resistance to the Chinese occupation.

- In 1989, people filled Tiananmen Square in China for several weeks for peaceful demonstrations demanding political reforms. On June 4th, the government sent in soldiers and tanks against these unarmed demonstrators, many of them students. Many were killed.

- China and North Korea are communist countries. South Korea is a democracy.

- Hong Kong, a small island off the southern coast of China, was ruled by Great Britain from 1841 until 1997, when it was turned back over to China. It had a major capitalist economy quite different from communist mainland China.

- The longest structure in the world is the Great Wall in China. It was originally begun by the first Chinese emperor over 2,000 years ago, in order to deter invasions from the north. It covers over 1400 miles, but curves make the wall over 4000 miles long.

- In China, red is the color for happiness and is used for any happy occasion.

- Ping-pong and kite flying are two favorite activities. Chinese also play soccer and basketball.

- The Chinese New Year marks the beginning of spring and the end of winter. Many festivals and parades are held.

- The bicycle is the main form of personal transportation in China and in many other Asian countries.

- Many shops in China still use an abacus to calculate costs of purchases.

- The giant panda only lives in the forests of western Sichuan province and eats a specific type of bamboo shoot that grows there. Because these forests are being cut down, there are only about 700 giant pandas left in the wild.

- The Chinese do not have an alphabet. They write using pictures called characters. There are over 60,000 characters in the Chinese language. Children must learn 400 to 500 characters per year in school!

Japan Close-Up

Fact File

Area: 145,800 square miles
Capital city: Tokyo
Main language: Japanese
Main religions: Shintoism, Buddhism
Currency: Yen
Government: Constitutional monarchy

Geography
Japan is an archipelago, "a group of closely scattered islands in any large body of water," in the Pacific Ocean. It consists of four large islands and some 3,000 smaller ones. The largest island is called Honshu. In several places there are active volcanoes. About seventy percent of Japan is mountainous and covered with forests. Most people live in coastal regions.

Climate
The climate is subtropical in the south and colder in the north.

Resources
Japan has almost no natural resources. Although it's a very industrialized nation, raw materials to make goods must be imported. Japan is the leading producer of cars in the world. They're also a leading exporter of electronic goods. Japan does have a major fishing industry, catching and selling tuna, squid, and octopus.

I Didn't Know That!

- Sumo wrestling is the top spectator sport in Japan. Wrestlers typically weigh over 330 pounds.

- Japanese are famous for their sophisticated gardens and bonsai trees. Other art forms include ikebana - the art of flower arranging; haiku and tanka poetry; and origami - the art of paper folding.

- The tea ceremony is an old ritual that women continue to learn. Few women ever master the entire tea ceremony though, as it's very complicated.

- Schools are very intense in Japan - students go 5 days per week with a short summer vacation. Many children also go to Juko, an evening cramming school, to help them keep up with regular school.

- Traditional colorful robes are called kimonos.

- The most common food in the Japanese diet is rice. Fish is the main source of protein.

- Japanese respect authority and family. They greet each other by bowing.

- March 3rd is the "Doll's Festival" which Japanese girls look forward to all year. This is their chance to display special dolls that may have been in their family for generations.

- The Japanese flag has a red circle, or "rising sun" on a field of white. The Japanese call their country "Nippon," which means "land of the rising sun."

Continent: Africa

Fact File

Size (in relation to other continents): second largest
Area: 11,700,000 square miles
Largest country: Sudan
Smallest country: Seychelles
Highest point: Mt. Kilimanjaro, Tanzania
Lowest point: Lac Assal, Dijibouti
Longest river: Nile, 4,145 miles long
Largest lake (in square miles): Lake Victoria
Deepest lake: Lake Tanganyika
Principal mountain ranges: Atlas Mountains in the far north and Drakensberg in the far south
Largest desert: Sahara Desert - largest in the world
Highest waterfall: Tugela Falls, South Africa - the second highest in the world (after Angel Falls)
Largest island: Madagascar, off the southeastern coast of Africa - fourth largest in the world

Geography

Africa stretches from the Mediterranean Sea and Atlantic Ocean in the north, and runs south past the Tropic of Capricorn. It's bordered on the east by the Indian Ocean, and by the Atlantic Ocean on the west. The equator almost divides Africa in half. Central Africa consists mostly of high plateaus. In eastern and southern Africa these plateaus are covered with rolling grasslands, known as "savannas." A long string of mountain ranges run north-south through eastern Africa, designating the Great Rift Valley. This valley is a series of cracks in the earth's surface. The steep-sided rift valleys have rich farmland and large lakes. Africa's coastlines tend to be either plains or mountains.

Climate and Vegetation

The Sahara Desert, which covers much of the northern half of the continent, experiences a hot, dry, windy climate. Dense, tropical rain forests with hot, rainy weather run across much of central Africa. Southern Africa has the large, dry Kalahari Desert, along with milder, temperate weather along coastal regions. Vegetation varies but includes tall, green, closely growing trees and plants with thick undergrowth in the rain forests, and short grass and thorny bushes in the north.

Natural Resources

Africa's great natural resources include vast mineral reserves like gold, silver, and copper. Gemstone deposits include diamonds, and huge rain forests produce mahogany. Energy resources include oil and coal. There are also immense areas of land almost devoid of resources, like deserts, where life is hard and people are poor.

Population

Africa has more countries than any other continent; most independent only since the 1950's. Traditionally, the Arab world has had great influence on the people in northern Africa, especially in Egypt. People in this region are mostly Muslim, and Arabic is widely spoken. South of the Sahara, natives are black, from many different tribes, and represent more than 1,000 languages/dialects! The country of South Africa has a large (minority) white population.

History

Africa has a tremendously rich and varied history dating back to long before the time of Arab, Muslim, Greek, and Roman influences. In the 19th century, Europeans began to discover Africa's immense natural resources and scrambled to colonize as much of Africa as possible.

By 1894, all but the Sahara region had been divided between seven European nations as some fifty separate kingdoms, states, or countries. These colonial boundaries continually changed with bargains and treaties. Often, enemy tribes found themselves together within a single country, and individual tribes were divided among several countries. Since European boundaries did not match important tribal boundaries, warfare and hardship abounded. Regardless, these boundaries laid the foundation for modern Africa's boundaries and present systems of administration. The 1950's saw the beginning of the end of the colonial period, as one African nation after another became independent.

There are over fifty countries in Africa. List the names and capitals of twenty of them.

Animals

When thinking of Africa, huge herds of animals come to mind including elephants, antelopes and zebras. Africa also supports a huge variety of fish, reptiles, and amphibians. Famous insects include the African dung beetle and the tsetse fly, purveyor of "sleeping sickness." Endangered species include rare mountain gorillas and the Congo peacock, Africa's rarest bird.

Current Events

I Didn't Know That!

- The Sahara Desert is roughly equal to the size of the United States!

- The bushmen of the Kalahari Desert are remarkably adept at finding water. They store this precious resource in empty ostrich eggs.

- The Pyramids at Giza in Egypt are the only of the Seven Wonders of the Ancient World still surviving.

- The largest diamond ever mined was found in South Africa in 1905.

- Long-distance running is popular in Kenya. Their athletes have won medals in the Olympics.

- Kenya is famous for Nairobi National Parks and other wild animal preserves where tourists can go on camera safaris.

- Swahili is the most common language in eastern Africa. Most people know Swahili along with their own ethnic language.

- Botswana's currency, pula, means "rain." Fresh water is hard to come by in many African countries. Collecting water from pumps is a common daily chore.

- A public policy, called "Apartheid," is a rigid system of racial separation that has caused political unrest and bloodshed in South Africa for many years. Although this system was officially abolished, it isn't as easy to abolish it in many people's hearts.

- In Nigeria, among the Yoruba ethnic group, an important guest is greeted by applause. The Yorubas also wink at their children if they want them to leave the room.

- Liberia was established by the colonization of freed American slaves. The capital, Monrovia, was named for President Monroe, who was instrumental in obtaining the land.

Liberia Close-Up

Fact File

Area: 38,250 square miles
Capital: Monrovia
Main Languages: English and about 20 tribal languages
Main Religions: Indigenous beliefs, Christian, Muslim
Currency: Liberian dollar
Government: Republic

Geography

Forest and woodland make up about sixty percent of the land of Liberia. The terrain is mostly flat with rolling coastal plains. The coastline facing the Atlantic Ocean has lagoons, mangrove swamps, and sandbars formed from river deposits. Inland, the grassy plateau provides for limited agriculture.

Climate

The climate of Liberia is warm year round with alternating dry and rainy seasons. It's typically hot and humid. Winter days are usually hot but evenings are cool. Summers are wet and cloudy. Liberia averages 150 inches of rain each year.

Resources

The climate is ideal for tree crops such as mahogany, walnut and Makere. Other resources include iron ore, diamonds, gold, lead, and hydropower.

Current Events

Tanzania Close-Up

Fact File

Area: 364,879 square miles
Capital: Dar es Sallaam (future move planned to Dodoma)
Language: Kiswahili (Swahili), English, Indigenous languages
Religion: Christian, Muslim, Indigenous beliefs
Currency: Tanzanian shilling
Government: Republic

Geography

Tanzania's terrain consists of plains along the coast, a central plateau, and highlands to the north and south. The highest point in Tanzania is Mt. Kilimanjaro. It is bordered by three of the largest lakes in Africa: Lake Victoria (the world's 2nd largest freshwater lake), Lake Tanganyika, (the world's longest freshwater lake and 2nd deepest lake), and Lake Nyasa. The Great Rift Valley cuts through the middle of the country running north and south.

Climate

The climate varies from tropical along the coast to temperate in the highlands.

Resources

Despite being one of the poorest nations in Africa, Tanzania is rich in natural resources. Tin, phosphates, iron ore, coal, diamonds, gemstones, gold and natural gas can be found in this nation. Its industry includes tobacco, sugar, sisal, and diamonds.

Animals

Tanzania has one of the largest wildlife populations in the world. Animals native to this region include; monkey, cheetah, crocodile, flamingo and more. Every April over 2 million wildebeests can be seen migrating across the Serengeti plains toward Kenya along with zebras, antelopes, gazelles and lions. Selous National Park is the largest game park in Africa and is home to more than half of the elephant population of Tanzania. In Zanzibar tourists can swim with the dolphins.

Map-It

On the outline map of Africa, locate the twenty countries from the list you made earlier. Number your list from one to twenty. Place the appropriate number in the correct location.

Color the Sahara Desert with orange stripes.
Color the Kalahari Desert with brown stripes.
Color Lake Victoria blue.
Color Lake Tanganyika green.
Color Lake Chad yellow.
Circle Madagascar purple.
Write in: Cairo, Casablanca, Cape Town.
Write in "M" for Mogadishu in Somalia.
Put green XXX's along the Great Rift Valley.
Put red XXX's along the Atlas Mountains.
Put brown XXX's along the Drakensberg Mountains.
Put a red triangle around Mt. Kilimanjaro.
Label the Red Sea, Indian Ocean, Atlantic Ocean, Gulf of Guinea, and the Mozambique Channel.
Put an "MS" in the Mediterranean Sea.
Color South Africa gold.
Put gold stripes through Egypt.
Draw the Tropic of Capricorn through Africa in brown.
Draw the Tropic of Cancer in orange.
Draw the Equator in black.
Draw the Nile River blue and the Niger River the color of your choice.

Continent: Australia

What's the difference between "Australia" and "Oceania"? In some atlases you'll read about the seven continents, including Australia. In other atlases you'll read about the seven continents that don't list Australia, but do list Oceania. Why is that? Australia is a very large land mass; therefore, historically it's been considered a continent. But recently some geographers have begun to include the islands surrounding Australia as a part of that continent and calling it "Oceania," because so much ocean exists between the bodies of land. When looking at other continents, surrounding islands have been included, so this is not unusual. (The British Isles are considered part of Europe, and the Caribbean Islands are part of North America.) So you'll run across both terms, although Australia is still more commonly referred to as one of the seven continents.

Fact File

Official name: Commonwealth of Australia
Size (in relation to other continents): smallest
Area: 2,966,155 square miles
Capital city: Canberra
Important cities: Brisbane, Perth, Melbourne, and Sidney
Highest point: Mt. Kosciusko in New South Wales
Largest lake: Lake Eyre
Longest river: Murray River
Population: about 18 million
Population density: 6.1 people per square mile - lowest of all populated continents
Government: parliamentary democracy
Currency: Australian dollar
Religion: Protestant and Roman Catholic

Geography

Australia faces the Indian Ocean in the west and south, and the Pacific Ocean in the north and east. The body of water between Queensland and New Guinea is known as the Coral Sea. The Tropic of Capricorn roughly runs through the center of Australia. It shares lines of latitude with the southern half of South America and with South Africa. It shares lines of longitude with Japan and the Philippines.

Climate and Vegetation

When the South Pole is tilted toward the sun, the sun's most powerful rays hit the southern half of the earth, and less sunshine hits the northern half. During that time, people in the Southern Hemisphere are having summer while people in the Northern Hemisphere are having winter. Naturally, when the South Pole is tilted away from the sun, the opposite occurs. So you can see that the two hemispheres always have opposite seasons. Australia is often called "the land down under," because it's under the equator!

Australia is the flattest and driest continent. Only about five percent of the land is more than 2,000 feet above sea level. The three main geographic regions are the Western Plateau, the Central Lowlands, and the Eastern Highlands.

Western Plateau: Covers two-thirds of the country and is mostly flat, with some low mountains, including Ayers Rock. Hot and dry with some vast deserts. Two of the deserts there are the Great Sandy Desert and the Great Victoria Desert. Surrounding the deserts and leading into the Central Lowlands are broad bands of semi-arid grasslands that support a huge livestock industry. This area sees temperatures regularly rising over 100°. Only a few native inhabitants, called "Aborigines," live in the deserts.

Central Lowlands: Run north-south between the Western Plateau and the Eastern Highlands. Consist mostly of dry grassland, but ranchers do have some water from wells.

Eastern Highlands or "Great Dividing Range": Run almost the length of the northeastern coast. Includes the highest peak, the Blue Mountains, the Australian Alps, and other ranges. Just beyond the mountains lie the eastern and southeastern coasts, where most of Australia's large cities are located. The Eastern Highlands and coastal areas receive plenty of rain along with sunshine. The eastern coast has a temperate climate.

Tasmania is an Australian state, but it's a separate, heart-shaped island about 150 miles off the southeast coast of Australia. It's mountainous and experiences heavy rainfall. Tasmania has about 4,000 lakes!

The interior of Australia is often called "the outback" or "the bush." Ayers Rock, Australia's most famous landmark, can be found there. This solitary rock, found in the middle of vast flatlands, is an enormous six miles around and 1,100 feet tall! It's considered a sacred spot to the Aborigines. Inside the rock are caves with Aboriginal paintings and carvings.

Australia is also known for another geographic feature - the Great Barrier Reef, located off the coast of Queensland in eastern Australia. It's the longest reef in the world and a very popular site for scuba diving (both for humans and Great White Sharks!).

History
Before the British came, Australia was inhabited with native people, referred to as Aborigines. Captain James Cook explored the eastern shores in 1770, and claimed Australia as a British possession. The British established six colonies in Australia from 1788 to 1859. Many of the new immigrants were convicts from the overflowing jails and poorhouses in England. Gold was discovered in the 1850's, and soon many free settlers arrived. When Australia became independent in 1901, the colonies became states. Sadly, the Aborigine population was devastated by European diseases and hostilities. In the early 1960's, official attitudes towards them began to change and full rights of citizenship were extended to remaining Aborigines.

States and Territories
Six states and their capitals in order of size:

STATE	CAPITAL
New South Wales	Sydney
Victoria	Melbourne
Queensland	Brisbane
Western Australia	Perth
South Australia	Adelaide
Tasmania	Hobart

Two Territories:
- Northern Territory: Darwin
- Australian Capital Territory: Canberra

Animals

Australia is home to a great assortment of odd animals. For example:

Dingoes: wild dogs that run in packs in the outback. Considered pests because they attack livestock, dingoes are hunted. The longest fence in the world - 62,000 miles - was erected to keep dingoes away from livestock!

Marsupials: like kangaroos and koala bears. Some kinds of kangaroos can weigh up to 185 pounds, jump twenty-eight feet in a single bound, and run fifty miles-per-hour.

Birds: like emus (big birds that can't fly), and kookaburras (birds with a loud cry that sounds like wild laughter), and eagles, parakeets, and cockatoos.

Platypus: the animal that has evolutionists stumped!

Tasmanian Devils: live in Tasmania and are as mean as they look. Their powerful jaws and sharp teeth can chew through bone.

Crocodiles, echidna, and poisonous snakes are common in Australia.

Current Events

I Didn't Know That!

- Lake Eyre is one of the world's strangest lakes. It lies in central Australia and fills with water only three or four times a century!

- Termites can build hills six feet high or higher. These are called magnetic termite hills because they're always built to face north-south!

- Boomerangs were developed by the Aborigines. The returning type of boomerangs were only used in sporting games and for killing birds. The larger hunting boomerangs did not return.

- The Sydney Opera House in New South Wales is a very unusual looking structure. Some people describe it as wings, some as sails, and some as seashells.

- In the Great Barrier Reef, which stretches 1,250 miles along the east coast, you can find sea cucumbers, blue and red starfish, and giant clams weighing more than 150 pounds each!

- Ayers Rock looks red in the afternoon and evening because of the sun hitting the layer of rusty red dust on its surface.

- Perth, the largest city in western Australia, has a tower of minerals in front of its Town Hall. Many minerals and gems are mined in this area. Australia is a huge exporter of minerals.

- Australia has about nine times as many sheep as people! Wool and lamb are two of its biggest exports. In fact, Australia is the world's leading producer of wool. Sheep and cattle stations can be unbelievably big.

- People can go snow skiing in the Victorian Alps, part of the Great Dividing Range.

- Alice Springs, often called the "Capital of the Center," is located just 265 miles from Ayers Rock. It grew from a tiny settlement into an important town, both for Aborigines and whites.

- Although Australians speak "English," they've certainly made it their own language! Englishmen and Americans visiting might be perplexed by words like:

bikkies:	biscuits (cookies)
chook:	chicken
earbash:	nonstop talking
icy-pole:	popsicle
lolly water:	soft drink
yahoo:	noisy person
barbie:	barbeque

- Aborigine words that have been incorporated in Australian English include: kangaroo, dingo, and billabong (a dry pond or river that fills with water only during heavy rains.)

- Over eighty-five percent of Aussies live in cities or towns. Other people live in rural areas, small farm settlements, or on isolated cattle and sheep stations. The Flying Doctor Service provides health care to folks in the Outback. It was founded by a missionary/minister in 1928.

- Children in remote areas receive their education in a unique form of homeschooling: they use two-way radios to talk with their teachers through the "School of the Air."

- Water sports are very popular, as much of the population live in coastal areas. Cricket, rugby, soccer, and golf are well loved, too. Cricket is the most popular summer team sport.

- Eighteen million people live in all of Australia - roughly the same amount that live in the state of New York!

Map-It

On your outline map of Australia, complete the following:

Draw the boundaries of the states and territories. Label each one. (Hint: the Australian Capital Territory is a tiny spot inside New South Wales, similar to Washington, D.C.)

Color the Great Sandy Desert and Gibson Desert with orange stripes.
Color the Great Victoria Desert with brown stripes.
Color Lake Eyre blue.
Draw a red triangle around Ayers Rock.

Put an "AS" by Alice Springs.
Color Tasmania yellow.
Write in: Sydney, Melbourne, Canberra, Perth, and Darwin.
Put large brown XXX's along the Great Dividing Range (it goes for a LONG way).
Put blue dashes along the Great Barrier Reef.
Label the Coral Sea, Indian Ocean, and Pacific Ocean.
Color the Cape York Peninsula silver.
Put small blue xxx's around the Gulf of Carpentaria.
Draw the Tropic of Capricorn through Australia in brown.
Draw the Murray-Darling River in blue (it ends in Adelaide).

Surrounding Areas that Make Up Oceania

Oceania is comprised of Australia, New Zealand, Papua New Guinea and approximately 25,000 other islands in the South Pacific, many of which are uninhabited. Some of the island groups are the Northern Marianas, Caroline Islands, Palau, Fiji, Solomon Islands, Polynesia, Cook Islands, and American Samoa.

Papua New Guinea Close-Up

This country is on the island of New Guinea, almost directly north of Australia. At 309,000 miles, it's second in size only to Greenland (excluding Australia, because Australia is considered a continent, not an island). New Guinea has some of the most rugged and remote areas in the world. The right, or eastern half is an independent country called "Papua New Guinea," which became independent from Australia in 1977. Over seven hundred languages are spoken there! Its capital is Port Moresby, and major products include coffee and timber. Copper is also mined there. The left, or southern half of the island is called Papua (formerly Irian Jaya) and is considered to be a part of Indonesia, not Oceania.

New Zealand Close-Up

This country is actually two large islands and a number of smaller islands located southeast of Australia. The two largest lands, North Island and South Island, are separated by the Cook Strait. Parts of North Island are volcanically active.

The economy is based on agriculture, and they export a tremendous amount of food. They're known for lamb and kiwi fruit.

New Zealand was settled by the British. The capital is Wellington. Their native inhabitants are called "Maoris," and the British extended full citizenship to them in the early 1800's. Race relations have been much better than those experienced in Australia. English is spoken and they use a New Zealand dollar. This country is known for its natural beauty.

New Zealand has a huge variety of wildlife, including the kiwi bird and the world's largest parrot.

Rugby and soccer are the games of choice in New Zealand.

Continent: Antarctica

Fact File

Size (in relation to other continents): fifth largest

Area: about 5,400,000 square miles

Highest point: Vinson Massif - 16,860 feet

Biggest glaciers: Lambert (the world's longest), Amundsen, and
  Beardmore

Snowfall: about twenty-five inches a year at the coast; only two
  inches a year on the plateau

Lowest temperature: -128.5 °F at Vostok Research Base in 1983

Volcano: Mt. Erebus, on the bottom tip of the Ross Ice Shelf

Number of countries: none, although several countries lay claim to parts of the continent

Geography

Antarctica is larger than either Europe or Australia. It's a landmass buried beneath a massive ice cap. Only a few mountains and rocks show above the ice.

Climate and Vegetation

The forbidding, icy landscape is known as a "hostile" environment where winds can blow up to 200 miles per hour! Antarctica is a very cold desert. The South Pole probably gets less than one inch of precipitation a year - compared to the Sahara Desert which averages about eight inches annually. Although a small number of plants, insects, and animals live there, no humans are native to Antarctica. Whiteouts are a weather condition that happen when harsh winds fill the air with snow, causing nearly a complete lack of visibility.

History

Although Antarctica wasn't officially sighted until the 1800's, Ancient Greeks actually gave it its name. They hadn't seen it, but they believed there had to be a southern land mass to "balance" the continents in the northern hemisphere. A well known constellation in the northern sky was Arktos, the bear. So the Greeks called this unseen southern landmass Antarktikos, meaning "opposite the bear."

In 1911, a Norwegian named Roald Amundsen led the first expedition to the South Pole. He beat a British expedition, led by Scott, by five weeks. (Scott and his men all died on the return journey home.) In 1929, Commander Byrd of the U.S. Navy flew over the South Pole for the first time. And in 1957-58, a British expedition made the first overland crossing of the continent.

The only "inhabitants" in Antarctica are visiting researchers and tourists. About 4,000 scientists might be living there at any one time. More tourists are beginning to come though, and that's causing some problems. Some are looking for souvenirs; frighten the animals, and leave behind trash or graffiti.

Some scientists believe that there may be a great deal of oil buried deep below Antarctica's cold waters. Might people be able to drill for oil there? If so, to whom would it belong? How can the tourism industry be handled in a such a way so as not to cause harm? These are important questions that are currently being asked.

Current Events

The Antarctic Treaty, signed by twelve countries in 1961 mandated that Antarctica would be used only for peaceful purposes. In 1991 the same nations agreed to a moratorium on mining to last for fifty years. Some of the nations wanted to make Antarctica the first world park, but other nations didn't want to give up the potential for its wealth or location for monetary and military purposes.

I Didn't Know That!

- Antarctica holds seventy percent of the world's entire supply of fresh water in its ice and snow.

- The Antarctic Regions support an abundance of whales and seals. Many of the sea animals feed on "krill," small shrimp-like sea creatures that live here in the billions. At night they glow a peculiar greenish-blue!

- Seven different types of penguins make their home here, including emperor penguins.

- Antarctica has only two flowering species of plants.

- Although many places have been discovered by accident, this seldom happens in Antarctica! One would have to plan and prepare carefully to make a discovery here!

- The Antarctic Treaty, signed by twelve countries back in 1961, allowed for cooperation between countries and their scientists and delayed settlement claims until 1991. It also mandated that Antarctica would be used for peaceful purposes only.

Map-It

Complete the following on your outline map of Antarctica:

Put brown XXX's along the Transantarctica Mountains (the whole mountain range, including individual mountains, running from the Antarctic Peninsula down to Victoria Land)

Color the Ross Ice Shelf yellow (where the McMurdo Station, a large U.S. Research Base, is located).

Color the Antarctic Peninsula light green.

Identify: Pacific Ocean, Indian Ocean, Atlantic Ocean.

Circle the Lambert Glacier.

Put a + by the Magnetic South Pole.

For Additional Information:

One Internet address that leads to other neat spots:
www.loc.gov/rr/international/frd/antarctica/education.htm

CONQUERING THE CONTINENTS: HIGH SCHOOL

CHAPTER 14

PURE GEOGRAPHY FOR HIGH SCHOOL

More than half of American schools do not teach geography or even require credit in geography for graduation. Yet our world is becoming more and more globally connected. In order for our students to fare well in the competitive business community it's imperative they have a solid foundation of geography.

This section is designed to provide solid basis for covering geography at the high school level. Completing these activities, as well as reading a variety of related non-fiction books, warrents at least one semester of credit. Remember to incorporate the five themes of geography and to provide abundant map activities.

At this level, the student should be filling out a blank map with finer details than is required of a middle school student. He should be able to understand how the geography of an area affects its culture, read thematic maps, and research information about any nation on earth. Keep good school atlases handy as well as good books on cultures of the world. If you're not using a geography textbook, be sure to obtain books from the library to use.

We've included reproducible map activity sheets and challenge questions for student use. They should research information needed using an almanac, atlas, encyclopedia, text book and library books. Answers to challenge questions are in Appendix B. Be asssured that if this study is fully completed, your students will have a solid geographic foundation from which to build.

Use your local and school library videos to help students to implant visual images of places around the world. National Geographic makes excellent videos available at most libraries. Watch for any other videos that may suit your geography needs and use them freely.

To order large-scale maps see the Continent Map Set in Resources in the back of this book.

Important note:

The very detailed, high school level, mapping assignments on the next pages may not fit well on a single 8.5" x 11" continent map from this book. Make several copies of each continent and have your student label one with rivers, one with place names, and another with physical features, etc. However, many students appreciate using large-scale outline maps to keep all information on one map.

Teachers, before you begin:

A step-by-step plan is listed below for your convenience.
1. Read pages 151-152, 199-200.
2. Ensure student has basic proficiency in use of atlases, almanacs and other reference materials.
3. Have an assortment of up-to-date atlases and other refer ence books available.
4. Read pages 55-60 about outline maps.
5. Copy pages 153-155, 201-218, and the seven continent outline maps in chapter fifteen. Assemble into a three-ring notebook.
6. Adapt suggestions from chapter thirteen, if desired.

Assign students to:

1. Review:
   • Geography Definitions Flashcards (chapter seventeen)
   • Stuff to Know by Heart (chapter seventeen)
   • Continent Fact Files (chapter thirteen)
2. Read chapter two before beginning outline activities.
3. Do "Almanac Trek" on page 240.
4. Complete selected (not all) Continental Essays on page 218 for each continent, either before or after performing outline map activity.
5. Complete all outline activities and Challenge Questions.
6. Work neatly and keep all papers in their binder.

Tips for labeling paper maps:

Use paper outline maps for the following activities.
• Establish a consistent color-code and format beginning with the first map assignment.
• Using red ink or underlining capitals is less cumbersome than using a star.
• Fine-tipped Stabilo Sensor #189 markers or Liquid Expresso Extra Fine Line Pen by Sanford are both excellent to use in label-ing on paper maps. They provide a fine tip, do not bleed, and are firm enough not to flatten.
• Remember, your student won't find everything he needs in any one atlas!
• Important Notice: spellings of place names vary greatly.

Your journey through the seven continents is about to begin.
Bon Voyage!

North America Outline Activity

1. Label each country and its capital city:

Bahamas	Dominican Republic	Mexico
Belize	El Salvador	Nicaragua
Canada	Haiti	Panama
Costa Rica	Honduras	Guatemala
Cuba	Jamaica	United States

2. Label the Canadian Provinces and Territories:

British Columbia	Quebec	Yukon Territory
Alberta	Newfoundland	Northwest Territories
Saskatchewan	New Brunswick	Nunavut Territory
Manitoba	Nova Scotia	
Ontario	Prince Edward Island	

3. Draw and label the following physical features:

Aleutian Islands	Panama Canal	Yucatan Peninsula
Baja California	Ellesmere Island	Vancouver Island
Cape Hatteras	Victoria Island	Baffin Island
Cape Farvel		

4. Establish and mark:

Lines of Latitude: 10° N, 20° N, 30° N, 40° N, 50° N, 60° N, 70° N, 80° N

Lines of Longitude: 20° W, 30° W, 40° W, 50° W, 60° W, 70° W, 80° W, 90° W, 100° W, 110° W, 120° W, 130° W, 140° W, 150° W, 160° W, 170° W, 180°

The Tropic of Cancer   The Arctic Circle

5. Draw and label rivers in blue:

Mississippi River	Missouri River	Red River
Rio Grande River	Colorado River	Mackenzie River
Columbia River	Yukon River	Nelson River
Saskatchewan River	St. Lawrence Seaway	Arkansas River
Peace River		

6. Draw and label bodies of water:

Atlantic Ocean	Pacific Ocean	Arctic Ocean
Bering Sea	Beaufort Sea	Gulf of Mexico
Caribbean Sea	Golfo de Panama	Gulf of California
Gulf of St. Lawrence	Baffin Bay	Hudson Bay
Lago de Nicaragua	Prudhoe Bay	Gulf of Campeche
Lake Superior	Lake Michigan	Lake Huron
Lake Erie	Lake Ontario	Great Salt Lake
Great Slave Lake	Great Bear Lake	Lake Winnipeg
Lake Athabasca	Foxe Basin	

6. Draw mountains with brown triangles and label:

      Mt. McKinley   Mt. Whitney   Mt. Logan
      Pico de Orizaba

7. Draw and label landforms and regions:

Rocky Mountains	Brooks Range	Alaska Range
Coast Mountains	Sierra Madre Oriental	Cascade Range
Coast Range	Appalachian Mountains	
Sierra Nevada	Sierra Madre Occidental	

8. Label the following cities:

Anchorage	Whitehorse	Edmonton
Vancouver	Montreal	New York
Miami	Houston	Denver
Chicago	Los Angeles	Your home town

Challenge: How Much Do You Know About North America?

1. What direction would you be traveling if you were on a ship passing through the Panama Canal from the Atlantic Ocean to the Pacific ocean?
2. When a ship traveling from New York to San Francisco passes through the Panama Canal instead of going around the southern tip of South America, how many miles are saved?
3. What's the largest inland body of water in Central America?
4. What's the one place in North America where you can see both the Pacific and Atlantic Oceans?
5. What's the oldest capital in the Americas?
6. What's the name for the land area that extends off southeastern Mexico, separating the Gulf of Mexico from the Caribbean Sea?
7. What's the oldest city in the USA to be founded by Europeans?
8. What's the largest island in North America?
9. What's the name given to the series of five large, freshwater lakes along the boundary between the United States and Canada?
10. Name the five Great Lakes.
11. Which of the Great Lakes is entirely within the borders of the United States?
12. Which waterway connects the ports on the Great Lakes with the Atlantic Ocean?
13. What country exports the largest percentage of the world's wood pulp and lumber?
14. What's the name for the vast, fertile region in central USA and Canada, a large part of which is drained by the Mississippi River and its tributaries?
15. What's the predominate landform running from Alaska, along the western United States, through Mexico and Central America?

South America Outline Activity

1. Label each country and its capital city:

Argentina	Brazil	Bolivia
Chile	Colombia	Ecuador
French Guiana	Guyana	Paraguay
Peru	Suriname	Uruguay
Venezuela		

2. Draw and label the following physical features:

Falkland Islands	Cape Horn	Galapagos Islands
Angel Falls	Tierra del Fuego	Atacama Desert
South Georgia		South Sandwich Trench

3. Establish and mark:

Lines of Latitude: 10° N , 10° S, 20° S, 30° S, 40° S, 50° S, 60° S

Lines of Longitude: 30° W, 40° W, 50° W, 60° W, 70° W, 80° W, 90° W

The Equator   Tropic of Capricorn

4. Draw and label rivers in blue:

Amazon River	Orinoco River	Tocanitins River
Paraquay River	Uruguay River	Rio Negro
Colorado River	Parana River	Madeira River
Rio de la Plata		Sao Francisco River

5. Draw and label bodies of water:

Atlantic Ocean	Pacific Ocean	Drake Passage
Strait of Magellan	Lake Titicaca	Caribbean Sea
Lake Maracaibo	Gulf of Venezuela	Others??

6. Draw mountains with brown triangles and label:

Mt. Aconcagua	Andes Mountains	Others??

7. On a separate map, color-code and label the following:

Mato Grosso Plateau	Patgonia	Guiana Highlands
Brazilian Highlands	Altiplano	Pampas
Llanos	Amazon Basin	Gran Chaco
Atacama Desert		

8. Label the following cities: Recife, Brazil   Rio de Janeiro, Brazil
                                                                 Stanley, Falkland Islands

Challenge: How Much Do You Know About South America?

1. What's the name of the river basin in northern Brazil that contains one-fifth of the world's fresh water and is home to the largest rain forest in the world?
2. What's the highest point in South America?
3. What sacred city, build by the Incas, lies high in the Peruvian Andes?
4. How many cubic feet of water flow into the Atlantic Ocean from the Amazon River each second?
5. What city in South America has the largest population?
6. What are the two most predominate climate zones in South America?
7. What geographic feature forms a natural boundary between Chile and Argentina?
8. What's the regional name given to the area covered with shrub, sparse grass, and wasteland in southern Argentina?
9. Approximately what percentage of world coffee production comes from South America?
10. Which South American country has the highest Gross Domestic Product (GDP)?
11. What three cities have the highest population density in South America?
12. What's the name of highest dam in South America? Where is it located and how high is it?
13. What's the name and location of the largest hydroelectric plant in the world?
14. What runner from Ecuador won the 20,000 meter walk event in the 1996 Summer Olympics?
15. What country won the gold medal in the 1996 Summer Olympics for women's beach volleyball?
16. What South American country has two capitals?
17. Based on the geography and location of Chile, what would you expect to be a major industry there?
18. What three natural disasters, prevalent along eastern South America, are associated with tectonic activity in the area?
19. Describe the general summer weather in the area around Santiago, Chile.
20. What's the predominate climate type in Peru, west of the Andes mountains?
21. What are the two major vegetation environments in South America?
22. What's the average population density in the Amazon River Basin?
23. What South American city lies due south of Chicago, Illinois?
24. Where in South America would you find places where no rainfall has ever been recorded?
25. What is the name for the flat, grassy plains found in the temperate regions of southern South America, east of the Andes?
26. What island, located 2,300 miles (3,700 km) west of Chile, is famous for its strange monuments - more than 600 stone faces scattered over the island, the earliest dating back more than 1,500 years?

Europe Outline Activity

1. Label each country and its capital city:

Albania	Greece	Poland
Andorra	Hungary	Portugal
Austria	Iceland	Romania
Belarus	Ireland	San Marino
Belgium	Italy	Slovakia
Bulgaria	Latvia	Slovenia
Bosnia & Herzegovina	Liechtenstein	Spain
Croatia	Lithuania	Sweden
Czech Republic	Luxembourg	Switzerland
Denmark	Macedonia	Ukraine
Estonia	Malta	United Kingdom
Finland	Moldova	Vatican City
France	Netherlands	Yugoslavia
Germany	Norway	

2. Draw and label the following physical features:

Sicily	Sardinia	Corsica
Islas Baleares	Malta	Crete
Cyprus	Faroe Islands	Shetland Islands
Hebrides	Rhodes	Balkan Peninsula
Mallorca	Eivissa	Cape Finisterre
Mizen Head	Lofoten Islands	Crimean Peninsula
Bornholm	Menorca	Iberian Peninsula
Dardanelles	Bosporus	

3. Establish and mark:

Lines of Latitude: 40° N, 50° N, 60° N, 70° N

Lines of Longitude: 20° W, 10° W, 0°, 10° E, 20° E, 30° E, 40° E,

Arctic Circle

4. Draw and label rivers in blue:

Rhine River (or Rhein)	Neman River	Danube River
Dnieper River	Thames River	Guadalquivir River
Ebro River	Tagus River	Po River
Seine River	Elbe River	Marne River
Oder River	Tiber River	Loire River
Rhone River	Saone River	Wisla River

5. Draw and label bodies of water with blue diagonal lines:

Atlantic Ocean	North Sea	Mediterranean Sea
Norwegian Sea	Baltic Sea	Tyrrhenian Sea
Ionian Sea	Aegean Sea	Adriatic Sea
Black Sea	Irish Sea	Sea of Marmara
Gulf of Bothnia	Bay of Biscay	English Channel
Strait of Gibraltar	Gulf of Lions	Gulf of Finland
White Sea (Beloe)	Moray Firth	Firth of Forth
St. George's Channel	Strait of Dover	Ligurian Sea

6. Draw mountains with brown triangles and label:

Mt. Mulhacen	Mt. Etna	Mt. Olympus
Mt. Blanc	Mt. Vesuvius	Mt. Kebnekaise
Mt. Grossglockner	Pyrenees	Appenines (Appennino)
Alps	Carpathian	Transylvanian
Iberian	Dinaric	Pindus
Sudetes	Ore	Massif Central
Cantabrian		

7. On a separate map, color-code and label the following:

Black Forest	Lapland	Great Hungarian Plain
Bohemian Forest		Great Northern European Plain

8. Label the following cities:

Edinburgh	Glasgow	Belfast
Birmingham	Marseille	Lyon
Toulouse	Barcelona	Bilbao
Valladolid	Seville	Malaga
Zaragoza	Naples	Palermo
Nice	Milan	Venice
Zurich	Hamburg	Frankfurt
Dresden	Cologne	Stuttgart
Gdansk	Odesa	Istanbul

Challenge: How Much Do You Know About Europe?

1. What are four official languages recognized in Switzerland?
2. What independent countries were once part of Yugoslavia?
3. What's the nickname for the tunnel that connects England and France under the English Channel?
4. How many national capitals are located on the Danube River?
5. What independent countries were once part of the Union of Soviet Socialist Republics (USSR)?
6. Why is Ukraine called the "Bread Basket of Europe"?
7. What mountain ranges divide the colder, wetter part of northern Europe from the sunnier Southern part?
8. What's the name of the climate found in southern Europe characterized by long, dry summers and short, rainy winters?
9. What's the predominant religion of Europe?
10. What's the name and size of the smallest independent country in Europe?
11. What natural resource, found in the North Sea off Scotland, has brought considerable wealth to the United Kingdom?
12. What city in Italy was covered with twenty feet of volcanic ash in 79 A.D. when Mt. Vesuvius erupted?

Asia Outline Activity

1. Label each country and its capital city:

Afghanistan	Jordan	Qatar
Armenia	Kazakstan	Russia
Azerbaijan	Kuwait	Saudi Arabia
Bangladesh	Kygyzstan	South Korea
Bhutan	Laos	Sri Lanka
Brunei	Lebanon	Syria
Cambodia	Malaysia	Turkey
China	Maldives	Taiwan
Cyprus	Mongolia	Tajikistan
Georgia	Myanmar	Thailand
India	Nepal	Turkmenistan
Indonesia	North Korea	United Arab Emirates
Iran	Oman	Uzbekistan
Iraq	Pakistan	Vietnam
Israel	Papua	Yemen
Japan	Philippines	

2. Draw and label the following physical features:

    Southwest Asia: Arabian Peninsula, Suez Canal, Socotra

    North/Central Asia: Kamchatka Peninsula, Sakhalin, Kurile Islands,
    Novaya Zemlya, Severnaya Zemlya,
    Taymyr Peninsula, Kola Peninsula

    South Asia: Maldives

    Southeast Asia: Andaman Islands, Nicobar Islands, Java,
    Philippine Trench, Java Trench, Borneo,
    Sumatra, Indochina, New Guinea

    East Asia: Hainan, Manchuria

3. Establish and mark:
    Lines of Latitude: 10° S, 0° , 10° N, 20° N, 30° N, 40° N, 50° N, 60° N, 70° N,
    80° N, 90° N

    Lines of Longitude: 30° E, 40° E, 50° E, 60° E, 70° E, 80° E, 90° E, 100°E, 110° E, 120°E,
    130° E, 140° E, 150° E, 160° E, 170° E, 180° , 170° W

    Arctic Circle   Equator   Tropic of Cancer

4. **Draw and label rivers in blue:**

Southwest Asia:	Tigris, Euphrates
North/Central Asia:	Volga, Ob, Don, Amu Darya
South Asia:	Ganges, Indus, Godavari, Brahmaputra
Southeast Asia:	Mekong
East Asia:	Yangtze, Huang, Amur

5. **Draw and label bodies of water with blue diagonal lines:**

Southwest Asia: Mediterranean Sea, Persian Gulf, Red Sea, Gulf of Aqaba, Strait of Hormuz, Gulf of Suez, Gulf of Oman, Gulf of Aden, Arabian Sea Aral Sea (formerly Lake Aral)

North/Central Asia: Sea of Okhotsk, Lake Baikal, Lake Balkhash, Laptev Sea, Black Sea, Barents Sea, Bering Sea, Chukchi Sea, Kara Sea, Caspian Sea

South Asia: Indian Ocean, Bay of Bengal

Southeast Asia: Pacific Ocean, South China Sea, Celebes Sea, Philippine Sea, Coral Sea, Java Sea, Sulu Sea Gulf of Tonkin, Strait of Malacca, Timor Sea Gulf of Thailand, Andaman Sea, Arafuru Sea

East Asia: Sea of Japan, Taiwan Strait, Yellow Sea, Korea Strait

6. **Draw mountains with brown triangles and label:**

Southwest Asia: Mt. Ararat, Zagros

North/Central Asia: Ural, Stanovoy Range, Altai, Yablonovy, Sikhote-Alin, Sayan, Caucasus, Verkhoyansk

East Asia: Mt. Fuji, Greater Khingan Range, Mt. Everest, Altun Shan, Himalayas, Qin Ling, Kunlun

7. On a separate map, color-code and label the following:

    Southwest Asia: Plateau of Iran

    North/Central Asia: Siberia, Caspian Depression, Gobi Desert, Ust-Urt Plateau

    South Asia: Great Indian Desert, Eastern Ghats, Deccan Plateau, Western Ghats

    East Asia: Plateau of Tibet, Tarim Basin, Szechwan Basin, Yunnan Plateau, North China Plain

8. Label the following cities:

    Southwest Asia: Jiddah

    North/Central Asia: Murmansk, Rostov-na-Donu, Volgograd, Niznij Novgorod, Perm', Groznyj, Novosibirsk Ekaterinburg, Omsk, Irkutsk, St. Petersburg

    South Asia: Karachi, Bombay, Bangalore, Madras, Kolkata (formerly Calcutta), Lahore

    Southeast Asia: Da Nang, Ho Chi Minh City

    East Asia: Shanghai, Pusan, Osaka, Hiroshima, Sapporo

Challenge: How Much Do You Know About Asia?

1. What physical structure was built in China to defend against invasions by the Huns?
2. Which two countries are linked by the Khyber Pass?
3. Name the Persian Gulf country that's actually a federation of seven Arab sheikdoms.
4. What's the desert area in the southern third of Saudi Arabia called?
5. What island volcanic eruption in 1883 has been called the loudest natural explosion in history?
6. At their closest point, how far apart are the Asian and North American continents?
7. What's the term used to identify the crescent-shaped area of fertile land running from Egypt's Nile Valley, along the eastern shore of the Mediterranean Sea, then through Mesopotamia (the land between the Tigris and Euphrates Rivers) to the Persian Gulf?
8. What region is known as the "Roof of the World"?
9. How long is the Trans-Siberian Railroad, and what two cities mark its beginning and end?
10. Which Asian country has the highest population density?
11. What percent of the world's population lives in Asia?
12. What's the highest point above sea level on Asia?
13. Asia contains the highest and lowest points on the earth's surface. Name them.
14. Asia contains the largest inland body of water. Name it.
15. Name the eight major world religions that originated in Asia.
16. What metropolitan area in Asia has the largest population?
17. Name the desert regions in Arabia and China that are uninhabited.
18. What's the name of the storm system that dumps much needed rain along the southeast and Indian Ocean coastal areas during the summer?
19. What percent of the population in China, India, and Indonesia are engaged in farming?
20. What's the most commonly grown crop in Asia?
21. What type of vegetation is most prevalent in the arctic and subarctic regions of Siberia?
22. What valuable hardwood is rapidly being cut in the tropical rain forests of Malaysia, the Philippines, Indonesia and Indochina?
23. What's the name given to the Chinese sailing ship that transports people and goods?

Africa Outline Activity

1. Label each country and its capital city. (Several countries have two capitals.)

Algeria	Ethiopia	Rwanda
Angola	Gabon	Sao Tome & Principe
Benin	Ghana	Senegal
Botswana	Guinea	Seychelles
Burkina Faso	Guinea-Bissau	Sierra Leone
Burundi	Kenya	Somalia
Cameroon	Lesotho	South Africa
Cape Verde	Liberia	Sudan
Central African Republic	Libya	Swaziland
Chad	Madagascar	Tanzania
Cote D'Ivoire	Malawi	The Gambia
Congo	Mali	Togo
*Dem. Republic of the Congo	Mauritania	Tunisia
Djibouti	Morocco	Uganda
Egypt	Mozambique	Western Sahara
Equatorial Guinea	Namibia	Zambia
Eritrea	Niger	Zimbabwe
	Nigeria	

*AKA Zaire

2. Draw and label the following physical features:

Rift Valley	Suez Canal	Cape of Good Hope
Comoros Islands	Seychelles	Cape Gwardafuy
Canary Islands (Islas Canarias)	Madeira Islands	Victoria Falls
Zanzibar Island		

3. Establish and mark:

Lines of Latitude: 30° S, 20° S, 10° S, 10° N, 20° N, 30° N, 40° N

Lines of Longitude: 20° W, 10° W, 10° E, 20° E, 30° E, 40° E, 50° E

Equator   Tropic of Cancer   Tropic of Capricorn

4. Draw and label rivers in blue:

West Africa: Senegal, Gambia, Niger, Volta, Benue
East Africa: White Nile, Blue Nile, Nile, Shabeelle, Pangani
Central Africa: Cuanza, Cuado, Zambezi, Limpopo, Zaire (Congo),
                  Kwango, Ubangi, Lomami, Lulalba, Kasai
Southern Africa: Okavango, Vaal, Limpopo, Orange

5. Draw and label bodies of water:

   Northern Africa: Atlantic Ocean, Gulf of Guines, Lake Volta, Lake Chad, Mediterranean Sea, Red Sea, Gulf of Aden, Lake Nasser, Indian Ocean

   Central/Southern Africa: Lake Bangweulu, Lake Victoria, Lake Kariba, Lake Tanganyika, Lake Nyasa (Malawi), Lake Kivu, Lake Albert, Lake Xau, Mozambique Channel,

6. Draw mountains with brown triangles and label:

   Northern Africa: Ahaggar, Tibesti, Atlas, Adamaoua, Air

   Central Africa: Mt. Kenya, Mt. Kilamanjaro (Kilimanjaro)

7. On a separate map, color-code and label the following:

   Northern Africa: Sahara Desert, Libyan Desert, Eastern Desert, Ethiopian Plateau

   Central Africa: Congo Basin

   Southern Africa: Kalahari Desert, Namib Desert, Cape Province, Drakensberg Escarpment, Lesotho, Swaziland

8. Label the following cities:

   West Africa: Bouake, Kumasi, Tema, Ibadan, Ogbomosho, Kano, Benin

   East Africa: Omdurman, Port Sudan, Berbera, Hargeysa, Dodoma, Mandera, Mombasa

   Central Africa: Tambura, Lobito, Pointe Noire, Bulawayo, Beira, Quelimane, Zomba, Kitwe, Lubumbashi, Kisangani

   Southern Africa: Port Elizabeth, Durban

Challenge: How Much Do You Know About Africa?

1. What's the vast plain of grassland, acacia bushes, forest and rocky outcrops located in northern Tanzania, east of Lake Victoria and west of Kilimanjaro called?
2. What's the largest inland delta in the world and where is it located?
3. What's unusual about the province of Cabinda?
4. What discovery in 1867 along the banks of the Orange River had a significant impact on the course of history for South Africa?
5. What African nation was founded by free American slaves in 1847?
6. What's the semi-arid vegetative region that separates the central African tropical rain forests and savanna from the Sahara Desert?
7. Which African country has the richest and most varied deposits of minerals in the world?
8. What's the largest lake in Africa?
9. What's the highest point above sea level in Africa?
10. What city in Africa has the largest population?
11. What percentage of the world's population lives in Africa?
12. Why can't most of the great rivers in Africa be used for transportation from the continent's coast to the interior?
13. What's the predominate climate region in Africa?
14. What percent of Africa is covered by desert?
15. Name three things that have changed parts of the Sahel from marginal land into barren wasteland.
16. Where are most of the commercial farms of Africa located?
17. What percent of Africans work in agriculture?
18. Which continent(s) are not self-sufficient for food?
19. What percent of Africa's land is suitable for grazing?
20. What is the most populous independent country in Africa?
21. What's the name for the chain of valleys in east Africa that runs from the Red Sea to Mozambique?
22. What natural feature is created in the desert when underground water comes to the surface?
23. What is the name and elevation of the highest point on the continent of Africa.
24. What is the traditional mode of transportation in the Sahara Desert?
25. What country in Africa has the highest per capita annual income?
26. Near which geographical feature are the highest concentration of inhabitants found?
27. What city in Africa has the highest mean annual temperature?
28. What are the two least urbanized countries in Africa?

Australia - Oceania Outline Activity

Use both the Australia and Pacific Rim outline maps to complete this activity.

1. Label each country or island group and its capital city. Indicate if the island is controlled by a particular country:

American Samoa	New Zealand	Wallis & Futuna
Australia	Nile	Western Samoa
Cook Islands	Northern Mariana Islands	Hawaiian Islands
Federated States of Micronesia	Palau	Midway Island
Fiji	Papua New Guinea	Wake Island
French Polynesia	Pitcairn	Guam
Kiribati	Solomon Islands	Easter Island
Marshall Islands	Tokelau	Japan
Nauru	Tonga	Philippines
New Caledonia	Vanuatu	Indonesia

2. Label the following continents if shown on your map:

North America   Asia   South America

3. Draw and label the following physical features:

Cape York Peninsula	Sandy Cape
Eyre Peninsula	Kangaroo Island
International Date Line	Kermadec Tonga Trench
Mariana Trench	Bougainville Trench
Archipelago of the Recherche	

4. Establish and mark:

Lines of Latitude: 40° S, 30° S, 20° S, 10° S, 10° N, 20° N, 30° N

Lines of Longitude: 110° E, 120° E, 130° E, 140° E, 150° E, 160° E, 170° E, 180°
                     170° W, 160° W, 150° W, 140° W, 130° W, 120° W

Equator   Tropic of Cancer   Tropic of Capricorn

5. Draw and label rivers in blue:

Darling River	Murray River	Lachian River
Daly River	Victoria River	Fitzroy River

6. Draw and label bodies of water:

Indian Ocean	Pacific Ocean	Timor Sea
Arafura Sea	Coral Sea	Tasman Sea
Shark Bay	Torres Strait	Halifax Bay
Gulf of Carpenteria	Jervis Bay	Bass Strait
Encounter Bay	Spencer Gulf	Geographic Bay
Great Australian Bight	Joseph Bonaparte Gulf	Bay of Plenty
Philippine Sea	Cook Strait	Foveaux Strait

7. Draw mountains with brown triangles and label:

Great Dividing Range   Mt. Bartle Frere
King Leopold Range   Mt. Cook
Hamersley Range   Mt. Kosciusko
Darling Range   Mt. Liebig
MacDonnell Range   Mt. Meharry
Nullarbor Plain   Mt. Ossa
Cape York Peninsula   Mt. Ruapehu
Southern Alps   Mt. Woodroffe
Ayers Rock

8. On a separate map, color-code and label the following:

Kimberly Plateau   Barkly Tableland
Great Sandy Desert   Tanami Desert
Simpson Desert   Gibson Desert
Great Victoria Desert

9. Label the following ocean currents with red arrows:

East Australian   Japan   California
North Equatorial   Peru   South Equatorial

10. Label the following cities:

Sydney   Melbourne   Adelaide
Darwin   Brisbane   Alice Springs
Wagga Wagga   Derby   Kalgoorlie-Boulder
Hobart   Auckland   Perth

Challenge: How Much Do You Know About Australia and Oceania?

1. What's the name for the large, red, oval-shaped rock, one of the largest monoliths in the world, in the plains of central Australia that rises 2,831 feet (863m)?
2. What's the name of the 1,181 mile (1,900 km) long coral reef system located off the northeastern coast of Australia?
3. What's the name of Australia's only island state?
4. What does the term "Oceania" mean?
5. How many of Oceania's countries have become independent since 1975?
6. On what island is Robert Louis Stevenson, author of *Kidnapped*, *Treasure Island*, and *Dr. Jekyll and Mr. Hyde*, buried?
7. Give the name and latitude of the two most southern national capitals of independent countries.

Antarctica Outline Activity

1. Draw and label the following physical features:

South Magnetic Pole	South Pole	Antarctic Peninsula
Lambert Glacier	Roosevelt Island	Thurston Island
Alexander Island	Adelaide Island	Berkner Island
George Coast		

2. Establish and mark:

   Lines of Latitude: 60° S, 70° S, 80° S

   Lines of Longitude: 90° W, 0°, 90° E , 180°

   Antarctic Circle

3. Draw and label bodies of water:

Atlantic Ocean	Pacific Ocean	Indian Ocean
Scotia Sea	Weddell Sea	Ross Sea
Amundsen Sea	Bellingshausen Sea	

4. Draw mountains with brown triangles and label:

Mt. Erebus	Mt. Kirkpatrick	Mt. Sidley
Transantarctic	Sor Rondane	Mulig Hofmann
Pensacola	Napier	Ellsworth

5. Draw and label highland orange, ice shelves yellow:

Amery Ice Shelf	Filchner Ice Shelf	Ronne Ice Shelf
American Highland	Larsen Ice Shelf	Ross Ice Shelf

6. Label the following lands:

Wilkes	Enderby	Queen Maud
Coats	Ellsworth	Graham
Marie Byrd	Victoria	

CONTINENTAL ESSAYS

As your high school students complete the questions and outline activities for each continent, choose a country or have them select a country in which to answer essay questions or to write a report. Below are suggestions for questions. **Don't** give students all essay questions, but do select two or three that best suit the nation.

Essay Questions
1. Describe any important historical event, battle, discovery or turning point in the history of this nation. Use facts and details.

2. If you lived there, how would its culture affect your lifestyle?

3. What place(s) would you most want to see during a visit? Explain why.

4. How was this nation settled? From where did the people originate, and how did immigration affect its culture?

5. Describe life in this country today. Give details.

6. How does this nation's religion affect its culture?

7. How does this country's climate affect lifestyle and culture?

8. Research a conflict between this nation and a neighboring country. Outline and describe the significance of the various geographic, economic, cultural, social, religious, ethnic, political, and military factors involved in the conflict.

9. How does this country interact with other nations of the world? Include import and export information. How do other nations view this country?

10. For what is the people of this nation most proud? Least proud? Explain the details, causes and effects.

Unit Five

Reproducibles for your GeoTreks

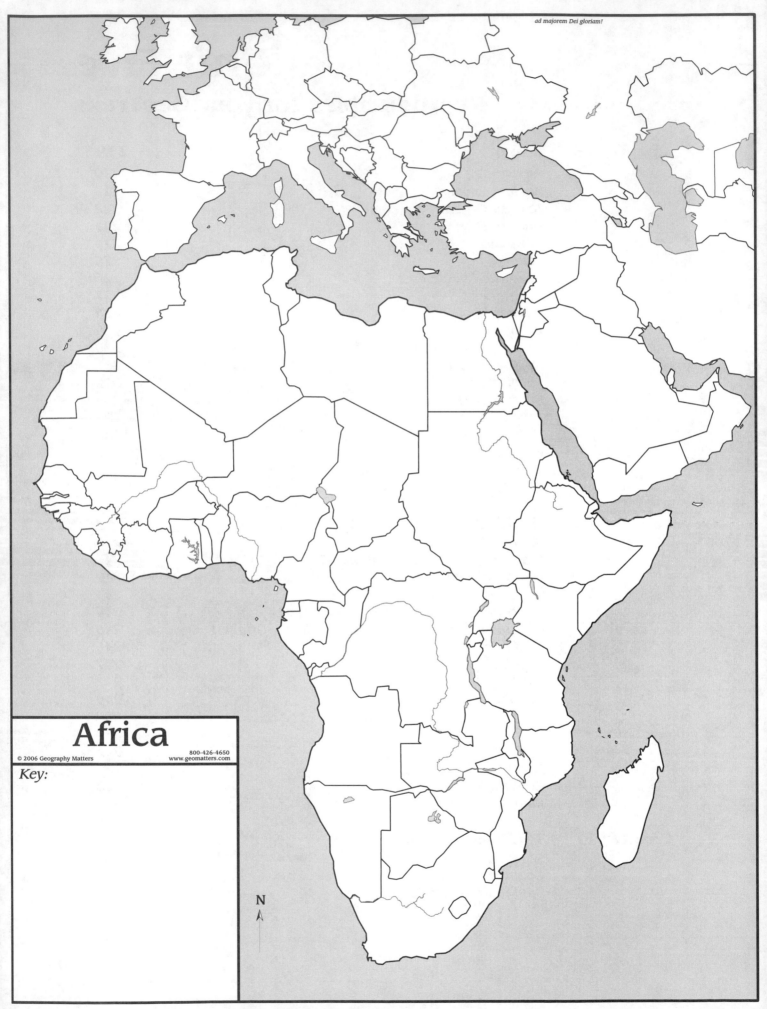

ad majorem Dei gloriam!

Africa

© 2006 Geography Matters

800-426-4650
www.geomatters.com

Key:

N

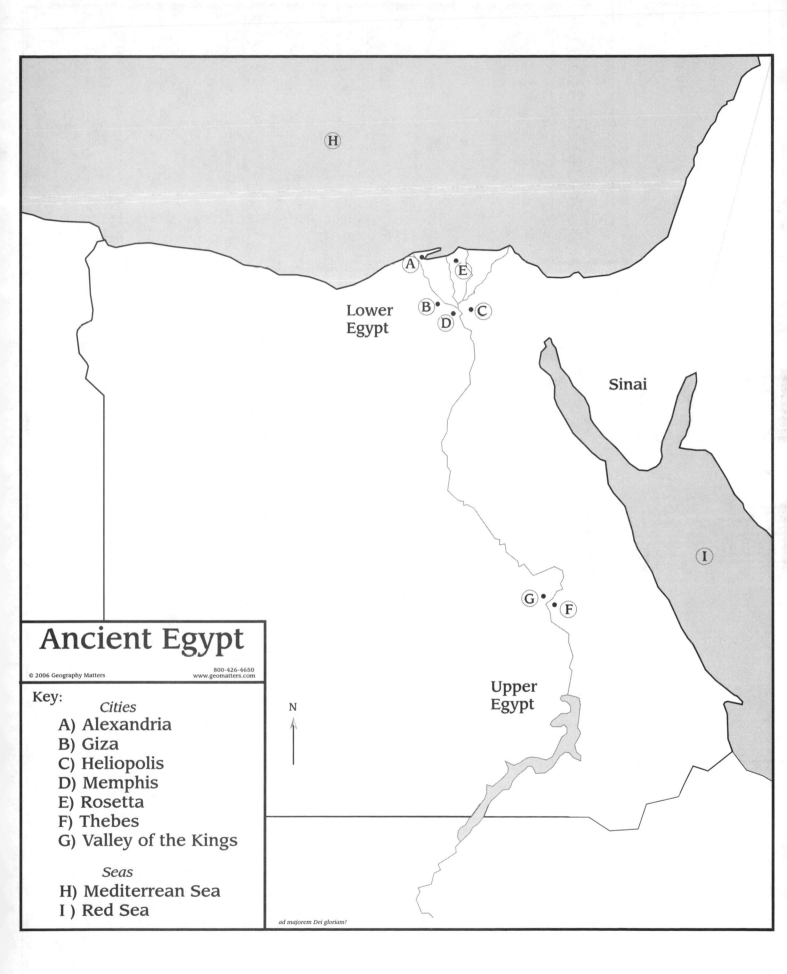

Ancient Egypt

© 2006 Geography Matters

800-426-4650
www.geomatters.com

Lower
Egypt

Upper
Egypt

Sinai

N

Key:

Cities

A) Alexandria
B) Giza
C) Heliopolis
D) Memphis
E) Rosetta
F) Thebes
G) Valley of the Kings

Seas

H) Mediterrean Sea
I) Red Sea

ad majorem Dei gloriam!

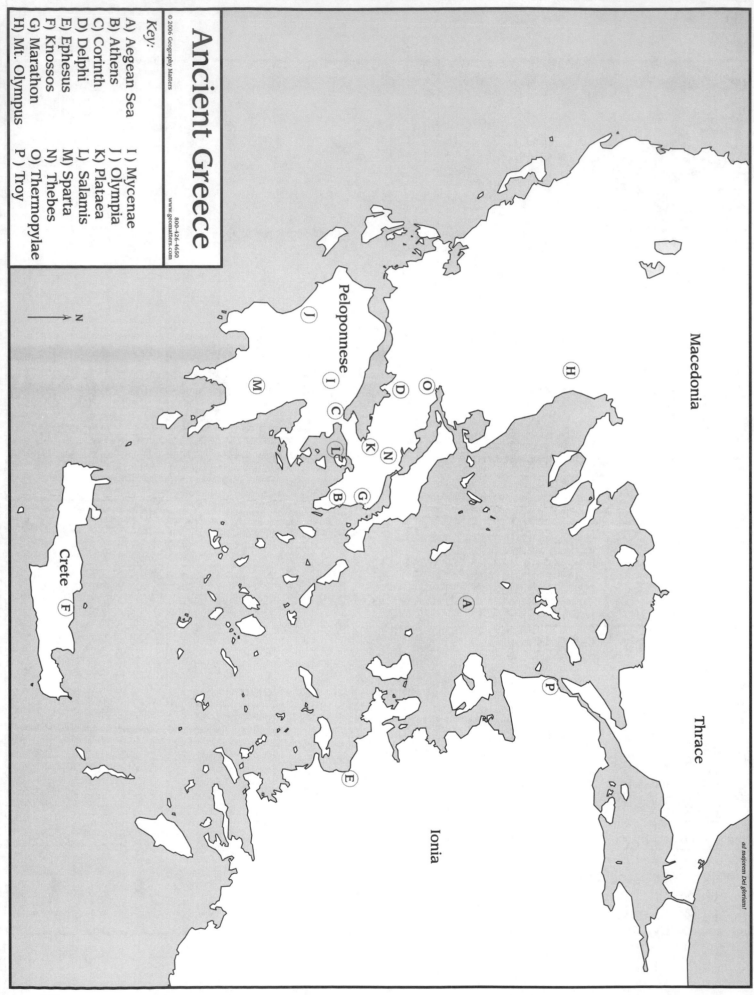

Ancient Greece

© 2006 Geography Matters

800-426-4650
www.geomatters.com

Key:

A) Aegean Sea
B) Athens
C) Corinth
D) Delphi
E) Ephesus
F) Knossos
G) Marathon
H) Mt. Olympus

I) Mycenae
J) Olympia
K) Plataea
L) Salamis
M) Sparta
N) Thebes
O) Thermopylae
P) Troy

N →

Macedonia

Thrace

Peloponnese

Crete

Ionia

ad majorem Dei gloriam!

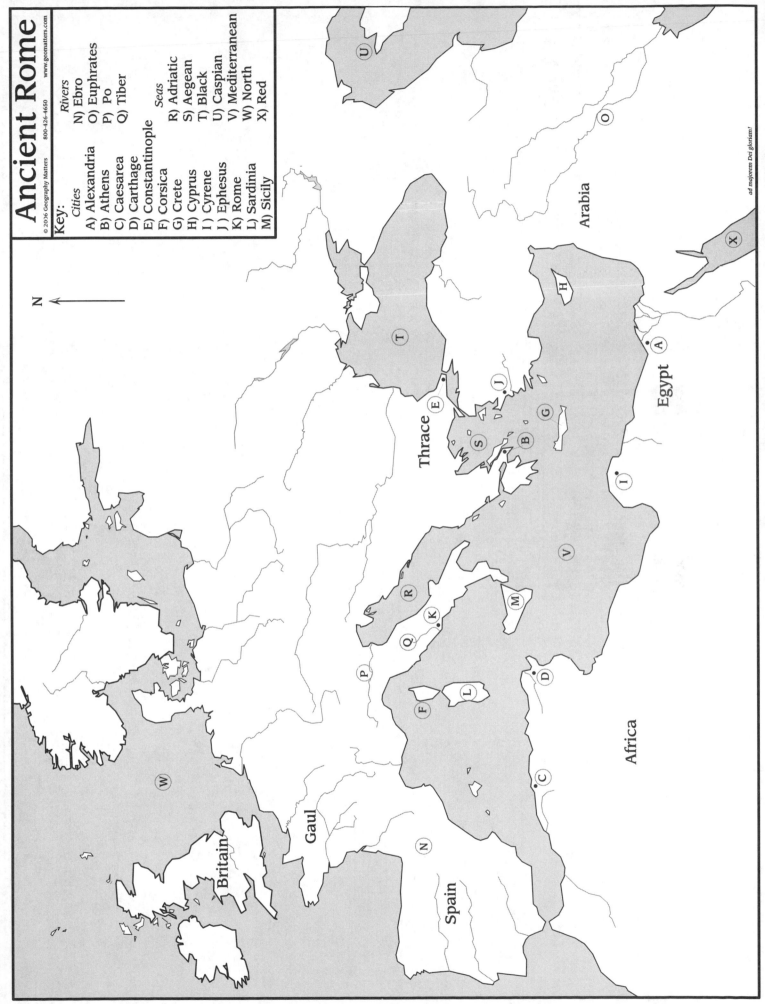

Ancient Rome

© 2006 Geography Matters   800-426-4650   www.geomatters.com

Key:

Cities
A) Alexandria
B) Athens
C) Caesarea
D) Carthage
E) Constantinople
F) Corsica
G) Crete
H) Cyprus
I) Cyrene
J) Ephesus
K) Rome
L) Sardinia
M) Sicily

Rivers
N) Ebro
O) Euphrates
P) Po
Q) Tiber

Seas
R) Adriatic
S) Aegean
T) Black
U) Caspian
V) Mediterranean
W) North
X) Red

N

ad majorem Dei gloriam!

Arabia

Egypt

Thrace

Africa

Gaul

Britain

Spain

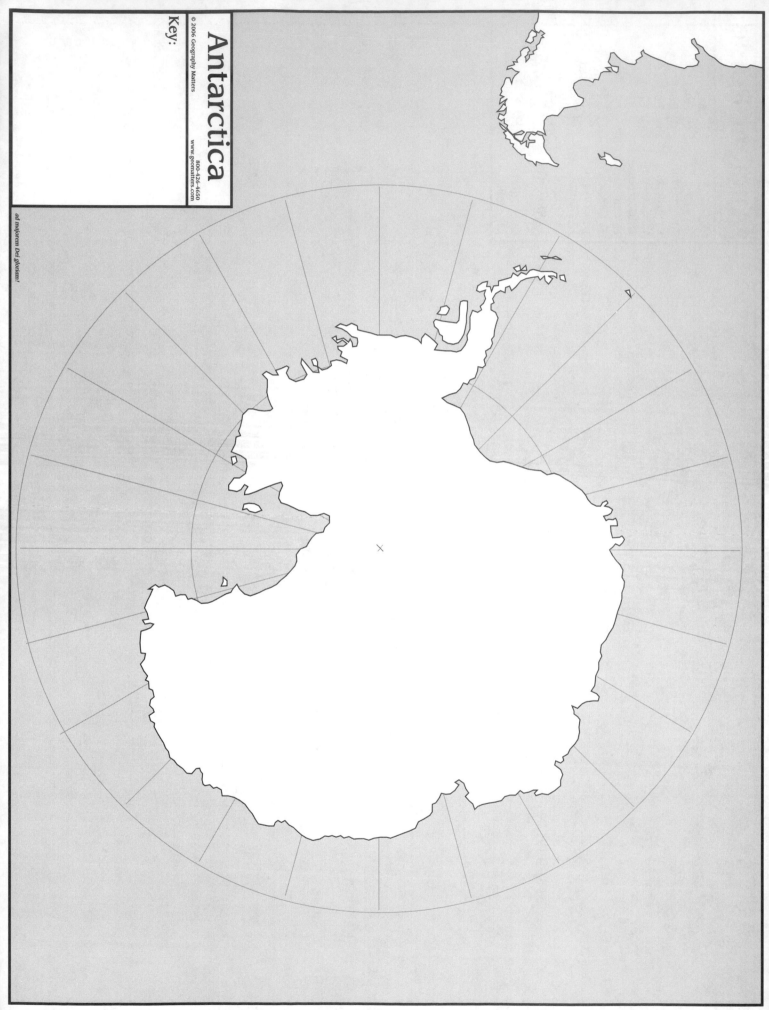

Antarctica

Key:

© 2006 Geography Matters
800-426-4650
www.geomatters.com

ad majorem Dei gloriam!

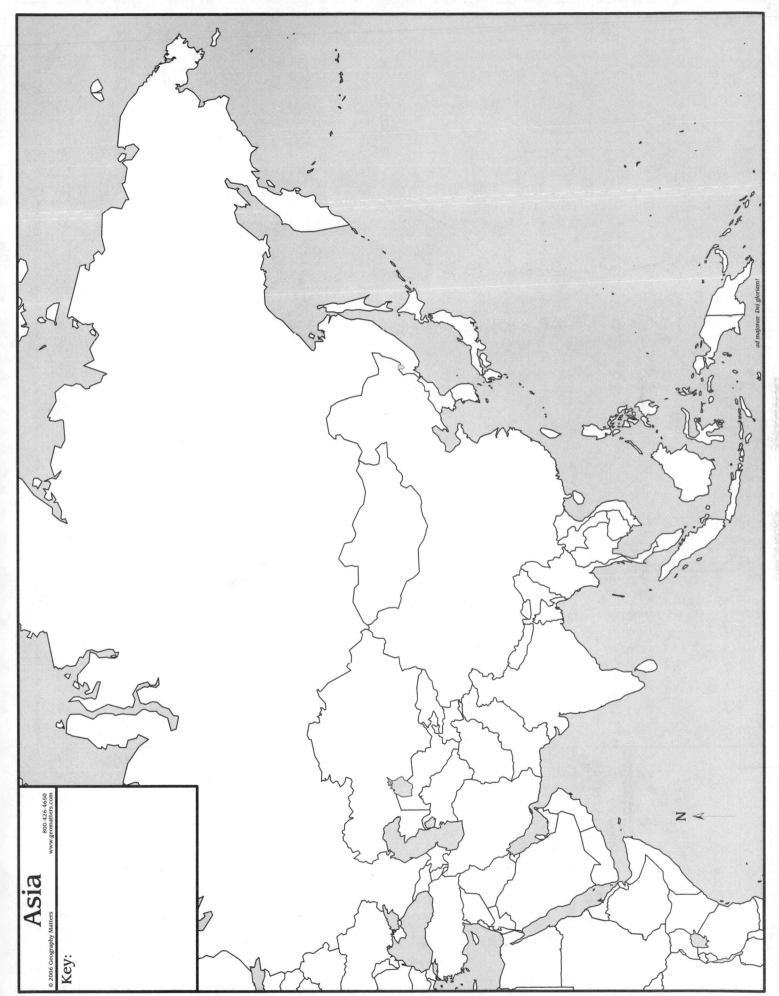

Asia

© 2006 Geography Matters

www.geomatters.com

800-426-4650

Key:

ad majorem Dei gloriam!

N

225

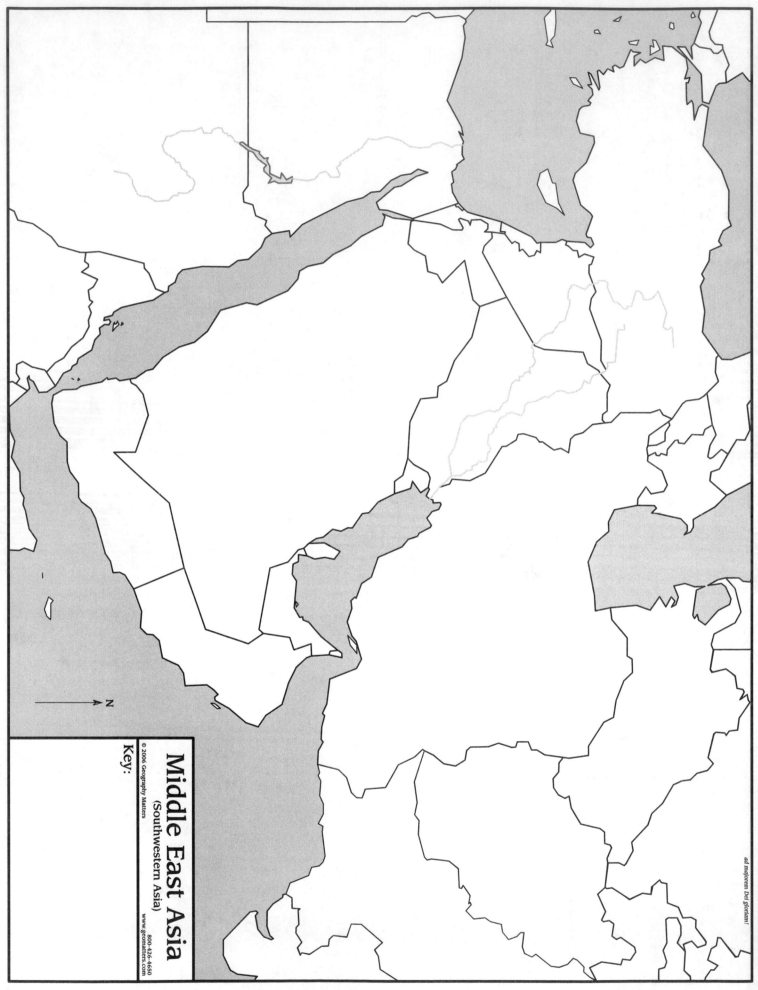

Middle East Asia
(Southwestern Asia)

Key:

© 2006 Geography Matters
800-426-4650
www.geomatters.com

N

ad majorem Dei gloriam!

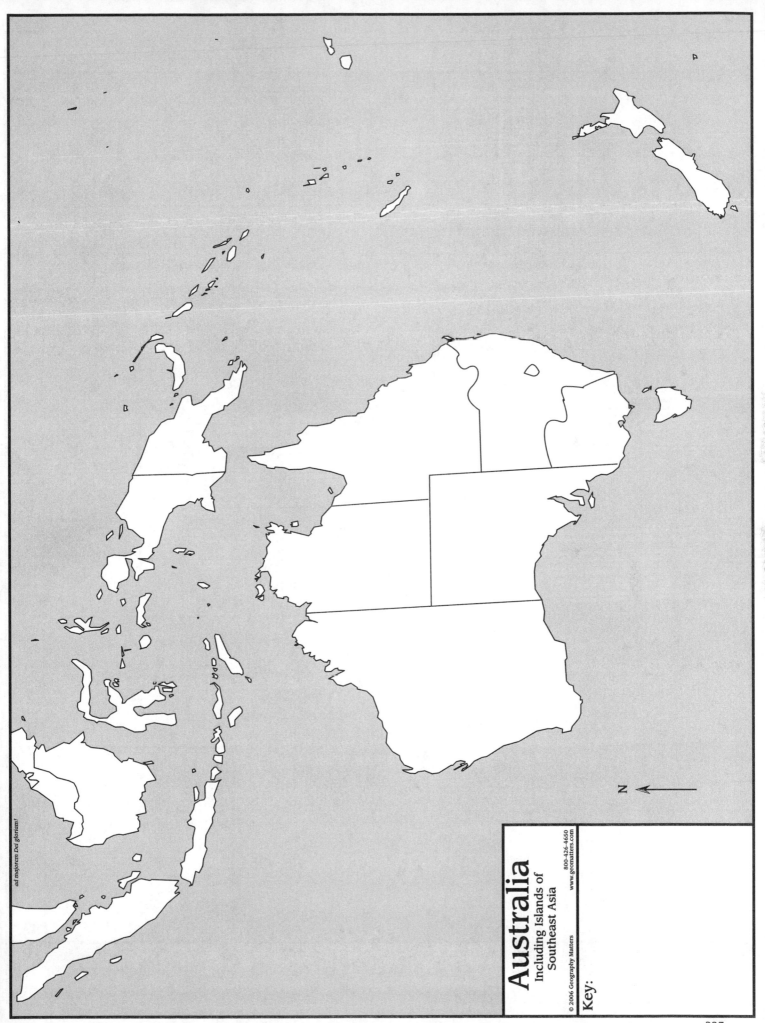

ad majorem Dei gloriam!

Australia
Including Islands of Southeast Asia

© 2006 Geography Matters

800-426-4650
www.geomatters.com

Key:

N ←

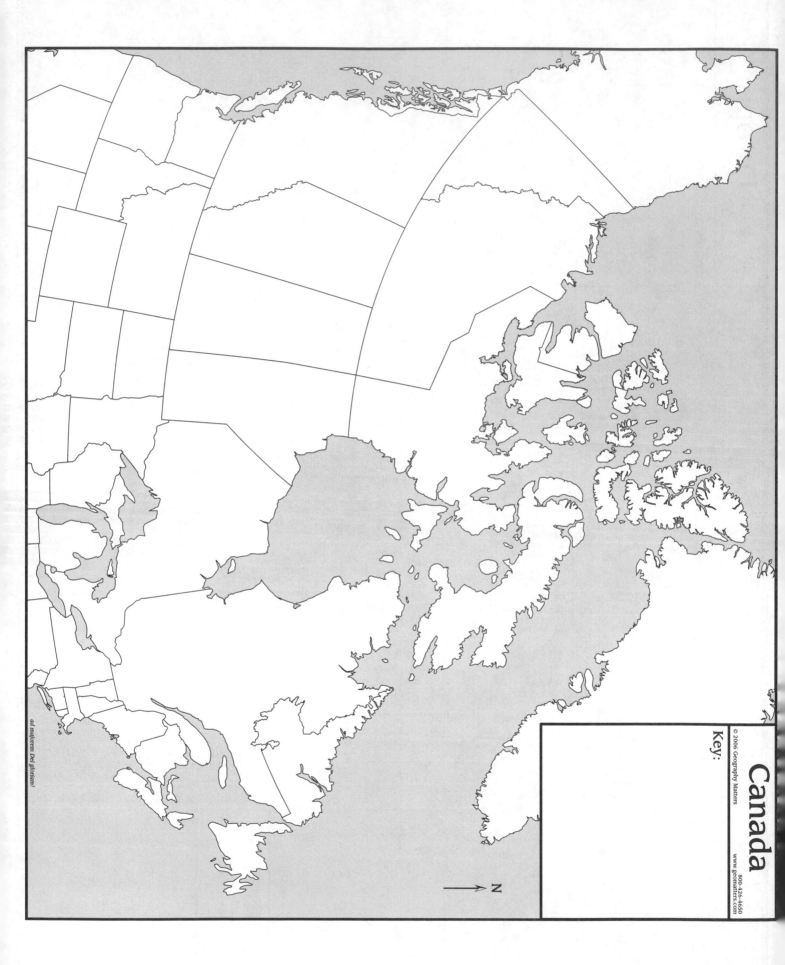

Key:

© 2006 Geography Matters

Canada

800-426-4650
www.geomatters.com

ad majorem Dei gloriam!

N →

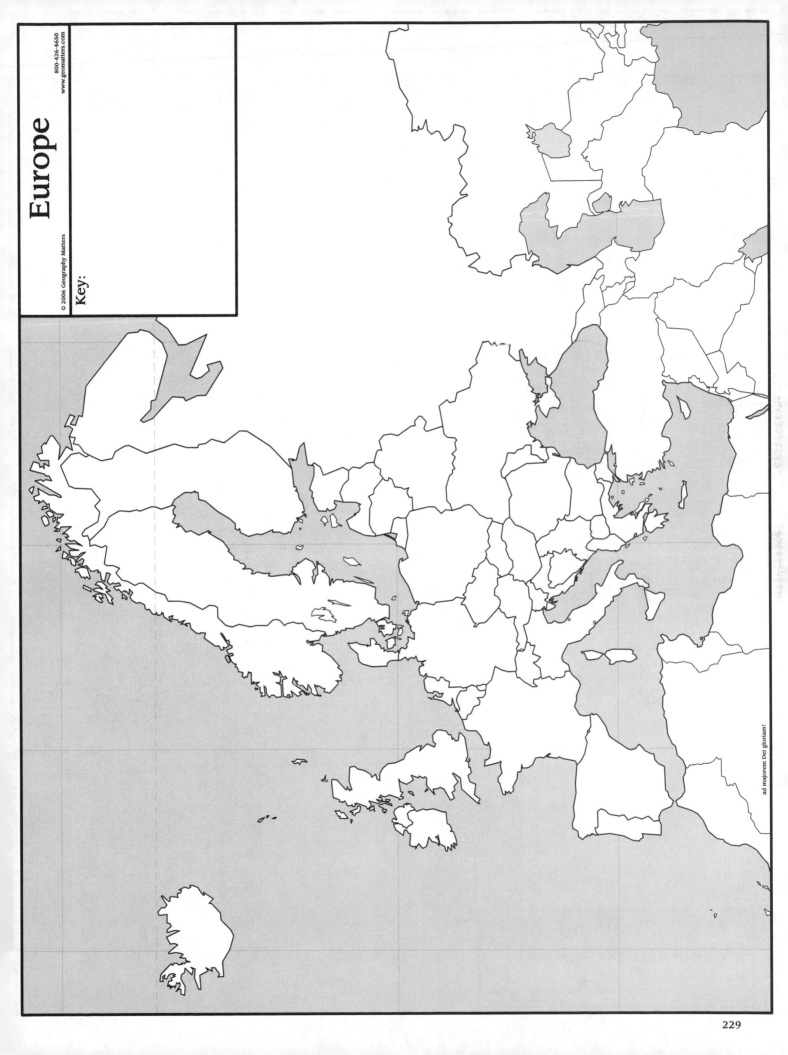

Europe

Key:

800-426-4650
www.geomatters.com

ad majorem Dei gloriam!

229

Map of Holland for
Hans Brinker Study

40 km

0   40 miles

800-426-4650
© 2006 Geography Matters   www.geomatters.com

ad majorem Dei gloriam!

230

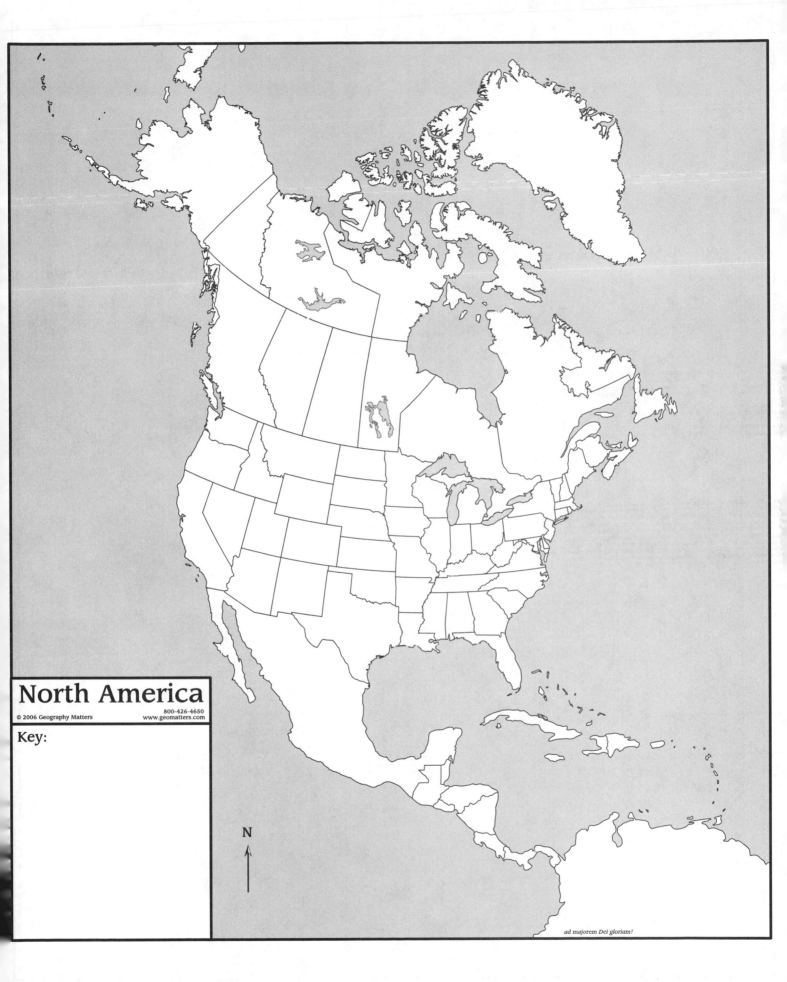

North America

© 2006 Geography Matters

800-426-4650
www.geomatters.com

Key:

N

ad majorem Dei gloriam!

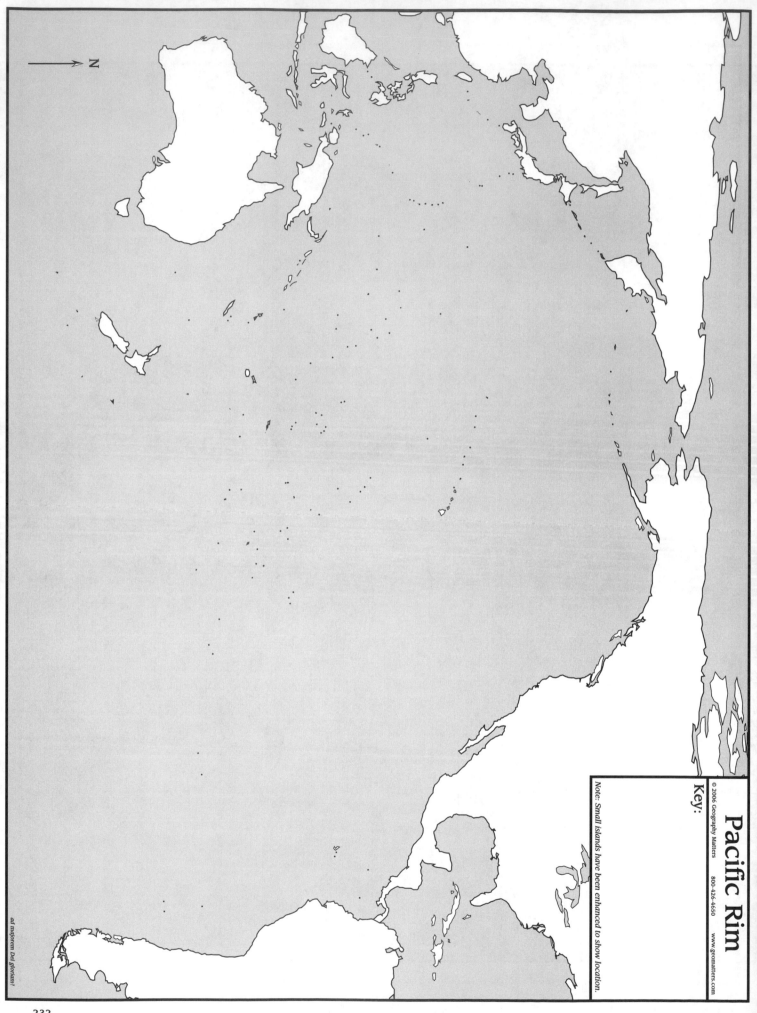

Key:

Pacific Rim

© 2006 Geography Matters   800-426-4650   www.geomatters.com

N

ad majorem Dei gloriam!

South America

© 2006 Geography Matters

800-426-4650
www.geomatters.com

Key:

N

ad majorem Dei gloriam!

233

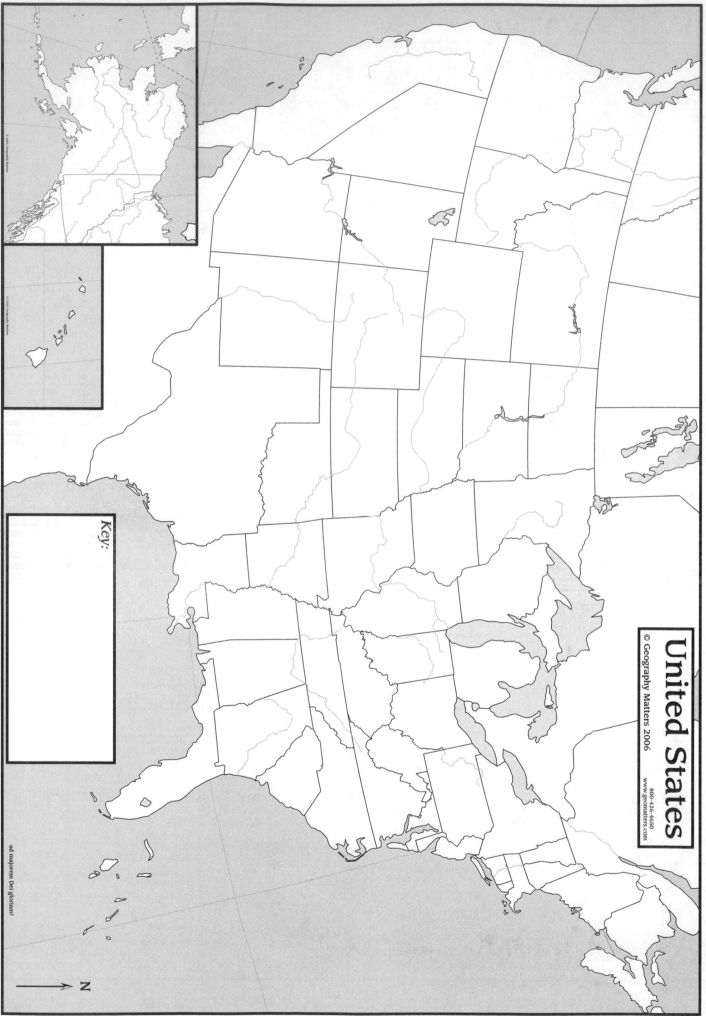

United States

© Geography Matters 2006

800-426-4650
www.geomatters.com

Key:

ad majorem Dei gloriam!

N

234

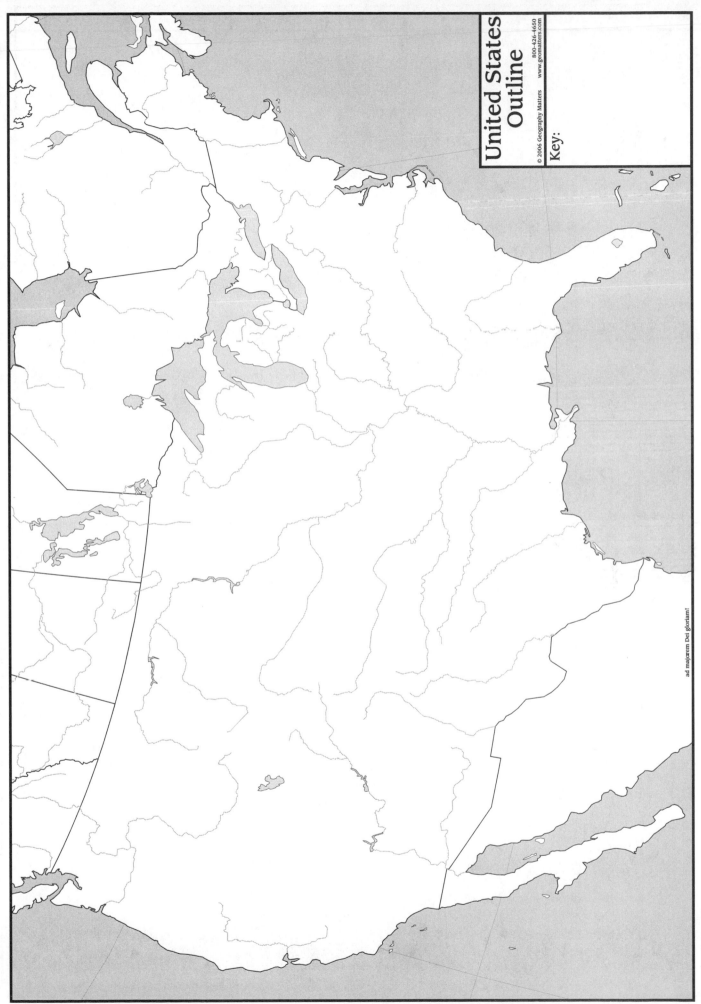

ad majorem Dei gloriam!

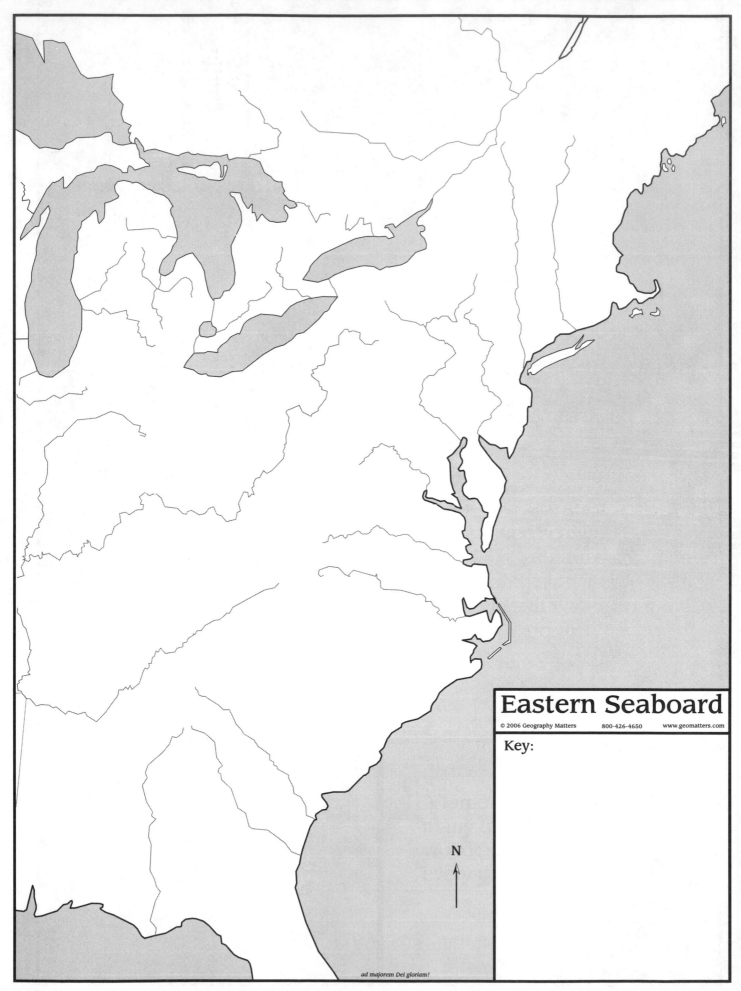

Eastern Seaboard

© 2006 Geography Matters   800-426-4650   www.geomatters.com

Key:

N

ad majorem Dei gloriam!

236

Eastern Seaboard
with current state boundaries

© 2006 Geography Matters

800-426-4650
www.geomatters.com

Key:

N

ad majorem Dei gloriam!

237

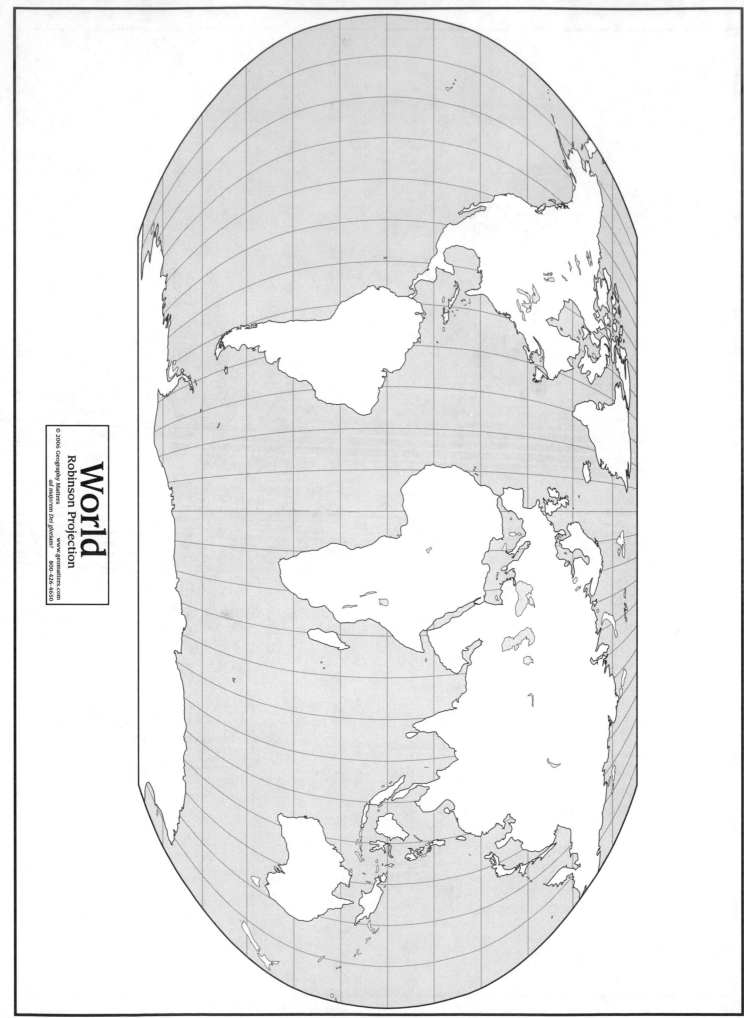

World
Robinson Projection

WALKING TOURS
CHAPTER 16

Notes Activity Sheets, Charts, Graphs and Grids

It's always fun to take a few side trips or walking tours. This chapter is full of all the different reproducibles mentioned throughout *The Ultimate Guide.* These will provide your students with the forms and activities they need to help round out their geography studies.

You'll find information regarding the use of each sheet on the page numbers indicated below. Answer keys for titles marked with an asterick (*) are located in Appendix B.

Almanac Trek

Student Name: _____   Date: _____

Name and year of almanac being used: _____

1. What United States Corporation had the largest revenue last year? _____

2. Will there be a total eclipse of the sun this year? _____

   If so, when? _____

3. Which movie won an Oscar for Best Picture last year? _____

4. What's the population of your state, according to the most recent census? _____

5. What's the zip code for Evansville, Indiana? _____

6. What's the chief religion of Brazil? _____

7. What's the address for the Geological Society of America?

           _____

           _____

           _____

8. Who won the Woman's World Champion Figure Skating Competition in 1966, 1967, and

   1968? _____

9. Who was the most recently appointed Justice of the United States Supreme Court?

   _____

10. What's the record low temperature recorded in Alaska? _____

What Do You Know About Maps?

Student Name: _____   Date: _____

MATCHING

Name	Definition
Scale	A group of symbols and what they mean.
Key	A line representing actual distance on earth.
Legend	A symbol on a map showing N, S, E, & W.
Compass Rose	A person who draws maps for a job.
Cartographer	This is another word for "key."

FILL IN THE BLANK:

If you're facing north, what direction is directly behind you?_____

The four cardinal directions are:_____, _____, _____, & _____.

MULTIPLE CHOICE:

A map scale is:
 a. something on a fish.
 b. a musical term.
 c. a line that tells how much distance is represented on a map.

A cartographer is:
 a. a cartoon character.
 b. someone who draw maps for a living.
 c. a person who designs cars.

DRAW A PICTURE OF A COMPASS ROSE:

TRUE OR FALSE:

___ A "legend" and a "key" are the same thing.
___ The sun appears to rise in the east.
___ A compass is the same as a compass rose.
___All maps show north pointing "up" like this:

N

NFL Mind Benders

Student Name: _____   Date: _____

1. What geographic region do the Patriots represent?
2. What mode of transportation does the AFC team in New York depict?
3. What animal, that was almost wiped out in the 19th century, does the northernmost New York state AFC team identify?
4. What transportation method is suggested by the race held on Memorial Day weekend in the Colts' home city?
5. Which NFL team is the only team to have a mascot with fins, and what bay is adjacent to the city?
6. Name the 3 rivers that converge at the home city of the AFC team in western Pennsylvania.
7. Name the bay associated with the Ravens and a seafood that's popular in that area.
8. What river flows by the city in Ohio whose mascot is orange with black stripes?
9. Name the plateau that runs through the easten part of the state the Titans call home.
10. Name the largest city in geographic area in the U.S. and the team it hosts.
11. What geographic feature is associated with many of the earthquakes that occur in the Raiders' home state?
12. What gulf lies off the coast of the Chargers' home city?
13. What AFC team is located at the highest altitude?
14. Name the interstate running east/west by the Chiefs' home stadium.
15. Name the mountains and national park that lie west of the Seahawks' stadium and the Sound that is east of it.
16. What's the capital of the state in which the New York Giants play their home games?
17. What river separates the home state of the Cowboys from the "Sooner" state?
18. What team plays in the city where Independence Hall is located?
19. What football team's home city residents cannot vote for U.S. Senate candidates?
20. Name the canyon that's located in the home state of the Cardinals' football team.
21. Name the capital of the country that's 50 miles north of the Packers' home city.
22. What European region does the mascot of the football team located in the land of 10,000 lakes represent?
23. Name the Great Lake that borders the home city of the Bears.
24. What's the largest fresh water lake in the home state of the Buccaneers?
25. What industry is most readily associated with the Lions?
26. What historical event does the San Francisco NFL team honor?
27. What musical style is associated with the Saints' home city?
28. Name the five states that border the state that the Falcons call home.
29. Name the mountain range that runs through the state where the Panthers play their home games.
30. Name the river that flows by the Rams' host city.
31. Name the NFL team that sits just east of 41°N and 82°W and the lake it borders.

Let the Games Begin!

Directions: Select an Olympic athlete and answer the following questions about his/her home nation. Information can be obtained from an encyclopedia, almanac, atlas, olympic broadcast, or other resources.

Student Name_____ Date_____

1. Current medal winning athlete and event:
   Name:_____ Country:_____
2. Event: _____
3. Just the Facts
   Continent: _____
   Latitude/Longitude:_____
   Capital: _____
   Time Zone of capital: _____
   This country's time when it's noon in your time zone: _____
   Type of Government: _____
   Area: _____ Life expectancy: _____ Population: _____

   HOST CITY: _____
   GAMES/YEAR: _____
   TIME ZONE: _____

   Currency: _____
   Your time zone: _____
   Language: _____

4. Past athletes from this nation who have won medals:
   Name: _____ Event: _____ Medal: _____
   Name: _____ Event: _____ Medal: _____
5. Interesting Facts
   Choose two other famous people from this nation and list their accomplishments:
   Name: _____ Known for: _____
   Name: _____ Known for: _____

   Choose one interesting historical event and describe below:
   _____
   _____
   _____
   _____
   _____
   _____
   _____

   Name one significant structure located in this nation:
   _____

6. Draw a picture of the nation's flag and currency and explain what the symbols mean. (You may use the back of this paper if necessary.)

FLAG   CURRENCY/COIN

Chocolate Chip Geological Dig

Geologist's Name: _____   Date: _____

Grid #1

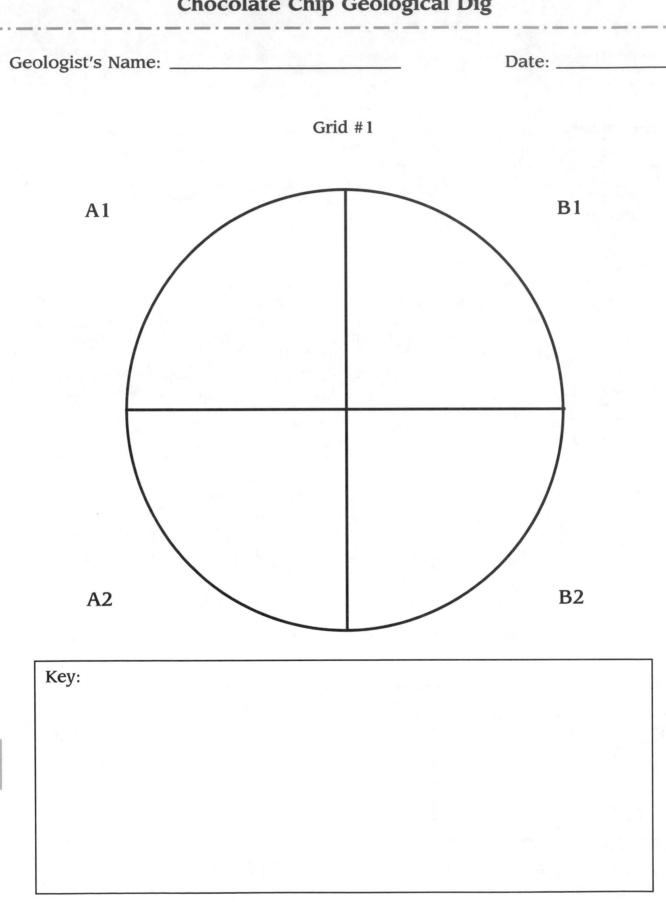

A1

B1

A2

B2

Key:

Chocolate Chip Geological Dig

Geologist's Name: _____   Date: _____

Items	A 1	A 2	B 1	B 2
Chocolate Chips				
Nuts				
Raisins				
M & M's				
Other				

Grid #2

Chocolate Chip Geological Dig

Geologist's Name: _____   Date: _____

Substance	Number of Particles	Weight

Grid #3

Novel Activity Sheet

Student Name: _____   Date Due: _____

Name of Novel: _____   Copyright: _____

Name of Author: _____

1. Where does this story take place?
   Continent: _____ Country: _____ City: _____
2. What is the latitude? longitude? _____
3. What is your own latitude? longitude? _____
4. What kind of climate is depicted?
   _____
5. How does the climate differ from your own?
   _____
6. What is the time period of the setting? _____
7. What other historical events were going on at this time in other places of the world?
   _____
   _____
   _____

8. What's on the northern border? _____
9. What's on the southern border? _____
10. What's on the eastern border? _____
11. What's on the western border? _____
12. Name all major water sources:
    _____
    _____

13. List any other important geographical features:
    _____
14. What types of transportation are used? _____
15. List any plants mentioned:
    _____
    _____

16. List any animals mentioned:
    _____
    _____

17. Name all regions you noticed:
    _____
    _____

18. What's the monetary unit for this country? _____

19. What foods are mentioned?
    _____
    _____

20. Describe the culture of the people. Include their language, religion, customs, etc.
    _____
    _____
    _____

Define geography terms and vocabulary words on separate paper.

WEATHER REPORT

TODAY

Skies:

Precipitation:

Temperature:

Wind Direction:

Wind Speed:

Other:

(Cloud types,
severe weather,
fog, etc.)

PREDICTION/FORECAST

Skies:

Precipitation:

Temperature:

Wind Direction:

Wind Speed:

Other:

(Cloud types,
severe weather,
fog, etc.)

SYMBOLS

Sunny:

Partly Cloudy:

Cloudy:

Rain:

Snow:

Sleet:

High/Low Temp:

Severe Thunderstorms:

Hurricane:

Tornado:

Floods:

Weather Person's Name

Date: _____

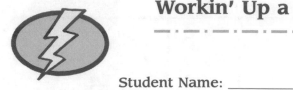

Workin' Up a Storm

Student Name: _____   Date: _____

Which type of storm best fits each description?

A. Thunderstorm   B. Hurricane   C. Tornado

1. ____ The smallest but most violent storm.
2. ____ The most destructive to islands and coastal regions.
3. ____ The most common type of storm in hot, unstable low latitudes and along fronts in middle latitudes.
4. ____ The most common type of storm on earth.

Use MORE or LESS to complete the following sentences:

5. _____   The equator receives _____ solar energy than do the poles.
6. _____   In the tropics, _____ solar energy is received than is lost to space.
7. _____   In the polar regions, _____ solar energy is received than is lost to space.

Complete the following sentences:

8. _____   When moist air flowing from the ocean meets a mountain barrier, the air is forced to_____.
9. _____   The higher the air rises, the more it _____.
10. _____   As moist air moves down the _____side of the mountain, it begins to warm up and become drier.

Match the letter with the most correct statement.

A. Orographic Effect   D. Weather   G. Humidity   J. Climate   M. Typhoons
B. Air Pressure   E. Evaporation   H. Westerlies   K. Doldrums   N. Trade Winds
C. Polar Easterlies   F. Precipitation I. Tornadoes   L. Condensation   O. Front

11. _____ Condition of the atmosphere at a given place or time.
12. _____ Weather conditions in an area over a long period of time.
13. _____ Measurement of the weight of air.
14. _____ Winds in low latitudes that blow from the east.
15. _____ Calm areas between the trade winds and equatorial zones.
16. _____ Winds in the middle latitudes that flow out of the Arctic and Antarctic regions.
17. _____ Winds in the high latitudes that flow out of the Arctic and Antarctic regions.
18. _____ The meeting zones of two different types of winds.
19. _____ The measurement of water vapor in the air.
20. _____ Condensed droplets of water vapor that fall to the earth's surface.
21. _____ Severe tropical storms, also called hurricanes, that sometimes form over the ocean waters of low latitudes and may travel into middle latitudes.
22. _____ Small, twisting storms that cause great destruction in their path.
23. _____ The effect of elevation that causes a difference in climate between the two sides of a mountain.
24._____ Process in which water in a liquid state or solid state passes into the vapor state.
25._____ Process of the change of matter in a gaseous state to the liquid or solid state.

Are You a Junior Volcanologist?

Student Name: _____   Date: _____

1. What's the funnel shaped opening at the top of a volcano called? _____

2. Scientists use a _____ _____ to measure volcanoes.

3. What's a volcano called that isn't active but could erupt again? _____

4. What's the name for a dead volcano that isn't likely to erupt again? _____

5. The spread of lava down a volcano is called a _____ _____.

6. Which volcanic rock can float on water? _____

7. Name the volcano in Washington State that erupted in 1980. _____

8. A _____ connects the magma chamber to the crater.

9. What's a volcano called that is likely to erupt at anytime? _____

10. What do we call the area around the edges of the Pacific Ocean where many of the

    world's volcanoes are located? _____ _____ _____

11. What are the fine particles of matter spewed from a volcano called? _____

12. A volcanic explosion is called an _____.

13. What's the red hot, melted rock beneath the earth's surface called? _____

14. What volcanic rock is black and glassy? _____

15. What's the hard outer layer of the earth called? _____

16. What's the name for scientists who study volcanoes? _____

Are You a Senior Volcanologist?

Student Name: _____   Date: _____

1. These openings can be active and bubbling, filled with water, or just rocky pits:

_____

2. What's the name of the device that measures the size of the swell of a volcano?

_____   _____

3. A quiet volcano is referred to as _____.

4. An inactive volcano not expected to erupt again is referred to as _____.

5. What's it called when magma hits the surface and begins spreading outward?

_____   _____

6. _____ is made from volcanic froth and is commercially used for polishing.

7. An example of a famous composite cone volcano is _____.

8. What's an opening for the escape of gas or liquid in the earth's crust called?

_____

9. The opposite of a dormant volcano is a(n) _____ volcano.

10. The _____--- ___ -- _____ is known for both volcanoes and earthquakes.

11. When Mt. St. Helens erupted, _____ fell like black snow over many western states.

12. What's an explosion of gas, ash, and lava called? _____

13. When _____, or melted rock, reaches the surface it's called lava.

14. This volcanic rock is formed when thick, sticky lava cools quickly: _____.

15. When magma breaks through the earth's _____, a volcano is born.

16. Unlike Spock, these scientists who study volcanoes don't hail from Vulcan!

_____

Student Name _____ **Title** _____ **Date** _____

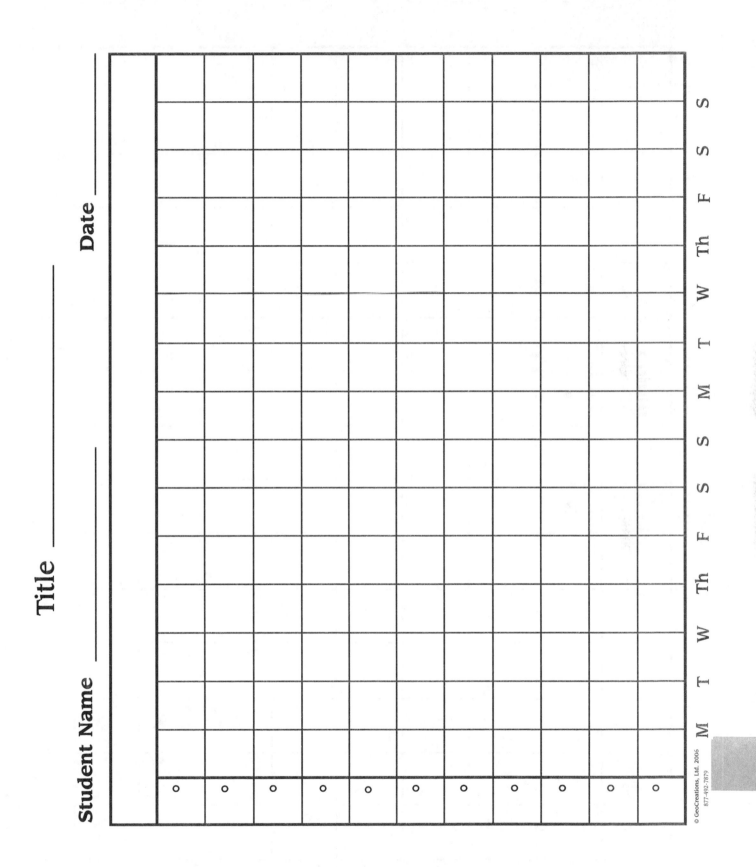

Temperature Graph

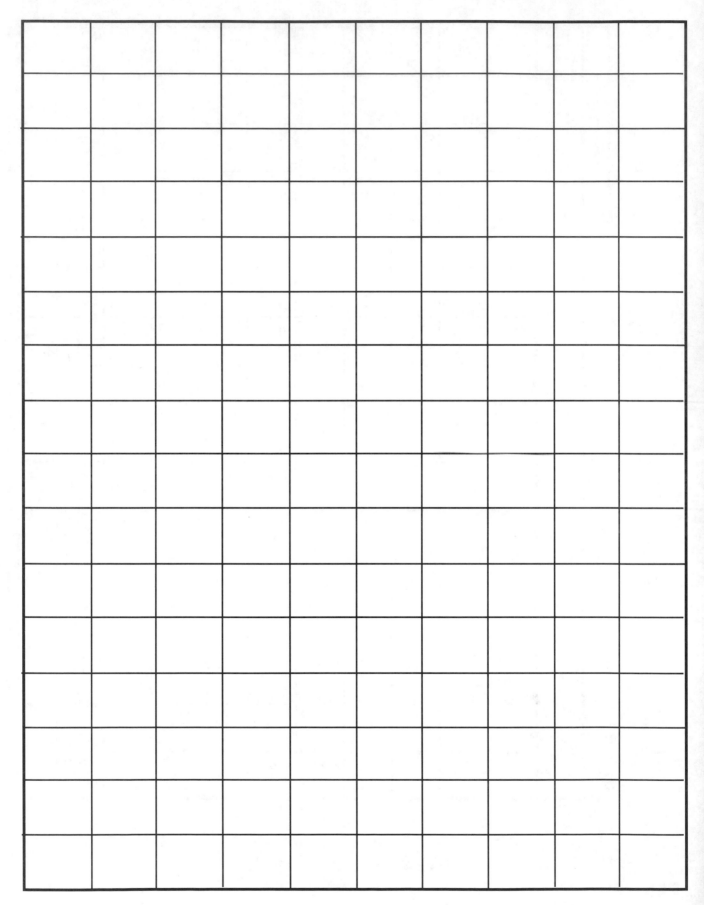

Grid

Student Name _____ Date _____

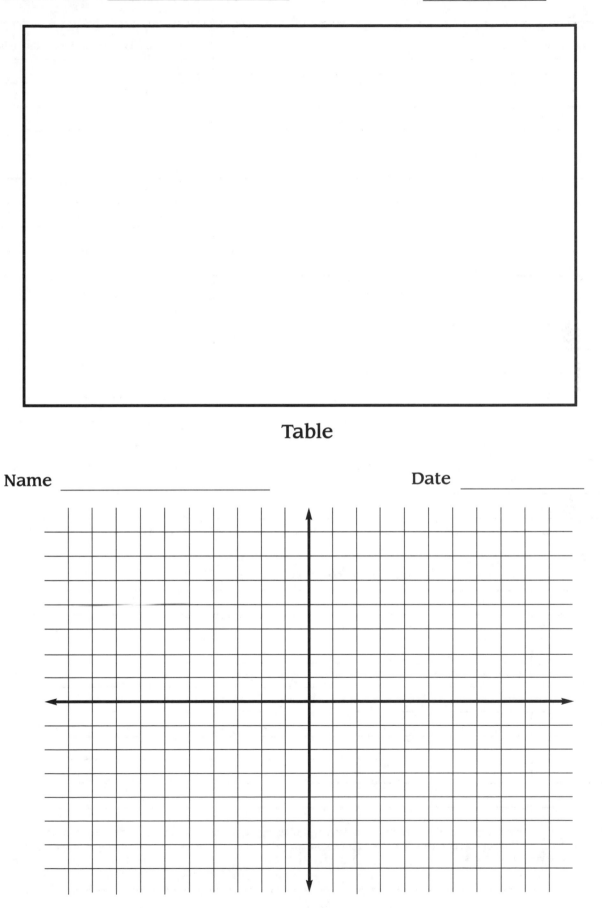

Table

Name _____ Date _____

Co-ordinate Grid

Map and Timeline Assignments

Map title:_____

Places & Events	Bodies of Water & Physical Features

Use coding on your maps: Countries (all capital letters), Capitals (red), Water (blue), Mountains (brown), Physical Features (green)

Timeline

Date	Person/Event - add interesting facts you have learned.

Color code details on your timeline: Europe (blue), USA (green), Africa (yellow), Asia (red), Middle East (orange) Science (purple). Feel free to choose your own colors.

TOOLS FOR THE TOUR GUIDE

CHAPTER 17

REPRODUCIBLE TEACHER TOOLS

Scope and Sequence Charts

These Scope and Sequence Charts are designed to help you:
- keep track of what geography you have covered and
- plan for each new school year

Copy one for each student and check off what you've covered each year. They're broken down into four grade levels and include not only pure geography but also a listing of what geographic topics you can teach through history, science, math and literature at each level. This is an extensive list; take what you want and use it as a guide.

Geography Definitions Flash Cards

These are two-sided flash cards. Copy onto card stock, laminate, and use to drill geography definitions. It's a good idea to have a geography terms chart available to enable the student to see these physical features in graphic form. Look in your student's atlas or geography books, or order a color chart from the order form in the back of *The Ultimate Guide*.

Good Stuff to Know by Heart

These are divided into sections; both to help organize information and to help the student succeed by memorizing small chunks at a time. Also, part of the "memorization" has to do with finding places quickly on a map rather than simply memorizing names. Copy these onto cardstock, laminate, and cut into sections. These handy little lists can be pulled out of the glove compartment, your wallet, or backpack, and time spent waiting can be turned into time spent learning.

GeoBit says:

If you copy the Geography Definitions Flash Cards one-sided, students can play a memory game matching the word with its definition.

Student's Name: _____

K through 6th Grade	K	1	2	3	4	5	6
GEOGRAPHY							
Introduction to Maps & Terminology							
Location: Home & School							
Make/Read Simple Map							
Compass Use							
Local Geography & Topography							
Flat Maps & Globes							
Read, Follow & Draw Maps							
U.S. Geography & Topography							
Identify: Seven Continents							
Major Bodies of Water							
Major Cities							
Regions of the World							
World Geography: Canada							
Mexico/Central America							
South							
Europe							
Asia							
Africa							
Time Zones							
Climatic Regions							
Natural Resources of the U.S.							
Earth's Resources							
Additional Map/Globe Skills							
LITERATURE							
Intro-Geography Thru Literature Approach							
Complete Several Books With This Approach							
MATHEMATICS							
Standard & Metric Measurements							
Time							
Weight							
Length							
Volume							
Shape							
Temperature							
Basic Chart & Graph Concepts							

GEOGRAPHY SCOPE & SEQUENCE

Student's Name:

K through 6th Grade	K	1	2	3	4	5	6
HISTORY							
Neighborhoods: Families Around the World							
Ancient Civilizations							
Maps Included With History							
Exposure to Foreign Cultures							
American Exploration & Discovery							
U. S. History: Colonial Life in America							
Pioneer Life in America							
Revolutionary War in America							
Westward Movement							
Industrial & Cultural Growth							
Life in U.S. & Its Possessions							
State History							
Memorize States & Capitals							
World Cultures							
Milestones in Human Achievement							
Transportation & Communication							
World Trade							
Political & Economic Systems							
SCIENCE							
Common Birds, Trees & Flowers							
Forest Plants							
Desert Plants & Animals							
Sea Plants & Animals							
Plant & Animal Habitats							
Environment of the Local State							
Ecosystems							
Weather & Climate							
Time & Seasons							
Water Cycle							
Food Cycle							
Geology							
Landforms							
Oceans							
Continents							
Pollution							

Student's Name: _____

6th through 8th Grade	6	7	8	Notes:
G E O G R A P H Y				
Ability to:				
Plan & Follow Route on a Road Map				
Articulate Directions Clearly				
Exposure to Compass & Its Use				
U. S. Geography				
World Geography				
Advanced Map & Globe Skills				
World Trade				
Know Location Around the World of:				
Countries, Mountains, Oceans, Lakes				
Ability to:				
Do Geography-Related Research				
Define Geography				
Complete Major Geography Project(s)				
Understand Interconnectedness Between Disciplines				
S C I E N C E				
Ecosystems				
Ecology & Environment				
Food Supply				
Ocean & Atmosphere				
Weather				
Effects of Weather & Climate				
Geology:				
Rocks, Soils & Minerals				
Composition of Earth				
The Earth's Movement				
Weathering & Erosion				
L I T E R A T U R E				
In-Depth Exposure to:				
Foreign Language				
Cultures				
M A T H E M A T I C S / E C O N O M I C S				
U.S. Economic System				

GEOGRAPHY SCOPE & SEQUENCE

Student's Name:

6th through 8th Grade	6	7	8	Notes:
H I S T O R Y				
Always Use Maps With History				
Western Hemisphere Countries/Cultures:				
North & South America				
Middle America & the Caribbean				
Eastern Hemisphere Countries/Cultures:				
Europe				
Asia				
Africa				
Australia, Pacific Ocean & Antarctica				
Ancient Civilizations				
Greek & Roman Civilizations				
Our Old World Backgrounds				
Exploration & Discovery				
Growth & Development of the U.S.:				
Colonial Life				
Struggle For Independence				
Westward Movement				
Civil War				
Reconstruction				
U.S. As a World Power				
Relationships Among Nations				
World Customs, Traditions & Beliefs				
Political & Economic Systems				
Milestones in Human Achievement				
Transportation & Communication				
World Trade & Resources				
Contemporary Problems & Issues				
Yesterday & Today Around the World:				
Middle East				
Far East				
Continental Europe				
Scandinavia				
British Isles				
Russia & the former Soviet Union				
Mediterranean				
Africa				

Student's Name:

9th and 10th Grades	9	10	Notes:
G E O G R A P H Y			
All Material Covered in K-8 Scope & Sequence			
World Geography			
Able to Identify:			
Majority of Countries on a World Map			
Capitals of Major Countries			
Completion of at Least:			
One Semester Geography Course			
One Major Geography Research Paper			
One Major Map Project			
Advanced Map & Globe Skills			
H I S T O R Y			
Earliest Civilizations			
Greek Civilization			
Roman Civilization			
The Middle Ages			
The Renaissance			
The Reformation			
The Rise & Fall of Monarchies			
The French Revolution			
Nationalism			
Imperialism			
World War I			
World War II			
The Korean War			
The Cold War			
The Vietnam War			
20th Century Wars in the Middle East			
Comparative Cultures & Religions			
Ethnic Studies			
Urban Studies			
World Interdependence			
World Problems & Issues			

Student's Name:

9th and 10th Grades	9	10	Notes:
S C I E N C E			
Earth History			
Earth Science			
Erosion			
Ecology			
Air & Water Pollution			
Weather & Climate			
Air Masses & Fronts			
Water & Its Uses			
Energy In Ecosystems			
Environmental Issues			
L I T E R A T U R E			
Cross-cultural Literature			
Folklore & Ballads			
Geographical Dialects			
Regional:			
Customs			
Traditions			
Folkways			
Language			
MATHEMATICS/ECONOMICS			
Elementary Economics			
Resource Management			
Conservation of Human Resources			

11th and 12th Grades	11	12	Notes:
G E O G R A P H Y			
All Material Covered In K Through 10 Scope & Sequence			
Changing Political Boundaries of Nations & States			
H I S T O R Y			
Age of Exploration & Discovery			
Colonization of America			
U.S. As a World Power			
World War I			
The Great Depression			
World War II			
The Cold War			
Urbanization			
Business & Industry in the U.S.			
International Relations			
American Foreign Policy			
International Organizations			
Literary, Social & Political Heritage of England			
S C I E N C E			
Agriculture			
Conservation			
L I T E R A T U R E			
Cross-cultural Literature			
World Literature			
M A T H E M A T I C S / E C O N O M I C S			
Family Economics & Management			
Economic Theory & Concepts			
Labor-Management Relations			
Taxation & Finance			
Distribution & Exchange			

AQUIFER	ARCHIPELAGO
ATOLL	BAY
BUTTE	CANYON
CAPE	CENSUS

A group of islands.

A layer of water-bearing rock through which groundwater moves.

Part of a lake or sea that is partly surrounded by the shore land.

A coral reef in the open ocean that appears as a low, ring-shaped island or ring of islets.

A deep, narrow valley having high, steep sides or cliffs.

Tall, steep-sided towers of rock. Smaller than a mesa.

A count of the population of a country, usually conducted by the government. It records the number of people and data such as age, gender, and occupation. A census can also be taken of plant or animal life.

A narrow part of land along a shore that sticks out into the water.

CHANNEL	COAST
CORE	CRUST
DELTA	DESERT
DIVIDE	ECOSYSTEM

Land along the sea.	A wide strait or waterway between two land masses that lie close to each other.
One of three main layers of the earth. The middle layer of hot rock, the mantle, is sandwiched between the inner layer, called the core, and the outer layer, called the crust.	One of three main layers of the earth. The middle layer of hot rock, the mantle, is sandwiched between the inner layer, called the core, and the outer layer, called the crust.
Very dry area of land that receives ten inches or less of precipitation a year. Deserts are found on every continent and cover about one-third of the earth's land area.	Land made by soil that drops from a river at its mouth, the place where it meets the sea.
Contraction of 'ecological system', a term used in classifying the earth's natural communities according to how living and non-living things and their environment function as a unit.	The high land that separates two river basins. A river drains the water from the land, and that land is its basin.

ELEVATION	EQUATOR
EQUINOX	ESCARPMENT
ESTUARY	FJORD
FOREST	FRONT

An imaginary line around the middle of the earth. Halfway between the North and South Poles, it divides the earth into Northern and Southern Hemispheres. It is the 0° line of latitude.

The distance above sea level.

A steep slope or cliff

Occurs twice a year when the sun appears directly overhead to observers at the equator. The periods of sunlight and darkness are nearly equal.

A deep, narrow inlet of the sea between high, steep cliffs.

A broadened seaward end of a river. Most estuaries contain a mixture of fresh water from the river and salt water from the ocean.

The boundary between two air masses of different temperature and humidity. There are three basic types of fronts: warm, cold, and stationary.

A large area of land where many trees grow. A forest or woodland gets much rainfall every year.

268

GEYSER	GLACIER
GRASSLAND	GROUNDWATER
GULF	HABITAT
HARBOR	HILL

A huge mass of ice that moves slowly over land.

A hot spring through which jets of water and steam erupt.

Water beneath the earth's surface from rain and melted snow that seeped down through soil and into pores and cracks in rocks.

A region where grass is the naturally dominant vegetation. A grassland occurs where there is not enough regular rainfall to support the growth of a forest, but not so little rain as to form a desert.

The natural environment of a plant or animal - the place where the plant commonly grows or the animal normally finds food and shelter.

A large area of the ocean or sea that lies within a curved coastline. It is a portion of the ocean that penetrates into land. Gulfs vary in size, shape, and depth. They are sometimes connected to the ocean by one or more narrow passages called straits.

A small area of land that is higher than the land around it.

A sheltered body of water where ships anchor and are safe from the winds and waves of storms at sea.

INLET	ISLAND
ISTHMUS	LAGOON
LAKE	LATITUDE
LONGITUDE	MAGMA

Land that is surrounded by water and smaller than a continent. There are four major kinds of islands: continental, oceanic, coral, and barrier.

A small strip of water that reaches from a sea or lake into the shore land.

A pool of shallow water linked to the sea by an inlet.

A narrow piece of land that joins two larger land areas and separates two bodies of water.

The distance north or south of the equator.

A body of water, usually fresh water, that is surrounded by land.

Molten rock inside the earth. It originates in the lower part of the earth's crust and in the upper portion of the mantle.

The distance east or west of the prime meridian. Lines of longitude, which meet at the Poles, are known as meridians. The one that runs through Greenwich, England is accepted as the 0° longitude, or Prime Meridian.

MANTLE	MARSH
MESA	MOUNTAIN
MOUNTAIN RANGE	OASIS
PENINSULA	PERMAFROST

A type of wetland forming a grassy fringe near river mouths, and along coastlines protected from open ocean. They are alternately flooded and exposed by the movement of the tides.

One of three main layers of the earth. The middle layer of hot rock, the mantle, is sandwiched between the inner layer, called the core, and the outer layer, called the crust.

Land that rises very high, much higher than the land at its base. Mountains are much higher than hills.

Broad, flat-topped landforms with steep sides. Found mostly in dry regions.

An area made fertile by a source of fresh water in an otherwise arid region. Water in an oasis comes from under-ground springs or from irrigation.

A row of mountains that are joined together. A mountain range makes a giant natural wall.

Permanently frozen layer below the earth's surface consisting of soil, gravel, and sand usually bound together by ice.

A three-sided piece of land jutting out into a lake or ocean.

PLAIN	PLATEAU
PRECIPITATION	PRIME MERIDIAN
RICHTER SCALE	RIVER
RAIN FOREST	ROCK

A large, relatively flat area thatstands above the surrounding land. Plateaus occupy about one-third of the earth's land and occur on every continent.

A large, relatively flat land, often covered with grasses.

The line of O° longitude, the starting point for measuring distance east and west around the globe. It runs through Greenwich, England.

A term that covers all forms in which water falls to earth from the atmosphere. The main types of precipitation are rain, snow, sleet, and hail.

A large, moving body of fresh water that starts at a source in higher land. It drains the water from an area called a basin. The river moves from the higher to the lower land and carries the water to its mouth, where it ends. That mouth is typically at a lake, ocean, sea, or another river.

Developed in the United States by seismologists Charles F. Richter and Beno Gutenburg, it is used to indicate the amount of energy released at the focus of an earthquake.

The material that makes up most of the earth. Rock is a natural substance composed of solid matter. Rocks are divided into three categories according to how they were formed: igneous, sedimentary, or metamorphic.

A moist, densely wooded area usually found in a warm, tropical wet climate.

SAVANNA	SEA
SILT	SOUND
STRAIT	SWAMP
TOPOGRAPHY	TAIGA

A large body of salt water nearly or partly surrounded by land. A sea is much smaller than an ocean.

A tropical grassland with clumps of grasses and widely scattered trees found in warm, tropical regions where rainfall is seasonal; a pro-longed dry season alternates with a rainy season.

A long and wide body of water. A sound connects two larger bodies of water or separates an island from a larger body of land.

A type of matter that water, ice, and wind transport and deposit. Silt is made up of particles of rocks and miner-als that are smaller than fine sand.

An area of land permanently saturated with water and sometimes covered by it. Typically dominated by trees.

A passageway of water that connects two large bodies of water.

A forest of the cold, subarctic regions that begins south of the tundra vegetation. Coniferous, or cone-bearing trees, such as spruce, pine, fir, are common in taiga.

The lay of the land- the shape of the surface features of a geographic area.

TRIBUTARY	**TSUNAMI**
TUNDRA	**VALLEY**
WATER TABLE	**WETLAND**

Ocean waves triggered primarily by movement of the ocean floor during strong earthquakes. Volcanic eruptions in or near the ocean may also cause them.

A stream or river that flows into a larger stream or river.

The lower land between hills or mountains.

A cold region characterized by low vegetation. Plant species are limited in number and are adapted to short growing seasons and cold temperatures. There are two kinds of tundra - the alpine tundra of high mountain ranges and the Arctic tundra of the polar area.

An area of land that is covered by water or that is saturated with surface water or groundwater for long enough periods to support vegetation adapted to wet conditions.

Water, seeping down through the soil under the force of gravity, reaches a zone where the pores in rocks and sediments are saturated, or filled with water. The area where zones of saturated and unsaturated rocks and sediments meet marks the water table.

Seven Continents
In order from largest to smallest in land size:

1. Asia
2. Africa
3. North America
4. South America
5. Antarctica
6. Europe
7. Australia

Four Major Oceans
In order from largest to smallest in area:

1. Pacific Ocean
2. Atlantic Ocean
3. Indian Ocean
4. Arctic Ocean

Extremes
Smallest Continent: Australia
Largest Continent: Asia
Largest Lake: Caspian Sea, Asia
Largest Desert: Sahara, Africa
Highest Waterfall: Angel Falls, Venezuela
Largest Island: Greenland
Longest River: Nile, Africa
Largest Ocean: Pacific
Highest Mountain: Mount Everest
(Himalayan Mountain Range, China/Nepal)

Largest Surface Lakes
Listed in order of area from largest to smallest. Can you find them quickly on a map?

1. Caspian Sea, Asia
2. Lake Superior, Canada/U.S.A.
3. Lake Victoria, Africa
4. Aral Sea, Asia
5. Lake Huron, Canada/U.S.A.
6. Lake Michigan, U.S.A.
7. Lake Tanganyika, Africa

(Note: out of the eight highest mountains, seven are in the Himalayas! Only the second highest, "K2," isn't. It's in the Karakoram Range in China/India.)

Water Facts

Amount of the earth's surface covered by water:	75%
World's largest ocean:	Pacific Ocean
Ocean that separates Europe from America:	Atlantic Ocean
Warmest ocean:	Indian Ocean
Smallest and coldest ocean:	Arctic Ocean
World's largest lake:	Caspian Sea
Europe's most important waterway:	Rhine River

Largest Deserts
How quickly can you find these on a world map?

1. Sahara Desert
2. Australian Deserts
3. Arabian Desert
4. Gobi Desert, central Asia
5. Kalahari Desert, southern Africa

Largest Islands
How quickly can you find these on a world map?

1. Greenland
2. New Guinea
3. Borneo
4. Madagascar
5. Baffin Island
6. Sumatra Island
7. Honshu

World's Longest Rivers
How quickly can you find these on a map?

1. Nile, Africa
2. Amazon, South America
3. Yangtze, Asia
4. Mississippi-Missouri, North America
5. Huang (Yellow), Asia

Rivers with Greatest Volume of Water

1. Amazon, South America
2. Congo, Africa

Although the Nile is slightly longer, the Amazon surpasses it in every other catagory.

Smallest Independent Countries in the World
Can you find them quickly on a map?

1. Vatican City
2. Monaco
3. Nauru
4. Tuvalu
5. San Marino

Largest Countries in the World
Can you find them quickly on a map?

1. Russia
2. Canada
3. China
4. USA
5. Brazil

States and Capitals

Montgomery, Alabama
Juneau, Alaska
Phoenix, Arizona
Little Rock, Arkansas
Sacramento, California
Denver, Colorado
Hartford, Connecticut
Dover, Delaware
Talahassee, Florida
Atlanta, Georgia
Honolulu, Hawaii
Boise, Idaho
Springfield, Illinois
Indianapolis, Indiana
Des Moines, Iowa
Topeka, Kansas
Frankfort, Kentucky

Baton Rouge, Louisiana
Augusta, Maine
Annapolis, Maryland
Boston, Massachusetts
Lansing, Michigan
Saint Paul, Minnesota
Jackson, Mississippi
Jefferson City, Missouri
Helena, Montana
Lincoln, Nebraska
Carson City, Nevada
Concord, New Hampshire
Trenton, New Jersey
Santa Fe, New Mexico
Albany, New York
Raleigh, North Carolina
Bismarck, North Dakota

Columbus, Ohio
Oklahoma City, Oklahoma
Salem, Oregon
Harrisburg, Pennsylvania
Providence, Rhode Island
Columbia, South Carolina
Pierre, South Dakota
Nashville, Tennessee
Austin, Texas
Salt Lake City, Utah
Montpelier, Vermont
Richmond, Virginia
Olympia, Washington
Charleston, West Virginia
Madison, Wisconsin
Cheyenne, Wyoming

Know Your Earth!

Distance around the equator:	24,901 miles
Distance to the center of the earth:	3,963 miles
Average distance: earth to sun:	93,210,000 miles
Average distance: earth to moon:	238,857 miles
Coldest recorded temperature:	Antarctica (-128.6° F)
Hottest recorded temperature:	Al Aziziyah, Libya (136 °F)
Highest average rainfall:	Mt. Waialeale, Hawaii
Driest place on earth:	Atacama Desert, Chile

Notes:

TIMELINE TREKKIN'

CHAPTER 18

TIMELINES FOR YOUR GEOTREKS

Why Use Timelines?

For most people, history was learned in chunks here and there, rarely in chronological order, and never in conjunction with all events in the world that were happening simultaneously. It wouldn't be possible to teach all cultures concurrently. Yet, all people can benefit in their understanding of geography and history when they actually see in a visual form the world's history chronologically.

Nothing puts history in perspective quite like a timeline. The benefits of using a timeline throughout your school year parallel those of utilizing outline maps. It's fascinating and sometimes shocking to discover familiar historical events occurred during the same time period or didn't occur as closely in time as you'd thought. It's common to attempt to teach history in neat, little packaged topics. Missing from the picture, however, is both chronology and a clear understanding regarding how one nation's events affected the history of another. Using timelines faithfully, fills in that gap.

Types of Timelines
There are basically two types of timelines. One is informational, and it comes complete with all dates of importance to the publisher. It may focus on the principal historical events of a particular nation or it may include other nations or topics as well. Informational timelines are sometimes found in your history curriculum, in a separate section of the book, or along the top of the page. Typically, only facts pertinent to the topic at hand are presented.

Of course, there are too many historical events to depict them all at once on any one timeline, although efforts to do so have resulted in the very thick book titled the *Timetables of History*.

The Wall Chart of World History is a fascinating 16 ft. accordian-fold timeline in an oversize book format.

This is a good reference for finding dates and information, but it wasn't designed to be used in an active, everyday way. Besides, you don't expect your students to remember every single date they learned during the course of twelve years in school. (At least we hope you don't!) But you do want them to grasp the important turning points in history, and to understand what else was happening in the world at the same time.

Activity Timeline

This is where the second type of timeline comes in. It's an activity timeline, and the rest of this chapter will be devoted to demonstrating its usefulness. An activity timeline will be blank or have very few details, and it's designed for students to add information to it regularly during the course of studies.

This timeline may be designed in strips with dates every fifty or one hundred years, or it may be done in poster form, a card file or notebook. The student places important information on the timeline in the form of fig- ures or pictures, or simply by writing in the proper place. An activity timeline will provide students with the hands-on learning experience that most often increases memory retention. This visual representation will aid the student's memory as well.

With an activity timeline, only what the student has learned or is learning is placed there. This is what you have deemed important for students to know and understand. Nothing insignificant is ever added to the timeline to distract attention or add confusion. If the student placed something on the timeline during another study, he now has a reference point with which to associate new information.

Activity Timeline
• Hands-on activity
• Custom and personalized
• Starts out blank
• Students add as they learn

Methods
• File Cards
• Strips
• Poster
• Notebook

An activity timeline may be used all year long for all subjects of study, not just during history. It can be prominently displayed for all to see, allowing students to take turns adding information, or allowing each student to keep their own notebooks or file card systems. As events are learned, the student places the key point to remember on the timeline at the location of the date when it occurred. It's recommended the same timeline be used year after year, to build the student's historical base of knowledge.

It's beneficial to put certain historical eras on the timeline at the beginning of the year in order to establish reference points. Some standard eras include the Renaissance, Reformation, Early Middle Ages (Dark Ages), Middle Ages, Enlightenment, Industrial Revolution, etc. It's appropriate to mention that these different ages are extracted and named according to the paradigm of the historian. This is a good reason to start with a blank timeline, adding information reflecting your own philosophy.

A Word About World Views!

Record of History Reflects Philosophy
Although history can appear to be simply a series of events and facts without room for opinion, this is far from the truth! All history is interpreted from the perspective, philosophy, and the world view of the historian presenting the facts. Timelines with pre-selected dates will reflect events of importance to the historian who designed it, but may not reflect your own understanding of history.

Example of Historical Perspectives
There's a distinct difference, for example, between the way a Christian historian and a secular historian view historic events. A Christian historian believes God is active in the unfolding of history. He may naturally associate the thinking of the people in 1215 and the signing of the Magna Carta as having been influenced by the fact that Alfred the Great had parts of the Latin Bible translated into English 300 years before. An historian who believes the Bible played no significant role in history would not view it as an influence on the Magna Carta. Instead, he may interpret events as resulting from other effects, or may not even deem the same events important at all.

Were the "Dark Ages" Dark?
Even the title given to historical eras reflect the world view of the historian who named it. Why were the Dark Ages so named? From the sound of it, you'd expect nothing positive or progres-sively significant happened during that period, from 500-1100 A.D. Yet, this was a time of spiritual awareness and developing skills. Buddhism spread in China and Japan. Islam was established by Mohammed and spread to Arabia, Spain, and northern India or to any area they conquered. Art was used for religious purposes. Benedictine monks taught that life should be filled with manual labor, prayer and worship. They provided medical care and preserved learning from the classical period by copying manuscripts. Vikings became Christians. Charlemagne founded schools in cathedrals and monasteries. In fact, by 1100 nearly all of Europe had accepted Christianity.

This was the period of time when monks copied books with beautifully decorated capital lettering. Germanic people were skilled at metal work and making gold and silver jewelry. The Chinese designed intricate porcelain and pottery and made the first printing press. Vikings were skilled wood carvers. Farm tools such as the scythe, sickle, flail and plows were designed and built of iron. Justinian laws were established that later influenced the laws of nearly all European countries. Would you have named this era the "Dark Ages?"

What was the Renaissance About?

Likewise, from the 1400's to 1600 A.D. is the time period historians designate the "Renaissance." New birth is depicted in this name. Interest in the arts and the learning of ancient Greeks and Romans surfaced anew. Man became interested in Greek medical manuscripts; the human body was venerated. The many beautiful pieces of art that came from this period demonstrate a mixture of Greek and Roman pagan ideals combined with Biblical ideas. It reflected the growing value system rooted in the belief that man is autonomous and therefore totally independent. The sculpture of David by Michelangelo is a clear example of the humanism of the day. There he is, man, with great confidence in himself for the future. Man is powerful. The painting, "Red Virgin," by Fouquet was the first to depict a likeness of the Virgin Mary in a disrespectful way. To those who view this era as a time of architectural advances, scientific achievement and artistic beauty, it was indeed a Renaissance. But to some Christians it may not have been considered a time of rebirth, but rather an irreverent turning away from dependence on God toward faith in mere man.

Activity Timelines Can Reflect Your World View

It's easy to see how your own philosophy and theology is reflected in the way historical events are taught. Whether you choose to call it the "Dark Ages" or "Early Middle Ages," or whether you choose to focus on the Renaissance or the Reformation that occurred almost simultaneously, is totally up to you. If you decide to establish a reference point on your activity timeline, a world view will be depicted in the way you prefer.

Examples of Eras

Although it's hard to designate exact eras of time, here are some suggestions. Exact start and stop dates vary according to different resources. Eras are listed, along with approximate dates that coincide with the name given to the period. Some historians prefer to use the newer B.C.E. and C.E. (before the Common Era and Common Era) instead of the traditional B.C. and A.D. (Before Christ and Anno Domini - in the year of our Lord.)

40,000 B.C. - 500 B.C.	Ancient World
40,000 B.C. -10,000 B.C.	Ice Age
5000 B.C. - 2000 B.C.	Stone Age
c.2000 B.C. - 3500 B.C.	Bronze Age
3500 B.C. - 500 A.D.	Ancient Civilization
499 B.C. - 500 A.D.	Classical World
500 - 1500 A.D.	Middle Ages
501 - 1100 A.D.	Early Middle Ages/Dark Ages
1101 - 1460 A.D.	Middle Ages
1461 - 1600 A.D.	Renaissance

Read More About It

Want more information about World Views? Try these enlightening books:
- *How Should We Then Live?* by Francis A. Schaeffer
- *Understanding the Times* by David Noebel
- *The Collapse of the Brass Heaven* by Zeb Bradford Long and Douglas McMurry

1517 - c.1600 A.D.   Reformation
1601 -1707 A.D.   Trade and Empire
1708 -1835 A.D.   Revolution and Independence
c.1715 - c.1789 A.D.   Enlightenment
1836 - 1914 A.D.   Unification and Colonization
1914 - 1949 A.D.   World at War
1950 - today   Modern World

American history can be divided into additional eras:

Exploration
Pilgrims/Colonization
Revolution
Western Expansion
Civil War
Reconstruction
Industrialization
World War Era
Modern Times

c. = circa
Used before dates, to reflect an approximate year when exact dates are unknown.

TERRIFIC TIPS ON CONSTRUCTING TIMELINES!

There are several methods for organizing historical events on a timeline. We give you four different ideas. Choose the system that best suits your fancy. You can keep a chronological card file, stretch out history strips across the wall, use a poster, or keep an ongoing timeline notebook.

Terrific Timeline #1: File Cards

Dates and events can be recorded on 3 x 5 cards and put in order in a file box. These cards can also be placed along the wall by stretching a piece of string or twine across the wall and attaching with nails or pushpins. Cards are then hung clothesline-style with paper clips. Allow cards to hang in a way so they can freely slide by the upper edge of the paper clip along the twine. When you want to add new dates, the old cards can simply slide over to make room for new ones.

Terrific Timeline #2: Strips

Another method uses a bulletin board border. Attach the border strips on the bulletin board or along a wall. Make hash marks vertically on the border every four to six inches. These hash marks can represent ten years, twenty-five years, fifty years or whatever you desire. This is a real advantage, since there are time eras you'll study up close and personal (such as the American Revolution or the Civil War), and there are broader spans of time that will be covered (such as Ancient Rome). This timeline can be adapted to fit your individual needs.

The best way to use this kind of timeline is to have students attach timeline figures to the strips representing the historical period or event being studied. There are over 300 different reproducible figures included in this unit, or students can draw their own from whatever materials you're studying. When using paper, it's a good idea to laminate figures or cover with clear contact paper to keep them looking fresh. The "poor man's lamination," clear, wide packing tape, works great with this size. Attach with rolled tape, glue stick or sticky tack.

Terrific Timeline #3: Poster

This same method can be used on a poster-type of timeline. The poster style doesn't take up as much space stretching across the room. Make your own with poster board or purchase an inexpensive, poster-style laminated timeline. (See Resources at the back of this book.) The laminated timeline has dates on one side and unlabeled hash marks on the reverse side for expanded studies. As your school year progresses students can write events, draw pictures, and place timeline figures on the poster.

The Mark-It Timeline of History poster is highly recommended. See Resources.

Terrific Timeline #4: Notebook

Another popular method is the notebook format. You can use the reproducible "Notebook Timeline of History" in the next chapter. Place the dates you want to cover on the upper shaded blocks. Label hash marks as you see fit. Each can represent one year, two years, five years, or whatever. Two lines are provided to enable your student to follow parallel events. For example, if you're studying European history and want to follow what's happening in America at the same time, place European events under the top line in the wide space provided and American events above the lower line.

See an example of a completed page of the notebook timeline on page 294.

Another fascinating approach to use with double lines is to track art, literature, music, or scientific breakthroughs as they flow through history. Lines below the timeline are provided for the student to record details of events he wants to remember. He may want to research other corresponding contemporary topics and record them by coloring in the icon (science, for example) and noting any scientific discovery that occurred at the same time next to that icon. Students can draw or tape pictures in the lower area as well.

Setting Up the Notebook

- Make copies of the "Notebook Timeline of History" from page 300.
- Mark and label dates, or perhaps add eras before you begin. (Later when you're ready to place information on the time-line you won't have to figure out where to put it.)
- Pages should be reproduced, labeled, and placed in a three-ring binder by the first week of school.
- You may choose to have students label the dates according to your instructions.

How Many Copies Do I Make?

1. Counting hash marks:

- Decide how many years you want each page to represent.

- If you want each page to represent 20 years, each hash mark would equal one year. (100 years? Each mark equals 5 years.)

- Divide the total number of years you want your timeline to cover by how many years each page represents. Now you know how many pages to copy for each student.

Notebook Timeline of History

Dates go here

Place events to remember here. There is plenty of room for figures, pictures, or overlapping events.

Track parallel events here.

Use these symbols to help identify topic of record

Write details, stories, summary paragraphs, drawings, diagrams or other information on these lines. See a segment of a completed timeline on next page.

© GeoCreations, Ltd. 1998

2. Here are some recommendations for how many years each page could cover:

- During dates B.C., each hash mark can represent twenty to one-hundred years. (Using twenty years, each page represents 400 years. If you're dating back to 5000 B.C., you'll need thirteen pages for dates.)

- During dates A.D. you may want each hash mark to equal two to five years.

- If hash marks equal twenty years during B.C. and two years during A.D., you'll need about 40 copies of the timeline page per student.

- It is not necessary to make every page represent the same number of years. Be flexible, do what works best for your need.

3. If you don't want all of history at your fingertips, just reproduce enough to get through the time period you're studying.

Please Note:
Don't expect every page of your timeline to have this much information. Some periods of history are not as action-packed.

SAMPLE COMPLETED NOTEBOOK TIMELINE PAGE

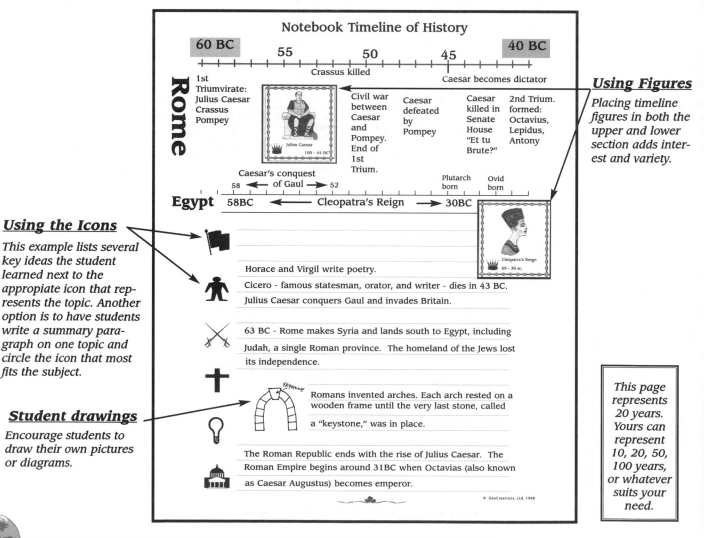

Using Figures

Placing timeline figures in both the upper and lower section adds interest and variety.

Using the Icons

This example lists several key ideas the student learned next to the appropiate icon that represents the topic. Another option is to have students write a summary paragraph on one topic and circle the icon that most fits the subject.

Student drawings

Encourage students to draw their own pictures or diagrams.

This page represents 20 years. Yours can represent 10, 20, 50, 100 years, or whatever suits your need.

FANTASTIC FIGURES!

The timeline figures in this book are designed for you to photo-copy. Each figure is encrypted with visual messages to help students absorb information with just a quick glance at the timeline.

The timeline figures in this book are also available in color on CD-ROM from Geography Matters. Using PDF files and Adobe Acrobat Reader, simply print the pages from your home computer.

- Note the variety of **borders** around the figures.
  The seven different borders represent the **era** during which the event occurred.
- Note the various small icons in the lower left corner.
  There are ten **icons,** each representing the **topic** covered.
- Copy on colored card stock. Each **color** represents a specific **geographical region** (continent.)

Then the location, era, and topic are visible at a glance.

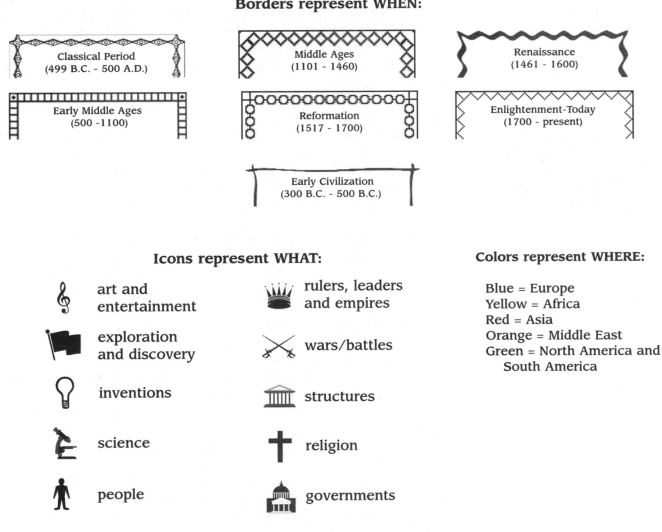

Borders represent WHEN:

Classical Period
(499 B.C. - 500 A.D.)

Middle Ages
(1101 - 1460)

Renaissance
(1461 - 1600)

Early Middle Ages
(500 -1100)

Reformation
(1517 - 1700)

Enlightenment-Today
(1700 - present)

Early Civilization
(300 B.C. - 500 B.C.)

Icons represent WHAT:

- art and entertainment
- exploration and discovery
- inventions
- science
- people
- rulers, leaders and empires
- wars/battles
- structures
- religion
- governments

Colors represent WHERE:

Blue = Europe
Yellow = Africa
Red = Asia
Orange = Middle East
Green = North America and South America

An option for the timeline figures: Copy onto adhesive paper. Highlight border only for color-coding. Let students color the figures. Cut, peel, and stick the timeline figures onto your timeline. This is especially fun for artistic students who enjoy coloring.

More Terrific Timeline Tips!

Don't expect everything to be placed in the exact date location when it happened. Sometimes overlapping events occur that prevent a fact from being placed in the exact spot. The goal is for students to visualize the chronology of history and to understand what events were contemporary with one another.

When studying a period of history close-up, such as the Revolutionary War or conquests of Alexander the Great, an expanded timeline with room for detail is just the ticket. Allow for an extra page or two to record the finer details. Each hash mark may now represent one year or one month. When the study is complete, return to the general timeline and let students choose the most interesting event to represent that in-depth study.

Use the "Map and Timeline Assignments" sheet in chapter 16 to list dates and events you wish your student to record on his timeline. Where do you get these dates and events? From the daily lessons! Whatever you are studying can be depicted on a timeline. Select important turning points or particular topics of interest. Add to the assignment sheet throughout the study. Recording appropriate information on an outline map at the same time is especially beneficial.

Color-code events on a timeline to aid the visual learner. Try this:
- Red for USA History
- Blue for World History
- Green for Science and Technology

Color-Coding and Graphics

Color-coding the timeline adds interest and enhances memory retention. If you're writing events on your timeline, color-code time eras or topics such as science and technology, structures, events, people, and explorers. Draw pictures and diagrams on the timeline or add timeline figures.

The figures in this book are arranged according to where events took place. If you copy the Europe pages in blue and the Americas in green, for instance, your students can tell at a glance where and when an event occurred. If you're copying them on white card stock, let students color the borders of each figure according to the color indicated.

Family Heritage

The blank timeline page can also be used for a family heritage research project. Make five to seven copies of "Notebook Timeline of History" sheets per student. Each sheet represents twenty years if each mark represents one year. Challenge students to locate family information related to the last one hundred years. Students can record births, deaths, anniversaries, accomplishments, movement/relocation, and other important events of parents, grandparents, great grandparents, and any other ancestors.

Use the "Family Heritage" timeline figures, and also obtain pictures of as many family members represented on the timeline as possible. If pictures are too delicate or rare to place in the notebook, make copies from a high quality copy machine. Even old color photos copy well on today's color copiers.

It's especially interesting to research historical events that occurred simultaneously and add to the timeline in words, pictures, or drawings. Pictures of the newest model of car, tractor, or current clothing of the day are great to place on the timeline. Any "new" inventions or fascinating facts will make this a meaningful project. It's a wonderful family treasure to cherish or give!

Please Note: Space does not allow representation of all family types and colors in our Family Heritage timeline figures. Encourage students to make figures of their family by drawing, using graphics, or copying family photos.

Making Your Own Figures

Can't find the exact figure you want? Adapt one of our generic figures to suit your needs. Encourage students to make their own figures to add to their timeline. Using the generic figures included in this set, students can trace or draw in the icons and appropriate border. Often, your textbook will have a great picture that the student can copy or trace. Don't forget to color in the border to represent which continent or area the event occurred.

Outline Maps

Timeline figures are great to use on outline maps! Place events of historical importance near the location on your map and draw a line to its origin. Use the many areas of the map not in use, like the border or the ocean, to tape the figure. (Or on laminate, use a removable glue stick.) Kinesthetic learners like to connect a string or piece of yarn from the figure to the map.

Note: For a chronological listing of the dates included in our set of figures see Appendix C. The additional separate alphabetical index for the timeline figures and Who Am I? cards makes finding them easy.

GREAT GAMES KIDS LOVE TO PLAY

Before and After (Using the Timeline Figures)

Copy the timeline figures on colored card stock, laminate, and cut along borders to form cards. Shuffle all the cards or use only the colored cards that represent the place you've chosen or those with the borders that represent the era you wish to play.

You may extend the length of time the game is played by dealing out more cards at the beginning of the game.

For two players or two teams:
- Deal five cards to each player. Place the rest of the cards face down as a draw pile.
- Player A takes one card from his hand and reads the event (not the date) on the chosen card. He asks player B: "Can you find an event from your cards that occurred BEFORE (or AFTER) this?"

- Player B takes a card from his own hand that he believes did occur BEFORE (or AFTER) A's card, and reads it.
- Both cards are shown and dates are compared to determine if player B was correct in his choice.
- If player B was correct, he keeps both cards and sets them aside. It is now player B's turn to ask.
- If player B was incorrect he draws from the draw pile, Player A keeps both cards aside, and gets to continue until he stumps his opponent. Then it becomes player B's turn.
- Cards are drawn from the draw pile only when the player answering the question is incorrect in his choice.
- Play continues until one player is out of cards.
- Points are scored by counting cards kept aside. Each card counts one point. Each card left in the hand at the end of play counts as one point against his total score.

This game can be played by more than two players. Players ask questions to the player on his left and answers questions from the player on his right.

Who Am I?

This game is designed to spark curiosity in students and will introduce them to many of the timeline figures in the next chapter. Players try to guess "who" or "what" from a list of clues. You can pick cards that reflect the era of history you're covering and play the game as an introduction to the course or use as a wrap-up to a study. Let students make their own "Who Am I?" clues and list them on the generic cards provided.

Scoring:
5 points for answering correctly on the first clue

4 points for answering correctly on the second clue.

3 points for answering correctly on the third clue

2 points for answering correctly on the fourth clue

1 point for answering correctly on the fifth clue

Here's how to play:
Copy the "Who Am I?" cards (in chapter 19) onto card stock and laminate, if desired. Make several copies of the score sheet. A caller can be designated or players can take turns asking the questions. All other players write their answers on their score sheet.

1. The first clue is given. Each player tries to answer the question based on the first clue alone and writes the answer on the first line. Have no idea? Place an X there, instead.
2. The second clue is given and players try again. Place the answer on line two of the score sheet, or place an X.
3. When all clues are given, the caller identifies the correct answer.

As with all of our games, feel free to adapt the rules to suit your own class or to include your own great ideas.

TOOLS FOR THE TIME TRAVELER

CHAPTER 19

Reproducibles for your Timeline

Notebook Timeline of History
Timeline Figures
Who Am I? Score Sheet
Who Am I? Game

300

AFRICA

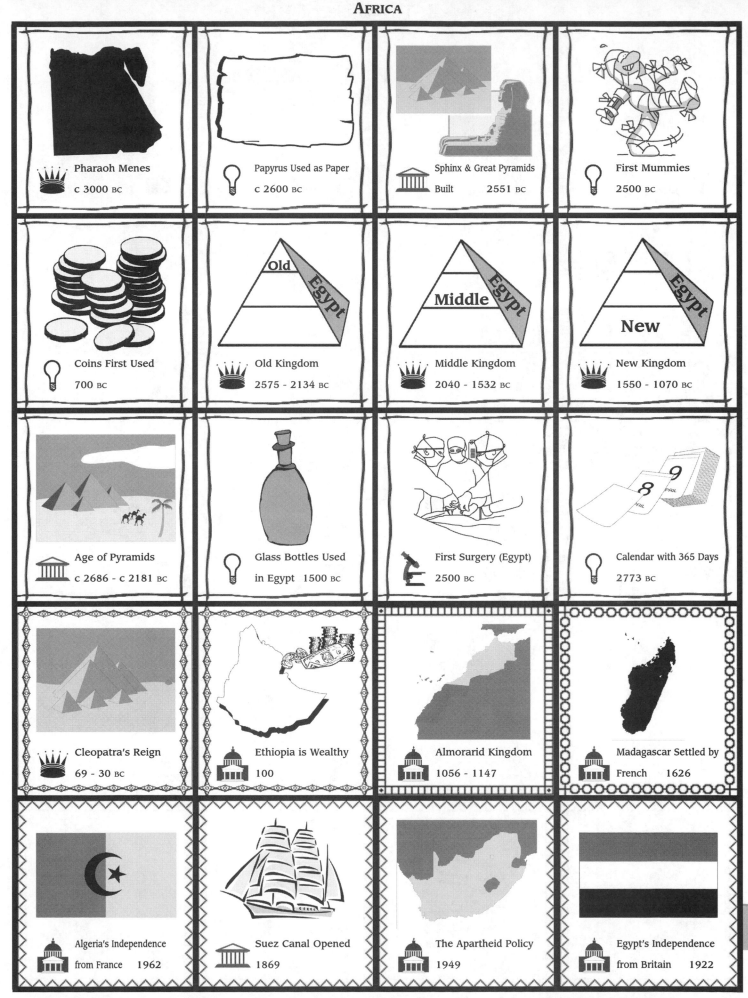

Pharaoh Menes
c 3000 BC

Papyrus Used as Paper
c 2600 BC

Sphinx & Great Pyramids Built
2551 BC

First Mummies
2500 BC

Coins First Used
700 BC

Old Kingdom
2575 - 2134 BC

Middle Kingdom
2040 - 1532 BC

New Kingdom
1550 - 1070 BC

Age of Pyramids
c 2686 - c 2181 BC

Glass Bottles Used in Egypt
1500 BC

First Surgery (Egypt)
2500 BC

Calendar with 365 Days
2773 BC

Cleopatra's Reign
69 - 30 BC

Ethiopia is Wealthy
100

Almorarid Kingdom
1056 - 1147

Madagascar Settled by French
1626

Algeria's Independence from France
1962

Suez Canal Opened
1869

The Apartheid Policy
1949

Egypt's Independence from Britain
1922

Print this sheet in <u>YELLOW</u> or color the borders <u>YELLOW</u>!   These events occurred in AFRICA.   **301**

Solar Eclipse
First Date in Chinese History   755 BC

Chinese Start Weaving Silk   c 2690 BC

First Chinese Language Dictionary   1100 - 900 BC

Chou (Zhou) Dynasty   1122 - 256 BC

China's First Zoo   2000 BC

First Kite   390 BC

Shang Dynasty   1500 - 1122 BC

Magnetic Compass   c 270

Great Gupta Empire   320 - 535

Silk Paintings & Pottery Figures   c 150 BC

Great Wall of China   218 - 204 BC

Buddhism Introduced in China   50 BC - AD 50

Han Dynasty   c 206 BC - AD c 221

Chin (Qin) Dynasty   221 - 207 BC

Buddha   563 - 483 BC

Imperial Canal Built   605 - 610

Age of Iron & Steel   900

First Mass Production of Books   932

Samurai   c 1000 - c 1877

T'ang Dynasty   618 - 907

302   Print this sheet in PINK or color the borders PINK!   These events occurred in ASIA.

Song Dynasty
960 - 1279

Wooden Blocks for Printing
(China)   593

Genghis Khan
1167 - 1227

Mongol Empire
1279 - 1368

Rockets Used in Battle
1232

Ming Dynasty
1368 - 1644

Peter the Great
1689 - 1725

Mongul Empire
1527 - 1803

Taj Mahal Built
1629 - 1650

JAPAN

Russia

Russo-Japanese War
1904 - 1905

Vladimir Lenin
1870 - 1924

Bolshevik Revolution
1917

People's Republic of
China   1946

Opium War
1839 - 1860

Empress Tzu Hui
1862 - 1908

Mahatma Gandhi
1869 - 1948

Manchu Dynasty
1644 - 1912

BRITAIN, FRANCE,
& TURKEY

Russia

Crimean War
1854 - 1856

Communist
Party

Karl Marx
1818 - 1883

C

Confucius
551 - 479 BC

Print this sheet in <u>PINK</u> or color the borders <u>PINK</u>!   These events occurred in ASIA.   303

First Day in Mayan Calendar 3372 BC

Mayan Golden Age 300 - 600

Tenochtitlan Founded 1325

African Slaves in America 1502

Hernan Cortes 1485 - 1547

Hernando de Soto 1500 - 1542

Virginia Colony Founded 1607

Pilgrims Reach Cape Cod 1620

Salem Witch Trials 1692

Boston Tea Party 1773

Revolutionary War 1776 - 1783

The Declaration of Independence 1776

Treaty of Paris 1783

George Washington 1789 - 1797

California Gold Rush 1849

UNION Confederates Civil War 1861 - 1865

Lewis & Clark Expedition 1804 - 1806

Thomas Edison 1847 - 1931

Airplane Invented 1903

Japanese Attack Pearl Harbor 1941

304 Print this sheet in <u>GREEN</u> or color the borders <u>GREEN</u>! These events occurred in AMERICA.

Henry Hudson ? - 1611	Quakers Settle Pennsylvania 1682	First College (Harvard) Founded 1636	Abortion Legalized 1973
First Space Shuttle 1981	The Telephone 1875	Titanic Sinks 1912	Prohibition 1919
Government Programs / The New Deal 1933 - 1945	Polio Vaccination 1954	Prayer from Schools 1962	Northwest Ordinance 1787
Indians Become American Citizens 1924	Booker T. Washington 1856 - 1915	U.S. War with Mexico 1846 - 1848	Louisiana Purchase 1803
Transcontinental Railroad 1869	Pony Express 1860 - 1861	Homestead Act 1862	Cotton Gin 1793

Print this sheet in <u>GREEN</u> or color the borders <u>GREEN</u>!   These events occurred in AMERICA.   305

Golden Gate Bridge 1937

Statue of Liberty 1886

First Mickey Mouse Cartoon 1928

George W. Bush 2001-

Henry Ford 1863 - 1947

Radio Broadcasting in U.S.A. 1920

Color TV 1950

Clara Barton 1821 - 1912

Man Walks on Moon 1969

Panama Canal Finished 1914

Martin Luther King Jr. 1929 - 1968

The Alamo 1836

U.S. Stock Market Crashes 1929

The Great Depression 1929 - 1932

Atom Bomb First Used 1945

Monroe Doctrine 1823

Salvation Army Founded 1865

Sequoya 1770 - 1843

Simon Bolivar 1783 - 1830

Albert Einstein 1879 - 1955

306   Print this sheet in <u>GREEN</u> or color the borders <u>GREEN</u>!   These events occurred in AMERICA.

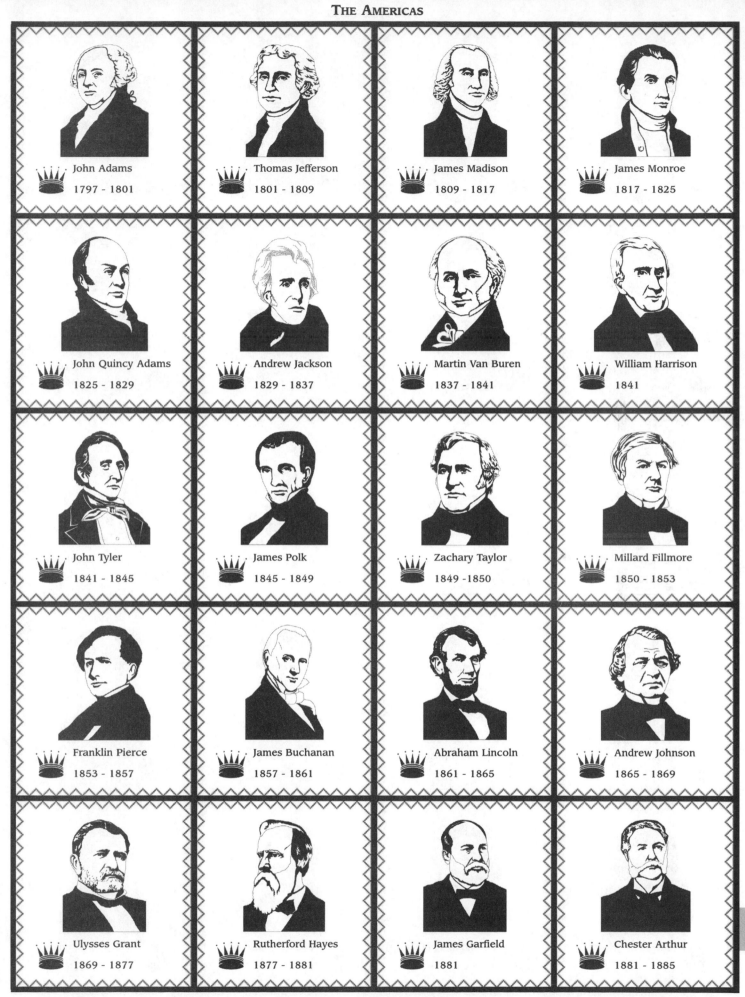

Print this sheet in <u>GREEN</u> or color the borders <u>GREEN</u>! These events occurred in AMERICA. 307

Print this sheet in <u>GREEN</u> or color the borders <u>GREEN</u>! These events occurred in AMERICA.

Leonardo da Vinci
1452 - 1519

Marco Polo
1254 - 1324

Paper First Made
c 1150

The Inquisition Begins
1233

Canterbury Tales
1388

Movable Type Used
1440

FRANCE

England

Hundred Years' War
1337 - 1453

Brother
Sun

Sister
Moon

St. Francis of Assisi
1182 - 1226

Bible Now in English
1380

Black Plague
1347 - 1353

Richard the Lion Hearted
1157 - 1199

Popes Dominated by
French   1309 - 1377

Magnifying Glass
1266

Byzantine Empire
395 - 1453

Joan of Arc
1412 - 1431

Pablo Picasso
1881 - 1973

King John

Magna Carta Signed
1215

Leaning Tower of Pisa
1174

Sir Walter Raleigh
c 1552 - 1618

Ireland

James Connoly
1870 - 1916

Print this sheet in <u>BLUE</u> or color the borders <u>BLUE</u>!   These events occurred in EUROPE.   309

Trojan Wars
c 1250 - 1240 BC

Iliad & Odyssey
c 700 BC

Stonehenge
2700 BC

First Olympic Games
776 BC

Athens 1st Democracy
508 BC

John Calvin
1509 - 1564

Nicolaus Copernicus
1473 - 1543

Mary Queen of Scots
1542 - 1587

Archimedes
c 287 - 212 BC

Constantine
c 280 - 337

Marc Antony
c 83 - 30 BC

Philip II
382 - 336 BC

Ptolemy
90 - 168

First Christian Persecution
54 - 68

Emperor Nero
37 - 68

Hippocrates
c 460 - 377 BC

Legendary King Arthur
c 503

The First Pope
42

Last Roman Emperor
Dethroned 476

The League of Nations
1919

310   Print this sheet in <u>BLUE</u> or color the borders <u>BLUE</u>!   These events occurred in EUROPE.

Microscope Invented
1590

Spanish Armada Defeated
1588

Johann Sebastian Bach
1685 - 1750

Isaac Newton
1642 - 1727

Pilgrim's Progress
1678

King James Bible
1611

Puritan Revolution (England)
1640

The Reformation Starts
c 1516

First Surgery
1528

Galileo's Telescope
1610

CATHOLICS

Protestants

Thirty Years' War
1618 - 1648

C ommonwealth of

I ndependent

S tates

The CIS (Russia)
1991

Our Family Heritage

Our Family Heritage

Our Family Heritage

Our Family Heritage

Our Family Heritage

Our Family Heritage

Our Family Heritage

Our Family Heritage

Print this sheet in <u>BLUE</u> or color the borders <u>BLUE</u>! These events occurred in EUROPE. 311

SPARTA

Athens

GREEKS

Persians

ROMANS

Carthage

Parthenon
477 - 432 BC

Peloponnesian War
431 - 404 BC

Persian War
c 490 - 479 BC

Punic Wars
264 - 146 BC

Alexander's Empire
Divided 323 - 319 BC

Aristotle
384 - 322 BC

Socrates
469 - 399 BC

Plato
427 - 347 BC

Rome Destroyed by Fire
64

Concrete First Used
in Rome c 200 BC

Julian Calendar
c 45 BC

Alexander the Great
356 - 323 BC

Greek Classical Period
480 BC

Golden Age of Athens
477 - 405 BC

Hannibal
247 - 183 BC

Julius Caesar
100 - 44 BC

ROME

Roman Empire
31 BC - AD 476

ROME

Roman Empire Divided
395

Octavian (Caesar Augustus)
63 BC - AD 14

John Wesley
1703 - 1791

312   Print this sheet in <u>BLUE</u> or color the borders <u>BLUE</u>!   These events occurred in EUROPE.

William Shakespeare
1564 - 1616

Ponce de Leon
1460 - 1521

First Watch
1504

Bartholomeu Dias
c 1450 - 1500

Modern Globe
1492

Galileo Galilee
1564 - 1642

Spain Established
1478

Holland's Independence
1587

Christopher Columbus
1451 - 1506

Spanish Inquisition
Starts   1478

Ferdinand & Isabella
1469 - 1516

Henry VIII Separates from
the Church   1534

Michelangelo Buonarroti
1475 - 1564

Queen Elizabeth
1558 - 1603

Henry VIII
1491 - 1547

Council of Trent
1545

Ferdinand Magellan
1480 - 1521

Martin Luther
1483 - 1546

Scientific Revolution
1543

John Wycliffe
1320-1384

Print this sheet in <u>BLUE</u> or color the borders <u>BLUE</u>!   These events occurred in EUROPE.   313

Vikings Settle Iceland
874

Lief Ericsson Discovers
North America   1003

Pope Nicolas I
858 - 867

Otto I of Germany
936 - 973

The Crusades
1096 - 1204

Charlemagne
771 - 841

Pope Gregory VII Challenges
Henry VI   1077

Treaty of Verdun
843

New Holy Roman Empire
962 - 1806

Catholic Church Divides
1054

West   East

Battle of Hastings
1066

William the Conqueror
1027 - 1087

Florence Nightingale
1820 - 1910

N ORTH
A TLANTIC
T REATY
O RGANIZATION
NATO
1949

Francis Ferdinand
? - 1914

Benito Mussolini
1883 - 1945

D - Day
1944

Miracle of Dunkirk
1940

Munich Agreement
1938

Y OUNG
M EN'S
C HRISTIAN
A SSOCIATION
YMCA Founded
1844

Print this sheet in <u>BLUE</u> or color the borders <u>BLUE</u>!   These events occurred in EUROPE.

Eiffel Tower 1889	**Balkan Wars** 1829 - 1913	**Greek Independence** 1829	**BRITAIN** *France* **Seven Years' War** 1756 - 1763
Poison Gas Used in War 1915	**Lusitania Sinks** 1915	**Tanks Used in Battle** 1916	**Berlin Wall Built** 1961
Ludwig Von Beethoven 1770 - 1827	**Napoleon Bonaparte** 1769 - 1821	**Captain James Cook** 1728 - 1779	**GERMANY** *France* **Franco - Prussian War** 1870 - 1871
ALLIES **Central Powers** **World War I** 1914 - 1918	**Adolf Hitler** 1889 - 1945	**Spanish Civil War** 1936 - 1939	**ALLIES** *Axis* **World War II** 1939 - 1945
French Revolution 1789 - 1799	FRANCE HUNGRY GERMANY ITALY **The Triple Alliance** 1882 - 1915	FRANCE RUSSIA UNTIED KINGDOM **The Triple Entente** 1890 - 1915	**Treaty of Versailles** 1919

Print this sheet in <u>BLUE</u> or color the borders <u>BLUE</u>!   These events occurred in EUROPE.   315

Hammurabi's Reign
1792 - 1750 BC

Earliest Known Map
c 3800 BC

Bronze First Used
c 3760 BC

Writing Appears
c 3200 BC

Wheeled Vehicles
c 3000 BC

First Iron Objects Made
c 3000 BC

Basis for Modern
Alphabet c 2000 BC

Windmills Used
600 BC

The Hanging Gardens
580 BC

N. Kingdom of Israel
Destroyed 722 BC

Fall of Babylon
539 BC

Cyrus of Persia
? - 529 BC

Birth of Jesus
c 4

Parchment Replaces Stone
Tablets   460 BC

Jerusalem Falls to Crusaders
1099

Mohammed (Muhammad)
570 - 631

Islam Introduced
622

Ottoman Empire
c 1300 - 1918

Persian Gulf War
1991

Resettlement of Israel
1909

316 Print this sheet in <u>TAN</u> or color the borders <u>TAN</u>!   These events occurred in THE MIDDLE EAST.

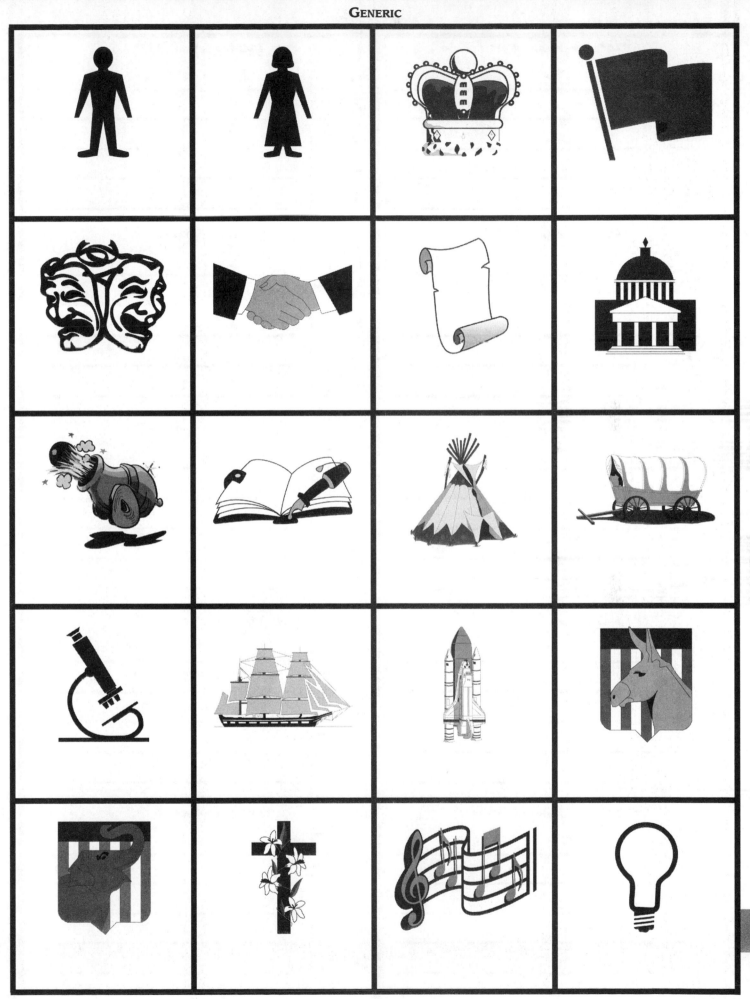

WHO AM I ?		**WHO AM I ?**
5 ☐ _____		5 ☐ _____
4 ☐ _____		4 ☐ _____
3 ☐ _____		3 ☐ _____
2 ☐ _____		2 ☐ _____
1 ☐ _____		1 ☐ _____

WHO AM I ?		**WHO AM I ?**
5 ☐ _____		5 ☐ _____
4 ☐ _____		4 ☐ _____
3 ☐ _____		3 ☐ _____
2 ☐ _____		2 ☐ _____
1 ☐ _____		1 ☐ _____

WHO AM I ?		**WHO AM I ?**
5 ☐ _____		5 ☐ _____
4 ☐ _____		4 ☐ _____
3 ☐ _____		3 ☐ _____
2 ☐ _____		2 ☐ _____
1 ☐ _____		1 ☐ _____

WHO AM I ?		**WHO AM I ?**
5 ☐ _____		5 ☐ _____
4 ☐ _____		4 ☐ _____
3 ☐ _____		3 ☐ _____
2 ☐ _____		2 ☐ _____
1 ☐ _____		1 ☐ _____

WHO AM I ?		**WHO AM I ?**
5 ☐ _____		5 ☐ _____
4 ☐ _____		4 ☐ _____
3 ☐ _____		3 ☐ _____
2 ☐ _____		2 ☐ _____
1 ☐ _____		1 ☐ _____

WHO AM I?

- I was a ten year war.
- I was fought between the Mycenaean and the Trojans.
- I ended with the burning of the city of Troy.
- I spanned from around 1250 - 1240 BC.

THE TROJAN WAR

WHO AM I?

- I was made up of three wars.
- I was caused over jealousy between Sparta and Athens.
- I ended with the destruction of the Athenian Navy.
- I spanned from 431 - 404 BC.

THE PELOPONNESIAN WAR

WHO AM I?

- I am one of the most elaborate megalithic monuments in Europe.
- It is thought I was built to mark midwinter's moon rise and midsummer's sunrise.
- I am located on the Salisbury Plain, England.
- I was finished around 2700 BC.

STONEHENGE

WHO AM I?

- My empire was the largest in the world.
- I conquered the Persians.
- I was the son of Philip II.
- I was 20 when I inherited the Macedon throne.
- I died at age 32.
- My life time was from 356 - 323 BC.

ALEXANDER THE GREAT

WHO AM I?

- I was widely read and memorized by the Greeks.
- I consisted of two poems.
- I was written by Homer who refined and rewrote many old stories and myths.
- I was composed around 700 BC.

THE ILIAD AND THE ODYSSEY

WHO AM I?

- I was known as the cruelest Roman Emperor.
- I was first to persecute the Christians.
- I had my mother and first wife murdered.
- It's rumored that I set Rome on fire and then blamed the Christians.
- I lived from 37 - 68.

NERO

WHO AM I?

- I was an event held to honor the gods.
- My participants were able to show off their athletic skills.
- I was held at the sanctuary of Zeus at Olympia, Greece.
- I was first held in 776 BC.

THE FIRST OLYMPICS

WHO AM I?

- I was known as the "Father of Modern Medicine."
- I used the power of observation to detect many different illnesses.
- I was born in Greece.
- I lived from around 460 - 377 BC.

HIPPOCRATES

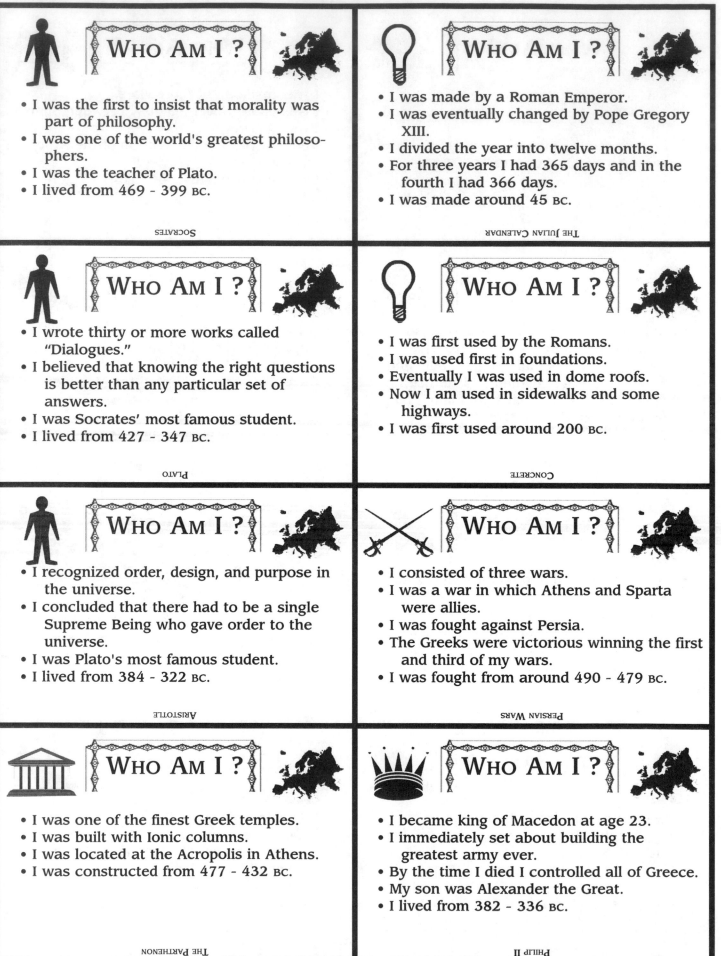

WHO AM I?

- I was the first to insist that morality was part of philosophy.
- I was one of the world's greatest philosophers.
- I was the teacher of Plato.
- I lived from 469 - 399 BC.

SOCRATES

WHO AM I?

- I was made by a Roman Emperor.
- I was eventually changed by Pope Gregory XIII.
- I divided the year into twelve months.
- For three years I had 365 days and in the fourth I had 366 days.
- I was made around 45 BC.

THE JULIAN CALENDAR

WHO AM I?

- I wrote thirty or more works called "Dialogues."
- I believed that knowing the right questions is better than any particular set of answers.
- I was Socrates' most famous student.
- I lived from 427 - 347 BC.

PLATO

WHO AM I?

- I was first used by the Romans.
- I was used first in foundations.
- Eventually I was used in dome roofs.
- Now I am used in sidewalks and some highways.
- I was first used around 200 BC.

CONCRETE

WHO AM I?

- I recognized order, design, and purpose in the universe.
- I concluded that there had to be a single Supreme Being who gave order to the universe.
- I was Plato's most famous student.
- I lived from 384 - 322 BC.

ARISTOTLE

WHO AM I?

- I consisted of three wars.
- I was a war in which Athens and Sparta were allies.
- I was fought against Persia.
- The Greeks were victorious winning the first and third of my wars.
- I was fought from around 490 - 479 BC.

PERSIAN WARS

WHO AM I?

- I was one of the finest Greek temples.
- I was built with Ionic columns.
- I was located at the Acropolis in Athens.
- I was constructed from 477 - 432 BC.

THE PARTHENON

WHO AM I?

- I became king of Macedon at age 23.
- I immediately set about building the greatest army ever.
- By the time I died I controlled all of Greece.
- My son was Alexander the Great.
- I lived from 382 - 336 BC.

PHILIP II

320

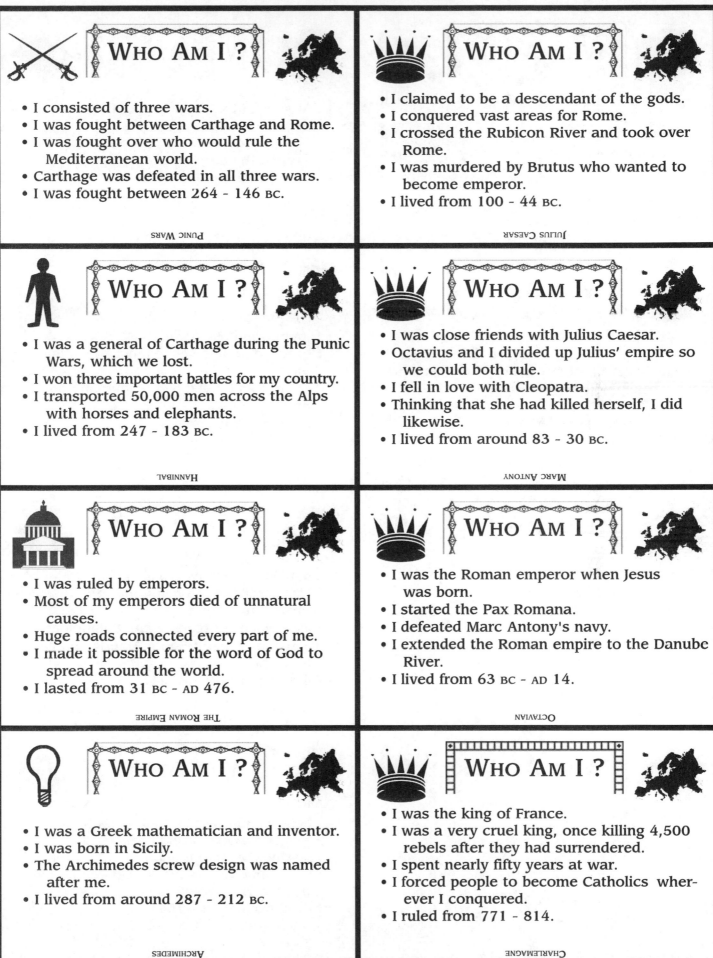

WHO AM I?

- I consisted of three wars.
- I was fought between Carthage and Rome.
- I was fought over who would rule the Mediterranean world.
- Carthage was defeated in all three wars.
- I was fought between 264 - 146 BC.

PUNIC WARS

WHO AM I?

- I claimed to be a descendant of the gods.
- I conquered vast areas for Rome.
- I crossed the Rubicon River and took over Rome.
- I was murdered by Brutus who wanted to become emperor.
- I lived from 100 - 44 BC.

JULIUS CAESAR

WHO AM I?

- I was a general of Carthage during the Punic Wars, which we lost.
- I won three important battles for my country.
- I transported 50,000 men across the Alps with horses and elephants.
- I lived from 247 - 183 BC.

HANNIBAL

WHO AM I?

- I was close friends with Julius Caesar.
- Octavius and I divided up Julius' empire so we could both rule.
- I fell in love with Cleopatra.
- Thinking that she had killed herself, I did likewise.
- I lived from around 83 - 30 BC.

MARC ANTONY

WHO AM I?

- I was ruled by emperors.
- Most of my emperors died of unnatural causes.
- Huge roads connected every part of me.
- I made it possible for the word of God to spread around the world.
- I lasted from 31 BC - AD 476.

THE ROMAN EMPIRE

WHO AM I?

- I was the Roman emperor when Jesus was born.
- I started the Pax Romana.
- I defeated Marc Antony's navy.
- I extended the Roman empire to the Danube River.
- I lived from 63 BC - AD 14.

OCTAVIAN

WHO AM I?

- I was a Greek mathematician and inventor.
- I was born in Sicily.
- The Archimedes screw design was named after me.
- I lived from around 287 - 212 BC.

ARCHIMEDES

WHO AM I?

- I was the king of France.
- I was a very cruel king, once killing 4,500 rebels after they had surrendered.
- I spent nearly fifty years at war.
- I forced people to become Catholics wherever I conquered.
- I ruled from 771 - 814.

CHARLEMAGNE

321

WHO AM I?

- I was born in Venice and I took a trip with my father.
- I wrote a book about my journeys.
- I was only 17 when I went on my four year expedition.
- I brought spaghetti to Italy from China.
- I lived from 1254 - 1324.

MARCO POLO

WHO AM I?

- I was given the command of three ships to explore the coast of Africa.
- Strong winds blew me off course and around the Cape of Good Hope.
- I drowned there near the Cape.
- I lived from around 1450 - 1500.

BARTHOLOMEU DIAS

WHO AM I?

- I got my name for being so fierce.
- Sir Walter Scott wrote about my heroics.
- I participated in the Crusades.
- The king of the jungle is in my name.
- I lived from 1157 - 1199.

RICHARD THE LION HEARTED

WHO AM I?

- I was born in Portugal.
- I believed I could get to India by sailing west.
- My trip was funded by the king and queen of Spain.
- I sailed west in three ships.
- I lived from 1451 - 1506.

CHRISTOPHER COLUMBUS

WHO AM I?

- I was in a superman movie.
- I was built in Italy.
- I don't stand perfectly vertical.
- Part of my name sounds like "pizza."
- I was built in 1174.

THE LEANING TOWER OF PISA

WHO AM I?

- I named the Pacific Ocean.
- I was credited with being the first to sail around the world.
- I died when we reached the Philippines.
- There is a strait in South America named after me.
- I lived from 1480 - 1521.

FERDINAND MAGELLAN

WHO AM I?

- I was fought over land.
- I was fought between France and Britain.
- During me, the English used long bows and gun powder.
- I was eventually won by the French with the help of Joan of Arc.
- My time period is 1337 - 1453.

THE HUNDRED YEARS' WAR

WHO AM I?

- I believed man was saved by faith alone, not by good works or indulgences.
- I started the Reformation.
- I nailed my Ninety-five Theses on the church door in Wittenberg.
- I lived from 1483 - 1546.

MARTIN LUTHER

WHO AM I ?

- I was born to a wealthy family.
- I gave up all I had to help the sick and poor.
- I believed that a friar should work for a living and only beg when he could not work.
- After my death I was made a saint.
- I lived from 1182 - 1226.

ST. FRANCIS OF ASSISI

WHO AM I ?

- My victims died within a couple of hours.
- I was spread by fleas first carried by rats and then by humans.
- I killed one-fourth the population of Europe and much of the Asian populations.
- I was a form of Bubonic Plague.
- I lasted from 1347 - 1353.

THE BLACK PLAGUE

WHO AM I ?

- I was French, yet the English killed me.
- I was only a young girl, yet I encouraged many soldiers.
- I believed I was God's instrument.
- I helped the French win against the English in the Hundred Years' War.
- I lived from 1412 - 1431.

JOAN OF ARC

WHO AM I ?

- I was invented by Roger Bacon.
- You could start fires with me.
- I made things appear larger.
- I was made in 1266.

THE MAGNIFYING GLASS

WHO AM I ?

- I was a professor of theology.
- I denounced the wealth and corruption of the Church.
- I translated the Bible into English.
- I lived from around 1320 - 1384.

JOHN WYCLIFFE

WHO AM I ?

- I wrote backward in my journals.
- I was an inventor, yet most of my ideas never worked while I was alive.
- People say I was born ahead of my time.
- I was also a great painter, artist, sculpturer, musician, architect, and engineer.
- I lived from 1452 - 1519.

LEONARDO DA VINCI

WHO AM I ?

- I was first printed in England by William Caxton.
- Although a poem, I am full of political messages.
- The English poet Geoffrey Chaucer wrote me.
- I was written in 1388.

CANTERBURY TALES

WHO AM I ?

- I was made up of the Eastern Roman Empire.
- My capital was Constantinople.
- I was the center of learning where Ancient Greek and the new Christian church were combined.
- I lasted from 395 - 1453.

THE BYZANTINE EMPIRE

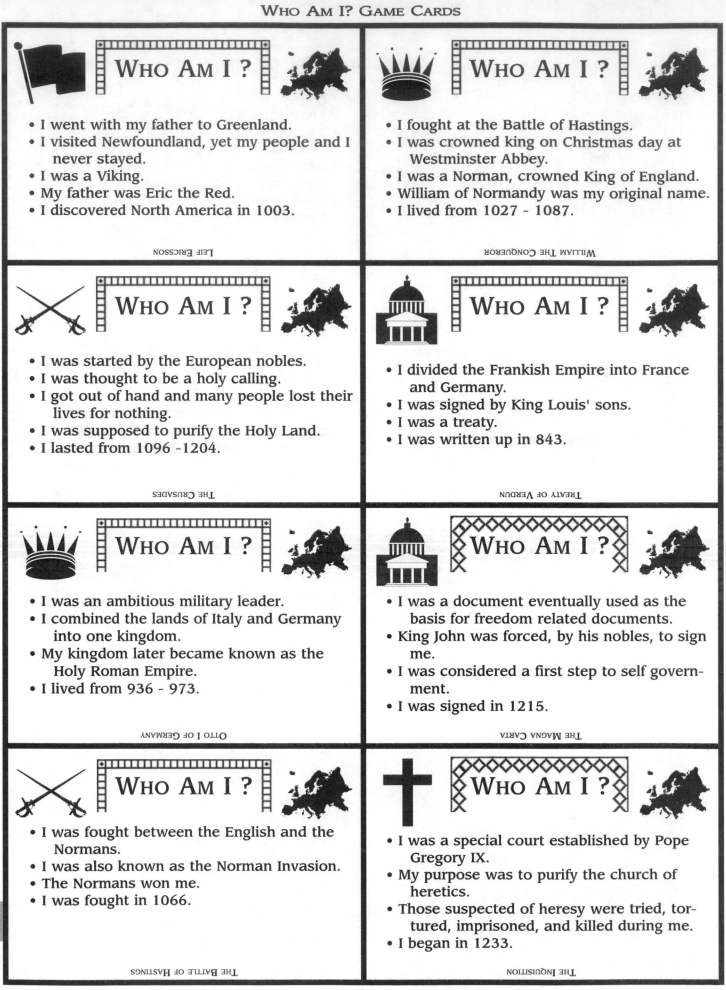

WHO AM I?

- I went with my father to Greenland.
- I visited Newfoundland, yet my people and I never stayed.
- I was a Viking.
- My father was Eric the Red.
- I discovered North America in 1003.

LEIF ERICSSON

WHO AM I?

- I fought at the Battle of Hastings.
- I was crowned king on Christmas day at Westminster Abbey.
- I was a Norman, crowned King of England.
- William of Normandy was my original name.
- I lived from 1027 - 1087.

WILLIAM THE CONQUEROR

WHO AM I?

- I was started by the European nobles.
- I was thought to be a holy calling.
- I got out of hand and many people lost their lives for nothing.
- I was supposed to purify the Holy Land.
- I lasted from 1096 -1204.

THE CRUSADES

WHO AM I?

- I divided the Frankish Empire into France and Germany.
- I was signed by King Louis' sons.
- I was a treaty.
- I was written up in 843.

TREATY OF VERDUN

WHO AM I?

- I was an ambitious military leader.
- I combined the lands of Italy and Germany into one kingdom.
- My kingdom later became known as the Holy Roman Empire.
- I lived from 936 - 973.

OTTO I OF GERMANY

WHO AM I?

- I was a document eventually used as the basis for freedom related documents.
- King John was forced, by his nobles, to sign me.
- I was considered a first step to self government.
- I was signed in 1215.

THE MAGNA CARTA

WHO AM I?

- I was fought between the English and the Normans.
- I was also known as the Norman Invasion.
- The Normans won me.
- I was fought in 1066.

THE BATTLE OF HASTINGS

WHO AM I?

- I was a special court established by Pope Gregory IX.
- My purpose was to purify the church of heretics.
- Those suspected of heresy were tried, tortured, imprisoned, and killed during me.
- I began in 1233.

THE INQUISITION

324

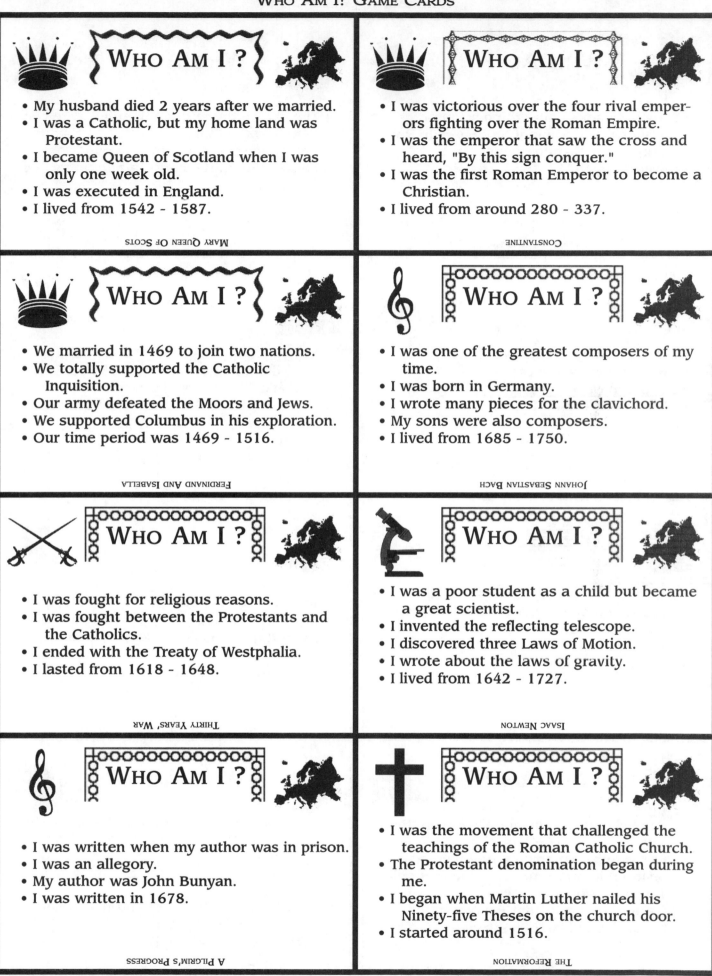

WHO AM I?
- My husband died 2 years after we married.
- I was a Catholic, but my home land was Protestant.
- I became Queen of Scotland when I was only one week old.
- I was executed in England.
- I lived from 1542 - 1587.

MARY QUEEN OF SCOTS

WHO AM I?
- I was victorious over the four rival emperors fighting over the Roman Empire.
- I was the emperor that saw the cross and heard, "By this sign conquer."
- I was the first Roman Emperor to become a Christian.
- I lived from around 280 - 337.

CONSTANTINE

WHO AM I?
- We married in 1469 to join two nations.
- We totally supported the Catholic Inquisition.
- Our army defeated the Moors and Jews.
- We supported Columbus in his exploration.
- Our time period was 1469 - 1516.

FERDINAND AND ISABELLA

WHO AM I?
- I was one of the greatest composers of my time.
- I was born in Germany.
- I wrote many pieces for the clavichord.
- My sons were also composers.
- I lived from 1685 - 1750.

JOHANN SEBASTIAN BACH

WHO AM I?
- I was fought for religious reasons.
- I was fought between the Protestants and the Catholics.
- I ended with the Treaty of Westphalia.
- I lasted from 1618 - 1648.

THIRTY YEARS' WAR

WHO AM I?
- I was a poor student as a child but became a great scientist.
- I invented the reflecting telescope.
- I discovered three Laws of Motion.
- I wrote about the laws of gravity.
- I lived from 1642 - 1727.

ISAAC NEWTON

WHO AM I?
- I was written when my author was in prison.
- I was an allegory.
- My author was John Bunyan.
- I was written in 1678.

A PILGRIM'S PROGRESS

WHO AM I?
- I was the movement that challenged the teachings of the Roman Catholic Church.
- The Protestant denomination began during me.
- I began when Martin Luther nailed his Ninety-five Theses on the church door.
- I started around 1516.

THE REFORMATION

325

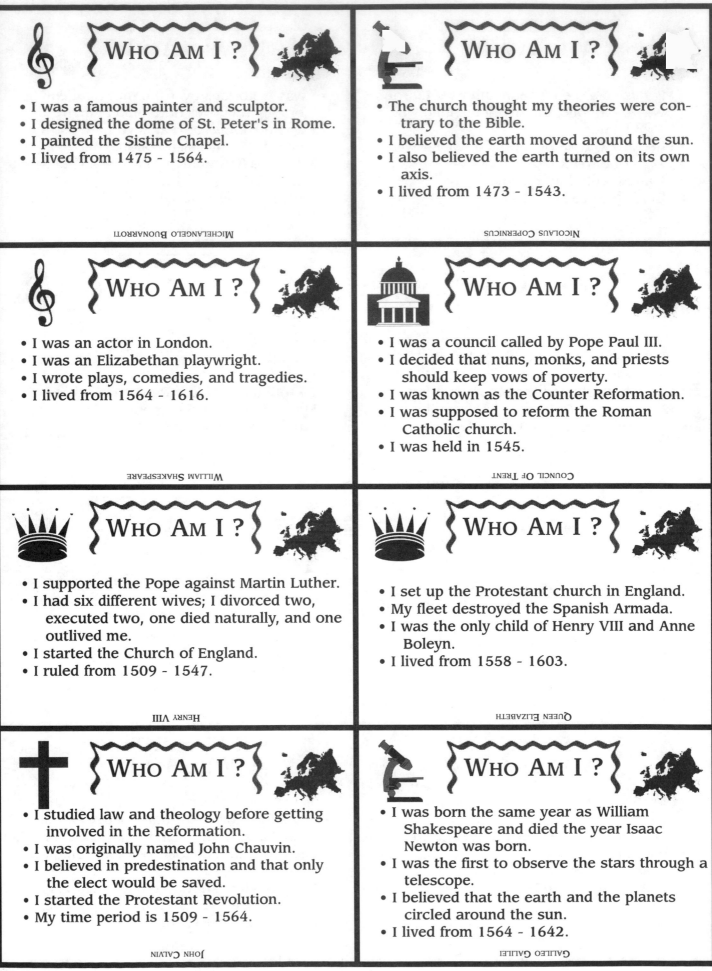

WHO AM I?

- I was a famous painter and sculptor.
- I designed the dome of St. Peter's in Rome.
- I painted the Sistine Chapel.
- I lived from 1475 - 1564.

MICHELANGELO BUONARROTI

WHO AM I?

- The church thought my theories were contrary to the Bible.
- I believed the earth moved around the sun.
- I also believed the earth turned on its own axis.
- I lived from 1473 - 1543.

NICOLAUS COPERNICUS

WHO AM I?

- I was an actor in London.
- I was an Elizabethan playwright.
- I wrote plays, comedies, and tragedies.
- I lived from 1564 - 1616.

WILLIAM SHAKESPEARE

WHO AM I?

- I was a council called by Pope Paul III.
- I decided that nuns, monks, and priests should keep vows of poverty.
- I was known as the Counter Reformation.
- I was supposed to reform the Roman Catholic church.
- I was held in 1545.

COUNCIL OF TRENT

WHO AM I?

- I supported the Pope against Martin Luther.
- I had six different wives; I divorced two, executed two, one died naturally, and one outlived me.
- I started the Church of England.
- I ruled from 1509 - 1547.

HENRY VIII

WHO AM I?

- I set up the Protestant church in England.
- My fleet destroyed the Spanish Armada.
- I was the only child of Henry VIII and Anne Boleyn.
- I lived from 1558 - 1603.

QUEEN ELIZABETH

WHO AM I?

- I studied law and theology before getting involved in the Reformation.
- I was originally named John Chauvin.
- I believed in predestination and that only the elect would be saved.
- I started the Protestant Revolution.
- My time period is 1509 - 1564.

JOHN CALVIN

WHO AM I?

- I was born the same year as William Shakespeare and died the year Isaac Newton was born.
- I was the first to observe the stars through a telescope.
- I believed that the earth and the planets circled around the sun.
- I lived from 1564 - 1642.

GALILEO GALILEI

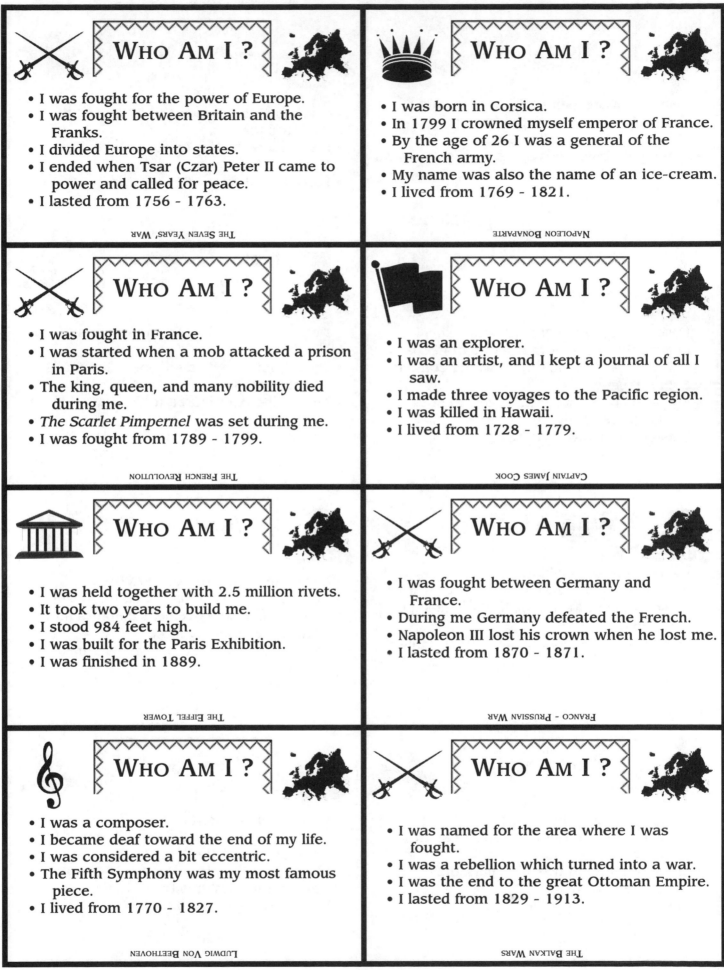

WHO AM I?

- I was fought for the power of Europe.
- I was fought between Britain and the Franks.
- I divided Europe into states.
- I ended when Tsar (Czar) Peter II came to power and called for peace.
- I lasted from 1756 - 1763.

THE SEVEN YEARS' WAR

WHO AM I?

- I was born in Corsica.
- In 1799 I crowned myself emperor of France.
- By the age of 26 I was a general of the French army.
- My name was also the name of an ice-cream.
- I lived from 1769 - 1821.

NAPOLEON BONAPARTE

WHO AM I?

- I was fought in France.
- I was started when a mob attacked a prison in Paris.
- The king, queen, and many nobility died during me.
- *The Scarlet Pimpernel* was set during me.
- I was fought from 1789 - 1799.

THE FRENCH REVOLUTION

WHO AM I?

- I was an explorer.
- I was an artist, and I kept a journal of all I saw.
- I made three voyages to the Pacific region.
- I was killed in Hawaii.
- I lived from 1728 - 1779.

CAPTAIN JAMES COOK

WHO AM I?

- I was held together with 2.5 million rivets.
- It took two years to build me.
- I stood 984 feet high.
- I was built for the Paris Exhibition.
- I was finished in 1889.

THE EIFFEL TOWER

WHO AM I?

- I was fought between Germany and France.
- During me Germany defeated the French.
- Napoleon III lost his crown when he lost me.
- I lasted from 1870 - 1871.

FRANCO - PRUSSIAN WAR

WHO AM I?

- I was a composer.
- I became deaf toward the end of my life.
- I was considered a bit eccentric.
- The Fifth Symphony was my most famous piece.
- I lived from 1770 - 1827.

LUDWIG VON BEETHOVEN

WHO AM I?

- I was named for the area where I was fought.
- I was a rebellion which turned into a war.
- I was the end to the great Ottoman Empire.
- I lasted from 1829 - 1913.

THE BALKAN WARS

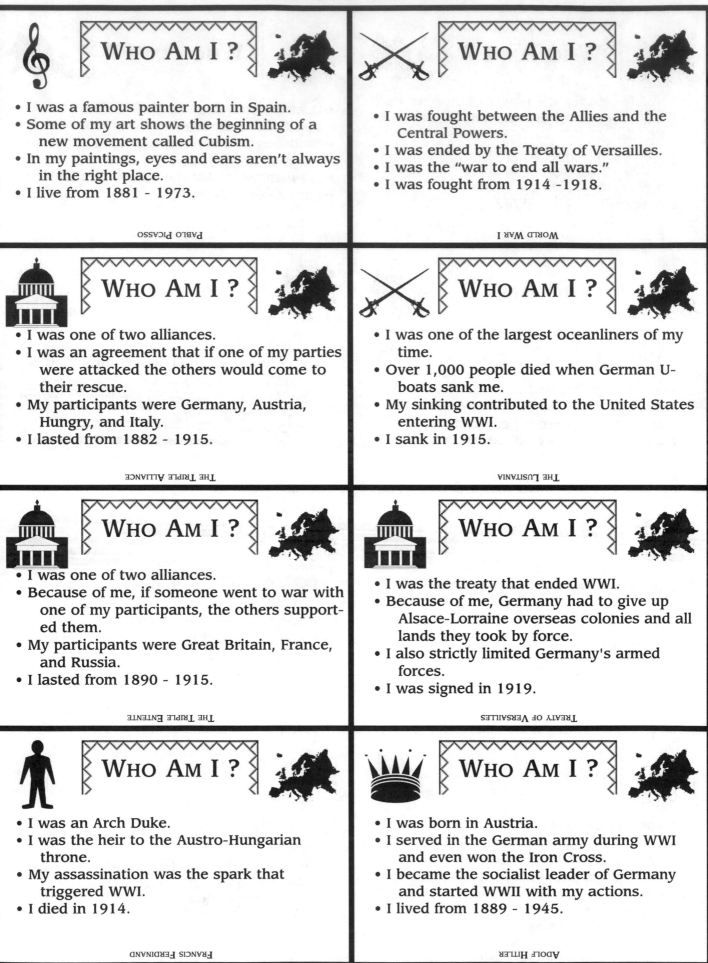

WHO AM I?
- I was a famous painter born in Spain.
- Some of my art shows the beginning of a new movement called Cubism.
- In my paintings, eyes and ears aren't always in the right place.
- I live from 1881 - 1973.

PABLO PICASSO

WHO AM I?
- I was fought between the Allies and the Central Powers.
- I was ended by the Treaty of Versailles.
- I was the "war to end all wars."
- I was fought from 1914 -1918.

WORLD WAR I

WHO AM I?
- I was one of two alliances.
- I was an agreement that if one of my parties were attacked the others would come to their rescue.
- My participants were Germany, Austria, Hungry, and Italy.
- I lasted from 1882 - 1915.

THE TRIPLE ALLIANCE

WHO AM I?
- I was one of the largest oceanliners of my time.
- Over 1,000 people died when German U-boats sank me.
- My sinking contributed to the United States entering WWI.
- I sank in 1915.

THE LUSITANIA

WHO AM I?
- I was one of two alliances.
- Because of me, if someone went to war with one of my participants, the others supported them.
- My participants were Great Britain, France, and Russia.
- I lasted from 1890 - 1915.

THE TRIPLE ENTENTE

WHO AM I?
- I was the treaty that ended WWI.
- Because of me, Germany had to give up Alsace-Lorraine overseas colonies and all lands they took by force.
- I also strictly limited Germany's armed forces.
- I was signed in 1919.

TREATY OF VERSAILLES

WHO AM I?
- I was an Arch Duke.
- I was the heir to the Austro-Hungarian throne.
- My assassination was the spark that triggered WWI.
- I died in 1914.

FRANCIS FERDINAND

WHO AM I?
- I was born in Austria.
- I served in the German army during WWI and even won the Iron Cross.
- I became the socialist leader of Germany and started WWII with my actions.
- I lived from 1889 - 1945.

ADOLF HITLER

Who Am I ?

- I was born in Italy.
- I was kicked out of the Socialist party because of my role in WWI.
- I became the dictator of Italy and entered WWII on the Axis side.
- I lived from 1883 - 1945.

BENITO MUSSOLINI

Who Am I ?

- I was the invasion of Normandy by the Allies.
- The Germans had a counter attack during me but they had to retreat.
- I began the end of the Nazis - reign of terror.
- I happened in 1944.

D - DAY

Who Am I ?

- I was a war fought in Spain.
- I was started over the question of political leaders.
- Francisco Franco was a great military leader during me.
- I was fought from 1936 - 1939.

THE SPANISH CIVIL WAR

Who Am I ?

- I founded the Methodist Church.
- I was one of the most famous men in English history.
- I led Europe in revival.
- I was one of nineteen children born to my mother, Susanna Wesley.
- I lived from 1703 - 1791.

JOHN WESLEY

Who Am I ?

- I was fought between the Allies and the Axis.
- I pulled the U.S. out of their Great Depression.
- The U.S. entered me when the Japanese bombed Pearl Harbor.
- I was fought from 1939 - 1945.

WORLD WAR II

Who Am I ?

- I was the leader of the Irish Citizen Army.
- I founded the Irish Socialist Republican Party in 1896.
- I was shot while in jail because of being involved in the Easter Rising.
- I lived from 1870 - 1916.

JAMES CONNOLLY

Who Am I ?

- I was signed by Hitler, Mussolini, Neville Chamberlain, and Edouard Daladier.
- Britain and France mistakenly believed I would keep Europe at peace.
- I established new boundaries in Europe after WWI.
- I was signed in 1938.

MUNICH AGREEMENT

Who Am I ?

- My verdict convicted many innocent people to hang on the gallows.
- It is believed that I began because of religious superstition.
- *The Crucible* was written about me.
- I occurred in 1692.

SALEM WITCH TRIALS

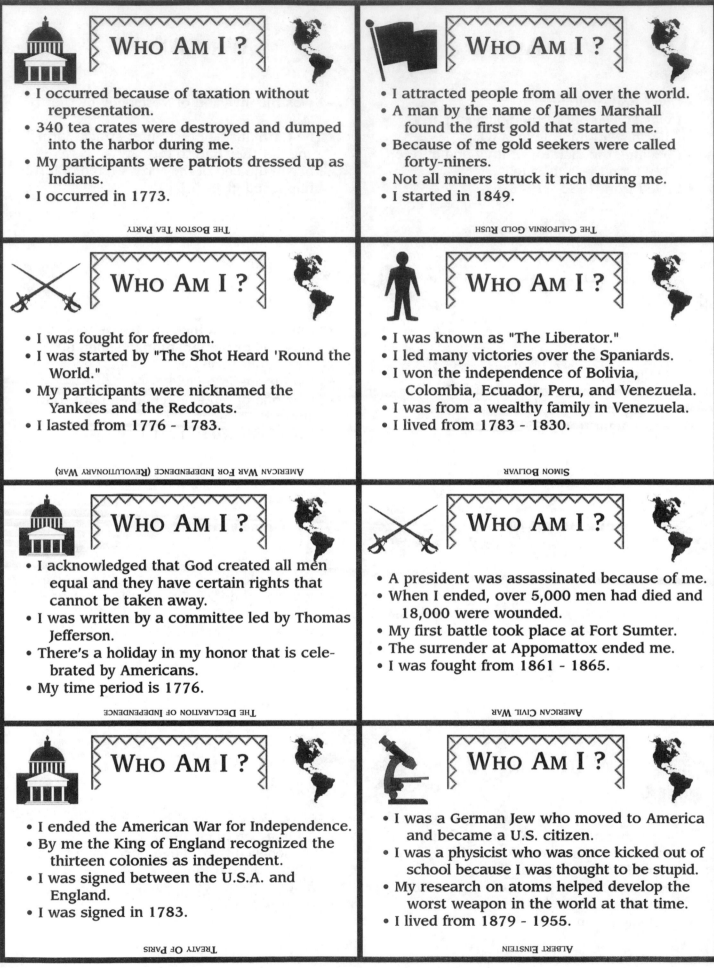

WHO AM I?

- I occurred because of taxation without representation.
- 340 tea crates were destroyed and dumped into the harbor during me.
- My participants were patriots dressed up as Indians.
- I occurred in 1773.

THE BOSTON TEA PARTY

WHO AM I?

- I attracted people from all over the world.
- A man by the name of James Marshall found the first gold that started me.
- Because of me gold seekers were called forty-niners.
- Not all miners struck it rich during me.
- I started in 1849.

THE CALIFORNIA GOLD RUSH

WHO AM I?

- I was fought for freedom.
- I was started by "The Shot Heard 'Round the World."
- My participants were nicknamed the Yankees and the Redcoats.
- I lasted from 1776 - 1783.

AMERICAN WAR FOR INDEPENDENCE (REVOLUTIONARY WAR)

WHO AM I?

- I was known as "The Liberator."
- I led many victories over the Spaniards.
- I won the independence of Bolivia, Colombia, Ecuador, Peru, and Venezuela.
- I was from a wealthy family in Venezuela.
- I lived from 1783 - 1830.

SIMON BOLIVAR

WHO AM I?

- I acknowledged that God created all men equal and they have certain rights that cannot be taken away.
- I was written by a committee led by Thomas Jefferson.
- There's a holiday in my honor that is celebrated by Americans.
- My time period is 1776.

THE DECLARATION OF INDEPENDENCE

WHO AM I?

- A president was assassinated because of me.
- When I ended, over 5,000 men had died and 18,000 were wounded.
- My first battle took place at Fort Sumter.
- The surrender at Appomattox ended me.
- I was fought from 1861 - 1865.

AMERICAN CIVIL WAR

WHO AM I?

- I ended the American War for Independence.
- By me the King of England recognized the thirteen colonies as independent.
- I was signed between the U.S.A. and England.
- I was signed in 1783.

TREATY OF PARIS

WHO AM I?

- I was a German Jew who moved to America and became a U.S. citizen.
- I was a physicist who was once kicked out of school because I was thought to be stupid.
- My research on atoms helped develop the worst weapon in the world at that time.
- I lived from 1879 - 1955.

ALBERT EINSTEIN

330

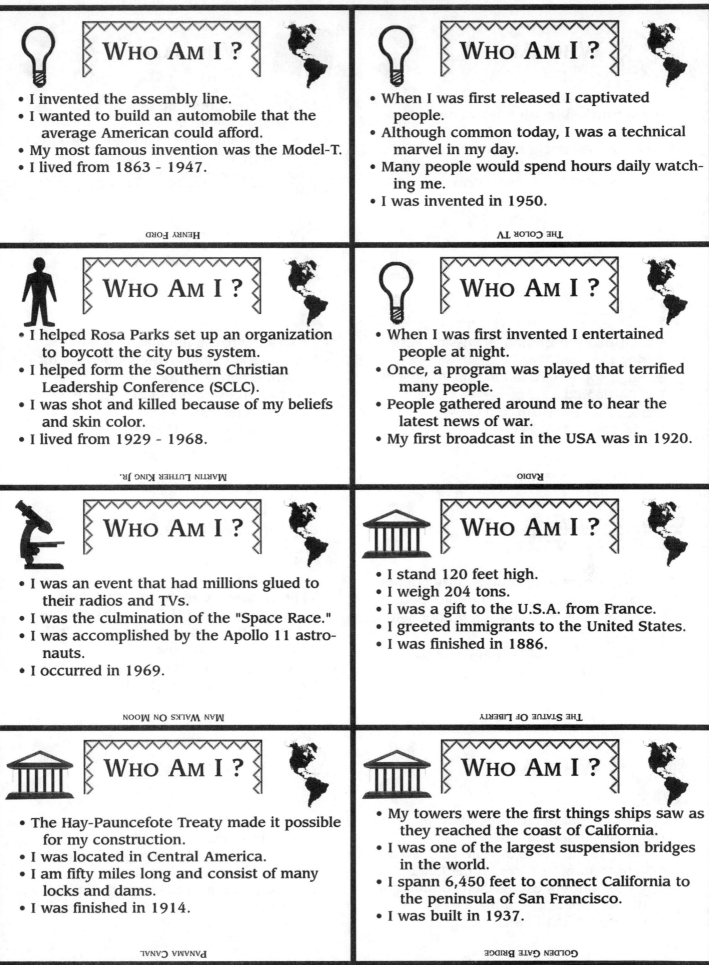

WHO AM I?

- I invented the assembly line.
- I wanted to build an automobile that the average American could afford.
- My most famous invention was the Model-T.
- I lived from 1863 - 1947.

HENRY FORD

WHO AM I?

- When I was first released I captivated people.
- Although common today, I was a technical marvel in my day.
- Many people would spend hours daily watching me.
- I was invented in 1950.

THE COLOR TV

WHO AM I?

- I helped Rosa Parks set up an organization to boycott the city bus system.
- I helped form the Southern Christian Leadership Conference (SCLC).
- I was shot and killed because of my beliefs and skin color.
- I lived from 1929 - 1968.

MARTIN LUTHER KING JR.

WHO AM I?

- When I was first invented I entertained people at night.
- Once, a program was played that terrified many people.
- People gathered around me to hear the latest news of war.
- My first broadcast in the USA was in 1920.

RADIO

WHO AM I?

- I was an event that had millions glued to their radios and TVs.
- I was the culmination of the "Space Race."
- I was accomplished by the Apollo 11 astronauts.
- I occurred in 1969.

MAN WALKS ON MOON

WHO AM I?

- I stand 120 feet high.
- I weigh 204 tons.
- I was a gift to the U.S.A. from France.
- I greeted immigrants to the United States.
- I was finished in 1886.

THE STATUE OF LIBERTY

WHO AM I?

- The Hay-Pauncefote Treaty made it possible for my construction.
- I was located in Central America.
- I am fifty miles long and consist of many locks and dams.
- I was finished in 1914.

PANAMA CANAL

WHO AM I?

- My towers were the first things ships saw as they reached the coast of California.
- I was one of the largest suspension bridges in the world.
- I spann 6,450 feet to connect California to the peninsula of San Francisco.
- I was built in 1937.

GOLDEN GATE BRIDGE

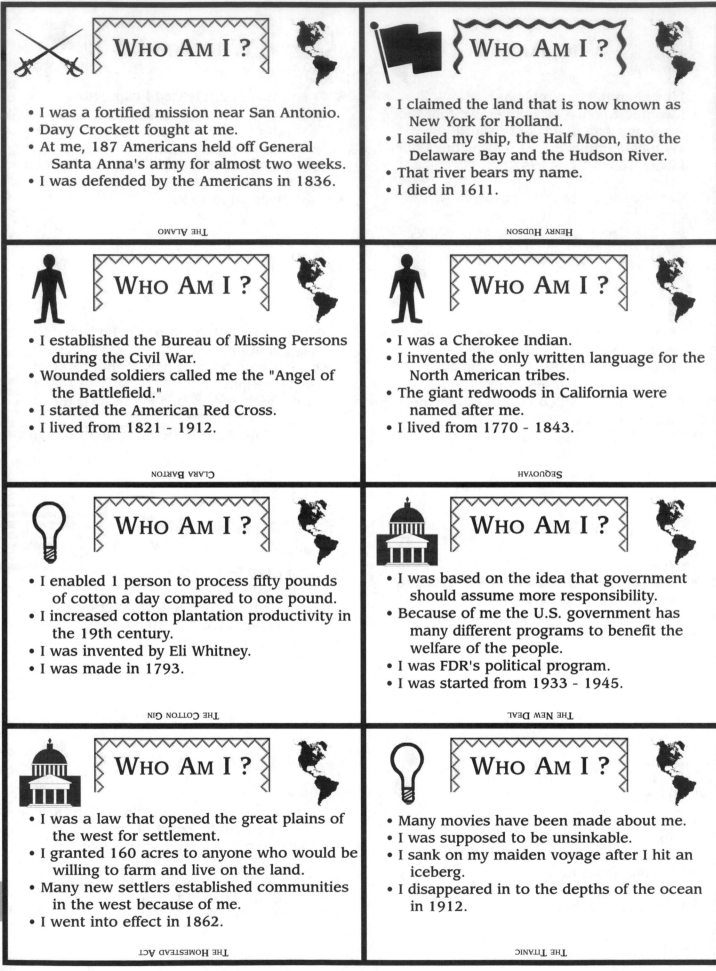

WHO AM I?

- I was a fortified mission near San Antonio.
- Davy Crockett fought at me.
- At me, 187 Americans held off General Santa Anna's army for almost two weeks.
- I was defended by the Americans in 1836.

THE ALAMO

WHO AM I?

- I claimed the land that is now known as New York for Holland.
- I sailed my ship, the Half Moon, into the Delaware Bay and the Hudson River.
- That river bears my name.
- I died in 1611.

HENRY HUDSON

WHO AM I?

- I established the Bureau of Missing Persons during the Civil War.
- Wounded soldiers called me the "Angel of the Battlefield."
- I started the American Red Cross.
- I lived from 1821 - 1912.

CLARA BARTON

WHO AM I?

- I was a Cherokee Indian.
- I invented the only written language for the North American tribes.
- The giant redwoods in California were named after me.
- I lived from 1770 - 1843.

SEQUOYAH

WHO AM I?

- I enabled 1 person to process fifty pounds of cotton a day compared to one pound.
- I increased cotton plantation productivity in the 19th century.
- I was invented by Eli Whitney.
- I was made in 1793.

THE COTTON GIN

WHO AM I?

- I was based on the idea that government should assume more responsibility.
- Because of me the U.S. government has many different programs to benefit the welfare of the people.
- I was FDR's political program.
- I was started from 1933 - 1945.

THE NEW DEAL

WHO AM I?

- I was a law that opened the great plains of the west for settlement.
- I granted 160 acres to anyone who would be willing to farm and live on the land.
- Many new settlers established communities in the west because of me.
- I went into effect in 1862.

THE HOMESTEAD ACT

WHO AM I?

- Many movies have been made about me.
- I was supposed to be unsinkable.
- I sank on my maiden voyage after I hit an iceberg.
- I disappeared in to the depths of the ocean in 1912.

THE TITANIC

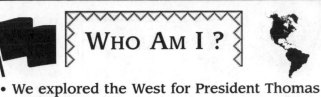 

WHO AM I?

- We explored the West for President Thomas Jefferson.
- We took an eighteen month exploration to the Pacific Ocean.
- One of us kept a detailed journal of all we found or saw.
- Our expedition lasted from 1804 - 1806.

THE LEWIS AND CLARK EXPEDITION

WHO AM I?

- I was a document that warned against the further colonization of the Americas by Europe.
- Any infraction of me would be considered an unfriendly act.
- I was issued by President Monroe.
- I went into effect in 1823.

MONROE DOCTRINE

WHO AM I?

- I am an inventor.
- My wife tapped Morse Code on my leg so I could understand plays and orations because I couldn't hear.
- I invented the light bulb, phonograph, kinescope and over 1000 other things.
- I lived from 1847 - 1931.

THOMAS EDISON

WHO AM I?

- I started at St. Joseph, Missouri, and went to San Francisco.
- I could reach my destination in ten days.
- I was the fastest mail service in the mid 19th century.
- The start of the transcontinental railroad ended my usefulness.
- I lasted from 1860 - 1861.

THE PONY EXPRESS

WHO AM I?

- I was born into a noble Spanish family.
- I grew up in the West Indies.
- I conquered the Aztecs.
- I lived from 1485 - 1547.

HERNAN CORTES

WHO AM I?

- I carried two-thirds of the U.S. internal trade.
- I was started by two different companies on opposite sides of the U.S.
- A Golden Spike marked my completion.
- I was the first railroad to cross the U.S.
- I was opened in 1869.

THE TRANSCONTINENTAL RAILROAD

 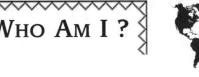 

WHO AM I?

- I was founded by William Booth.
- I was established to help the poor improve their lives.
- I am still active today.
- I started in 1865.

THE SALVATION ARMY

WHO AM I?

- I educated the black community and taught them to live without government aid.
- I fought for better education for my black brothers.
- I founded Tuskegee Institute in Alabama.
- I lived from 1856 - 1915.

BOOKER T. WASHINGTON

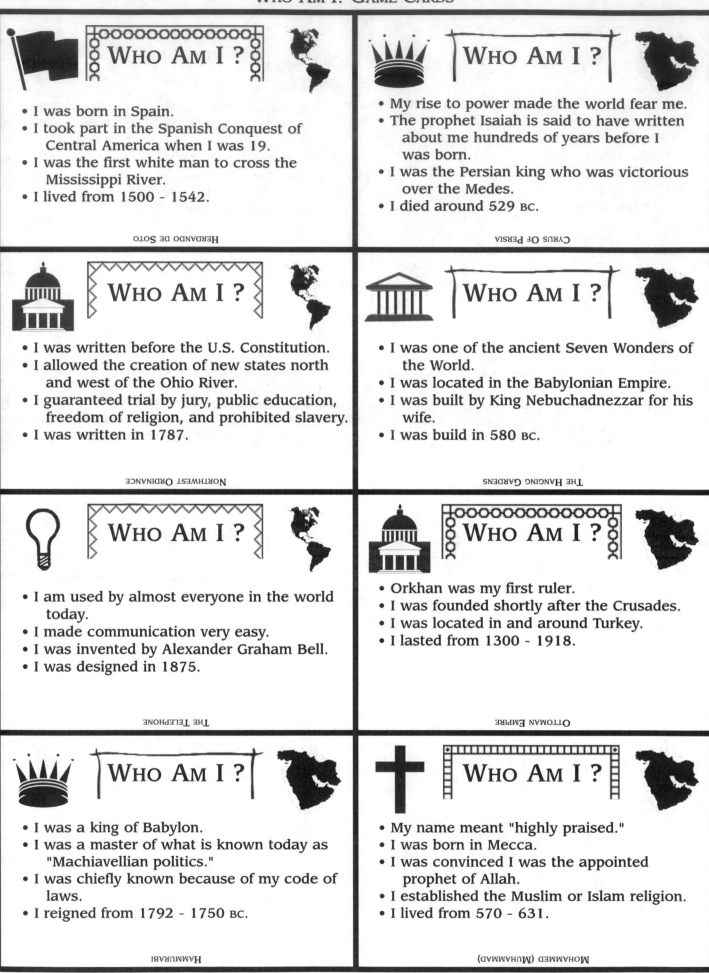

WHO AM I?

- I was born in Spain.
- I took part in the Spanish Conquest of Central America when I was 19.
- I was the first white man to cross the Mississippi River.
- I lived from 1500 - 1542.

HERDANDO DE SOTO

WHO AM I?

- My rise to power made the world fear me.
- The prophet Isaiah is said to have written about me hundreds of years before I was born.
- I was the Persian king who was victorious over the Medes.
- I died around 529 BC.

CYRUS OF PERSIA

WHO AM I?

- I was written before the U.S. Constitution.
- I allowed the creation of new states north and west of the Ohio River.
- I guaranteed trial by jury, public education, freedom of religion, and prohibited slavery.
- I was written in 1787.

NORTHWEST ORDINANCE

WHO AM I?

- I was one of the ancient Seven Wonders of the World.
- I was located in the Babylonian Empire.
- I was built by King Nebuchadnezzar for his wife.
- I was build in 580 BC.

THE HANGING GARDENS

WHO AM I?

- I am used by almost everyone in the world today.
- I made communication very easy.
- I was invented by Alexander Graham Bell.
- I was designed in 1875.

THE TELEPHONE

WHO AM I?

- Orkhan was my first ruler.
- I was founded shortly after the Crusades.
- I was located in and around Turkey.
- I lasted from 1300 - 1918.

OTTOMAN EMPIRE

WHO AM I?

- I was a king of Babylon.
- I was a master of what is known today as "Machiavellian politics."
- I was chiefly known because of my code of laws.
- I reigned from 1792 - 1750 BC.

HAMMURABI

WHO AM I?

- My name meant "highly praised."
- I was born in Mecca.
- I was convinced I was the appointed prophet of Allah.
- I established the Muslim or Islam religion.
- I lived from 570 - 631.

MOHAMMED (MUHAMMAD)

334

WHO AM I?

- We could be compared to the knights of the Middle Ages.
- We would be willing to fight to the death for our daimyos (overlords).
- We were the warrior class in China.
- We were from around 1000 - 1877.

SAMURAI

WHO AM I?

- For eighteen months I observed Europe's industry bringing information to Russia.
- I jerked backward Russia into a mighty European power.
- In a war with Sweden I obtained Estonia and Livonia.
- I ruled from 1689 - 1725.

PETER THE GREAT, CZAR OF RUSSIA

WHO AM I?

- I changed my name from Temujin when I was 39 years old.
- I conquered northern China and overran Afghanistan, Persia, and Turkestan.
- I became leader of my tribe at age 13 when my father was poisoned.
- In some ways my empire was greater than Alexander the Great's.
- I lived from 1167 - 1227.

GENGHIS KHAN

WHO AM I?

- Babur founded me when he invaded India from Afghanistan.
- I covered most of India at one point.
- The Taj Mahal was built during me.
- I lasted from 1527 - 1803.

MONGUL EMPIRE

WHO AM I?

- My name means "brightness."
- My first ruler was Hung Wu.
- My emperors were great builders.
- My period is known for my blue and white porcelain.
- I lasted from 1368 - 1644.

MING DYNASTY

WHO AM I?

- I was the first war in which the public was kept informed by photographs and reports.
- I was a struggle over territory because of the collapse of the Ottoman Empire.
- Florence Nightingale was a nurse during me.
- I lasted from 1854 - 1856.

THE CRIMEAN WAR

WHO AM I?

- I was located in Agra, India.
- I was built with white marble inlaid with detailed patterns of semi-precious stones.
- I was built for the Mongul ruler, Shah Jahan's favorite wife.
- It took twenty-one years to complete me.
- I was built between 1629 - 1650.

THE TAJ MAHAL

WHO AM I?

- I was started because Russia expanded into Manchuria.
- I was between the Russians and the Japanese.
- At the Battle of Tsushima the Russians were defeated.
- I lasted from 1904 - 1905.

THE RUSSO - JAPANESE WAR

335

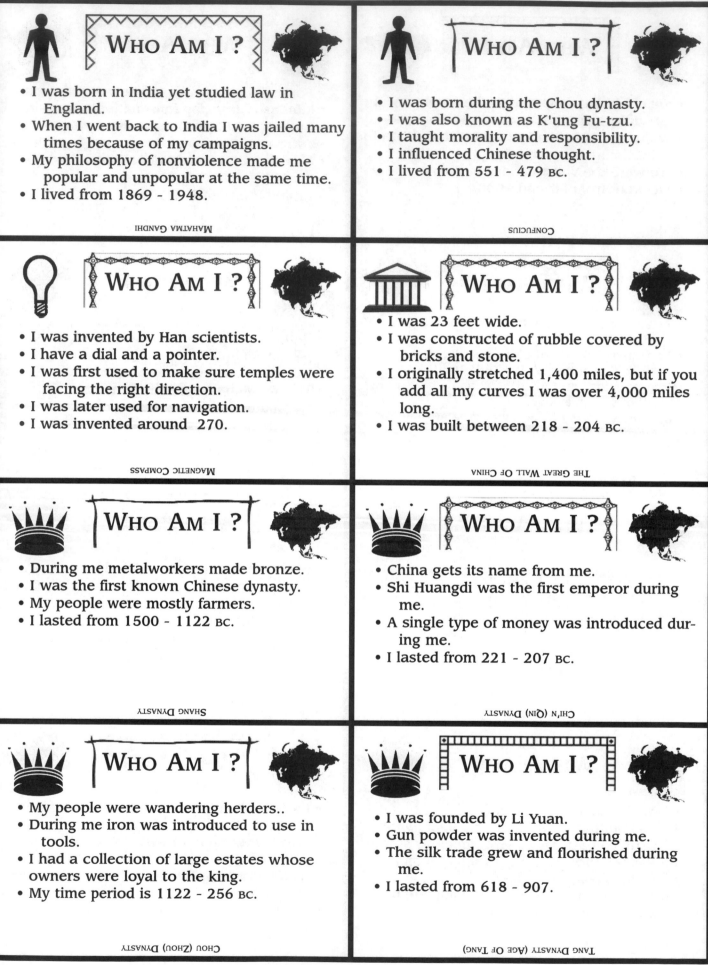

WHO AM I?
- I was born in India yet studied law in England.
- When I went back to India I was jailed many times because of my campaigns.
- My philosophy of nonviolence made me popular and unpopular at the same time.
- I lived from 1869 - 1948.

MAHATMA GANDHI

WHO AM I?
- I was born during the Chou dynasty.
- I was also known as K'ung Fu-tzu.
- I taught morality and responsibility.
- I influenced Chinese thought.
- I lived from 551 - 479 BC.

CONFUCIUS

WHO AM I?
- I was invented by Han scientists.
- I have a dial and a pointer.
- I was first used to make sure temples were facing the right direction.
- I was later used for navigation.
- I was invented around 270.

MAGNETIC COMPASS

WHO AM I?
- I was 23 feet wide.
- I was constructed of rubble covered by bricks and stone.
- I originally stretched 1,400 miles, but if you add all my curves I was over 4,000 miles long.
- I was built between 218 - 204 BC.

THE GREAT WALL OF CHINA

WHO AM I?
- During me metalworkers made bronze.
- I was the first known Chinese dynasty.
- My people were mostly farmers.
- I lasted from 1500 - 1122 BC.

SHANG DYNASTY

WHO AM I?
- China gets its name from me.
- Shi Huangdi was the first emperor during me.
- A single type of money was introduced during me.
- I lasted from 221 - 207 BC.

CHI'N (QIN) DYNASTY

WHO AM I?
- My people were wandering herders..
- During me iron was introduced to use in tools.
- I had a collection of large estates whose owners were loyal to the king.
- My time period is 1122 - 256 BC.

CHOU (ZHOU) DYNASTY

WHO AM I?
- I was founded by Li Yuan.
- Gun powder was invented during me.
- The silk trade grew and flourished during me.
- I lasted from 618 - 907.

TANG DYNASTY (AGE OF TANG)

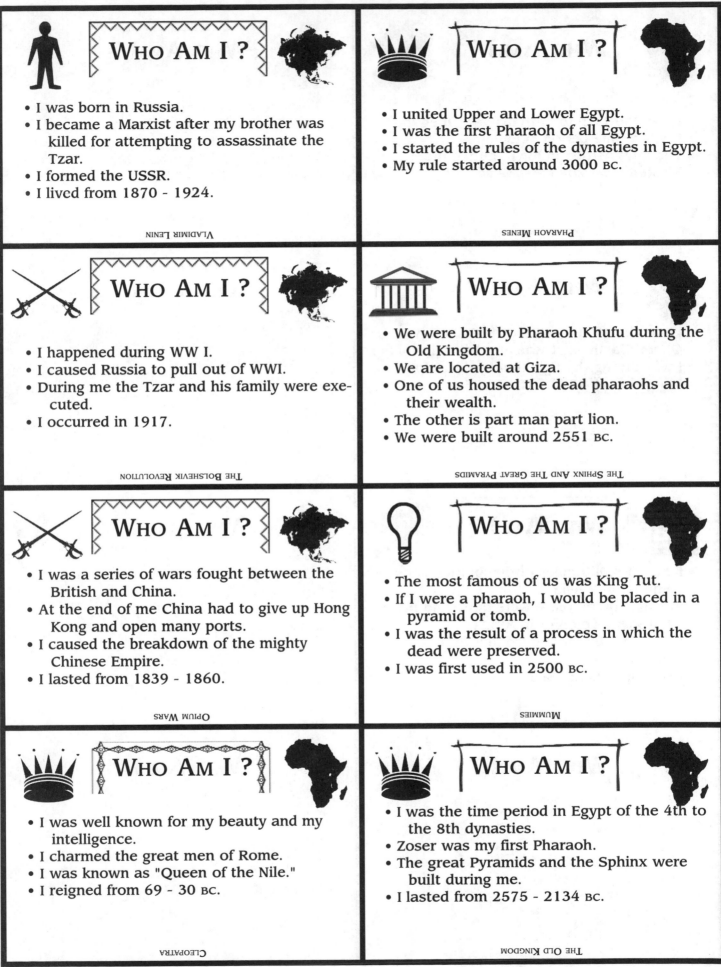

Who Am I?
- I was born in Russia.
- I became a Marxist after my brother was killed for attempting to assassinate the Tzar.
- I formed the USSR.
- I lived from 1870 - 1924.

Vladimir Lenin

Who Am I?
- I united Upper and Lower Egypt.
- I was the first Pharaoh of all Egypt.
- I started the rules of the dynasties in Egypt.
- My rule started around 3000 BC.

Pharaoh Menes

Who Am I?
- I happened during WW I.
- I caused Russia to pull out of WWI.
- During me the Tzar and his family were executed.
- I occurred in 1917.

The Bolshevik Revolution

Who Am I?
- We were built by Pharaoh Khufu during the Old Kingdom.
- We are located at Giza.
- One of us housed the dead pharaohs and their wealth.
- The other is part man part lion.
- We were built around 2551 BC.

The Sphinx And The Great Pyramids

Who Am I?
- I was a series of wars fought between the British and China.
- At the end of me China had to give up Hong Kong and open many ports.
- I caused the breakdown of the mighty Chinese Empire.
- I lasted from 1839 - 1860.

Opium Wars

Who Am I?
- The most famous of us was King Tut.
- If I were a pharaoh, I would be placed in a pyramid or tomb.
- I was the result of a process in which the dead were preserved.
- I was first used in 2500 BC.

Mummies

Who Am I?
- I was well known for my beauty and my intelligence.
- I charmed the great men of Rome.
- I was known as "Queen of the Nile."
- I reigned from 69 - 30 BC.

Cleopatra

Who Am I?
- I was the time period in Egypt of the 4th to the 8th dynasties.
- Zoser was my first Pharaoh.
- The great Pyramids and the Sphinx were built during me.
- I lasted from 2575 - 2134 BC.

The Old Kingdom

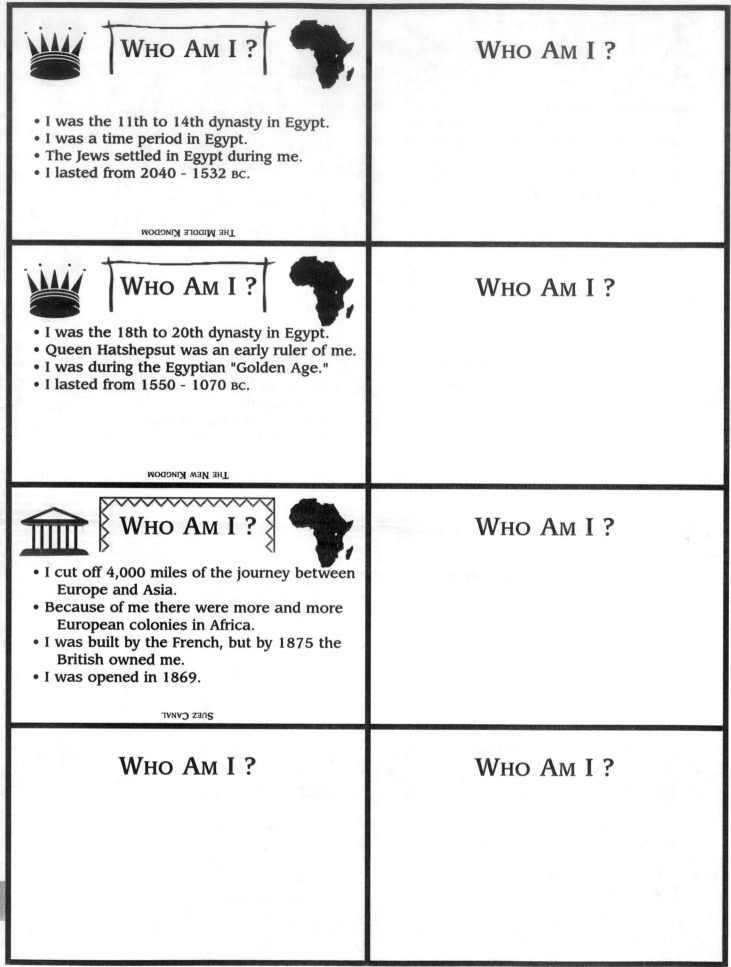

WHO AM I?

- I was the 11th to 14th dynasty in Egypt.
- I was a time period in Egypt.
- The Jews settled in Egypt during me.
- I lasted from 2040 - 1532 BC.

THE MIDDLE KINGDOM

WHO AM I?

WHO AM I?

- I was the 18th to 20th dynasty in Egypt.
- Queen Hatshepsut was an early ruler of me.
- I was during the Egyptian "Golden Age."
- I lasted from 1550 - 1070 BC.

THE NEW KINGDOM

WHO AM I?

WHO AM I?

- I cut off 4,000 miles of the journey between Europe and Asia.
- Because of me there were more and more European colonies in Africa.
- I was built by the French, but by 1875 the British owned me.
- I was opened in 1869.

SUEZ CANAL

WHO AM I?

WHO AM I?

WHO AM I?

338

Geography Terms Defined

Note: Most of these terms can also be found as Geography Definitions Flashcards in chapter seventeen.

Aquifer - A layer of water-bearing rock through which groundwater moves.

Archipelago - A group of islands.

Atoll - A coral reef in the open ocean that appears as a low, ring-shaped island or ring of islets.

Bay - Part of a lake or sea that is partly surrounded by the shore land.

Butte - Tall, steep-sided towers of rock. Smaller than a mesa.

Canyon - A deep, narrow valley having high, steep sides or cliffs.

Cape - A narrow part of land along a shore that sticks out into the water.

Census - A count of the population of a country, usually conducted by the government. It records the number of people and data such as age, gender, and occupation. A census can also be taken of plant or animal life.

Channel - A wide strait or waterway between two land masses that lie close to each other.

Coast - Land along the sea.

Core - One of three main layers of the earth. The middle layer of hot rock, the mantle, is sandwiched between the inner layer, called the core, and the outer layer, called the crust.

Crust - One of three main layers of the earth. The middle layer of hot rock, the mantle, is sandwiched between the inner layer, called the core, and the outer layer, called the crust.

Delta - Land made by soil that drops from a river at its mouth, the place where it meets the sea.

Desert - Very dry area of land that receives 10 inches or less of precipitation a year. Deserts are found on every continent and cover about one-third of the earth's land area.

Divide - The high land that separates two river basins. A river drains the water from the land, and that land is its basin.

Ecosystem - Contraction of "ecological system", a term used in classifying the earth's natural communities according to how living and non-living things and their environment function as a unit.

Elevation - The distance above sea level.

Equator - An imaginary line around the middle of the earth. Halfway between the North and South Poles, it divides the earth into Northern and Southern Hemispheres. It is the 0° line of latitude.

Equinox - Occurs twice a year when the sun appears directly overhead to observers at the equator. The periods of sunlight and darkness are nearly equal.

Escarpment - A steep slope or cliff.

Estuary - A broadened seaward end of a river. Most estuaries contain a mixture of fresh water from the river and salt water from the ocean.

Fjord - A deep, narrow inlet of the sea between high, steep cliffs.

Forest - A large area of land where many trees grow. A forest or woodland gets much rainfall every year.

Front - The boundary between two air masses of different temperature and humidity. There are three basic types of fronts: warm, cold, and stationary.

Geyser - A hot spring through which jets of water and steam erupt.

Glacier - A huge mass of ice that moves slowly over land.

Grassland - A region where grass is the naturally dominant vegetation. A grassland occurs where there is not enough regular rainfall to support the growth of a forest, but not so little rain as to form a desert.

Groundwater - Water beneath the earth's surface from rain and melted snow that seeps down through soil and into pores and cracks in rocks.

Gulf - A large area of the ocean or sea that lies within a curved coastline. It's a portion of the ocean that penetrates into land. Gulfs vary in size, shape, and depth. They are sometimes connected to the ocean by one or more narrow passages called straits.

Habitat - The natural environment of a plant or animal; the place where the plant commonly grows or the animal normally finds food and shelter.

Harbor - A sheltered body of water where ships anchor and are safe from the winds and waves of storms at sea.

Hill - A small area of land that is higher than the land around it.

Inlet - A small strip of water that reaches from a sea or lake into the shore land.

Island - Land that is surrounded by water and smaller than a continent. There are four major kinds of islands: continental, oceanic, coral, and barrier.

Isthmus - A narrow piece of land that joins two larger land areas and separates two bodies of water.

Lagoon - A pool of shallow water linked to the sea by an inlet.

Lake - A body of water, usually fresh water, that is surrounded by land.

Latitude - The distance north or south of the equator.

Longitude - The distance east or west of the prime meridian. Lines of longitude, which meet at the Poles, are known as meridians. The one that runs through Greenwich, England is accepted as the 0° longitude, or prime meridian.

Magma - Molten rock inside the earth. It originates in the lower part of the earth's crust and in the upper portion of the mantle.

Mantle - One of three main layers of the earth. The middle layer of hot rock, the mantle, is sandwiched between the inner layer, called the core, and the outer layer, called the crust.

Marsh - A type of wetland forming a grassy fringe near river mouths and along coastlines protected from open ocean. They are alternately flooded and exposed by the movement of the tides.

Mesa - Broad, flat-topped landforms with steep sides. Found mostly in dry regions.

Mountain - Land that rises very high; much higher than the land at its base. Mountains are much higher than hills.

Mountain range - A row of mountains that are joined together. A mountain range makes a giant natural wall.

Oasis - An area made fertile by a source of fresh water in an otherwise arid region. Water in an oasis comes from underground springs or from irrigation.

Peninsula - A three-sided piece of land jutting out into a lake or ocean.

Permafrost - Permanently frozen layer below the earth's surface consisting of soil, gravel, and sand usually bound together by ice.

Plain - A large, relatively flat land, often covered with grasses.

Plateau - A large, relatively flat area that stands above the surrounding land. Plateaus occupy about one-third of the earth's land and occur on every continent.

Precipitation - A term that covers all forms in which water falls to earth from the atmosphere. The main types of precipitation are rain, snow, sleet, and hail.

Prime Meridian - The line of O° longitude, the starting point for measuring distance east and west around the globe. It runs through Greenwich, England.

Richter scale - Developed in the United States by seismologists Charles F. Richter and Beno Gutenburg, it is used to indicate the amount of energy released at the focus of an earthquake.

River - A large, moving body of fresh water that starts at a source in higher land. It drains water from an area called a basin. The river moves from the higher to the lower land, and it carries the water to its mouth, where it ends. The mouth is typically at a lake, ocean, sea, or another river.

Rain forest - A moist, densely wooded area usually found in a warm, tropical wet climate.

Rock - The material that makes up most of the earth. Rock is a natural substance composed of solid matter. Rocks are divided into three categories, according to how they were formed: igneous, sedimentary, or metamorphic.

Savanna - A tropical grassland with clumps of grasses and widely scattered trees found in warm, tropical regions where rainfall is seasonal; a prolonged dry season alternates with a rainy season.

Sea - A large body of salt water nearly or partly surrounded by land. A sea is much smaller than an ocean.

Silt - A type of matter that water, ice, and wind transport and deposit. Silt is made of particles of rocks and minerals that are smaller than fine sand.

Sound - A long and wide body of water. A sound connects two larger bodies of water or separates an island from a larger body of land.

Steppe - An area covered mainly by short grasses. Steppes occur where there are distinct seasonal variations in temperature. Usually associated with Asia and southeastern Europe.

Strait - A passageway of water that connects two large bodies of water.

Swamp - An area of land permanently saturated with water and sometimes covered by it. Typically dominated by trees.

Taiga - A forest of the cold, subarctic regions that begins south of the tundra vegetation. Coniferous, or cone-bearing, trees such as spruce, pine, and fir are common in taiga.

Topography - The lay of the land; the shape of the surface features of a geographic area.

Tributary - A stream or river that flows into a larger stream or river.

Tsunami - Ocean waves triggered primarily by movement of the ocean floor during strong earthquakes. Volcanic eruptions in or near the ocean may also cause them.

Tundra - A cold region characterized by low vegetation. Plant species are limited in number and are adapted to short growing seasons and cold temperatures. There are two kinds of tundra: the alpine tundra of high mountain ranges and the arctic tundra of the polar area.

Valley - The lower land between hills or mountains.

Water table - Water, seeping down through the soil under the force of gravity, reaches a zone where the pores in rocks and sediments are saturated, or filled with water. The area where zones of saturated and unsaturated rocks and sediments meet marks the water table.

Wetland - An area of land that is covered by water or that is saturated with surface water or groundwater for long enough periods to support vegetation adapted to wet conditions.

Answer Keys

"How Much Do You Know About North America?" (page 202)
1. Southeast
2. 7,800 miles (12,600 km.)
3. Lake Nicaragua in Nicaragua
4. Irazu, a volcano in Costa Rica
5. Mexico City
6. The Yucatan Peninsula
7. St. Augustine, Florida
8. Greenland
9. The Great Lakes
10. Superior, Michigan, Huron, Erie, Ontario
11. Lake Michigan
12. The St. Lawrence Seaway
13. Canada - wood pulp: 32% and lumber: 42%
14. The Great Plains
15. The Rocky Mountains

"How Much Do You Know About South America?" (page 204)
1. Amazon Basin
2. Mt. Aconcagua
3. Machu Picchu
4. 6,180,000 cubic feet
5. Sao Paulo, pop. 9,393,753 (1991 est.)
6. Tropical rain forest & tropical savannas
7. The Andes Mountains
8. Patagonia
9. 45%
10. Brazil
11. Buenos Aires, Rio de Janeiro, Caracas
12. The Guavio on the Orinoco River in Colombia at 820 feet (250 meters)
13. Itaipu on the Brazil-Paraguay border
14. Jefferson Perez
15. Brazil
16. Bolivia - Sucre & La Paz
17. Fishing
18. Earthquakes, volcanoes and tsunamis (tidal waves)
19. Moderate, dry summer
20. Desert
21. Forest & grassland
22. Under two people per square mile
23. None
24. The Atacama desert in northern Chile
25. The pampas
26. Easter Island

"How Much Do You Know About Europe?" (page 207)
1. German, French, Italian and Romansch
2. Prior to 1991, Yugoslavia was comprised of six republics: Bosnia and Herzegovina, Croatia, Macedonia, Montenegro, Serbia, and Slovenia. In 1991-92 Bosnia and Herzegovina, Croatia, Macedonia, and Slovenia declared independence. Now the republics of Montenegro and Serbia make up Yugoslavia.
3. The Chunnel
4. Four: Bratislava - Slovakia; Budapest - Hungary; Vienna - Austria; Belgrade - Yugoslavia
5. When the USSR broke up in 1991, all 15 republics became independent countries: Armenia, Azerbaijan, Belarus, Estonia, Georgia, Kazakstan, Kyrgyzstan, Latvia, Lithuania, Moldova, Russia, Tajikistan, Turkmenistan, Ukraine, Uzbekistan.
6. The Ukraine's main geographic feature is its flat plains, or steppes. This area has very fertile soils that make it outstanding for agricultural production. It produces a large number of crops including wheat, rye, barley, corn, and potatoes.
7. The Pyrenees, Alps, and Carpathian Mountains
8. Mediterranean climate
9. Christianity
10. Vatican City - 0.2 square miles (0.4 sq km.)
11. Oil
12. Pompeii

"How Much Do You Know About Asia?" (page 211)
1. The Great Wall of China
2. Afghanistan and Pakistan
3. The United Arab Emirates (The sheikdoms are: Abu Dhabi, Ajman, Dubai, Fujeirah, Sharjah, Umm al-Qawain, and Ras al-Khaimah.)
4. The Empty Quarter - it covers 250,00 square miles (647,000 square km) and is the world's largest continuous body of sand
5. The eruption of Krakatau, an island volcano between Java and Sumatra
6. 56 miles - at the Bering Strait
7. The Fertile Crescent

Answer Keys

8. Tibet - with an average elevation of 15,000 feet (4,600 km)
9. 5,764 miles (9,297 km) from Moscow in the east to Nakhodka on the Pacific coast
10. Singapore - 17,814 people per square mile (6,879 per sq km)
11. 60%
12. Mt. Everest - 29,028 feet (8,848 m) in China (Tibet)-Nepal
13. Mt. Everest and the Dead Sea (Israel-Jordan)
14. The Caspian Sea
15. Buddhism, Christianity, Confucianism, Hinduism, Islam, Judaism, Shinto, & Taoism
16. Tokyo-Yokohama, Japan
17. Arabia - Rub' al Khali and China - Takla Makan
18. Monsoon
19. Two-thirds
20. Rice
21. Tundra
22. Teak
23. A junk

"How Much Do You Know About Africa?" (page 214)
1. The Serengeti or Serengeti National Park
2. The Okavango River Delta has its origins in the mountains of central Angola and runs 1,000 miles (1,600 km) to the northwest corner of Botswana, where it cascadesover the Gomre Faults and spreads out into a swampy delta covering approximately 4,000 square miles (10,350 km).
3. Cabinda is a province of Angola in western Africa that's cut off from the rest of Angola by a corridor of land belonging to Zaire.
4. A 21-carat diamond was discovered. This set off an enormous diamond rush as thousands of people headed to South Africa in a mad rush to explore for diamonds.
5. The country of Liberia. Liberia is derived from the Latin word "liber," meaning "free."
6. The Sahel, a semiarid savanna with tall grasses in the south and short grasses in the north
7. South Africa has the largest known deposits of chromite, platinum, vanadium, and manganese. It leads the world in the production of gold, vanadium, chromite, and platinum metals.
8. Lake Victoria
9. Kilimanjaro, Tanzania

10. Cairo, Egypt
11. One-seventh
12. A high plateau covers much of the continent. The boundaries of the plateau are marked by escarpments (steep slopes) over which many of these great rivers plunge as falls or rapids, thereby prohibiting water travel by boat or ship.
13 The Sahara desert
14. One-third
15. Drought, over-farming, and over-grazing
16. Throughout central and southern Africa
17. Three out of four
18. Only Africa
19. One-fourth
20. Nigeria with a population of 128,285,000
21. The Great Rift Valley
22. An oasis
23. Kilimanjaro, Tanzania at 19,340 feet (5,895 m).
24. The camel (or one-humped dromedary)
25. South Africa
26. Water - near the coast, lakes and rivers
27. Dalol, Ethiopia - 94 F (34 C).
28. Burundi - 5% and Rwanda - 6%

"How Much Do You Know About Australia and Oceania?" (page 216)
1. Ayers Rock, or as it is now called by its Aboriginal name, Uluru
2. The Great Barrier Reef
3. Tasmania
4. "Oceania" refers to the widely scattered islands of the Pacific Ocean. It generally extends from the Midway Islands in the north to New Zealand in the south, and from Easter Island in the east to Palau in the west. The three main island groups of Oceania are: Polynesia, Melanesia, and Micronesia. The islands of New Zealand and the continent of Australia are some times considered part of Oceania.
5. Eight: Papua New Guinea - 1975; the Solomon Islands and Tuvalu - 1978; Kiribati - 1979; Vanuatu - 1980; the Marshall Islands and the Federated States of Micronesia - 1986; and Palau in 1994.
6. Upolu in Western Samoa
7. Wellington, New Zealand is the southernmost national capital in the world at 41°18' south latitude. In second place is Canberra, Australia, which lies at 35°17' south latitude.

Answer Keys

Workin' Up a Storm (page 112)
1. C
2. B
3. A
4. A
5. More
6. More
7. Less
8. Rise
9. Cools
10. Back/other
11. D
12. J
13. B
14. N
15. K
16. H
17. C
18. O
19. G
20. F
21. M
22. I
23. A
24. E
25. L

Answer key for both:
"Are You a Junior Volcanologist?" (page 114)
"Are You a Senior Volcanologist?" (page 115)
1. Crater
2. Tilt meter
3. Dormant
4. Extinct
5. Lava flow
6. Pumice
7. Mt. St. Helens
8. Vent
9. Active
10. Ring of Fire
11. Ash
12. Eruption
13. Magma
14. Obsidian
15. Crust
16. Volcanologists

NFL Mind Benders (page 242)
1. Northeast, North Atlantic, New England (Any of these are correct.)
2. Air transportation (Jets)
3. Buffalo (Bills)
4. Automobiles (Indianapolis Colts)
5. Miami (Dolphins), Biscayne Bay
6. Ohio, Allegheny, & Monongahela Rivers (Pittsburgh Steelers)
7. Chesapeake Bay, crabs (Baltimore)
8. Ohio River (Cincinnati Bengals)
9. Cumberland Plateau (Tennessee Titans)
10. Jacksonville, Jaguars
11. San Andreas Fault (Oakland)
12. Gulf of Santa Catalina (San Diego)
13. Denver Broncos in Colorado, Mile High Stadium
14. Interstate 70 (Kansas City)
15. Olympic Mountains, Olympic National Park, Puget Sound (Seattle)
16. Trenton (the Giants play at the Meadowlands in New Jersey)
17. The Red River separates Oklahoma and Texas (Dallas)
18. Philadelphia Eagles
19. Washington, D.C. (Washington Redskins)
20. The Grand Canyon (Arizona)
21. Ottawa, Canada (Green Bay Packers - Wisconsin, USA)
22. Scandinavia - homeland of the Vikings (Minnesota Vikings)
23. Michigan (Chicago)
24. Lake Okeechobee (Tampa Bay, Florida)
25. Automobile industry (Detroit, Michigan)
26. The Gold Rush of 1849 (49'ers)
27. Jazz (New Orleans, Louisiana)
28. Florida, Alabama, Tennessee, N. & S. Carolina (Atlanta, Georgia)
29. Blue Ridge Mountains (North Carolina)
30. Mississippi River (St. Louis, Missouri)
31. Cleveland Browns, Lake Erie

Chronological Listing of Timeline Figures

c 3800 BC	Earliest Known Map
c 3760 BC	Bronze First Used
3372 BC	First Day in Mayan Calendar
c 3200 BC	Writing Appears
3000 BC	Wheeled Vehicles
c 3000 BC	First Iron Objects Made
c 3000 BC	Pharaoh Menes
2700 BC	Stonehenge
c 2600 BC	Papyrus Used as Paper
2773 BC	Calendar with 365 Days
c 2690 BC	Chinese Start Weaving Silk
2575-2134 BC	Old Kingdom (Egypt)
c 2686-2181 BC	Age of Pyramids
2551 BC	Sphinx & Great Pyramids Built
2500 BC	First Mummies
2500 BC	First Surgery (Egypt)
2040-1532 BC	Middle Kingdom (Egypt)
c 2000 BC	Basis for Modern Alphabet
2000 BC	China's First Zoo
1792-1750 BC	Hammurabi's Reign
1500 BC	Glass Bottles Used (Egypt)
1550-1070 BC	New Kingdom (Egypt)
1500-1122 BC	Shang Dynasty
c 1250-1240 BC	Trojan War
1100-900 BC	First Chinese Language Dictionary
1122-256 BC	Chou (Zhou) Dynasty
776 BC	First Olympic Games
755 BC	First Date in Chinese History
722 BC	N. Kingdom of Israel Destroyed
700 BC	First Coins Used
c 700 BC	Iliad & Odyssey
600 BC	Windmills Used
580 BC	The Hanging Gardens
563-483 BC	Buddha
551-479 BC	Confucius
539 BC	Fall of Babylon
?-529 BC	Cyrus of Persia
508 BC	Athens 1st Democracy
c 490-479 BC	Persian War
480 BC	Greek Classical Period
477-432 BC	Parthenon
477-405 BC	Golden Age of Athens
469-399 BC	Socrates
460 BC	Parchment Replaces Stone Tablets
c 460-377 BC	Hippocrates
431-404 BC	Peloponnesian War
427-347 BC	Plato
390 BC	First Kite
384-322 BC	Aristotle
382-336 BC	Philip II
356-323 BC	Alexander the Great
323-319 BC	Alexander's Empire Divided
c 287-212 BC	Archimedes
264-146 BC	Punic War
247-183 BC	Hannibal
221-207 BC	Chin (Qin) Dynasty
218-204 BC	Great Wall of China
c 206 BC-AD 221	Han Dynasty
c 200 BC	Concrete First Used (Rome)
c 150 BC	Silk Paintings / Pottery Fig.
100-44 BC	Julius Caesar
c 83-30 BC	Marc Antony
69-30 BC	Cleopatra's Reign
63 BC-AD 14	Octavian (Caesar Augusts)
50 BC-AD 50	Buddhism Introduced
c 45 BC	Julian Calendar
31 BC-AD 476	Roman Empire
c 4	Birth of Jesus
42	The First Pope
54-68	First Christian Persecution
37-68	Nero
64	Rome Destroyed by Fire
90-168	Ptolemy
100	Ethiopia Wealthy
c 270	Magnetic Compass
c 280-337	Constantine
300-600	Mayan Golden Age
320-535	Great Gupta Empire
395	Roman Empire Divided
395-1453	Byzantine Empire
476	Last Roman Emperor Dethroned
c 503	Legendary King Arthur
570-631	Mohammed (Muhammad)
593	Wooden Blocks Used for Printing (China)
605-610	Imperial Canal Built
618-907	T'ang Dynasty
622	Islam Introduced
771-841	Charlemagne
843	Treaty of Verdun
847	Vikings Settle Iceland
858-867	Pope Nicholas I

900	Age of Iron & Steel	1542-1587	Mary Queen of Scots
932	First Mass Production of Books	1543	Scientific Revolution
960-1279	Song Dynasty	1545	Council of Trent
936-973	Otto I of Germany	c 1552-1618	Sir Walter Raleigh
962-1806	The New Holy Roman Empire	1558-1603	Queen Elizabeth
c 1000 - 1877	Samurai	1564-1616	William Shakespeare
1003	Leif Ericsson Discovers North America	1564-1642	Galileo Galilei
1027-1087	William the Conqueror	1587	Holland's Independence
1054	Catholic Church Divides	1588	Spanish Armada Defeated
1056-1147	Almorarid Kingdom	1590	Microscope Invented
1066	The Battle of Hastings	1607	Virginia Colony Founded
1077	Pope George VII Challenges Henry IV	?-1611	Henry Hudson
1096-1204	The Crusades	1610	Galileo's Telescope
1099	Jerusalem Falls to Crusaders	1611	King James Bible
c 1150	Paper First Made (Europe)	1618-1648	The Thirty Years' War
1157-1199	Richard the Lion Hearted	1620	Pilgrims Reach Cape Cod
1174	Leaning Tower of Pisa	1626	Madagascar Settled by French
1182-1226	St. Francis of Assisi	1629-1650	Taj Mahal Built
1167-1227	Genghis Khan	1636	First College, Harvard
1215	Magna Carta Signed	1640	Puritan Revolution, England
1232	Rockets Used in Battle	1642-1727	Isaac Newton
1233	The Inquisition Begins	1644-1912	Manchu Dynasty
1254-1324	Marco Polo	1678	Pilgrim's Progress
1266	Magnifying Glass	1682	Quakers Settle Pennsylvania
1279-1368	Mongol Empire	1685-1750	Johann Sebastian Bach
c 1300-1918	Ottoman Empire	1689-1725	Peter the Great
1309-1377	The Popes Dominated by French	1692	Salem Witch Trials
1320-1384	John Wycliffe	1703-1791	John Wesley
1325	Tenochtitlan Founded	1728-1779	Captain James Cook
1337-1453	Hundred Years' War	1756-1763	Seven Years' War
1347-1353	Black Plague	1769-1821	Napoleon Bonaparte
1368-1644	Ming Dynasty	1770-1827	Ludwig Von Beethoven
1380	Bible Now in English	1770-1843	Sequoya
1388	Canterbury Tales	1773	Boston Tea Party
1412-1431	Joan of Arc	1776	Declaration of Independence
1440	Movable Type Used (Europe)	1776-1783	Revolutionary War
c 1450-1500	Bartholomeu Dias	1783	Treaty of Paris
1451-1506	Christopher Columbus	1783-1830	Simon Bolivar
1452-1519	Leonardo da Vinci	1787	Northwest Ordinance
1460-1521	Ponce de Leon	1789-1797	George Washington
1469-1516	Ferdinand & Isabella	1789-1799	The French Revolution
1473-1543	Nicolaus Copernicus	1793	Cotton Gin
1475-1564	Michelangelo Buonarroti	1797-1801	John Adams
1478	Spain Established	1801-1809	Thomas Jefferson
1478	Spanish Inquisition	1803	Louisiana Purchase
1480-1521	Ferdinand Magellan	1804-1806	Lewis & Clark Expedition
1483-1546	Martin Luther	1809-1817	James Madison
1485-1547	Hernan Cortes	1817-1825	James Monroe
1491-1547	Henry VIII	1818-1883	Karl Marx
1492	Modern Globe	1820-1910	Florence Nightingale
1500-1542	Hernando de Soto	1821-1912	Clara Barton
1502	African Slaves in America	1823	Monroe Doctrine
1504	First Watch	1825-1829	John Quincy Adams
1509-1564	John Calvin	1829	Greece Independence
c 1516	The Reformation Starts	1829-1837	Andrew Jackson
1527-1803	Mongul Empire	1829-1913	Balkan Wars
1528	First Surgery (Europe)		

Chronological Listing of Timeline Figures

1836	The Alamo
1837-1841	Martin Van Buren
1839-1860	Opium War
1841	William Harrison
1841-1845	John Tyler
1844	YMCA Founded
1845-1849	James Polk
1846-1848	U.S. War with Mexico
1847-1931	Thomas Edison
1849	California Gold Rush
1849-1850	Zachary Taylor
1850-1853	Millard Fillmore
1853-1857	Franklin Pierce
1854-1856	Crimean War
1856-1915	Booker T. Washington
1857-1861	James Buchanan
1860-1861	Pony Express
1861-1865	Abraham Lincoln
1861-1865	Civil War
1862-1908	Empress Tzu Hui
1862	Homestead Act
1863-1947	Henry Ford
1865	The Salvation Army
1865-1869	Andrew Jonson
1869	Suez Canal Opened
1869	Transcontinental Railroad
1869-1877	Ulysses Grant
1869-1948	Mahatma Gandhi
1870-1871	Franko-Prussian War
1870-1916	James Connoly
1870-1924	Vladimir Lenin
1877-1881	Rutherford Hayes
1875	The Telephone
1879-1955	Albert Einstein
1881	James Garfield
1881-1885	Chester Arthur
1881-1973	Pablo Picasso
1882-1915	The Triple Alliance
1883-1945	Benito Mussolini
1885-1889	Grover Cleveland
1886	Statue of Liberty
1889	Eiffel Tower
1889-1893	Benjamin Harrison
1889-1945	Adolf Hitler
1890-1915	The Triple Entente
1893-1897	Grover Cleveland
1897-1901	William McKinley
1901-1909	Theodore Roosevelt
1903	Airplane Invented
1904-1905	Russo-Japanese War
1909	First Resettlement of Israel
1909-1913	William Taft
1912	The Titanic Sinks
1913-1921	Woodrow Wilson
?-1914	Francis Ferdinand
1914	Panama Canal Finished
1914-1918	World War I
1915	The Lusitania Sinks
1915	Poison Gas Used in War
1916	Tanks Used in Battle
1917	Bolshevik Revolution
1919	The League of Nations
1919	Prohibition
1919	Treaty of Versailles
1920	Radio Broadcasting in U.S.
1921-1923	Warren Harding
1922	Egypt's Independence from Britain
1923-1929	Calvin Coolidge
1924	Indians Become American Citizens
1928	First Mickey Mouse Cartoon
1929	U.S. Stock Market Crashes
1929-1932	The Great Depression
1929-1933	Herbert Hoover
1929-1968	Martin Luther King Jr.
1933-1945	Franklin Roosevelt
1933-1945	The New Deal
1936-1939	Spanish Civil War
1937	Golden Gate Bridge
1938	Munich Agreement
1939-1945	World War II
1940	Miracle of Dunkirk
1941	Japanese Attack Pearl Harbor
1944	D-Day
1945	Atom Bomb First Used
1945- 1953	Harry Truman
1946	People's Republic of China
1949	The Apartheid Policy
1949	NATO
1950	Color TV
1953-1961	Dwight Eisenhower
1954	Polio Vaccination
1961	Berlin Wall Built
1961-1963	John Kennedy
1962	Prayer Removed from Schools
1962	Algeria's Independence from France
1963-1969	Lyndon Johnson
1969	Man Walks on Moon
1969-1974	Richard Nixon
1973	Abortion Legalized
1974-1977	Gerald Ford
1977-1981	Jimmy Carter
1981	First Space Shuttle
1981-1989	Ronald Reagan
1989-1993	George Bush
1991	Commonwealth of Independent States
1991	Persian Gulf War
1993-2001	William Clinton
2001-	George W. Bush

Index of Timeline Figures and Who Am I? Cards

F = Timeline Figure
C = Who Am I? Card

Index of Timeline Figures and Who Am I? Cards

F = Timeline Figure
C = Who Am I? Card

All American History Volume I   Exploration -- 1840

Both classical and hands-on, *All American History* reads like a good book -- bringing America's story to life piece by piece. Containing hundreds of images and dozens of maps, All American History is a complete year's curriculum for students in grades 5 - 8 when combined with the *AAH Student Activity Book* and *AAH Teacher's Guide*. Adaptable for younger & older students.

32 weekly lessons-- each lesson contains three sections examining the atmosphere, event, and impact.
- All American History Student Reader, hardcover 464 pages.
- All American History Student Activity Book, pbk. 224 pages.
- All American History Teacher's Guide, pbk. 272 pages.

The Mystery of History - Volume I

Classical, Chronological, Complete. A User-Friendly Family Curriculum. Written for 4th - 8th graders, adaptable for older & younger students. *The Mystery of History* provides a historically accurate, Bible-centered approach to learning ancient history. The completely chronological lessons shed new light on who walked the earth when, as well as on where important Bible figures fit into secular history. Pbk. 496 pages.

The Mystery of History - Volume II

The story continues with The Early Church and The Middle Ages (A.D. 30 – 1460). Pbk. 752 pages.

Hands-On Geography

Take another look! This long-time favorite introduction to geography went through a massive revision. New look and layout, loads more ideas and activities make this a book worth getting excited about! Enough material to last families for several years. Written from a Christian perspective, *Hands-On Geography* will motivate you to teach an oft-neglected subject. Includes specific instructions for activities, games, and projects. Pbk. 144 pages, K-5.

Christian Kids Explore Series

The 35 weekly lessons are well organized and easy-to-follow. The schedule calls for teaching twice-weekly while still allowing time for projects, exploration of resource books, field trips, etc. The conversational style gives students the basic information needed, making this an ideal first course in science; especially useful for those following a classical approach. Filled with activities, book lists, lessons, experiments, coloring pages and much more.

- Christian Kids Explore Biology   Grades 1 – 6
- Christian Kids Explore Earth & Space   Grades 1 – 6
- Christian Kids Explore Chemistry   Grades 4 – 8

From Basic to Baghdad: A Soldier Writes Home

Written by a homeschool graduate, JB Hogan chronicles his life from enlisting in the Army on a whim just before 9/11, through his tour of duty as part of the 3rd Infantry Division. Both scathingly funny and deeply poignant, this coming-of-age story is a book for America. Hardcover 250 pages.

The Scientist's Apprentice

A one-year science curriculum that is understandable and exciting for K-6th grade students. Experiments, games, crafts, recipes, writing, and songs teach to different learning styles. Reinforces orderly thinking skills. Reproducible pages and easy-to-follow directions make this a practical program families will love. More interesting than a text book and easier than a unit study. We've done all the work for you! The four topics studied are: Astronomy, oceanography, anatomy, and earth science. Pbk. 200 pages.

Over Our Heads in Wonder

Discover God's "Wonders in the Sky," and His love and power on earth! Parents will appreciate the simplicity of this book while students enjoy the great activities. Includes 25+ readings/discussions and 50+ projects/experiments encompassing science, the Bible, writing, math, and language arts. Suitable for multi-level teaching, these "any day -anywhere" assignments utilize common household materials. Pbk. 96 pages, K-5.

Student History Notebook of America

Many homeschool approaches call for students to keep their own notebooks. Witness improvements in the quality of students' work as they record information, artwork, daily assignments and more. Book includes pages for essays, drawings, vocabulary, presidents, states and capitals, maps and much more. Great addition to any prepackaged US history curriculum or use as the basis for your own units. Pbk. 112 pages, K-12.

To order these resources use the order form on the following page or contact Bright Ideas Press.

Bright Ideas Press Order Form

Mail check or money order to:

Bright Ideas Press
P.O. Box 333
Cheswold, DE 19936

Toll Free: 877.492.8081

Visa & MasterCard orders are accepted. See below for information.

SHIPPING TABLE

Up to $50.............$6.00
$50-$150...............10%
over $150.............free
Out of Country.......call

Item	Title	Price	Qty.	Total
BIP-1	Hands-On Geography	$14.95		
GC-100	The Ultimate Geography and Timeline Guide	$34.95		
BIP-5	The Mystery of History - Volume I	$44.95		
BIP-7	The Mystery of History - Volume II	$49.95		
BIP-81	All American History Vol. 1 Student Reader	$44.95		
BIP-82	All American History Vol. 1 Student Act. Book	$16.95		
BIP-83	All American History Vol. 1 Teacher Guide	$18.95		
BIP-10	From Basic to Baghdad: A Soldier Writes Home	$14.95		
BIP-6	Christian Kids Explore Biology	$29.95		
BIP-9	Christian Kids Explore Chemistry	$29.95		
BIP-11	Christian Kids Explore Earth & Space	$29.95		
BIP-2	The Scientist's Apprentice	$26.95		
BIP-6	Gifted Children at Home	$24.95		

Special! FREE SHIPPING on *orders* over $150.00

Sub Total	
Shipping Cost See Shipping Table	
Total Amount Due	

SHIP TO ADDRESS: Please PRINT clearly

Name: _____

Address: _____

_____

Phone: ( ) _____

Email: _____

Credit Card Information

___ MasterCard   ___ Visa

___ - ___ - ___ - ___
Card #

_____ / _____
Exp. Date

_____
Signature

Uncle Josh's Color Maps with Outline on Reverse
Beautiful color maps perfect for use in any home or school. Double-sided maps include a vivid color, labeled map with physical terrain demonstrated in shaded relief on one side and a simple black and white outline map on the reverse. Basic labeling of states, countries, and capitals keep maps free from clutter. Laminated for unlimited write-on and wipe-off uses. Add more places while you learn. Choose the U.S. or the World. 23" x 34"

Uncle Josh's Outline Map Book or CD-Rom
Reproducible outline maps have a myriad of uses in the home, school, and office. Uncle Josh uses only quality digital map art which shows rivers and surrounding boundaries. Students see the place they are studying in context. (No map of Germany "floating" in the center of the page, here!) The book has over 100 reproducible maps, and the CD-ROM includes an additional 75+ maps for easy printing from your home computer. (Uses PDF files and Adobe Acrobat Reader.)

Trail Guide Series
The Trail Guides are easy-to-follow resources to help you teach essential geographical facts and features. Students learn about their world with the 5-minute daily drills, mapping, building their own geography notebooks, and choosing from a wide variety of projects. Each *Trail Guide* is written for three different levels and can be used for several years. The literature unit provides a thrilling way to drive home the relevance of knowing geography. (Printable *Trail Guide* student notebooks are also available in CD-ROM or eBook.) 2nd-12th grades

- *Trail Guide to U.S. Geography* – organized by region and covers all 5o states. Literature unit covers the Lewis and Clark Expedition with *The Captain's Dog*, by Roland Smith.
- *Trail Guide to World Geography* – organized by continent. Literature unit with *Around the World in 80 Days* by Jules Verne.
- *Trail Guide to Bible Geography* – Organized by the chronology of the Bible from Abraham through Paul. Literature unit with *The Bronze Bow* by Elizabeth George Speare.

Galloping the Globe
Word searches, mazes, maps, and more...clues, puzzles, and animals galore! This literature-based geography unit study covers all seven continents while integrating science, history/biographies, activities, mapping, Internet, notebooking, and more. K-4th grades

Cantering the Country Country
A U.S. version of *Galloping the Globe* teaches character qualities taken from official state mottoes. Language arts uses preambles to state constitutions and includes a CD-ROM of printable activities and individual state outline maps. 1st-6th grades

Eat Your Way Through the USA and *Eat Your Way Around the World*
These cookbooks provide delicious recipes for a full meal using ingredients or typical dishes that would be served in each state or country.

Teaching Geography Through Art
A great way to learn about the world and the U.S. is through art. Complete instructions for art projects including, sculpture, drawing, pinata, and oh so many more. Organized by continent, all instructions for art projects in the *Trail Guide* series are in this book.

Continents Map Set
Includes (approx.) 17" x 22" maps of Africa, Europe, North America, South America, 23" x 34" 3A Map (Asia/Australia/Antarctica double-sided map), PLUS bonus USA map. Great to use for "Conquering the Continents" mapping assignments.

Mark-It Timeline of History
Students record historical events on the timeline to gain a broader perspective of history and to enhance memory retention. Two and one half inches between lines provide ample space for depicting overlapping events. Side one is marked with dates, side two is undated for any in-depth study. Laminated, durable, and reusable when using water-based (Vis-a-Vis) pens. Use as poster or cut in strips to stretch out for 21 feet of history! 23" x 34"

Historical Timeline Figures CD-ROM
Print the same Timeline Figures as found in *The Ultimate Geography and Timeline Guide* in color from your home computer. Includes the Who Am I? game cards and an additional set of figures without the borders. (Uses PDF files and Adobe Acrobat Reader.)

Geography Terms Chart
Full color laminated landscape picture with geography features labeled. 150 terms are defined on back. 12" x 18"

To order these resources use the order form on the following page or contact Geography Matters.